Library of
Davidson College

Norman Meller

CONSTITUTIONALISM
IN MICRONESIA

". . . like clay in the potter's hands, the shape of future political status would emerge as the powers and structures of the new Micronesian government were decided upon and the polity took shape."

CONSTITUTIONALISM IN MICRONESIA

CONSTITUTIONALISM IN MICRONESIA

Norman Meller

with the assistance of Terza Meller

published by
The Institute for Polynesian Studies
Brigham Young University—Hawaii Campus
funded by the
Polynesian Cultural Center

Library of Congress Cataloging in Publication Data
Meller, Norman.
  Constitutionalism in Micronesia.
  Includes index.
  1. Pacific Islands (Trust Territory)—Constitutional history. 2. Pacific Islands (Trust Territory)—Politics and government. I. Meller, Terza. II. Title.
JQ6240.A2M45   1985   320.996′5   85-14537
ISBN 0-939154-39-0

Copyright © 1985 The Institute for Polynesian Studies
All Rights Reserved
Manufactured in the United States of America
ISBN 0-939154-39-0

Distributed for The Institute for Polynesian Studies
by the University of Hawaii Press:

Order Department
University of Hawaii Press
2840 Kolowalu Street
Honolulu, Hawaii 96822

Contents

Introduction vii

Prologue 1

                Part I.   The Setting 5
Chapter 1.   Micronesia 7
Chapter 2.   Trust Territory Government 29
Chapter 3.   Future Status 51
Chapter 4.   Breakage at the Periphery 71

                Part II.   Scenario and Characters 105
Chapter 5.   Confusion Compounded 107
Chapter 6.   Delegates and Delegations 131
Chapter 7.   Confusion Confounded 145

                Part III.   Act I 173
Chapter 8.   The Palauan Ploy 175
Chapter 9.   The Issues Take Shape 193

                Part IV.   Entr'acte 213
Chapter 10. Crises at the Recess 215

                Part V.   Act II 233
Chapter 11. The Shape of the Government to Come 235
Chapter 12. Traditional Leaders and Customary Rights . . 261
Chapter 13. The Micronesian Way 287

                Part VI.   Epilogue 315
Chapter 14. Farewell Micronesia, Fare Well 317

                Appendices 355

Index 385

Photographs follow page 167

MICRONESIAN CONSTITUTIONAL CONVENTION

OFFICERS

President . . . . Tosiwo Nakayama
Vice President, Mariana Islands District . . . Lorenzo I.G. Cabrera
Vice President, Marshall Islands District . . . . Carl Heine
Vice President, Palau District . . . . John O. Ngiraked
Vice President, Ponape District . . . . Leo A. Falcam
Vice President, Truk District . . . . Chutomu Nimwes
Vice President, Yap District . . . . Petrus Tun
Floor Leader . . . . Luke M. Tman
Convention Secretary . . . . Victorio Uherbelau
Assistant Convention Secretary . . . . Asterio R. Takesy
Chief Sergeant-at-Arms . . . . Sintaro Ezra

DELEGATES

Mariana Islands District
Olympio T. Borja
Lorenzo I.G. Cabrera
Jose R. Cruz*
Luis M. Limes
Benjamin T. Manglona
Alonzo Igisomar
Francisco T. Palacios*
Joaquin I. Pangelinan*
Alfonso C. Rasa

Ponape District
Kikuo Apis
William Eperiam
Leo A. Falcam
Heinrich Iriarte
Nahnmwarki Max Iriarte⁺
Hirosi Ismael
Apinel Mateak
Bailey Olter
Tadao P. Sigrah
Nahniken Heinrich Stephen⁺
Daro Weital
Strik Yoma

* Resigned
⁺ These are the preferred spellings of these Ponapean titles.

Marshall Islands District
Kinja Andrike
Carl Heine
John Heine
Hemos A. Jack*
Langue Kalles
Wilfred Kendall
Tom Kijiner
Iroij Jeltan Lanki
Isaac Lanwi
Mary Lanwi
Tipne Philippo
Iroij Litokwa Tomeing

Palau District
Chief Ibedul Y. Gibbons
Tosiwo Nakamura
John O. Ngiraked
Santos Olikong
Lazarus E. Salii
Jacob Sawaichi
Acting Chief Reklai
 Termeteet
Johnson Toribiong

Truk District
Chiro Albert
Chief Fichita Bossy
Soukichi Fritz
Sasauo Haruo
Kotaro Heldart
Chief Kintoky Joseph
Soiter Mwety
Tosiwo Nakayama
Frank Nifon
Chutomu Nimwes
Maketo Robert
Iskia Sony
Manuel Sound
Tatasy Wainit
Hans Wiliander

Yap District
Samuel Falanruw
Chief Belarmino Hathey
Chief Francisco Luktun
Hilary Tacheliol
Luke M. Tman
Petrus Tun

* Resigned

Introduction

In the summer of 1965, I played a minor role in the establishing of the Congress of Micronesia, the first legislative body with jurisdiction extending throughout the Trust Territory of the Pacific Islands. My study on the development of the legislative process in the Trust Territory, published as the "Congress of Micronesia," had its genesis in this experience. A decade to the day after the organizing of the Congress, and extending over a period of the next four months, I served as the consultant and director of research in the drafting of a constitution for all the peoples of the Trust Territory. From the latter participant-observation originated this work on constitutionalism in Micronesia, with attention centered on the Micronesian Constitutional Convention which met on Saipan in 1975.

Conceptually, both studies are concerned with similar, if not nearly identical, political institutions. The Congress of Micronesia[1] dealt with the founding and functioning of what is popularly called a "legislature," this with a "constitutional convention." The two bodies employ a common collegial process and embody a comparable representational character. Their differences are arguably more of degree than of kind: a convention normally has a short-term life with a single-goal objective, while the legislature is a continuing, multi-purpose body. But they need not always be so constituted. Almost coterminous in time with the Micronesian Convention, and geographically abutting, the House of Assembly in Papua New Guinea metamorphosed into a convention to debate and adopt a constituent document; once these Melanesian delegates had completed their constitutional labors, they returned to serving as legislators, first for the territory/trusteeship and then the new, independent nation. None of this is to deny that there are distinguishable dissimilarities between legislature and convention in action. They primarily stem, however, from differing aims and the group processes reflective of their distinctive membership. Perhaps if the names "legislature" had been reserved for the political genus with "parliament" and "convention" for the subordinate species, the close relation of the latter two would by now have been acknowledged. Or so at least I thought, and so still believe, and saw myself as returning in 1975 to the Micronesian boards which I had quitted a decade earlier.

My concluding words to the workshop held immediately before the Micronesian Constitutional Convention were a quotation from the Preface to *The Congress*:

> On July 9, 1965, the workshop which preceded the convening of the Congress of Micronesia drew to a close. When I would next see all thirty-three members-elect assembled, they would be congressmen. Many of them were former students at the University of Hawaii, a few even members of my class on legislatures. That memorable Friday afternoon was the eve of their receipt of the power to determine the destiny of the Trust Territory. I held then no reservation about their competence to assume that awesome responsibility--nor do I now.²

Ten years later, I was voicing the same sentiments to some of the same people, but applying them now to delegates-elect of a constitutional convention. From the events to be chronicled, the reader may judge for himself the degree to which the repetition of these words in 1975 concealed a political hyperbole necessitated by the circumstances under which they were uttered.

In retrospect, by what prerogative did I interject myself into the Micronesian constitutional process? At best, fundamental values of one culture can only be groped at by members of another, but never fully comprehended. It was the Micronesians, and they alone, who had to resolve the dimensions of their own nationality, and the basic questions of whether and how they would bridge their differences to form a union. As they considered these problems, everything, like the reflected images in a barbershop with four mirrored walls, continued to recede farther and farther back into the interstices of cultural truisms so as to be lost to all but Micronesians, who saw what to an

American could not even be sensed due to his own cultural myopia. The concepts I employed, for all I knew, narrowed or expanded those which their different cultures could have mustered. My logic was not necessarily theirs: I wryly smile at having placed the delegates in a situation requiring mutually exclusive, seriatim decisions of "yes" or "no," a logic they unconsciously abandoned for more culturally compatible modes as critical issues were reached. The positing of the diverse Micronesians acting as one, their very meeting to consider the prospect, was culturally incongruous. Only the Micronesians in their own way could join their diverse pasts with the demanding present, so as to prepare themselves to meet the unknown political future.

The establishment of the Congress of Micronesia represented a dissimilar problem. It was time and purpose specific: the Congress had to be created to meet the pressures for expanding self-government being brought to bear on the United States. To serve effectively as one of the three branches of the Trust Territory government whose legitimacy was accepted both by the other branches and Washington, the Congress would best be structured in the American model. The Micronesians appreciated that their values were subordinate; then, as a technician I was competent to identify the necessary constraints. Little of this applied in the context of drawing up a Micronesian constitution. Not only was its juridical frame different, but its political setting far broader. While I might draft as the delegates directed, the very reduction to writing symbolized the relativity of culture and the concomitant incapacity of Americans and Micronesians to communicate across fundamental cultural boundaries. All persons are not born equal, nor are they endowed with inalienable rights, or are they?

Why then pen this account? The answer is manifold. Records and memories are notoriously transient in Micronesia. The Congress contains references to documents and official communications of which no copies are today extant. Deliberately or unconsciously, over time it will be advantageous for some Americans and Micronesians to be selective in their recollections, whether for individual or collective benefit. History thus furnishes its own rationale for preparing an orderly account while the possibility still exists. But the compelling reason probably lies in my being a close observer of the flow of events which are still vivid enough for the suspense to be recalled and the vision of apparent success to be savored. The background leading to the holding of the Micronesian Constitutional Convention, the daily course of the Convention itself, and the repercussions which have continued without surcease, all partake of the essence of high drama. And the uncertainty which has characterized the Micronesian quest for constitutional self-government provides a unifying theme for this book.

. . . . .

It is only fitting that I acknowledge my indebtedness to many persons for a wide range of assistance received, so many in fact as to preclude my naming any in order to avoid slighting others undesignated. However, I should note here my gratitude to the Rockefeller Foundation for making available the beauty and tranquility of the Villa Serbelloni at Bellagio to facilitate restructuring the chaos of my notes into orderly manuscript; to the Pacific Islands Studies Program of the University of Hawaii which helped reproduce that manuscript; and to The Institute for Polynesian Studies of Brigham Young University--Hawaii Campus for undertaking its publication.

----
1. Norman Meller, *The Congress of Micronesia* (Honolulu: University of Hawaii Press, 1969).

2. *Ibid*, p. x.

Prologue

"This Convention, Mr. President, has a problem. It has gone nowhere. It has not worked. So far it has been a complete failure.

"Mr. President, this Convention has failed because individual Delegates and Delegations came here unprepared. It has failed because it has too many committees. It has failed because its Rules of Procedure are too cumbersome and complex, designed to allay the timidity of whoever suggested them in the first place, rather than to assist the work of this Convention. The Convention has failed because of the poor staff support that the Delegates have received. It has failed because it has taken a piecemeal approach to the drafting of the Constitution, providing no framework to place and evaluate individual proposals.

"...The system we have now has been used for six weeks. And, as we say in Palau, it's NOT working. Individual committees look to the Convention for answers. The Convention looks to the committees for answers. Back and forth we go, with nobody getting any answers....

"...I regret to observe that there has been an appalling lack of professionalism among some Convention staff. Some staff members ... have enormous emotional investments in the outcome ... and preconceived ideas of what the outcome ought to be. The staff are not here to mastermind the Convention, not here to direct or steer us. They are here to render professional services. If they cannot give us their services without promoting their emotional and philosophical considerations, they should--and this Convention should--reconsider their position.

"...The Palau Delegation came to this Convention prepared.... We told you what we required of you if Palau was to be part of you. Out of all the Delegations here, none has responded to us. Out of all the Delegates, I know of only three individual responses....

"...To us, the mere fact of joining you is a big sacrifice. And so to you, who complain about this, we say that the question is not how much--or how little--Palau is willing to offer for the unity of Micronesia. The question we have put forth to you and which requires an answer from you is will--or will not--Palau be able to be part of you....

"To the officers of this Convention, I say that if you want this Convention to ... work, you should stay right here after the rest of us go in recess, and ... prepare for the implementation of two steps...:

"First ... abolish all the standing committees and create a single constitutional drafting committee ... [and] I further suggest that the Palau draft be the basis of the work of this drafting committee.

"Second, let us cut our staff to a workable size...."[1]

What had gone wrong? This was Senator Lazarus E. Salii, prime mover in the status negotiations with the United States, and long outspoken supporter of Micronesian unity denouncing the Convention. It was he who had championed the enabling legislation, calling for the holding of the constitutional convention, as a means to strengthen the Micronesian status position. Later, he had served as Congressional Coordinator for the preliminary arrangements necessary to start Convention planning underway. As delegate to the Convention, why was he now attacking its members, its working procedures, and above all, its staff? A year and a half previously, even before the Convention bill had cleared the Congress, in response to my query he had written that the Convention would definitely need my assistance. Now as consultant to the Convention, and director of its research and drafting section, his charge of inept rules, unprofessional staff, and, indeed, the whole lack of fit of the Convention format to Micronesia pointed accusingly at me. The forty-second day of the Convention--nearly half of its life consumed--and not a single provision agreed upon as the delegates prepared to recess and go home. There was no alternative but to offer my resignation.

1. *Journal of the Micronesian Convention of 1975*, Vol. I (Saipan, T.T., 1975), pp. 173-74 (hereafter referred to as *CCM Journal*).

PART I. THE SETTING

Each act of man occurs within its own setting, and the Micronesian Constitutional Convention of 1975 is no exception. A playwright enjoys the advantage of deliberately shaping this frame so as to accommodate the planned unfolding of his plot. For the Convention, however, the backdrop of the stage had long since been fixed, so that it was the drama of the constitution which would remain malleable. Just as the experienced critic has no need of a theatre program as guide to the setting disclosed on the raising of the stage curtain, so anyone fully familiar with the Trust Territory may well abjure the detail of this Part. However, those who do rely upon its contents to set the frame of the constitutional drama should remember that as a conscious ordering of history, it cannot avoid the human fallibility which hedges all social description in subjectivity.

. . . . .

When originally peopling the oceanic region to be known in the twentieth century as the Trust Territory of the Pacific Islands, Micronesians developed a life-style ideally appropriate to their isolated existence. Limited living space and paucity of resources contributed to a subsistence closely bounded by the vicissitudes of nature and the ravages of human enemies. After European contact, the Micronesians again adapted, now adjusting to the kaleidoscope of Western culture. Material goods produced elsewhere, supplemented by modern communications and transportation, freed them from day-to-day dependence upon the vagaries of nature. The sanctions of distant metropolitan government enforced local peace and order. Substituted for the vulnerability of traditional life was a reliance upon the uncertain bounty of a world economy to supplement their livelihood, and the protection of at least one major power for their physical security. However, the setting of Micronesia had always been and remains one of obvious dependency. The only real differences over time are to be found in the character of that dependency and the degree to which Micronesian volition has been a component.

Chapter 1. Micronesia

Since World War II, a gradually strengthening current of political change has been carrying the dependent peoples of the South Seas[1] along the path of self-determination. The integration of Hawaii into the American Union as a coequal state formally marked the beginning, and the independence of Fiji, Nauru, and Western Samoa, together with associated state status for the Cook Islands, evinced the force of the movement in the 1960s. During the course of the 1970s, Papua New Guinea, the British Solomons, Kiribati, and Tuvalu (the latter two, respectively, the components of the former Gilbert and Ellice Islands Colony) would be declared independent, and Niue would opt for associate state status with New Zealand. As the decade drew to a close, the New Hebrides was prepared to follow suit. Paralleling these island polities but in the northern hemisphere--geographically covering some 3 million square miles of ocean extending from the equator northerly to the Tropic of Cancer and from the international date line westerly for several thousand miles--the future political status of the Trust Territory of the Pacific Islands was similarly taking shape.

Like Western Samoa, Nauru, and New Guinea, the peoples of the Micronesian islands dotting this wide swath of the Pacific had been governed as a Class C Mandate of the League of Nations between the two World Wars. Again without their consent, they were then made a United Nations Trusteeship. In 1975, with the independence of Papua New Guinea, the Trust Territory of the Pacific Islands became the last of the eleven trusteeships created under United Nations auspices. From its inception, the TTPI had been unique as the only strategic trusteeship, a status which permitted its American Administration to cordon off portions for secret military purposes. Always a ready target for censure, the TTPI was now fatally vulnerable to all those forces in the U.N. opposed to colonialism in any form. Despite the remonstrances of some Micronesians that the area was not yet adequately equipped for sustaining self-government, comparable objections which had not previously deterred the Australians and British from severing ties with their respective island possessions in the Pacific, the United States announced to the world that the year 1981 would see the termination of the trusteeship. However, unlike the other administering powers, the United States has been unwilling to withdraw its military presence from the islands of the Pacific. How, then, to reconcile Micronesian self-determination, the security needs of the United States, and the termination of the Trust Territory of the Pacific Islands? Part of the answer was to lie in the geographic and demographic composition of Micronesia.

Three great archipelagoes were joined to form the Trust Territory of the Pacific Islands.[2] The low, coral atolls of the Marshall Islands bounding the east of the Trust Territory are scattered along two parallel north-south axes, most with thin, meandering loops of palm-topped, sandy-soiled islets joined by low-lying reefs encircling extensive lagoons. Collectively, they formed an administrative district of the same name, with Majuro as its headquarters, and at the time of the Micronesian Constitutional Convention accounted for about one-fifth of the Trust Territory's population, and one-tenth of its land area. The Northern Marianas serve as part of the Trusteeship's western boundary at the other edge of the TTPI, a single chain along a north-south line. Ignoring political differentiation, they share a common geological heritage of dramatically uplifted limestone shelf and rich volcanic soil with Guam, the anchor island of the chain, but the legal delineation of the TTPI was so drawn as to exclude Guam. An acquisition of the Spanish American War, Guam had long been under United States rule as an American possession. The Northern Marianas are the converse of the Marshalls--more sparsely populated, with a quarter of the Trust Territory's land area occupied by half that fraction of its people. They are governed from Saipan, the largest island, to which the High Commissioner of the Trust Territory and his central administration were moved in 1962. The failure to have placed the Headquarters at a location more central to the whole of the TTPI was later to complicate Micronesia's transition to self-government.

Both high and low islands comprise the Carolines, the third archipelago which juts out to the southwest under Guam, and then in a wide band extends eastward over an arc of some two thousand miles toward the Marshalls. It was long divided into the remaining four administrative districts of the Trust Territory containing some seven distinct cultural groupings, and even more languages and sub-dialects. After the Micronesian Constitutional Convention, in 1977, an additional administrative district was to be formed around the island of Kusaie, a factor which was to prove crucial to the political future of a majority of the Micronesians.

In size of population and land area, Palau, at the westerly tip of the Carolines is almost indistinguishable from the Northern Marianas. Like the Marianas, too, its peoples shared disproportionately in the staffing of the TTPI Headquarters; while the Saipanese may have predominated in numbers, the Palauan educated elite held a near monopoly on its top administrative posts. Palau is administered from Koror, and was formerly the headquarters of the entire Mandate during the Japanese era, an historical antecedent which was to plague modern efforts to draw a constitution for Micronesia.

Several hundred miles to the northeast of Palau, four high islands, so closely conjoined as to seem as one, provide the ancestral home of the Yapese. Together with the people occupying the low islands stretching farther eastward for hundreds of miles, who once acknowledged their suzerainty under the Yap Empire, they are administered from the district center at Colonia. At the time of the Micronesian Constitutional Convention, the Yap District comprised about 7 percent of the population in the Trust Territory, and almost the same share of its land area. A small, culturally conservative area, its allegiance to Micronesian unity was to bulwark the efforts of the Convention.

In the center of the Carolines, the Truk District presents the anomaly of the Trust Territory's largest population (nearly 28 percent at the time of the Convention) living on as limited a land area as that of Yap, the smallest. Following traditional forms of subsistence usage, supplemented by copra cash cropping, some of the inhabited islands on the outer fringes of the Truk District have about reached their carrying capacities. The district takes its name from the vast Truk lagoon, and the location of the district headquarters on Moen, one of the many submerged mountain tops which have become islands within its fringing reef.

Truk's demographic pressures stand in sharp contrast to either those of the Northern Marianas or Palau, and superficially even to Ponape, nearly four hundred miles to the east. However, the Ponape district, which in 1975 was about the same in land area as the Northern Marianas or Palau, supported over double their proportion of the Trusteeship's population. At that time the separate administrative district of Kosrae (Kusaie) had not yet been formed, and the bulk of the single high islands of Ponape and Kusaie deceptively distorted the district's resources. In fact, several of the small islands in the Ponape District were facing the prospect of their populations outrunning food production. Resettlement on Ponape Island had already occurred of peoples from Pingelap and the equator-hugging atolls of Kapingamarangi and Nukuoro, both Polynesian outliers, and as such, cultural variants in Micronesia.

With district citizenry and land resources ill-matched, a population growth burgeoning at the annual rate of nearly 4 percent, and some of the outlying islands approaching their total utilization, the spector of human tragedy potential in failure accompanied all steps toward shaping the future governance of the Trust Territory. And complicating the task, the reality that is Micronesia was cloaked by a deception inherited from the Western world, which had posited a cultural commonality around which political integrity could be built.

When first contacted by Europeans, the tiny islands[3] scattered across the broad stretch of the North Pacific sustained peoples whose physical and ethnic similarities appeared to distinguish them from the rest of the world. The islands' minimally diverse resources supported a Stone Age style of life adapted to a tropical ocean location. Variance in language and culture was attributed to isolation over time, all subordinated to a basic similitude which was assumed to characterize these peoples collectively as Micronesians. So the abstraction remains to this day.

In fact, first contact with Micronesia encountered a myriad of minescule political units, with a range of social stratification filling the gamut in Sahlin's[4] classical gloss between the egalitarian "big man" of Melanesia and the chiefs of Eastern Polynesia's highly structured societies. A circumscribed empire, competing confederations, hereditary "kings," clan leaders of extended descent groups, all were distinctive political diversities which differentiated the islands when they were arbitrarily given collective names in honor of King Charles (Carolines) and Queen Regent Mariana de Austria (Marianas) of Spain, and the English captain of the vessel Scarborough for the Marshalls, who contacted them on his return voyage from carrying England's convicts to Australia. Over the interim of the four and a half centuries which have elapsed since Magellan, much of the traditional political structure was replaced by the imposed governments, but for the most part the underlying cultures which supported them only accommodated and did not disintegrate, nor did their attendant social stratification disappear.

Today, social and cultural heterogeneity still characterizes Micronesia. Even when living together on the same island, or within a single island chain, the various peoples of Micronesia continue to regard each other as different, and sometimes even as odious, while understanding little of any other island tradition beside their own. Their daily lives are a combination of customary and introduced ways, mostly concealed by an ever-thickening veneer of Western adaptation which hides and canalizes, but rarely completely supplants the traditional. "Though he may answer to the call of Palauan, Trukese, or Kusaien, [each Micronesian] sees himself more often than not as part of an extended family, a clan, a caste, an island community, a group that shares certain lands or titles or ceremonial wealth, or a constituency that gives support to and is served by a hereditary leader."[5]

It was the West which forcibly brought these island peoples together into larger political units, ignoring cultural and linguistic barriers, and simultaneously equipped them with the techniques necessary to sustain government over such an expanded area. Similarly, it has been the West which nourished the development of a commonality of political values unknown to Micronesians at the time of contact. It is to the Western intrusion that the concept of Micronesian political unity is indebted, initially as superimposed under the dominion of distant nations, and then as a growing aspiration of younger Micronesians caught up in the impetus of administering a single Micronesia. What tends to be forgotten, is well expressed by Philip W. Quigg, "the Trust Territory of the Pacific Islands, like so many political entities today, is an historical accident of the colonial period and therefore an artificial creation."[6]

The impact of the West at the outset appeared most prominently in the modification of physical Micronesia, the result of the genes, germs, and goods of explorers, whalers, and traders. To these early times can be traced the ever growing dependence of Micronesia on externalities. The superior military might of the West soon restricted the permissible scope of indigenous leadership, but for most of Micronesia the loss of formal political power was late occurring. Although the island of Guam, at the southern end of the Marianas had become the port of call of Spanish galleons outbound to the Philippines before the seventeenth century, and the pitifully small remnant of revolting Chamorros had been removed from the Northern Marianas to Guam by the eighteenth, the Hispanicizing of the Chamorros under centuries of Spanish rule had no parallel elsewhere in Micronesia. Only toward the end of the nineteenth century, when Germany challenged Spain's claims to suzerainty, did the latter begin to assert administrative authority over the Carolines, while Germany remained in the Marshalls. The Spanish-American War in 1898 saw military control of Guam transferred to the United States without violence, and over time the implanting there of an American set of political norms and forms. For the rest of the Hispanicized Chamorros who had resettled in the Northern Marianas in the 1800s, and the Carolinians both there and in Palau, Yap, Truk, and Ponape, the German Kaiser soon became their ruler by purchase of the area from Spain. During the ensuing fifteen years, for the most part Germany continued the indirect rule observed by Spain outside of the Marianas, seeking to maintain peace and promote economic development through the islands' traditional political structures. If these efforts had continued, most probably Micronesia would not have presented the disparity of culture change which was to undercut the attempt over a half century later to shape an all-encompassing constitution.

The labors of the Germans in achieving economic growth were truncated by Japanese seizure of the islands in World War I, and later were fully eclipsed. The Japanese purpose of eventual incorporation of Micronesia into its empire was to be fulfilled through colonization, aggressively supported by economic development. Resident Japanese, Okinawans, and Koreans came to outnumber the indigenes, and Japanese-style administration was instituted in the urbanized district centers of the major islands where the bulk of the colonists resided. For the outlying areas, with their predominantly Micronesian population, government was executed through the Japanese police, with local leaders keeping the peace, collecting taxes, maintaining vital statistics, and otherwise implementing their directions, frequently employing the mechanisms of the traditional social structure for the purpose. By utilizing great ingenuity and heavy subsidization, much of the latter hidden, the Japanese extensively exploited the islands' resources of sun, soil, and sea. This primarily took the form of sugar and copra production, phosphate and alumina mining, and a highly diversified marine industry. In retrospect, Japanese experience, like that of the predecessor colonial powers, was to point up Micronesia's physical limitations and the failure of the area's human resources to quickly or easily adopt Western-style modes of production. These same factors were to trouble the entire period of the American administration after World War II, compounded by the nostalgic legacy left by the Japanese of a golden era now lost to the Micronesians.

Accompanying the demographic and economic buildup, the Japanese installed the transportation, communication, and related supporting infrastructure necessary to sustain the development of Micronesia and to make the islands sufficiently attractive to encourage colonists to immigrate. In the outlying islands reliable scheduling assured the inflow of trade goods and the transshipment of the waiting copra and marine products before they spoiled. In the district centers, utilities designed for Japanese industry and commerce, and tending to the comforts of colonists, furnished electric, telephone, and water service to some indigenous consumers as well. Most of the physical improvements built by the Japanese to further their colonization efforts were either destroyed during World War II, or had deteriorated to a state of unusability by the end of hostilities. Military-related construction from which civilian benefit might be realized--the harbor improvements, docks, warehouses, water and fuel storage, airfields and seaplane ramps--was targeted for Allied demolition during the course of the war, and civilian buildings in their vicinity suffered the same attacks. After the transfer of Micronesia to American rule, the first decade and a half saw little more than temporizing repair of the remaining Japanese physical infrastructure, and conversion of the facilities which the American military had hastily erected in aid of their own war efforts. By the end of the 1930s, Japanese concentration upon economic development had been superseded by preparation of Micronesia as a base for launching World War II, and eventually all activity not devoted to winning the war was curtailed. At the termination of hostilities, Micronesia was in collapse, the Japanese military having commandeered the remaining civilian goods and facilities, and both colonists and indigenes were reduced to literal subsistence. The economy in Micronesia would not have regained its prewar dynamism, diversity, or productivity, nor civilian life its lost glitter, by the time the constitutional convention delegates were to gather on Saipan in 1975.

The Spanish devoted great care to the missionary field, and little to the economic development of Micronesia. The converse was true for the Germans and Japanese, and the Americans have paid relatively little attention to either.

The Trust Territory has held small economic attraction to the United States, and initial American policy was to encourage an indigenous living standard commensurate with the potential of Micronesia's known natural resources. The "most favored nation" clause of the Trusteeship Agreement was interpreted to limit investment to Micronesians and citizens of the United States. Not until 1974 were permits granted to individual and commercial investors of foreign countries, and then under conditions assuring the security of the area. The application of United States tariffs to imports from the Trust Territory and the policy of security clearance discouraged all but a few Americans from entering Micronesia to engage in private enterprise. For long, the Van Camp Seafood Company's tuna catching and freezing plant in Palau represented the only significant industrial development of the postwar American period. It would be several years after the Constitutional Convention before the $3 million copra processing plant in Palau, with a capacity for handling all of Micronesia's copra, was to open, the largest, privately financed industrial undertaking in the Trust Territory. From the mid-1940s, through the following decade, and into the 1960s, with the Japanese-built infrastructure in ruins, and lacking the private entrepreneurs and skilled artisans who were withdrawn when the Asian colonists were repatriated, the Micronesian economy limped along, giving rise to the sobriquet of "Rust Territory."

Some of the difficulties which the Micronesian Constitutional Convention faced in 1975 traced directly back to decisions made decades before in Washington in allocating responsibility for governing the Trust Territory. To the United States Navy was first assigned the responsibility for administering the war-conquered Pacific islands. It encouraged the Micronesians to reestablish normal routines of life, and to revive copra, trochus, and handicraft production as sources of money income. For a while the export of scrap metal also contributed to helping rebuild the Island economy. The supplies at first provided by the American forces to alleviate Micronesian suffering gradually became a steady stream of imported food and trade goods sold directly by government and by governmental instrumentality, and then through Micronesian trading cooperatives managed by Americans. In many functional areas, the range of governmental services reestablished by the Navy never equalled those provided normally by the Japanese. Later, when, under the rhetoric that it could govern more efficiently, the Department of Interior replaced the Navy in 1951, and civilian succeeded military administrators, government activities further contracted, and for a decade thereafter the Trusteeship "made do" on a spartan budget. The true cost to the United States treasury of the initial Navy years has never been fully computed, since various support services were rendered as incidental to maintaining the American military presence in the Pacific. Over the period 1952-62, the federal grant to the Department of Interior for administering the far-flung Trust Territory averaged $5.2 million annually under an authorization ceiling fixed at $7.5 million by Congress. A compensating factor, if so it be treated, is that of the entire time under the American flag, during this decade Micronesia most closely lived within its own economic capacity, as measured by the imbalance of the area's imports and exports.

What David Nevin[7] calls a tactical shift--the original strategy of maintaining Micronesia as part of the American defense zone in the Pacific never changing--the National Security Council in 1962 decided to scrap the Trusteeship's cover of security. Instead, through developing the islands, the Micronesians would be so favorably influenced that they would affiliate permanently with the United States. Symbolizing this intent, Headquarters of the High Commissioner for the first time was located within the Trust Territory, occupying the quarters vacated on Saipan when the CIA terminated its training program there for Asian agents and guerrillas. "The economy would be improved. Self-government, with elected district legislatures and a territorial congress, would be advanced. Education, health, and social welfare would be stressed. Transportation would be improved. Water systems, sewer systems, landing strips, hospitals, housing, would be built."[8] All semblance of slowly reestablishing a postwar Micronesia, with an economy based on the region's own natural wealth and entrepreneurial skills, and a government scaled proportionately, was to be abandoned. Just the year previously, the United Nations Visiting Mission had criticized the United States for failing to prepare Micronesia for self-determination and to develop the Territory's resources. Now, in part through massive monetary infusions, the political future of Micronesia was to be secured.

For fiscal year 1962-63, the federal grant for the Trust Territory rose an extraordinary 150 percent to $15 million under a budget ceiling of $17.5 million, and in irregular jumps thereafter the United States Congress continued to increase Territorial authorizations and appropriations for operating expenses of government and for capital improvements. The classified 1963 Solomon Report, which was concerned with implementing the National Security Council's decisions, recommended raising the TTPI's budget to an average annual $360 per capita over a four year period; this was doubled by 1971. While locally realized revenues gradually grew, they met only a small fraction of all public expenditures, amounting to about 12 percent by the summer of 1975, when the Micronesian Constitutional Convention was to meet. At this point of time, United States "aid" to the Trust Territory totalled about $80 million annually, representing the highest per capita U.S. economic assistance furnished to any underdeveloped foreign area. As a fit complement to this monetary effort, more Peace Corps Volunteers in relation to size of population had been introduced into Micronesia than any other country in the world.

During the first fifteen years of the Trust Territory, probably the profoundest impact on Micronesian life was made in the field of education. Markedly enlarging the limited, severely tracked Japanese system, American education laid a foundation of knowledge and values which gradually undermined satisfaction with a village life-style based upon subsistence farming supplemented by income earned from copra marketing, and constrained by the remaining hierarchical premises of tradition. With the proliferation of schools, by the time of the Micronesian Constitutional Convention severe problems of demoralization among the young and a surplus of educated unemployed were appearing.

In the second fifteen years of the Trust Territory, the primacy of education was overtaken by mushrooming governmental expenditures and the manifestation of their efforts in an ever-expanding consumer economy in which the average Micronesian came to enjoy an artificially inflated standard of living. Wages paid indigenes and export income mainly from copra, which had not much more than doubled in the decade 1952-61, quintupled in the next. By mid-1975, not alone did agriculture constitute the main economic activity of only about half the households in Micronesia, but indigenous production had failed to keep pace with the expansion of the Territorial population. During the five years just before the Micronesian Constitutional Convention it is doubtful that any real economic growth had occurred, with the larger federal government grants which went mostly into salaries accounting for the 12 percent growth registered in Gross Domestic Product. Exacerbating these disruptive economic changes, the supplying of a seeming inexhaustible cornucopia of free social services by government had helped to establish a welfare state psychology.

As governmental expenditures mounted to between 60 and 70 percent of the Gross Domestic Product of Micronesia--double the rate in the United States --the public bureaucracy multiplied. Concomitantly, the population shifted to the islands having the district headquarters, so that the annual growth rate of resident populations at these centers between the two last censuses (1967-1973) was double that of the Territory as a whole. At the time of the Constitutional Convention, government was by far the largest single employer and its payrolls accounted for about three-fourths of all wages earned. With public employment reputedly non-taxing, and with the average Micronesian governmental wage earner receiving over double the salary of his private counterpart (1975),[9] the preference for government employment required little explanation. In addition, servicing the public bureaucracy had become the mainstay of secondary industry in the island district centers. A reaction, seeking to move Micronesia toward a production-oriented economy through trimming the large cadre of highly paid government workers and eliminating activities considered non-productive, was just beginning to take shape among the Micronesian elite about the time the Convention delegates assembled on Saipan. To bring this to pass, however, they would have to provide for a government possessing the means for controlling the full gamut of public expenditures, a power not yet exercised by Micronesians.

During the Japanese era, economic development had been most extensive in the Mariana and Palau districts. The continued presence of the U.S. Navy in the Northern Marianas until 1962, and the higher level of governmental services and capital expenditures it brought to the district while the rest of the Trust Territory suffered the penury of the Department of Interior's administration, resulted in the Marianas being materially better off and psychologically less traumatized than Palau. Indeed, the U.N. Visiting Missions in 1961 presciently warned that the differential treatment being afforded to the Marianas would discourage the future unity of Micronesia. It did not allude to a contributing cultural factor: that Chamorros from the Marianas had been used as supervisors in other districts during preceding colonial administrations, so that the ill-will early generated was only being exacerbated. The final placing of all Micronesia under the Department of the Interior did not terminate what appeared as favorite treatment for the

Marianas, and particularly for Palau, it represented a further reverse. The Japanese had governed their Mandate from Koror in the Palau District; now, the Trust Territory Headquarters on Saipan in the Northern Marianas assured that the latter district would be the first to feel the impact of expanded governmental expenditures and services. So sparked, the pace of development would be fastest in the Marianas, and the shift there to a consumer economy most pronounced.

By the time of the Micronesian Constitutional Convention, half of the Trust Territory Operating Budget was being allocated to Headquarters and the Marianas, and per capita Gross Domestic Product in the district ($2,713) was over two and a half times greater than that of the Trust Territory as a whole ($1,051). Put in perspective, while the Marianas alone accounted for one-third of the total GDP of the Territory, its area constituted but one-fourth of the Territory's limited land, and its population only one-eighth. The explanation for the disparity lay in the high proportion of the Territory's wage income earned in the Marianas (37.1 percent), particularly in the private service sector (43.1 percent). Conversely, copra production had now nearly been abandoned. Palau, too, showed little interest in producing copra, but its slightly above average per capita GDP ($1,103) was hardly sufficient to compensate for the loss of the higher economic status it enjoyed during the Japanese era, nor to warrant the general air of superiority with which Palauans characteristically viewed other Micronesians. All of this contributed to the volatility of tensions which separated these two districts from the rest of the Trust Territory. As an added factor, the deriving of half of the territory's internally-levied income tax yield from the Marshalls, primarily due to the presence of Americans at the Kwajalien missile testing base, without a corresponding share of benefits voted by the Congress of Micronesia, had alienated that district. These three districts at the periphery of the Trust Territory regarded those in the center as unduly benefitting at their expense, and with the Administering Authority building few bonds of countervailing interdependence, economic development during the American period offered little to unifying the TTPI.[10]

The Micronesians' relations with Americans have long embraced a considerable degree of ambivalence, arising from a number of causes. The friendliness and egalitarianism of American troops contrasted sharply with the behavior of the Japanese military in the latter days of World War II, so Micronesians early welcomed the Americans. Once civilian administration was established, fraternization was never discouraged nor colonial caste line recognized. On the other hand, many of the wartime personnel who remained on in governmental service regarded the indigenous inhabitants as incapable of upgrading through technical training and culturally unqualified for assignments of responsibility, an attitude shared by some who later joined the Trust Territory service. Much of the daily administration at district and territorial headquarters appeared directed to the comforts of the resident Americans, so that the latter conspicuously enjoyed superior living conditions as well as higher pay. Micronesian mastery of technical and professional skills started slowly, and then quickened. Of necessity, even with the emphasis upon "localization," this meant expatriates continued to fill the billets in the Territory demanding specialized services, in later years frequently as nominal assistants to the Micronesians who have risen to staff the higher administrative posts. Inevitably this bolstered the sentiment, early spawned by reaction to those Americans who depreciated Micronesian ability, that Micronesians were being denied access to governmental opportunities rightfully theirs, particularly the more lucrative posts. That expatriates in 1975 still made up about 7 percent of the governmental work force after three decades of American rule, and on the average were far more highly paid, but served to confirm the belief. It was only to be regarded as retributive justice that the burden of the Territorial income tax relatively fell most heavily upon the expatriate in Micronesia.

Another factor contributing to the Micronesians' state of ambivalence arose from cultural conditioning in their dealing with four different colonial administrations. Over that period, Micronesians became adept at seemingly concurring with, but subtly manipulating the expatriate administrator. Coupled with Island distaste for precipitate decision-making, the practice of basing agreements upon consensus rather than fiat, and the need for accommodating family and cultural pressures of little moment to the expatriate, the Micronesian approached the administration of government somewhat differently than did the American counterpart, frequently to their mutual annoyance.

A final factor was the growing Micronesian suspicion, in many cases spilling over into distrust, and in some instances, manifest hatred, arising out of the American presence. At the time of the Constitutional Convention, approximately 60 percent of the land of the Trust Territory was classified as "public," this despite the objections of Micronesians that much had been acquired through duress in previous administrations, and large tracts were still traditionally claimed. For the American Administration to justify its continuing to hold these lands as being in the best interest of the Micronesians was only to be interpreted as an insincere delaying ruse to achieve other objectives. Similarly, the long postponed payment of war claims and the equally drawn out negotiations over future status led many Islanders to conclude that the motives of the United States must be perpetually questioned, and American policy always dealt with at arms length. At even greater depths of feeling, the whole tragedy of nuclear testing in the Pacific, with Micronesians subject to atomic fallout, entire island populations displaced, and with some returned only to be resettled, gave rise to the horrendous charge that the United States was deliberately experimenting with Micronesians as human guinea pigs to measure the effects of atomic exposure in its various forms.

During the course of both the Spanish and German periods, armed rebellion by Micronesians had challenged their rule. While the motives for the burning of the Congress of Micronesia chambers and the High Commissioner's residence on Saipan in 1971 have yet to be determined, there is no suggestion that they were part of an organized resistance to continuation of the American presence. Rather, action centering on the subject of future status was all on the level of the oral and written word, sometimes accompanied with the using of verbal maneuvers reminiscent of wrestling holds, as Micronesians applied pressure by appearance before the Trusteeship Council, the point of the United States' greatest vulnerability. Public clamor and mass demands were absent. The unusual spectacle in 1970 of twenty Micronesian students and their American supporters demonstrating outside a Honolulu hotel with banners demanding "Freedom for Micronesia," while Vice-President

Spiro T. Agnew addressed the annual Associated Press Managing Editors Conference within, had been quickly swallowed up in the pouring rain which drenched them. Instead, after the United States succeeded to the governance of the islands, opposition to its perpetuation took the form of unstructured and sometimes discordant Micronesian attitudes toward the United States. In the Constitutional Convention they were to become the basis for such diverse actions as the declaration of the sovereignty of the people of Micronesia and at the same time almost exclusive reliance upon American political philosophy and practice in structuring the new government to be erected. Unfortunately for achieving political unity, this anti-American phase of Micronesian ambivalence was to prove a poor substitute for a more positive premise, such as might have been supplied by a common traditional heritage,[11] to bind together all the peoples of the Trust Territory.

Few of the island polities within the Pacific are favored with proven economic resources which assure them a prosperous future. Those of Micronesia have normally been treated as particularly constrictive, and as incorporating the risk of political precariousness into any aspiration for independence. In the view of the 1973 U.N. Visiting Mission Report, "Complete self-sufficiency for Micronesians, except at a standard of living which would be unacceptable to most of its people, is doubtless unattainable."[12] But such judgments are out of harmony with the realpolitik of today, for political change occurring in the Pacific has not waited upon economic viability. In addition, in Micronesian minds, the value of their island resources is incalculable, that is, beyond current pricing, and as such can serve as a foundation for any new political entity they may wish to launch. In truth, there is enough vagueness about the area's known resources, and uncertainty about the dimensions of the unknown, as to permit undermining the credence of any challenge opposing the Micronesian position. In any event, it had become an important element in all political maneuvering accompanying the termination of the Trusteeship.

On land, Japanese exploration had disclosed traces of gold, silver, and manganese, the limited presence of iron, copper, and lignite, and more extensive bauxite deposits. Under American aegis the phosphate deposits on Angaur continued to be exploited until they could no longer be safely removed, but all other mining ceased. Precious coral has been the only mineral developed in commercial quantities from the Pacific ocean floor, but the abyssal deep is known to have calcareous ooze potentially suitable for industrial uses. In addition, in the Pacific there are areas of red clay containing alumina, and fields of nodules composed of manganese, cobalt, copper, and nickel. And there is always the possibility of discovering petroleum on land or through drilling on the ocean floor. The future, while enigmatic, remains inviting.

More readily to hand is the income to be earned from exploitation of the Trust Territory's marine resources. Foreign live-bait skipjack vessels and longline fishing boats taking yellow-fin tuna from Micronesian waters have established the creditability of this natural asset. Even without islanders themselves manning the fishing craft, there are royalties to be obtained from the awarding of fishing rights, and spin-off benefits to be gained from the operation of cold storage, canning, and other supporting shoreside facilities. When the Congress of Micronesia in 1974[13] sought to declare Micronesia an archipelagic state, permitting the drawing of lines connecting the outermost islands, and claiming internal sea jurisdiction as well as an economic zone for two hundred miles outside the baseline, it appeared a mere gesture taken in support of its negotiating committee at the United Nations Law of the Sea Conference. Subsequently, however, Fiji declared itself such an archipelagic regime and the various other island areas in the Pacific[14] have similarly taken steps to profit from their ocean resources. While the value of access to Micronesian waters for fishing nations such as Japan has at times been idly bandied in astronomically large economic terms, a monetary return of more modest proportions is assured to Micronesia so long as the fish supply and the tuna market hold.

Paradoxically, it is those very physical aspects of Micronesia's location which make its administration difficult and its economic development so tenuous which also provide its greatest potential for deriving external assistance sufficient to support viable self-government. Its siting in the Western Pacific, distant from heavily populated areas, its own population widely dispersed over

3 million miles of ocean, has caused the western section to be touted for the location of a multi-billion dollar petroleum storage and petrochemical industry mainly serving Japan. Similarly, a trial balloon has been floated proposing the setting up of a nuclear fuel storage and reprocessing facility for the Pacific in Micronesia, to be jointly constructed and shared by Japan, Australia, and Southeast Asian countries. But by far the most potent source for obtaining external aid is the capitalizing upon Micronesia's strategic position at the center of the geopolitical figure formed by the four super-powers of the Pacific, the United States, Soviet Union, Japan, and China. The Micronesian islands in Hanson W. Baldwin's words, "can provide both barriers and bases for any Pacific strategy,"[15] and as such are essential to the United States maintaining any forward position in the Western Pacific. In the lengthy negotiations between Americans and Micronesians over future political status, both the obtaining of access by United States military forces for specific missions and fall-back bases, and the denial of all Micronesia to any unfriendly power comprised the fundamental, even if sometimes not so articulated, American objectives. Of course, much of this has been conditioned upon the strategy and tactics of previous wars, rapidly becoming outdated, so that inherent even in the Micronesian "asset" of situs is an element of the same uncertainty implicit in the other resources upon which Micronesians must rely.

All of this provided the background for the drama of the Micronesian Constitutional Convention of 1975, without an understanding of which the play would be unintelligible. As I saw it then, I believe it mustered all of the major structural components. Upon reflection, I am no longer so positive, and more particularly, that I was competent to assign valences which corresponded with those affixed by Micronesians. About all of which I can be certain is that the delegates and I viewed the constitutional acts as they unfolded against the same world backdrop in which the community of nations had mushroomed since World War II to include an ever expanding group of ministates. Before the War, there had been only about six insular countries; by the third quarter of the twentieth century there were now some thirty, and the future held the prospect of their numbers doubling, with a majority in the Caribbean and Pacific. Both I and the Micronesians knew that there appeared to be no requisite minimal geographic size, population, or economic capacity for international recognition. Notwithstanding Micronesia's very modest proven assets, its leaders could embark upon a course of self-determination which would carry its peoples to independence, or some other status short of that.

----

1. Sailing to the Northwest Coast of North America, and then down to Acapulco, Mexico, the Spanish galleons headed northeast from Manila, and followed a route running north of Hawaii. Anything south of this sailing route is the "South Seas."

2. Subsequent to the adjournment of the 1975 Constitutional Convention of Micronesia, the Northern Marianas were withdrawn from the jurisdiction of the High Commissioner and placed under separate administration, while awaiting the termination of the Trusteeship. Also, a new district--Kosrae --was formed in 1977 by detaching the island of Kusaie from the Ponape District. However, the setting of the Constitutional Convention was that of the six administrative districts as described in the text.

3. Giving the basis for "Micronesia," coined out of the Greek words *mikros* (tiny) and *neso* (islands). Actually, the Gilberts at the conjunction of the dateline and equator, and the minescule Nauru lying just below the equator are also classed as Micronesian. While ethnologically related, their governance as distinctive island units has distinguished them from the region above the equator, so that in a political sense, "Micronesia" and "Trust Territory of the Pacific Islands" have come to be almost synonymous, and are so used in the text.

4. Marshall D. Sahlins, "Poor Man, Rich Man, Big-Man, Chief: Political Types in Melanesia and Polynesia," in Ian Hogbin and L.R. Hiatt (eds.), *Readings* in *Australian* and *Pacific* *Anthropology* (London: Melbourne University Press, 1966), p. 159.

5. Leonard Mason, "The Many Faces of Micronesia," 1971, p. 33. Unpublished manuscript.

6. Philip W. Quigg, "Coming of Age in Micronesia," *Foreign* *Affairs* 47:3 (April 1969), 493, at p. 495.

7. David Nevin, _The American Touch in Micronesia_ (New York: W.W. Norton & Company, 1977), p. 113.

8. _Idem_, p. 112.

9. To complete the record, at the same point of time, the average salaries of expatriates in governmental service were four-and-a-half times greater than those of expatriates in private employment, and, incidental to matters yet to be considered. They were also four-and-a-half times greater than the average wage of Micronesians on the public payroll.

10. At the 1,231st meeting of the Trusteeship Council on June 2, 1964, the High Commissioner was queried about what the American Administration was doing "to foster a homogeneous national feeling among the people of the Trust Territory." He responded with a reference to development of transport, adoption of a flag symbolizing Micronesia, radio broadcasting stations, inter-district schooling, and seminars and meetings at which people from various districts gathered. Absent was inclusion of any reference to economic activity which would aid integration of Micronesia. See T/SR. 1231, p. 47, par. 28.

11. A political myth of positive nature with potential for uniting Micronesia emerged a year before the Constitutional Convention, but was never exploited. A review of Micronesian oral history conducted by the staff of the Congress of Micronesia was found to indicate the existence of a prehistory political structure consisting of several large political entities. The Palau and Marshall islands were each distinct entities, although this was not clearly established. The rest of the Micronesian islands were united in a single polity called the "Kachau Empire" embracing all of the Carolines (excluding Angaur and the islands north in Palau) and all of the Marianas. The central figures were a series of chiefs called "Soukachau" who resided on Kusaie (old name "Kachau") and great navigators, named "Poluelap," who consolidated the empire and ruled the sea. The empire had fragmented by the advent of the Spanish. See Congress of Micronesia, _Micronesian Navigation Island Empires, and Traditional Concepts of Ownership of the Sea_, Fifth Congress, 2nd Reg. Session, January, 1974.

12. United Nations Visiting Mission Report on the Trust Territory of the Pacific Islands, May, 1973, par. 206, T/1748, p. 45.

13. S.J.R. No. 80, Fifth Congress of Micronesia, 2nd Session, 1974.

14. See *Epilogue*, p. 20, for disagreement between the United States and Palauan negotiators over archipelagic provisions of the Palau Constitution.

15. Hanson W. Baldwin, *Strategy for Tomorrow* (New York: Harper and Row, 1970), p. 279.

Chapter 2. Trust Territory Government

Viewed from the perspective of hindsight, the interregnum of the United States in Micronesia may be faulted in a number of respects.[1] Arrayed as a countervailing factor--as of the Micronesian Constitutional Convention--stood three decades of political growth, with Micronesians enjoying an ever greater involvement in an expanding scope of power never experienced in any of the previous three colonial periods. Brought to the fore was as politically capable an educated elite as could be found anywhere in the islands of the Pacific. The whole course of the Micronesian future status negotiations, with the Americans finding themselves continually retreating, bore full witness to this development. The Convention of 1975 and the events which immediately preceded its meeting were to provide ample opportunity for the display of Micronesian political sophistication, whether measured in modern or traditional terms.

In technical delineation, the United States established a unitary, three-tiered, American-style political system in Micronesia with highly differentiated public offices, a bureaucratic system of administrative command, and a variety of means for exercising authority through the imposition of sanctions which ultimately depend upon secular force. Emphasized early were institutions embodying political "representation." However, the introduction of the "separation of powers" principle along with a presidential-type chief executive were unaccompanied by a complementary attention to "checks and balances." For the most part, all of this was structured outside the stratified political order of tradition, so that those occupying roles of authority under Micronesian custom were assured no comparable place in the new institutions. The American presence marked a major break with former colonial government and raised a further challenge to custom.

The cultures of Micronesia embodied no fundamental egalitarianism which would serve as the basic underpinning for the building of a democratic polity. In the main, it waited upon the American

Administration after World War II to nourish political implants which subsumed that the future course of Micronesia was to be along the path of democracy, with all of its citizens to be treated as political equals. The Americans reconstituted local government, set up district administrations in which Micronesians came to play an important part, and embarked upon a course of gradually transferring the running of the central government into the hands of the Territory's citizens, always with control reserved in Washington. Nominally at least, demonstration of capacity determined the bureaucratic choice of Micronesian civil servants, while the secret ballot decided between aspirants for political office. Beneath the surface, friction continued between the remaining stratification of traditional society, premised upon status, and the introduced forms and processes of democracy. Normally, it was far from apparent. The influence of the traditional leader continued strongest in the municipality, received polite, but somewhat condescending acknowledgment in most of the district governments, and only formalistic recognition at the Hicom level of the Territory. In the drafting of the Micronesian constitution this underlying tension was to open a basic cleavage among the delegates.

The advent of the U.S. Naval Government with World War II temporarily returned to positions of authority in community and district government those traditional chiefs still acceptable to their people, but reserved all higher administrative and judicial positions for Americans. Over time, most of these prescriptive leaders voluntarily retired from their governmental posts in favor of the younger and better educated. Meanwhile, the shape of community government was formalized with the Trust Territory parceled up into municipalities whose boundaries for the most part preserved the customary, geopolitical divisions. These municipalities continued to remain the basic unit of government, closest to most people in Micronesia, and bounding the political perspective of many.

Each municipality came to have a magistrate (a few urbanized municipalities use the title of "mayor"), secretary, a council, most a municipal judge, and some limited additional personnel including policemen and a miscellany of municipal employees. Nearly all elect their magistrate and

councilors, introducing their peoples to American
precepts and practices, even if elections were
a mere formality when first instituted.[2] Clan
or kin group ties may still be instrumental in
achieving success at the polls, just as they can
influence election to higher office, and undoubtedly
helped determine the choice of some Convention
delegates. At last count there were 115 recognized
units of local government in the Trust Territory
of which two-fifths were formally chartered. Initially undertaken with great fanfare, chartering
accomplished little more than to assure use of
the election mechanism for choosing officers, and
observance of greater standardization of form and
training in the procedures of Westernized local
government. Municipalities construct minor local
improvements and exercise a limited range of designated powers in conducting municipal affairs.
Ordinances are adopted by council and magistrate,
where the former are elected, and by act of the
magistrate in the minority of the communities where
the councilors remain merely advisory. The magistrate has long provided liaison between community
and the executive branch of the regional administration and has been generally responsible for seeing
that laws and administrative orders are observed.
Particularly in the Outer Islands, he and the other
municipal officers perform few duties that would
not have been expected of local government more
traditionally structured, but they now receive
out of municipal taxes and fees a remuneration
for services which formerly would have been gratuitously rendered. Concomitantly, this serves
to exhaust a major part of the meager resources
available for financing municipal affairs.

From the beginning of district government
under the United States Navy, an administrator
accountable to the central government headed the
executive branch. After a few years, the familiar
American tri-partite form emerged, although lawmaking powers were not granted when district legislatures were first chartered. Representation in
these district legislatures was only broadly predicated upon population, varying from district to
district to reflect the desire to accommodate severally a maximum number of islands irrespective
of their size. Originally the district legislatures
brought both traditional leaders and elected Micronesian representatives into an advisory role at
this intermediate level of government, but in all
of the districts with chiefs, the assumption of

law-making power by the legislatures was eventually accompanied by reduction of their participation. By the time of the Constitutional Convention they held seats in only two district legislatures, Palau and the Marshalls--in the former without right of vote and in the latter only by virtue of having been elected as chiefs. Once possessed of legislating powers, bills adopted by a district legislature required the approval of the district administrator, and with his veto overridden, the impasse was raised to the High Commissioner for resolution. The imposition of district taxes and fees, the funding of public improvements, and the exercise of the police power for the maintenance of the public peace, health, and safety pretty well delineated the parameters of power set by legislative charter and Territorial law.

The executive branch at this district level closely paralleled that at Trust Territory Headquarters, with the latter's departments and staff agencies in many cases structurally replicated. Of the eight Headquarters departments existent at the time of the Constitutional Convention, four were concerned with direct services to individuals (Education, Health Services, Public Works, and Transportation and Communications), and another two with aspects of development (economic: Resources and Development; political: Public Affairs). The remaining two Headquarters departments (Finance and Personnel) filled more appropriately with the large number of staff and auxiliary agencies at Headquarters, which included an Executive Officer, Attorney General, Program and Budget Officer, Territorial Planner, Internal Auditor, and a shifting mix of special consultants and special assistants. Comparable functions were being performed at the Trust Territory and district levels, very frequently by similarly named offices of government. To the extent the district agencies were controlled by their counterparts at Headquarters, they tended to conduct themselves as field stations of the central government, outside of the effective direction of the District Administrator. However, the Territory had long vacillated over the degree of authority and responsibility to be allocated to the districts. Most recently there had been a devolution to the district, and a consonant growth in the stature of the District Administrator. With the exercising of greater discretion over the selection of personnel and the reallocation of funds within the district, he was in line to becoming central to the implementation of all governmental policy within his district. Such delegation of authority, of course, could occur no faster than permitted by the relaxation of the personnel, contracting, and policy mandates from Washington over the High Commissioner's administration of the whole Trust Territory. These, too, had varied over time from the one extreme of treating the Trust Territory as somewhat akin to a foreign government, to the other of holding the High Commissioner as closely accountable to Washington as the civilian head of any United States possession.

The third branch of district government--the judiciary--early incorporated an American system of jurisprudence administered by Micronesian judges under the watchful eye of the expatriate-staffed Trust Territory High Court. Appeals lay to the district courts from the approximately one hundred community courts which normally had jurisdiction over misdemeanors and minor civil suits, comparable to justices of the peace in the United States. To the district judges was also early assigned responsibility for trying the more serious criminal offenses and the civil cases of larger monetary import, with major felonies and actions of greater technical difficulty reserved to the original authority of the High Court. Over the three decades of American rule, to this large body of untrained judges under the guidance of the American jurists in the High Court had fallen the duty of reconciling Micronesian custom with introduced Western law. For the most important matters, whatever their nature, this task had been directly assumed by the Chief Justice and Associate Justices, either in the Trial or Appellate Divisions of the High Court. This judicial structure of the Trusteeship differed from some of the Polynesian areas of the Pacific where Land and Title Courts staffed by indigenous judges have been appended outside of the regular hierarchy of courts for the resolution of traditional issues. Rulings of the High Court with respect to customary obligations and, particularly, land matters in Micronesia had given rise to regional pockets of dissatisfaction with American law. In this was to lie much of the reason for the extended debate in the Constitutional Convention over the system of Jurisprudence to be recognized by the Micronesian constitution and the provision to be made for recognition of traditional rights.

From its inception the court system in Micronesia was independent of directions from the High Commissioner, as later it was to be from the Congress of Micronesia. Similarly it was not subject to external review, for its decisions were not appealable to the United States courts. The Chief Justice and the Associated Justices of the High Court have owed their appointments to the Secretary of the Interior, the district judges to the High Commissioner, and the community court judges to the District Administrators. However, all of the courts remained under the administration and technical supervision of the Chief Justice. The mystique of the law seemingly inherent in common law jurisdictions has long adorned the Micronesia courts, and has added to the prestige of judges and justices in the Trust Territory. Possibly because of this, together with the emphasis upon the judiciary as the bastion of individual protection against arbitrary government as taught in the area's American-style educational system, the delegates came to the Constitutional Convention in 1975 imbued with the value of an independent judiciary, outside the vicissitudes of political maneuver, much along the lines of the then existing model.

The cost of funding the courts represented the smallest expense of all major programmatic operations of the TTPI. Actual budgets of federal grant funds[3] show that for Fiscal 1975 the Judiciary was totally eclipsed by expenditures for Education, Health Services, and Public Works, and far exceeded by all others. (See Table 1, p. 41.)

When the Micronesian Constitutional Convention delegates met on Saipan, government in the Trust Territory was performing most all functions found publicly rendered on the mainland United States, including almost exclusively furnishing some which the citizens of the fifty states regard as primarily falling within the domain of the private economy. Among the latter were utilities, communication, and the total range of health care. Federal agencies were directly providing postal services, navigational assistance, defense and emergency protection, and enforcement of a modicum of United States regulatory acts applicable in Micronesia, this in addition to the activities of public servants of the municipal, district, and Headquarters levels of the Trust government. That many of these public services tended to be enjoyed mostly around district centers, so that life on the distant islands was less directly affected, in no way negates the familiarity with government in action which the delegates brought with them to the Micronesian Convention. They were conversant with the potential ranges of government which could be encompassed within the document they were charged to draft--even those who were minimally schooled and lacked personal encounter with the operations of government outside of the geographical boundaries of Micronesia.

The delegates had no comparable opportunity to be prepared within the Trust Territory for making choices between alternative systems of government, or even understanding the political processes which underpin the different forms of democracy functioning in the world. While Japan had been governed under a limited parliamentary system during the period of the Mandate, the older delegates to the Constitutional Convention could probably have recollected little other than an autocratic rule in which Micronesians were expected to give unquestioned obedience to the representatives of the Emperor serving in the South Seas. After World War II, it was primarily the American model of government with which these island peoples became acquainted through the example of political institutions introduced into the Trust Territory and the education received in Territorial schools. There was no censorship which kept published materials out of the Territory, but its cultures are oral and do not encourage individualized learning through recourse to the written word. With few foreign visitors permitted admission, there was little opportunity through that source of contact for the spread of information about other political systems. Foreign travel and advanced education received outside of the Trust Territory introduced some Micronesians to the mysteries of comparative government, but for most of them, this was mainly a taxonomic exercise. News media supplied topical snapshots rather than analytic assessment of foreign political institutions. Few pondered more than superficially whether so complicated and inherently discordant (to most of Micronesia) a system of government as the American, with its separation of powers and checks and balances, its reliance upon majority rule rather than consensus, and its insistence upon political equality, best met the needs of Micronesia. Even fewer were prepared to question all democratic systems of the West and consider whether an alternative should be adapted for Micronesia. With three decades devoid of personal experience providing meaningful appraisal of any other than the American political system, the delegates were conditioned to approach their drafting tasks from this single frame of reference. Probably most were unaware that as long ago as 1969 this had been tacitly recognized by Micronesia's spokesmen in their negotiations with the United States on future political status:

> Whatever our particular evaluations of the American administration in Micronesia may be, we feel that one contribution has been indelible, one achievement almost unqualified: the idea of democratic, representative, constitutional government.... We endorse this system--which was brought to us by America, and which we have come to know as an essentially American system. (Congress of Micronesia, Report of the Future Political Status Commission, Third Congress, 2nd Session, July 1969, p. 8.)

Prevailing in mid-1975 was a general dissatisfaction within the Trust Territory respecting its scale of government and the manner in which it was being administered. This the delegates brought with them to the Constitutional Convention. Without comprehending all contributing details, they were cognizant, and most appeared to accept the veracity, of the objection that disproportionate attention had been given by the American Administration to education, health, and other direct personal services. Such skewing, it was believed, had adversely limited the allocating of federal funds for fostering economic growth sufficient to support a viable Micronesian self-government. For the fiscal year just ended, in terms of actual money budgeted for operations and capital improvements, the Health Services and Education Departments had together received about three and a half times as much as did the Department of Resources and Development, a distribution which at least superficially appeared to substantiate the complaint. However, most were unaware that comparing FY 1975 with the funds budgeted for 1966-67 disclosed that economic development was now receiving greatly expanded attention and relatively had jumped 1,000 percent, while Health Services and Education had not even doubled over the same decade. Probably a sounder observable factor contributing to the general sense of discontent over the budgeting of the federal grant was the obvious burgeoning of the governmental work force, without Micronesians personally experiencing a corresponding growth in services received. This disproportion was well demonstrated by the fact that the expense of administering Headquarters and district executive offices had increased 1,000 percent over the period of the prior decade. The delegates could concur with the High Commissioner, without necessarily having to reach agreement on all details, that the Trust Territory government "as a whole ... [was] too large, too complex, [and] too costly in terms of operational costs as compared with programme costs."[4]

Delegation of functions to the districts and placing responsibility for adequacy of their performance closer to the people to be affected was widely believed by the delegates to be one way for improvement of administration in the Trust Territory. The Solomon Report in 1963 had generalized that an obstacle to the overall development of Micronesia was the "quasi-colonial bureaucracy in the present Trust Territory government."[5] Devolution of government to the districts would reverse the colonial tendency to centralize power. And not so incidentally, only a highly decentralized administration appeared to offer any promise for holding Micronesia together.

So implicitly was it accepted by the delegates that an additional way to improve the quality of Territorial administration was to place the running of the government in Micronesian hands, that it needed no exposition. The expansion of governmental services after 1962 had brought an increasing number of Micronesians into governmental administration at both district and Headquarters levels, and at ever higher positions of operational responsibility. By mid-1975, localization of the executive branch saw Micronesians serving in the chief administrative posts of all six districts, and in the directorships of the eight Headquarters' departments on Saipan. Nevertheless, Washington maintained the ability to direct the operations of government in the Trust Territory through filling with expatriates the highest positions in the executive and judicial branches and clearing the appointment of senior Micronesians, retaining final control over the federal purse, and reserving ultimate legislating power in the Secretary of the Interior.

Contrasted with this, the Congress of Micronesia displayed the prototype of total Micronesian involvement devoid of American control.

Outside of the district centers, government at the local level in Micronesia retained an element of tradition which offset taking the American-innovated municipal forms too seriously. District governments, also, were long regarded as but field stations transmitting the orders of a distant American Administration. It was only after the Congress of Micronesia came to serve as the Micronesians' counterfoil that the district legislatures, and the many boards and commissions thereafter spawned at both district and territorial levels, began to provide Micronesians with a sense of sharing meaningfully in the running of the government. Symbolically, the convening of the Congress of Micronesia in 1965[6] marked the Islanders' transition from experimental observation to active participation in governing all of Micronesia.

The Congress of Micronesia was American in form and process, and so may be considered its role in the governance of Micronesia. To the extent variances existed from the American model, they mainly embodied the Islands' consensus ways which continued to influence the conduct of the Congressmen. Its small original size--twelve members in the Senate, twenty-one in the House of Representatives--was deliberately chosen by the Micronesians to incorporate the American federal compromise of population representation in one house and regional representation in the other, with two Senators for each of the six administrative districts. A simple system of standing committees served as the screening device for all legislation. Much as in any American legislative body, the committee hurdle proved the hardest for proposed measures to overcome; most difficult floor decisions tended to be deferred until the last few days of each Congressional session. As one of the results of this parallelism, Micronesian legislators had come to be singularly at ease when lobbying the United States Congress in Washington.

Initially, as the sole Territory-wide political institution staffed by Micronesians, its membership elected from among the most educated men of the Trust Territory, the Congress of Micronesia became the focus of popular attention, and it was engulfed by an overwhelming public euphoria. July

12, the day on which it first met, became a "national" holiday. In turn, its symbolism was much later to unite the members of the Micronesian Pre-Convention Committee in the decision to convene the Constitutional Convention on the same day.[7] After the burning of its quarters on Saipan, when the Congress started meeting in the various district centers, public welcomes signalled the Congressmen's arrival. The scheduling of the 1972 Special Session on Ponape saw a crowd, complete with bank, awaiting at the airport, an automobile parade through Kolonia, and gala receptions and parties on the days following. Time was to prove that the status of the Congress was to have a trickle-down effect upon the regional legislatures functioning in the districts, more immediately in encouraging the formalizing of their procedures, and, less obviously, in contributing to the raising of their standing within their respective districts.

During the decade which followed its founding, the members of the Congress came to master the intricacies of the legislative process. No longer would a committee report, as did an early Senate Education Health and Social Affairs Committee:

> Of course it is a good bill, but each member of your Committee has a different point of view on the subject measure and could not compromise to come to one conclusion. One member says, "Kill it;" another one says, "Put it on the chair to sit on it," but the Chairman of the Committee says, "Bring it back to the Floor for each and every member of the Senate shall (sic) discuss and make a final decision on its passage on Second and Final Reading."[8]

The Congressmen also learned to flex their legislative powers to maximum advantage in securing desired responses from the American Administration, even when the Secretarial Order serving as the Congress's charter did not grant it authority to so act. They became skillful in the use of joint resolutions to express their views on subjects beyond their jurisdiction, as well as on matters certain to be vetoed by the High Commissioner if adopted as legislation, recognizing that the impact of a resolution voicing a Congressional position, while not legally binding, could often be as politically effective.

The statistics on Congressional bills introduced and enacted show that the High Commissioner continued to wield a strong threat of veto, negating 10 to 20 percent of the Congressional product. (See Table 2.) What the statistics do not reveal is that each succeeding session witnessed a greater volume of member-initiated measures introduced. In addition, the Congress did not hesitate to add amendments to Administration-sponsored legislation, testing how far it could advance its own position into controversial areas. Should a veto result, a compromise bill could then be enacted with the High Commissioner's approval assured. There was ever more occasion for the Administration and the Congress not to see eye-to-eye. On the other hand, the High Commissioner's policy discretion was gradually curtailed. By the time of the Constitutional Convention, it seemed that only those measures having implications external to the Trust Territory would be destined for review by the Secretary of Interior, should the High Commissioner's veto be overridden. After House Bill 3 of the Fifth Congress on investments was returned by the High Commissioner, the Congress proceeded to adopt it over his veto. Still strongly disapproving of the measure as discriminatory against Micronesians, the High Commissioner then signed the measure, stating he could not justify forwarding the legislation to the Secretary of the Interior. In contrast, Senate Bill 94 of the same Congress, concerned with admiralty and maritime law in the Trust Territory, after being vetoed eventually wound up in Washington and was disapproved by the Secretary as "...not fully consistent with the obligations of the United States in international conventions relating to shipping and, therefore, as written, exceeds the legislative authority of the Congress."[9] Where the High Commissioner might once have vetoed legislation solely upon his own policy preferences, by mid-1975 an added element normally would have had to be present.

The work of its committees signally contributed to the saliency of the Congress of Micronesia. All during the year, even when the Congress was not in session, single-house standing committees continued to meet on an intermittent basis. In addition, assembling by authorization of bill or resolution, joint legislative committees on such politically volatile subjects as territorial resources and development, program and budget planning, administrative appointments, and future political

Table 1. Actual Budgets by Program Area, 1975 ($000)

Government	Operations	Capital Improvements	Total
Judiciary	737	-0-	737
Health Services	8,085	4,545	12,630
Education	13,120	1,467	14,587
Public Affairs	1,996	-0-	1,996
Resources and Dev.	7,743	80	7,823
Prot. to Pers. & Pr.	2,349	-0-[a]	2,349
Administration	6,021	390[b]	6,411
Transp. & Coms.	3,718	5,139	8,857
Public Works	9,475	3,186[c]	12,661
	$53,244	$14,807	$68,051

(a) Legal affairs. (b) General Support – $40; Maintenance and Rehabilitation – $350.
(c) Community Development – $1,392; Water, Sewer, Power – $1,794.
Source: Congress of Micronesia, *Trust Territory of the Pacific Islands – Five Year Indicative Development Plan (1976-1981)*, July 1976, pp. 26, 27.

Table 2. A Decade of Congressional Action

Years	Bills Introduced	Passed	%	Signed	% Effective	Vetoed	% Vetoed
1965-66	226	44	19.5	40	90.0	4	10.0
1967-68	445	99	22.2	78	78.8	21	21.2
1969-70	435	77	17.7	62	80.5	15	19.5
1971-72	478	96	20.1	87	90.6	9	9.4
1973-74	689	106	15.4	90	84.9	16	15.1

status became the foci of the Territory's news media. Although normally warranting less news coverage, Congressmen also sat on the Bank of Micronesia's Board of Directors and various mixed membership committees monitoring actions of the executive branch. Seemingly ever more frequently, congressmen found occasion for committees to travel to various parts of the world on public business. Cumulatively, the annual cost of the interim activities consumed a large share of the Congressional budget. While the experience so gained outside the Territory added a polish to the developing sophistication of the Congress, and finesse to the role it assumed as protector of Micronesian interests, to their constituents these external trips of Congressmen also took on the character of junkets at public expense.

Succinctly put, over the decade since its founding, the Congress emerged as a countervailing force to the American-led Trust Territory Administration. The fact that the Congress openly criticized the High Commissioner or the United States government initially stirred the Micronesians so long accustomed to the tactics of covert opposition. It was observed, too, that the Congress gradually was receiving ever-increasing deference from the Administration. Leadership meetings with the High Commissioner began shaping policy, particularly after unilaterally-proposed American measures were rejected or modified by the Congress. The execution of Territorial laws was subjected to continuous oversight by the Congress, and the Congressmen were not overly gentle in voicing their complaints. The Micronesians could not be cognizant of the impact of the Congressional insistence on the terminating of federal civil service hires and their replacement by local personnel at all levels of government. Later, the significance of the Congress was further emphasized by the need of the High Commissioner to obtain the advice and consent of a Congressional joint committee to his major administrative appointments. Rejection, publicly reported in the Administration's own media, testified to Congressional review not being a rubber-stamp activity. The participation of the Congress in the fixing of salaries and pay scales for territorial employees provided it additional leverage. Joint committee examination of budget proposals, the budget estimates for the ensuing fiscal year, and the proposed program of action for that year and the following four introduced Micronesian-articulated political elements into the monetary plans of the Territory. Even though the final decision on the federal grant remained with Washington, Micronesian legislators appeared before U.S. Congressional committees in support of the Trust Territory budget. By mid-1975, with Micronesians holding high administrative positions, the ambience of legislative-executive relationships in the Trust Territory had come to approximate that in any state capital where personality rather than party politics prevail.

While probably understanding few of the proposed implementary details, the Micronesian voter became accustomed to Congressmen stressing the need for economic development within the Trust Territory. The Congress itself considered a wide range of legislation designed to foster economic growth. Marine resources, commercial agriculture, the attraction of external capital, and the regulation of foreign investment were all subjects of Congressional action. It adopted legislation founding District Fishing Authorities, a Copra Processing Authority, and the Bank of Micronesia as a developmental bank for the Territory. Loan funds made investments in Micronesian enterprise, under Congressional authorization. Friendly critics have charged that in the attempt to safeguard Micronesian resources when adopting such legislation, the Congress overreacted, so that "most of the legislation passed regarding the economy have (sic) tended to be overprotective and a hindrance to national economic development."[10]

Most impressive to the outside observer, even though probably less well appreciated within the Trust Territory, was the strong thrust into external affairs by the Congress of Micronesia. Congressmen extensively participated in international conferences pertinent to Micronesian concerns, annually appeared as special advisors to the United States delegation to the U.N. Trusteeship Council, and took part in the meetings of the South Pacific Commission. It was the Congress which sought United States aid in sponsoring the Islanders' membership in the Asian Development Bank, just as it urged on an apparently reluctant Administration to facilitate the United Nations Development Program's services in the Trust Territory. The stance of the Micronesian delegation at the Law of the Sea Conference did not coincide with that of the United States delegation. While over the years the State Department had criticized the Interior Department in its administration of the territories[11] and been sympathetic to the Micronesians' drive for greater self-government, in foreign affairs the State Department found itself resisting the Micronesian challenge. Once, Islander presence in international meetings merely served to legitimate the position of the United States, so far as it applied to the Trust Territory. By mid-1975, the Micronesian Congressmen were actively involved, publicly declaiming the Micronesian view even when at variance with that of the United States.

The year 1972 about marked the apogee of the Congress of Micronesia. When it first met in 1965, salaries of members and legislative expenses were included in the federal grant to the Trust Territory. After 1969, Territorial revenues became available for this purpose, and by 1972 the Congress informed the United States that it had no further need of Federal moneys for running the legislative branch of the Territorial government. Henceforth, it would rely upon revenues raised within Micronesia. In so emphasizing the independence of the Congress, this decision also removed the Congressional costs of operation from scrutiny by the Administering Authority's auditors and the employment of staff from review by the Territory's personnel agency. Although in the abstract the importance of the Congress to the Territory continued, its relative standing in Micronesian eyes gradually began to decline, starting approximately from the time self-sufficiency was announced. Perhaps this was inevitable, as it was impossible for any mortal group of men to remain upon the pedestal to which the Congress was originally elevated. There were also institutional explanations for this fall from grace.

No comparable development of a supporting political infrastructure accompanied the maturation of the Congress of Micronesia. Political parties bridging all six districts failed to materialize. Intra-district parties did appear in Palau and the Marianas, where they enjoyed a near monopoly, so that only one independent succeeded in being elected to the Congress from either district during the first decade of its life. However, these parties had no political role in the other four administrative districts. Within Palau and the Marianas their respective differences tended to mirror parochial squabbles, so that they exacerbated rather than facilitated the internal working of the Congress. Territory-wide interest groups, too, were slow to organize. Petitions and delegations might bring public pressure to bear upon the Congress, but public opinion was extremely diffuse and mostly regional in character. Consequently, each Congressman had to rely upon personal linkages for political support, cultivating clan ties and island loyalties. Meanwhile, the expanding scope of Congressional duties both kept him ever more away from his district and removed his activities from the understanding of his constituents. By maintaining a public presence through occasionally twisting the tail of the American tiger, and endeavoring to secure pork-barrel benefits for his home district, he could attempt to sustain a grass-roots following. But rivals in the district legislature could similarly perform, and demand ever greater attention for their region than the Congress afforded. Institutionally, these legislatures came to be competitors of the Congress. Eventually, the most effective challenge to the Congress was to be led by several of its own members, Congressmen aligned with, if not controlling, their district legislatures and championing district values over Territory-wide concerns.

As their power increased, the Congressmen fell victim to its corrupting influence, or so it began to appear to their constituents. Trust Territory loan funds found their way into business ventures headed by Congressmen. While individually they were among the best credit risks in the Territory, having the widest experience, their private profiting through governmental aid helped dispel the diffuse political support surrounding the Congress. The lack of a full audit, once the Congress began to depend upon its own funds, resulted in its members never being called to account for per diem and "representation" (entertainment) advances. Within the perspective of the total moneys so allocated, misused funds never amounted to a significantly large sum, but to those Micronesians already annoyed by Congressional "junketing," it became a further irritant.

Most provoking proved to be the distribution of taxes levied under Congress of Micronesia aegis, including the Congress's reserving of a large share to meet its own expenses. For CoM Fiscal Year 1975, which ended just before the Constitutional Convention, the Congress collected some $7.5 million in taxes, of which $1.5 million was returned directly to the districts for expenditure by their legislatures. Of the other $5.6 million, almost half (45 percent) funded the internal operations of the Congress; from the balance, $2.1 million was appropriated to the districts for designated capital improvement projects and development loans, and the remainder used for scholarships and Territory-wide programs.[12] Here the district legislators were confronted in dollar and cents terms with the exercise of Congressional judgment over actions they could have taken if the moneys raised in their districts had been left within their control. In the case of the Marshalls, ten times as much was retained under Congressional direction as was remitted to the Nitijela (Marshall district legislature) for its expenditure. Congressional funding of requested capital improvements might indirectly return tax moneys to their district of source, but at best it only helped assuage and did not eliminate the institutional competition.

An important component of the growing negative reaction to the Congress of Micronesia derived from the expansion of the Westernized political elite, with a younger, educated element seeking its place in the sun and challenging the older professionals. The turnover in the membership of Congress, on the whole, had been peripheral to the leadership, and the same group continued to direct Congressional policy.[13] Not until after the Constitutional Convention was there to be a major challenge to that leadership within the Congress, sparked by the large infusion of new members into the House of Representatives of the Seventh Congress, and it proved unsuccessful. Meanwhile, several Congressmen, who never were part of the Congressional inner circle, came to occupy more potent roles as leaders of the counter political elites at the district level.

The new generation of politicos could find their place in the district legislatures, just as the latter were emerging as centers of importance in their respective areas. Taking the Congress as a model, these bodies expanded the scope of their concern both with policy and in the detail of district administration. In part because of the increasing revenues returned under Congressional enactments, augmented funds were available for district appropriation. Simultaneously, the cost of the district legislatures began to expand, and materially contributing were the larger salaries district legislators now drew. First in the Marianas District, and then in Ponape, legislators became full-time office holders, like Congressmen, and the precedent was set for all other district legislatures to follow.

With the members of the Congress reduced to mere human status, some with discernible feet of clay, and the position of the district legislatures elevated so as to furnish a ready platform for the espousing of district-oriented positions, it became only a matter of time before the Congress of Micronesia was to be openly and fundamentally confronted. Sharing of the Territorial income tax became one of the issues, and the return of public lands to district control provided the source of another. The Congress temporized, and failed to satisfy the Marshalls' demand that it receive a larger tax share; this intransigence of the Congress, while retaining the funds, proved to be a Pyrrhic victory. On the dispute over returning public lands to the Micronesians, at the Honolulu meeting called by the United States in December 1974, delegations from the Marshalls and Mariana Islands supported the approach of the Secretary of Interior; those from Ponape, Truk, and Yap were in favor of the Congress of Micronesia's position; and the Palau group was split. The subsequent action taken unilaterally by the Secretary ran counter to the stand of the Congress. But of all issues, most important was the objection raised in the district legislatures of the Marianas, the Marshalls, and then in Palau to the leadership of the Congress in the negotiations on Micronesia's future political status.

> ...[T]his Congress is no longer the sole spokesman in Micronesia on this status question. The districts are beginning to assert the role in this regard and whether we like it or not, the districts are getting the attention of the Administering Authority, ... [U]nless we take serious note of this fact in Micronesia, we may wake up very soon to find out that this Congress exists only on paper and doesn't exist as a meaningful instrument....[14]

In 1973, the United Nations Visiting Mission opined that for a territory of some one hundred thousand people, the Micronesians had a representational system, "especially at the local level, which is top-heavy with too many legislators representing, proportionately, too few people."[15] To critics bent on censoring the United States for its administration of the Trust Territory, the objective of the over-representation was merely a facade to foster the impression of democracy. On balance, to hold this implant of American political institutions as only a cosmetic cover for the maintenance of United States imperialism is to ignore the crucial role that Micronesians elected as representatives have played in helping shape public policy within the Trust Territory, and eventually to challenge continuation of the American presence. And as the proper perspective for evaluating the U.N. Mission's statement, could the Micronesian Constitutional Convention have undertaken so taxing an exercise of self-determination as independently drafting a constitution for all of Micronesia without the long preparatory conditioning of so many Islanders through their representational institutions at all levels of government?

---

1. The works faulting the Trust Territory are nearly legion. See Stanley De Smith, *Micro-States and Micronesia* (New York: New York University Press, 1970); Donald F. McHenry, *Micronesia: Trust Betrayed* (New York: Carnegie Endowment for International Peace, 1975); David Nevin, *The American Touch in Micronesia* (New York: W.W. Norton & Company, Inc., 1977); Harold F. Nufer, *Micronesia Under American Rule* (Hicksville, N.Y.: Exposition Press, 1978); Roger W. Gale, *The Americanization of Micronesia* (Washington, D.C.: University Press of America, 1979). For a seminal "foresight" study, mostly ignored, see Douglas L. Oliver (ed.), *Planning Micronesia's Future* (Cambridge: Harvard University Press, 1951).

2. Under the Palauan Constitution adopted in 1980, local governments (now called "states") have adopted their own "constitutions." Many depart from the standard municipality form sponsored by the Trust Territory Administration and reintroduce traditional structures and processes.

3. The $68 million figure does not include expenditures of the $14 million of Federal funds otherwise derived; the some $7 million raised by the Congress of Micronesia during the latter's

FY 1975 in the form of territorial income taxes, import and export taxes, and from other sources; nor the probably $3 million raised by the districts and municipalities and disbursed directly by them.

4. Quotation is from a statement of High Commissioner Adrian P. Winkel before the U.N. Trusteeship Council on June 14, 1977 (reproduced in *Highlights*, July 1, 1977, p. 2).

5. Reproduced in McHenry, *op. cit.*, p. 234.

6. The story of the creation of the Congress of Micronesia is told in Norman Meller, *The Congress of Micronesia* (Honolulu: University of Hawaii Press, 1969).

7. Further demonstration of the symbolic importance of July 12 is found in its designation as the date in 1978 for the holding of the referendum on the proposed Federated States of Micronesia Constitution (see *Epilogue*).

8. Congress of Micronesia, SCR No. 62, *Senate Journal*, First Congress, 3rd Regular Session, 1967, p. 457.

9. Congress of Micronesia, *Senate Journal*, Fifth Congress, 1st Special Session, 1974, pp. 203-204.

10. "Micronesia: A New Frontier in Political, Social and Economic Outlook," A Special Report to the Congress of Micronesia, Special Session, 1972, p. 9.

11. Ruth G. Van Cleve, *The Office of Territorial Affairs* (New York: Praeger, 1974), pp. 175-79.

12. See Appendix A, Table 3. Data on distribution of Congress of Micronesia tax revenues from Congress of Micronesia, *Trust Territory of the Pacific Islands--Five Year Indicative Development Plan (1976-1981)*, July 1976, p. 32.

13. Representative Bethwell Henry and Senator Tosiwo Nakayama served as presiding officers of their respective houses for most of the life of the Congress.

14. Statement of Senator Lazarus Salii in Congress of Micronesia, *Senate Journal*, Sixth Congress, 1st Session, 1975, p. 263.

15. United Nations Visiting Mission Report on the Trust Territory of the Pacific Islands, May 1973, par. 192, T/1748, p. 41.

Chapter 3. Future Status

The genesis of the Trust Territory of the Pacific Islands embodied a temporary truce between the military hawks in the United States, ascendant at the conclusion of World War II, and the One-World doves who correctly foresaw a future intolerant of colonies, particularly those secured through force of arms. This uneasy compromise stagnated within the executive branch of the American government until the Kennedy Administration adopted a course of action designed to Americanize the Micronesians. Presumably, they would eventually opt for political joinder with the United States. Whether it be due to the inertial appeal of Micronesian tradition, negative reaction to the specific methods employed, the kernel of sheer contrariness which underlies the spark of independence in human nature, or all three, the American purpose came to be paralleled by a Micronesian counterforce which in its formulated expression aimed toward separate nationhood. A review of the whole history of future political status negotiations between Americans and Micronesians reveals a continuing search for a formula which would somehow bring the conflicting viewpoints into juxtaposition. All outside of Micronesia and most within were agreed that the Trust Territory of the Pacific Islands must soon end. Unilaterally, the United States announced that date to be 1981. For almost a decade prior to the Constitutional Convention, the form of the political entity to replace the Trusteeship had remained in dispute. The Convention delegates who assembled on Saipan in 1975 were fully conscious of their crucial part in helping to resolve the existing impasse. "[A] Constitution drawn up by our own people would be an invaluable tool and could conceivably help dictate the future course of our negotiations, giving our people of Micronesia a real voice in their future."[1]

Within a year of its organization, the Congress of Micronesia was petitioning the President of the United States to establish a commission to "study and critically assess the political alternatives open to Micronesia." A prolonged legislative clearance process then ensued,[2] and with no definitive response forthcoming from Washington, the Congress itself took action. At the next regular session (1967), Senate Joint Resolution No. 25 vested in six Micronesian Congressmen the responsibility of studying the subject of future status for Micronesia. Thus, practically from its inception, the Congress began serving as spokesman for Micronesian political aspirations and counterfoil to the American intention to integrate the whole area into the United States. While unanimity never existed within the Congress, and it functioned under the disadvantage of leading rather than responding to constituents' desires, Micronesian negotiators persisted in their efforts within the zigs and zags of Congressional policy directives. Only as the political myth of a unified Micronesia began to shatter, and district spokesmen with conflicting positions entered the negotiations, did the Congress falter. Charged with being unrepresentative of the people, in 1975 it sought popular sanction through a territorial referendum for retaining its self-designated role. Contemporaneously, the holding of the Constitutional Convention promised a new avenue for reestablishing a unified Micronesian position. The journal of the Convention contains disappointingly little debate on the subject of future political status. Nevertheless, the question furnished the matrix upon which the tapestry of the constitution was woven, while the near decade of study and negotiations provided many of the patterns which emerged in the final design.

After inquiring into the possible options available to Micronesia, and the experiences of other comparable areas, the original Future Political Status Commission recommended in 1969 to the Congress the two alternatives of free association with the United States and independence. The analogue of the Cook Islands and their relations with New Zealand, which had met with United Nations General Assembly approval under the guidelines of Resolution 1541, supplied ample precedent for free association status.[3] Internal government would be a wholly Micronesian affair; defense and foreign relations,[4] as their scope might eventually be negotiated, would remain with the United States; and as the capstone, the relationship would be unilaterally terminable. To adapt Rupert Emerson's comment made with respect to the original Trusteeship, the attempt to combine the two divergent elements of a nearly independent Micronesia with virtually full-blown United States sovereignty in military and security matters would be "an experiment to be watched with the closest attention."[5] Independence would be an alternative, but only if a satisfactory free association relationship with the United States could not be forged.

The first report made clear that the Administering Authority was not to hand down a Micronesian constitution.[6] Rather, the United States Congress was requested to adopt an "enabling act" which would authorize its writing. The future government of Micronesia would be democratic and representative, and offer a maximum degree of decentralization at the district level. At least initially, the executive authority of the central government might be vested in an "executive council representing all districts." And although not expressly stated, the report contemplated an internally self-governing Micronesia, which would negotiate the free association relationship with the United States. As the outline of the compact gradually took shape in the many meetings between Americans and Micronesians over the following years, the prospect of a self-governing Micronesia replacing the Congress in the negotiations became remoter. Only with the collapse of the talks, and the drafting of the Micronesian constitution, did this option again assume viability. Later events were to see not one but three self-governing Micronesian polities, each under its own constitution, continuing the negotiations until finally a compact was completed in 1982.

The Congress of Micronesia, without endorsing either free association or the proposal for enabling legislation, accepted the report and created a Political Status Delegation to bargain further, implied within the two options of free association or independence. The Micronesian Delegation brought an eleven-point proposal with it to Washington in September 1969. Heading the list was: "That the people of Micronesia will draft and adopt their own constitution." The United States generally agreed in principle with the basic position of the Micronesians, the outstanding exception being land control. That topic, to which there was express objection, called for renegotiation of land held by the federal government, and assured

Micronesians that there would be no confiscation of their land and no military bases in the islands without fair compensation, full consultation, and the consent of the government of Micronesia.[7] The importance of all these details to the people of Micronesia was to be reinforced by the attention given to them in the Constitutional Convention.

Four months later, when the negotiators next met informally on Saipan, the Department of Interior submitted the draft of an organic act which would have brought Micronesia into the United States as an unincorporated territory, much like Guam and the Virgin Islands. Territorial status would have placed the internal government of Micronesia under the control of the United States Congress, and the observance of the organic act route would specifically foreclose the possibility of holding a constitutional convention. The Micronesian Delegation concluded that the proposed bill would be "in manifest conflict with the intent of the Trusteeship Agreement, with the direction pointed by the Congress of Micronesia in its mandate..., and with the basic premises upon which the Delegation had opened discussions in Washington."[8] From that point on, the option of status as an American territory was rejected, nor was it ever revived for the later discussions with the separate district delegations.

The modern mind is accustomed to frame propositions in alternatives or triads. More rarely are quadrads employed. In this last category falls the set of four fundamental principles which the Micronesian delegates brought to the second formal negotiation session in May 1970, and which served as the benchmark for all further meetings. One of the propositions declared "that the people of Micronesia have the right to adopt their own constitution, and to amend, change or revoke any constitution or governmental plan at any time."[9] Sovereignty, the inherent right to choose independence or self-government, and unilateral termination of any free association pact comprised the remaining three propositions. Recognition of these four principles was stated to be "an essential and non-negotiable component of any Free Association" compact.[10] Here first appeared the reference to non-negotiability which later was to plague the Constitutional Convention when the Palauan delegates employed the same technique. Perhaps it was no coincidence that Senator Lazarus Salii, who had headed all of the Micronesian negotiations, also served as a member and tactician of the Palauan constitutional delegation.

Countering the Micronesians' delineation of an acceptable form of free association, the United States offered a modified commonwealth status. Now Puerto Rico was to provide the model upon which American-Micronesian ties would be built. The commonwealth proposal went far to meet the eleven points originally raised by the Micronesians, including the calling of a constitutional convention. However, the retention by the United States of the power of eminent domain, and the integration of Micronesia into the American nation erected major impediments. It was also objected that the proposal only "authorized" the people of Micronesia to adopt their constitution, and within certain limitations, without recognizing that it existed as a matter of right.

While communicating the commonwealth offer to the Congress of Micronesia, the Micronesian Delegation rejected it out-of-hand. So, too, did both houses of the Congress when they met in August of 1970 (HJR 90), and they also endorsed the four "non-negotiable" principles which were to underpin all further status discussions. Simultaneously, as the Congress of Micronesia was repudiating commonwealth, the Mariana Islands District Legislature approved of the concept, and invited the United States to proceed with its implementation in the Marianas. This cleavage over commonwealth was to metamorphose into the splintering of Micronesian unity.

In its 1970 report to the Congress, the Delegation reiterated the call for a constitutional convention to consider the internal arrangements necessary for each form of status that might be applicable to Micronesia. The convention would not make final decisions, but by meeting before the resolution of the status question, more Micronesians would be involved in determining their future. The Delegation also declared that the separation of powers system introduced by the United States was inappropriate to Micronesia, at least during the transition to self-government. To replace it, while the Trusteeship continued, it proposed that at the Territorial level there be an Executive Council with membership drawn from the Congress of Micronesia and senior officers of the Administration, presided over by the High Commissioner. Such an innovation necessarily waited upon the approbation of both the Congress and the Administering Authority. It obtained the support of neither, unlike some of the other suggestions for interim expansion of Micronesian participation in internal government which did receive approval. Eventually, the Constitutional Convention was to reject all further effort aimed at establishing a plural executive.

One of the "non-negotiable" principles enunciated at the 1970 meetings, which came to underlay the actions of the Constitutional Convention, was a declaration "that sovereignty in Micronesia resides in the people of Micronesia and their duly constituted government." From this was to flow the galaxy of specifics in the negotiations to follow, defining and delimiting the delegations to the United States of foreign relations and military defense functions. Only much later in the discussions was the problem of financial assistance to engender a comparable quantum of detail and finally to prove a more troublesome stumbling block.

At the 1970 session of the Congress of Micronesia, the Political Status Delegation was replaced by a twelve-member Joint Committee on Future Status. The third and longest-lived of the Congressional groups responsible for negotiating the Micronesian future status, the Joint Committee was to labor until superseded after the Constitutional Convention in 1975. One of its original charges directed it to study alternative forms of internal government for use by a future constitutional convention. While performing yeoman bargaining service, the Joint Committee minimized its role with respect to this aspect of Micronesian political education. If the preparation of the delegates who attended the Constitutional Convention of 1975 is an adequate measure, Micronesians continued to have little comprehension of or interest in any other than the American system of government, and incomplete knowledge of that.

Over a year was to elapse before the Third Round of status talks occurred. On the Micronesian side, the external front of unanimity had been weakened by the growth of the independence movement within the Trust Territory[11] and the Mariana District's opting for closer ties with the United

States. On the other hand, Washington elevated the status of the American delegation, heading it with a "Personal Representative of the President of the United States" holding the rank of ambassador. He tacitly withdrew all previous American offers and tilted more favorably toward much of the Micronesians' position on associated status. In reviewing the Hana, Maui, talks of 1971, the Joint Committee concluded partial agreement was reached on the sovereignty principle and the right of self-determination. With respect to sovereignty, both sides basically concurred over land and other internal matters, but not on foreign affairs and defense. Agreement on the principle of self-determination was only within the frame of associated state status. Unilateral termination was considered rejected by the American negotiators. Solely with regard to the fourth non-negotiable principle--the Micronesian constitution--did it appear to report satisfaction:

> ...[T]he United States proposes that there be two limitations on the Micronesian constitution, the compact and protection of fundamental rights. Otherwise, Micronesia would be free to adopt and change any system of government desired. In the view of the Joint Committee, this represents a basic agreement of this principle, and that the Micronesian people would be free to structure their constitution and government so as to best meet their needs.[12]

Although not extensively discussed, it was incidentally suggested by the Micronesian Joint Committee that the compact assume the form of a treaty. Much later, instead of being an unimportant nuance, the compact vehicle was to become crucial, for treaties, as acts of government, were to be declared to be invalid by the Federated States of Micronesia Constitution when in conflict with its provisions.

The Fourth and Fifth Rounds of negotiations, held within the span of approximately three months in 1972, brought both sides closer together and succeeded in producing a partial draft. The status compact would be based on the sovereign right of the people of Micronesia to choose their own future. Reaffirmed was their right to adopt a constitution of their own, and its legal force would be "derived from the sovereign power of the Micronesian people." The qualifying condition was retained that the constitution could not be in conflict with the compact, just as the latter would set out the scope of authority to be exercised by the United States over foreign affairs and defense. Not alone would both the Micronesian Congress and the United States Congress have to approve the compact, but also so would the people of Micronesia. Adhering to a policy reminiscent of medieval scholasticism, the United States carefully refrained from acknowledging the sovereignty of Micronesia as a state or of its government.[13] However, the stumbling block of the symbolism associated with sovereignty was mainly eroded away, while the pragmatic position of the United States held firmly to retention of its fundamental interests in Micronesia. Similarly, assured of the lands it would expressly designate under the compact, the United States agreed to forego any reserved rights of eminent domain. Once the compact was enforced, resort would be to Micronesian law to meet any additional American needs. Obviously, it was assumed the new Micronesian government would retain the ability to employ the power of eminent domain. Only in the heat of the 1975 Convention deliberations did the error of this ready assumption become evident.

With modifications, the partial draft sketched in Washington at the Fifth Round in the summer of 1972 reappeared as the first portion and as several of the Appendices of the nearly complete draft presented at the Seventh Round in late 1973. In the interim, the inconclusive Sixth Round held in the fall of 1972, and the following gap of a year, publicly marked the adjusting of both groups of negotiators to the emergence of independence as a bargaining alternative. But its potential failed to materialize, and discussions continued within the context of an associated state status, terminable after a still disputed number of years had elapsed and the delaying restrictions met. During the same period, the tangential issue of public lands also festered, and the Micronesians pressed for its resolution as a condition to resuming official negotiations. Then, with the principles governing the return of public lands agreed upon, it became the position of the Joint Committee at the Seventh Round that it could not consider the balance of the nearly complete draft presented by the American delegation until first there was agreement on its Titles dealing with finance and termination of associated status. Notwithstanding, the structure and most of the detail of the American's presentation contained the bulk of the tentative agreement initialed by American and Micronesia representatives a year later in Honolulu, in October 1974, after a number of informal meetings. Even though its terms now called for greater American financial assistance, it yet remained parsimonious in the opinion of the Congress of Micronesia which met early in 1975. But complicating factors also fueled the ire of the Congress. The United States was continuing to meet separately with the Marianas, despite the remonstrances of the Congress. As a further matter which counselled delay, the Micronesian Constitutional Convention was now scheduled to assemble in mid-year. In addition, the means adopted by the Secretary of the Interior for returning public lands to Micronesian control had so angered the Congressmen as to assure most any new compact proposal, whatever its terms, would be met with an indignant reception.

The public lands issue had ancient roots in Micronesia. The United States classed some three-fifths of the dry land of the Trust Territory as public. Marine lands were also considered part of the public domain. Excluding the small amount of real estate which the Trust Territory government had itself acquired for public purposes, most of these holdings represented succession to the rights held by the previous Spanish, German, and Japanese administrations. Private Japanese properties seized after World War II also were controlled and disposed of in the same manner as public lands, and administratively treated alike. Ever since the beginning of the Trust Territory, Micronesians had objected to this designation of the public domain, contesting the original acquisition of title in the previous colonial eras upon which the claim of the United States rested. Until late in the status negotiations, the United States adamantly delayed redressing what Micronesians considered as denial to them of their rightful lands. Before the United Nations, the American position was that the lands were held in trust for all of the indigenous inhabitants and ought not be returned to specific claimants; the Micronesians countered that the United States was more interested in retaining the land to further its own security needs. They particularly pointed to the retention lands in Micronesia under use and occupancy of the Defense Department, nearly fourteen thousand acres of public lands. Organized resentment over this surfaced in the Palau District in 1972, with the demand that all status negotiations be suspended until the public lands in the district were returned. The leaders in the Congress of Micronesia responded by adopting this position as applicable to all of the Trust Territory, and it became an ultimatum voiced by the Joint Committee on Future Status.

At the Seventh Round of negotiations held at the end of 1973, the United States agreed in principle to the return of the public lands before the termination of the Trusteeship, but ringed with a number of protective clauses. Some of these conditions were designed to assure access to areas which would be desired for security purposes; others sought to guarantee maintenance of adequate eminent domain powers, at least during the life of the Trusteeship; and still others looked to the orderly transference of the land as a safeguarding of Micronesian benefits. As finally contained in the Secretary of the Interior's policy statement, the Congress of Micronesia would be charged with enacting the enabling legislation, and for this purpose he submitted the draft of a suggested bill. When finally adopted by the 1974 Special Session, modifications insisted upon by the Congress over the strong objections of the Administration assured a veto. This was followed by an extraordinary meeting of Micronesian leaders in Hawaii, at which they put their case to no avail. On December 26, 1974, Secretarial Order 2969 amended the Trust Territory Code so as to authorize district legislatures to establish entities capable of receiving and administering the public lands, all under the conditions originally set in agreeing to the transfer. Not alone was the Administering Authority seen as challenging the Congress over a fundamental matter, but it accomplished by executive action what the leadership of the Congress strongly asserted was a legislative prerogative. By expressly amending the Territory's statute law, insult was added to injury in a raw demonstration that legislative power still resided in the United States notwithstanding the creation of the Congress of Micronesia nearly a decade earlier. Angered by such treatment, the Congress was in little mood to consider with equanimity the draft compact presented to it in January of 1975.

One need not have been omniscient to understand that the whole subject of land, including public leases and eminent domain, was to remain at issue in the Constitutional Convention. An additional element, moreover--the role of the traditional leader--was also presaged by this controversy over land. The initiating action originating from Palau called for the return of the district's public lands to its traditional leaders. Later, when in 1974 the Second Micronesian Traditional Chiefs Conference met in Truk, it had adopted a resolution "that it is the sense of all the Micronesian Traditional Chiefs that titles to all public lands in Micronesia should be returned to them in their respective districts."[14] Neither American general principles of governance nor the more specific goals of the Congressmen were congenial to such a resurgence in the role of the traditional leadership of Micronesia. Both the ill-fated Congressional legislation and the Secretarial Order which followed called for the creation of a custodial corporate entity in each district to opt for receipt of its area's public lands. It is possible that when the Palau District Legislature endorsed the traditional leaders as being qualified to accept title in trust for all the people of Palau, it was only mirroring a byplay between Palau's two political parties for the support of the chiefs, and did not contemplate that implicit might be reestablishment of their political powers. Nevertheless, the seeds were planted and their flowering at the Truk meeting of traditional leaders was but prelude to the demand of the chiefs for a greater place in the governance of Micronesia, so strongly voiced in the Constitutional Convention.

The presentation of an almost complete draft compact to the Congress of Micronesia at the beginning of 1975 was the direct outcome of putting agreed specifics to paper, a practice embarked upon at the earlier rounds of negotiations. By October of 1974, despite the intervening vicissitudes, most of the details appeared fleshed out. The explanation for this achievement partially lies in the two principals--Ambassador Franklin Haydn Williams for the United States and Senator Lazarus E. Salii, the latter sole or joint head of all Micronesian negotiating groups of the Congress--maintaining working contact, and with each exerting a major influence over the bargaining stance of his respective delegation.

Title One of the draft recognized the Micronesians' right to adopt their own constitution and form of government, but express conditions insured not alone concordance with the provisions of the compact, but that the constitution and laws "guarantee to the inhabitants of Micronesia their fundamental rights and ... establish a governmental structure consistent with the principles of democracy."[15] As Mussolini at one time described Fascism as an "organized, centralized, and authoritarian democracy," and Hitler his political system as a "real" democracy,[16] reference to consistency with democratic principles at the very least carried an overtone of ambiguity. "Fundamental human-rights" identify an area of concern which assumed major proportions of conflict during the course of the Constitutional Convention. The same Title also recognized the right of Micronesians, upon termination of the compact, freely to choose any future political status. However, other provisions of the 1974 draft compact, spelling out procedures on termination, effectively narrowed options of choice.

Titles Two and Three of the draft compact granted the United States "full responsibility for and authority over" defense matters in Micronesia and its foreign affairs. Supplemented by appended Annexes, the compact also spelled out the foreign affairs activities which might be undertaken by the Micronesian government and the acreage and location of lands in the Marshall Islands and the Palau District to be reserved for the United States armed forces. By this time the separate Marianas negotiations had been progressing so well that all reference to the Marianas district had been deleted from the compact.

For the antecedents to Title Five and the remaining portions of the draft, recourse must be had to the proposal which the United States brought to the Seventh Round, and on which the Micronesians refused to negotiate at that time. Title Five committed the government of Micronesia to adopt legislation effectuating international agreements applicable to Micronesia and to take appropriate measures to protect United States personnel and property. Such subjects as environmental protection by the United States, trade and commerce, currency, citizenship and nationality, immigration and travel, the exchange of representatives for consultation, and dispute settlement through negotiation were then covered in this and following Titles.

Unilateral termination under Title Eleven of the draft compact could occur only after the expiration of fifteen years, the giving of notice, and the entering into of a mutual security agreement. In addition, any district which disapproved of the termination by a two-thirds' vote was to remain subject to the compact, a provision which philosophically underlay the Constitutional Convention's later consideration of a district's right of secession under the constitution. The final Title Twelve called for a 55 percent majority vote of the electorate to approve the compact. Here, again, seeds of secession were nurtured by the inclusion of a provision permitting any district disapproving of the compact by a two-thirds' vote to enter into separate negotiations with the United States on that district's future political status. It was no coincidence that the enabling legislation enacted by the Congress of Micronesia for the calling of the Convention for a while adopted a similar two-thirds' vote for district rejection of the constitution.

When the Congress of Micronesia considered this draft compact early in 1975, it took major umbrage over the monetary provisions in Title Four, which detailed the American financial commitments for five districts. (The separate Marianas talks now called for that district to be funded separately.) During the six-year transition period before the end of the Trusteeship, some $400 million in capital improvements would be supplied, in addition to covering the ongoing costs of government. Over the compact's term of fifteen years, thereafter, the United States would appropriate an additional $690 million, plus federal agency services costing about $2.5 million a year. Since adjustments for inflation were to be made annually, based on the fiscal 1975 dollar, this total figure would surely rise another half to a full billion dollars more before the termination of the fifteen-year period. Included in these financial provisions of the compact were operational grants which at first increased and then gradually decreased; similar treatment of grants for capital improvements; and a fixed item of $5 million yearly for development loans, once the compact went into effect. Originally, in 1972, the Micronesians had proposed that the United States fund the operations of the Micronesian government at $100 million a year. Their negotiators scaled this proposal down at the Seventh

Round in 1973. A comparison of these reduced figures with those in Title Four of the 1974 draft reveals that there would have been provided in total over the compact's proposed fifteen-year period about what the Micronesians had previously sought for ten years. Over and above all these financial commitments, the United States would pay an unstated amount of compensation for land required under the compact's defense responsibilities.

Despite the magnitude of the sums proposed, in the judgment of the Micronesian Congressmen they were insufficient. In repudiating Title Four, it was charged by Representative Ekpop Silk, Co-chairman of the Joint Committee, that the levels of financing proposed, "... instead of working towards the goal of sufficiency,... will in fact achieve the opposite effect--to make us more, and not less, dependent upon outside assistance."[17] The Congressmen demanded assurance that during the transition period before termination of the Trusteeship, and in the next fifteen years of the compact, American dollars would build an economic infrastructure sufficient to support an independent Micronesia, should that option then be chosen. Negotiations were now stalemated, and the prospect of holding the Constitutional Convention in July promised to strengthen the Micronesian bargaining position. Meanwhile, if it were not for the threatened dissolution of Territorial unity, time appeared on the side of the Micronesians.

In the initial stages of the status negotiations, the United States' offers of territorial and then commonwealth status were refused by the Micronesians. At that time, free association was conceived of as akin to a permanent relationship with the United States. By the time the draft compact had taken what appeared to be a nearly definitive form at the end of 1974, free association was being regarded by the Micronesian negotiators as but an interim period. At some future date, an independent, fully sovereign Micronesia might be the destiny of its people. Meanwhile, no options were to be foreclosed. But what status the people themselves desired remained unknown, and all indications pointed to the existence of great indecision outside of the Marianas.

During the course of the status talks, the Trust Territory Administration mainly kept to the sidelines, providing information as requested and evidently attempting to refrain from decisions which might prejudice the United States position. As applicable, directives from the Department of Interior to the High Commissioner were shaped by the strategy and tactics of the status negotiations, and some actions, such as his vetoing particular bills, could be attributed to them. Charges were occasionally heard that the American negotiators were directly intervening in the Trust Territory's internal administration. The relationship of the High Commissioner with the leader of the American negotiating team remained correct but distant.

The United States in a general way encouraged the Micronesians to understand the workings of their Territory's administration and of the principles underlying self-government. Dissemination of information by the Administration on future status mainly consisted of the publishing of summaries and the distribution of the transcripts of negotiations, and for long represented a matter of relatively low priority. This reflected in part the inability of the contending federal factions in Washington to concur, in part the Micronesians' own disagreement over the form future political status should take, and gradually the latter's coming to suspect any American effort to influence political attitudes. At the beginning of 1974, with the concurrence of the Congress of Micronesia and using augmented federal funds, an accelerated campaign for emphasizing political education was launched. Central and district task forces were set up under the Education for Self-Government (ESG) banner, and they aggressively embarked upon a program heavily utilizing the mass media. The first phase was designed to prepare Micronesians to choose a new future political status; the second phase was directed at general civic education "for whatever political status is selected."[18] Caught in the interface of Washington oversight and Micronesian suspicion, the ESG effort was pitched toward the academically neutral. It had only started to encourage mass popular interest before the advisory referendum in 1975 was to ask for an expression of Micronesian preference on future status. By that time the Marshalls District was boycotting all Congress-inspired status activity, and in Palau, the influential Senator Roman Tmetuchl, together with the district legislature, was advising the people in that district to refrain from voting in the referendum at all.

Faced with the imminent prospect of a commonwealth covenant being submitted to the voters of the Marianas, the Congress of Micronesia felt constrained to "do something." It reacted by asking the whole Trust Territory to register its status preferences in an advisory general referendum. "Free association," "commonwealth," and "independence" were three of the options it placed on the referendum ballot. Because "statehood" had been discussed early in 1967-68, and continuation of "present status" under the Trusteeship might be preferred over any of the alternatives offered, they were also included. For good measure, "other status" was added. But the voting instructions adopted by the Congress failed to direct whether more than one affirmative choice was to be registered, so that tallies counted on a single ballot ranged from expressions of "yes" or "no" under all six status columns to affirmative indication of but a single preference, and the remainder of the ballot left blank.

About half of the Territory's registered voters (excluding the Mariana District which had just publicly approved commonwealth) went to the polls.[19] The vote cast overwhelmingly negated statehood and commonwealth; expressed in other terms, the delegates to the Convention were informed that the people disapproved of Micronesia's integration with the United States. "Present status" drew the largest affirmative vote across the Territory (10,148), followed by strong, almost equally affirmative expressions for free association (7,705) and independence (7,486). Those who voted in the Marshalls preferred the status quo; a little less positively, free association appeared to be the Yapese choice. In the other three districts--Palau, Ponape, and Truk--the vote tended to be distributed over those three choices.

Further complicating the interpretation of the returns, it was claimed that the translation of the various options into the indigenous languages resulted in the people confusing "self-government" with one or more of the choices given, and erroneously casting votes accordingly. Significantly, many voters revealed uncertainty over the differences between the status choices offered. The act providing for the Future Status Referendum had directed the High Commissioner to fix its date for sometime before July 12, evidencing the linkage with the Constitutional Convention scheduled to meet on that day. Rather than being of aid, however, the uncertainties over the future status of Micronesia, as heritage of the stalled negotiations, were left unresolved by the referendum. The Constitutional Convention had no alternative but to proceed without any clear mandate from the voters. Once underway, the first public hearings scheduled by its General Provisions Committee were to be on the subject of future political status.

----

1. Senator Lazarus E. Salii, Congress of Micronesia, <u>Senate Journal</u>, Fifth Congress, 2nd Regular Session, 1974, p. 100. For general discussion of political status negotiations, see McHenry, <u>op</u>. <u>cit</u>. For events since 1975 see <u>Epilogue</u>, especially changes made to the compact before it was finally concluded.

2. Ruth G. Van Cleve, <u>op</u>. <u>cit</u>., p. 142.

3. While the United Kingdom entered into an associated state relationship with its Caribbean possessions, it did not obtain the sanction of the United Nations General Assembly. Later, New Zealand copied the model of the Cooks in terminating the colonial ties of Niue, and like its predecessor, received UN concurrence.

4. In later negotiations, foreign relations, insofar as they did not involve security matters, were included under the jurisdiction of the Micronesian governments.

5. Rupert Emerson et al., <u>America's Pacific Dependencies</u> (New York: American Institute of Pacific Relations, 1949), p. 9.

6. So, too, did General Assembly Resolution 1541, which declares that an "associated territory should have the right to determine its internal constitution without outside interference in accordance with due constitutional processes and the freely expressed wishes of the people."

7. Congress of Micronesia, <u>Report of Political Status Delegation of the Congress of Micronesia</u>, Third Congress, 3rd Regular Session, 1970, p. 3.

8. <u>Ibid</u>., p. 4.

9. *Ibid.*, p. 11.

10. *Idem*. Note that General Assembly Resolution 1541 a decade earlier had posited that "Free Association must be the result of a free and voluntary choice and must include the right unilaterally to change that status on the part of the associated state" (*op. cit.*).

11. Micronesian independence as a subject of negotiations is an entire topic of itself. Suffice it to briefly note for the prelude to the writing of the Micronesian constitution that "independence" as a future status for Micronesia was not included in the draft of the Trusteeship Agreement, but added as an amendment on the instigation of the Soviet member of the Security Council. The United States delegate qualified the amendment by noting it could not "possibly be achieved within any foreseeable future." See Meller, *op. cit.*, pp. 386-87. By 1971 the "foreseeable future" appeared imminent, for an Independence Coalition had formed in the Congress of Micronesia, claiming a loose membership of eleven out of the thirty-three members. At the Second Regular Session of the Fourth Congress, in early 1972, the Coalition had grown to include half the membership. As it favored moving to independence through entering into an interim agreement of free association, it did not advocate outright independence. (See Hans Wiliander, "Independence as a Political Alternative," in Frances M. Smith, ed., *Micronesian Realities: Political and Economic* [Santa Cruz, Calif.: Center for South Pacific Studies, 1972], p. 21 at p. 23.) In August of the same year, Senator Lazarus E. Salii's challenger for leadership of his Liberal Party of Palau, Senator Roman Tmetuchl, succeeded in having the Congress pass a resolution directing the Joint Committee to begin negotiating for independence as well as free association. When in September 1972, at the Sixth Round of talks, Salii asked the United States negotiators to discuss independence, so that the Micronesians might be presented with a full range of options, Ambassador Haydn Williams responded that they had no instructions and were not prepared to do so. According to Donald McHenry (*op. cit.*) the "United States delegation was specifically instructed to avoid a discussion of independence. In addition, in a not too veiled threat (which would later lead to United Nations chastisement) the United States let the Micronesians know that United States stra-

tegic requirements would not countenance independence" (p. 112). By November of 1973, inclusion of independence as an option in a plebiscite on future status in Micronesia was approved by President Nixon (*idem*), and after President Carter reviewed the long-stalled negotiations in 1977, independence was expressly declared to be a permissible option on which the United States was prepared to negotiate (see Epilogue). Meanwhile, the inclusion of a provision permitting unilateral termination of a compact for associated state status in the tentative draft decisions reached in 1973 served to accommodate the Micronesian advocates both of associated status and independence, for to the supporters of independence the compact would control for only an interim period. Within the Congress, the ranks of the Independence Coalition had thinned, and the preserving of Micronesian unity had become a more immediate issue.

The long reluctance of the United States to consider independence as a viable option in its negotiations with the Micronesians stands in sharp contrast to New Zealand's termination of its trusteeship in Western Samoa. There the Samoans expressed the desire for a "Tongan relationship" with New Zealand, referring to England's exercise at that time of certain controls over the Kingdom of Tonga and the provision of specified services. Instead, the New Zealand government substituted an "independence approach" which posited unqualified independence, and not simply self-government, with which position the Western Samoans finally concurred. See Mary Boyd, "The Decolonization of Western Samoa" in Peter Munz (ed.), <u>The Feel of Truth</u> (Wellington: A.H. & A.W. Reed, 1969), p. 74.

12. Congress of Micronesia, <u>Draft Report of the Joint Committee on the Third Round of Negotiations in Hana, Hawaii</u>, Fourth Congress, 2nd Regular Session, 1971, p. 21.

13. On the other hand, see 1974 statement of Mary Trent, State Department Representative in the Trust Territory: "The first principle enunciated by the Micronesians was that sovereignty resides in the people of Micronesia and in their government. That is a principle recognized by the United States." In Benjamin F. Bast (ed.), <u>The Political Future of Guam and Micronesia</u> (Agana, Guam: University of Guam Press, 1974), p. 44. Providing a further complication, the TTPI Attorney General

had ruled that sovereignty resided in the United Nations. If this view were to hold, affirmative action in the U.N. approving the termination of the Trusteeship would appear a *sine qua non*, to which the United States has refused to commit itself. See statement of Robert J. McCloskey of the State Department in U.S. Congress, Senate, Committee on Foreign Relations, *Commonwealth of the Northern Mariana Islands, Hearings before the Committee on Foreign Relations on H.J. Res. 549*, 94th Congress, 1st Session, 1975, p. 109.

14. Resolution MTL-2-006-TK; Second Annual Micronesian Traditional Chiefs Conference, "Unity of Micronesia," (Truk: November 11-15, 1974), pp. 101, 109.

15. The draft initialed in 1980 dropped these conditions, as by then the constitutions had already been adopted.

16. Henry Mayo, *An Introduction to Democratic Theory* (New York: Oxford University Press, 1960), p. 21.

17. Congress of Micronesia, *House Journal*, Sixth Congress, 1st Regular Session, 1975, p. 482.

18. Public Information Office, Trust Territory, "Task Force on Education for Self Government," 1974, p. 1.

19. The Congress of Micronesia act (Public Law 6-20) calling for the General Referendum on Future Status was signed April 9, 1975. The High Commissioner delayed until May 15 to designate the date for holding the referendum, and then fixed it for July 8, 1975. Meanwhile, the Secretary of the Interior had issued a proclamation calling for a plebiscite in the Marianas on the Commonwealth Covenant to be held on June 17. The full returns of the 1975 General Referendum on Future Status are reported in Appendix B.

Voter instructions had appeared on a sample General Referendum ballot distributed by district election officials a month prior to the vote, but were then removed, "this deletion apparently having been ordered pursuant to an Attorney General's legal opinion." See Summary Record of the Committee on General Provisions, 9th Meeting, August 8, 1975, p. 1.

Chapter 4. Breakage at the Periphery

Great Britain's attempt to form a federation of its holdings in the Caribbean after World War II nicely illustrates the political phenomenon of peripheral cleavage. Before planning of the proposed polity had more than commenced, the Bahamas, British Honduras, and British Guyana all declined to join. Three years after the West Indian Federation began functioning, Jamaica--the most westerly of the island territories--voted to withdraw. Next to secede was Trinidad and Tobago, at the southwest "end" of the Federation. A glance at the map of the Caribbean shows that it was the initial opting out of some and the later withdrawal of the other areas at the edges of the region which spelled the dissolution of the Federation.[1] Over a century and a half earlier, one of the urgent reasons for the reformation of the American Articles of Confederation was the rumored secession of the state of Vermont at the northeast corner of the United States. The same centrifugal pulls made their appearance in the Trust Territory as the status talks ground on, and in the end were to see the disintegration of Micronesian unity.

Until the negotiating session in October of 1971, the United States' precise military interests in Micronesia's lands were unknown. It could be assumed that the closeness of Palau with the Philippines and Southeast Asia, and the juxtaposition of the Northern Marianas with Guam, made both districts of strategic military importance. The heavy American missilery investment in the Marshalls assured continuing military interest in at least Kwajalein. But in the near paranoia which engulfed the subject, at one time or another almost every piece of Micronesian real estate was identified by island leaders as coveted by the United States. Given the penchant of the military mind to plan for each new war in the paradigm of its predecessor, the Micronesians may have had cause for their fears. As a result of all this, the declaration in 1971 that only the three outer administrative districts contained lands whose use was of military interest to the United States--with by far the major base to be located on the single island of Tinian in the Mariana District--had a two-fold effect. One of the causes conducive to the suspicion of American motives was removed, and the negotiations over military lands could now enter the stage of hard bargaining. More important for Micronesia's unity, the "have" districts were separated from the "have not." It was now a matter of public knowledge that except for permitting freedom of passage and otherwise remaining neutral, Ponape, Truk, and Yap played no part in the foreseeable defense plans of the United States. Contrastingly, the Marshalls, Palau, and particularly the Marianas, were now each afforded distinctive bargaining stances. In their respective ways, and at their own pace, all three proceeded to avail themselves of the opportunity. Already presaged, the process of breakage at the periphery now had more than an ideological motive force.

President Nyerere of Tanzania once opined[2] that in forming a federation out of a group of colonies, chances of success were greater when starting with a central government rather than having the colonies each become separate political entities, and then trying to combine. An analogous problem of optimal means emerged in the Trust Territory in the form of a question over whether district constitutions should be drawn before tackling that of the central government. During a radio dialogue in November 1974, I had urged that district delegations not be sent to Saipan bound by finalized district constitutions, this in order to obtain maximum maneuverability within the Micronesian Constitutional Convention. In rebuttal, the <u>Micronesian Independent</u> editorialized, "The people of Micronesia must find themselves first in their own particular community and secondly in their relations with other communities. By defining the districts on a district level first, the secondary national constitution would be tailored to meet those existing criteria ... [T]he establishment of District level constitutions should be encouraged, not stifled."[3] Unarticulated was the premise that the dimensions of the future Micronesian union, whatever it might be called, could be definitively shaped by this decision on priorities. At the time of the exchange, the District of Palau was just embarking upon the writing of the first of its many constitutions. Except for Palau, the drafting of constitutions in the other districts did not begin until after the Micronesian Convention had concluded.

In Palau, the charges and counter charges arising out of the district's parochial politics had long contributed to confusing the entire issue of the Territory's future status. Internal district stresses helped fuel the public castigation of United States perfidy. Politicians were quick to seize the opportunity for local advantage offered when it appeared that the Congress of Micronesia leadership was faltering. "It is out of desperation that the Marianas and the Marshalls are trying to secede. We are sinking [,] so abandon the boat and seek survival."[4] Emanating from John Ngiraked, a spokesman for Palau's Progressive Party, its implied targets were the two Senators from the opposing Liberal Party serving on the Congress of Micronesia Joint Committee; paradoxically, one of them was leading the Territory's status efforts, and the other was promoting independent Palauan action.

Stung by such criticism, a questioning of the Congress of Micronesia which was also emerging elsewhere in the Trust Territory, the Congressmen took the occasion of the General Referendum on Future Status in 1975 to obtain popular endorsement for their continuing to negotiate the political future status of the Trust Territory. Of all matters on the ballot, this recorded the largest number of responses tallied, and overall (five districts, excluding the miniscule returns of the Marianas) 70.2 percent were in the affirmative. However, the Marshall District registered a small majority of votes in the negative, and if to this were added those Micronesians who boycotted the entire referendum, the district stood strongly opposed. The Palau response was more ambiguous, but was hardly as positive as the district's affirmative vote at first appeared to indicate; like the Marshallese, Palauans deliberately stayed away from the polls, although not in as great a proportion, and of those who did go to vote, a third expressed no preference at all on Congressional leadership. And of course by this time, the Marianas' adoption of their own covenant had effectively registered that district's rejection of any further Congressional involvement. The Congressional leadership over termination of future political status was being massively challenged in the three districts, witness to how far the breakage at the periphery had proceeded.

Mariana Islands District. Regardless of the Chamorro's probably related, if not common, origins with the rest of the Micronesian peoples, more than three centuries under Spanish rule had fundamentally altered Chamorro physical appearance and so Hispanicized their culture as to deflect them sharply from all others. Then the world's rapacious appetite for colonies divided the Marianas between the United States (Guam) and Germany (Northern Marianas), but common language, kin, and culture continued to identify all Chamorros as a group apart. The settlers from the Central Carolines, admitted to the Northern Marianas in the nineteenth century, remained a denegrated minority, which only emphasized the differentiation of Chamorros from other Micronesians. This distinctive history resulted in the Chamorros being more receptive to Western ways and more closely attuned to association with the Western world.

From the beginning of the American thrust into the Northern Marianas, the indigenous inhabitants cooperated closely with American military forces in World War II. Chamorros helped police the Japanese civilian detention camp on Saipan, and accompanied the U.S. Marines in their sweeps of the hills for Japanese military stragglers. After civil government was established under the Trusteeship, "... on numerous occasions [there was] expressed both formally and informally to the Government of the United States and to the United Nations through petitions, resolutions adopted by the District Legislature and Municipal Councils, and in referenda, the strong desire that the people of the Northern Mariana Islands become a part of the United States."[5] Once the district legislators threatened secession from the Trust Territory by force of arms, if necessary.[6]

Initially the Northern Marianas had proposed reintegration with Guam.[7] American rule would bring higher minimum wages, social security benefits, and a miscellany of other federal welfare gains. Reunification of the two areas might have been the course pursued if the voters of Guam in 1969 had not expressed their rejection of joinder. Preparations on Guam for the advisory referendum were inadequate, the polls poorly attended, and at least for the immediate future, the people of the Northern Marianas will not combine their fortunes with those of their kinsmen on Guam.

The explanation for Chamorro interest in a linkage with the United States, in lieu of remaining with the rest of the Micronesians of the Trust Territory, also lay in the material advantage they had already gained. Almost from the beginning of the American occupation, the Northern Marianas received relatively munificent treatment. During the period 1951 to 1962, when the Navy administered the area, the quality of paved roads, utilities, and other supportive services dramatically marked the area off from the deteriorating facilities in the remainder of the Trusteeship. A completely monetized economy developed, heavily dependent upon government employment, and more people came to live in the district center or closely adjacent than in any other administrative district. In keeping with the devil-theory held by many Micronesians, this differentiation was deliberate: the Machiavellian United States at no time ever intended to surrender its control of the Northern Marianas.

By 1960, two political parties were contesting the elections in the Northern Marianas. Both favored political ties with the United States. One proposed to secede from the rest of Micronesia, the other to work with all of the other districts, but to the same end of closer American affiliation. Over time, the voters frequently ignored these basic party distinctions, being more impressed by the qualities of the individual candidates and the kinship appeal of their family ties. A few politicos, too, did not hesitate to switch parties, and to reverse their announced stands on commonwealth. Nevertheless, underlying the give and take of local politics in the Marianas was the goal of establishing an association with the United States. Eventually, this objective gained the support of most Chamorros and an unknown minority of the Carolinian residents in the Marianas.

From the start, one or more representatives from the Marianas District sat on each of the future status negotiating bodies of the Congress of Micronesia. The offer of commonwealth by the Department of Interior's spokesman in 1970 struck a responsively favorable chord among the Chamorros, even though it was rejected by the other Congress of Micronesia negotiators. The political temper of the times was suggested by the victory of the

Popular Party in the 1970 Congressional elections on a platform advocating that the Mariana Islands become a separate commonwealth. Lest too much weight be attributed to this single plank, the Party also opposed the income tax which the Congress was considering, a very popular stand in the Marianas. Disagreement within the Congress over issues internal to the Trust Territory and the destruction by arson of the Congressional chambers served to further separate the Marianas representatives from the Congressmen of the other districts. Several months later, when the Congress of Micronesia convened in special session on Truk, the Marianas delegation initially boycotted the meeting in support of its declared objective to integrate the district with the United States. The abandonment of the boycott under a somewhat ignoble explanation did not signal an end to the delegation's intent to work for a separate political relationship.

During all of this time, both officially and unofficially the United States held to the position that the future of Micronesia was to be determined as a single unit, rebuffing the Marianas approaches. When late in 1971 the United States specified its future military needs in the Trust Territory, and it was evident that the bulk lay within the Marianas, the die was cast. Unlike most of Micronesia, the majority of the people in the district had no objection to the reestablishment of a military presence, particularly in view of the augmented income anticipated. Nor had they any desire to finance the rest of the Trust Territory out of the tax revenues to be derived from the increased economic activity. For a while longer, they might be willing to allow the Congressional Joint Committee to continue negotiations for free association or independence, but upon their conclusion, the Northern Marianas were to be free to arrange their own association with the United States. Both the American negotiators and Marianas Congressmen at the 1971 talks understood that commonwealth was the Marianas' preference, and the former informally assured the latter that the United States did not propose to insist upon any future status for the district not acceptable to it. Shortly after, even the compromise of unified Congressional negotiations collapsed. In April of 1972, during the Fourth Round of discussions in Koror, Palau, separate talks were requested by the Marianas representatives, with commonwealth the objective. The willing concurrence of the American negotiators formally set underway the disintegration of Micronesian unity which, until that time, the efforts of the Congress of Micronesia had succeeded in forestalling.[8]

One month later, in May of 1972, the Marianas District Legislature created its own status commission. Starting in December of the same year, and semiannually thereafter, negotiations steadily progressed. By October of 1974 it became necessary to conclude them rapidly, for with July 12, 1975, now fixed for the holding of the Micronesian Constitutional Convention, it was essential that the Marianas Covenant be signed and voted on before that date. Agreement was reached on a final commonwealth draft in February of 1975. All during this period and until he was defeated in the senatorial contest of late 1974, the Chairman of the Marianas Status Commission, Edward D.L.G. Pangelinan, remained one of the twelve members of the Micronesian Joint Committee. A comparable straddling was later to see Marianas delegates divided over service in the Constitutional Convention even though the people of their district had already voted for separate commonwealth status. And while all this was transpiring, the position of the United Nations, as represented by the 1973 United Nations Visiting Mission, steadfastly held that "although the Micronesians ... must work out for themselves what kind of future links they wish to have with one another, the [American] Administration is still at this stage obligated to promote national unity in every way possible."[9]

The Marianas Covenant purports to integrate[10] the Northern Marianas into the United States, and with some qualifications, places the area under the legislative authority of the U.S. Congress. While the American negotiators scaled down their original terms for acquiring the whole of Tinian Island, they obtained access to as much as two-thirds under a long-term lease, with any unused portion to be temporarily rented back at a nominal rate should the lease be entered into. The United States also secured varying rights to other, much smaller areas, and retained eminent domain power for the gaining of additional lands. In view of the compelling rationale underlying the status negotiations for all of Micronesia, it is probably superfluous to add, the Covenant expressly lodged complete authority over foreign affairs and military defense matters in the United States. On the other side of the balance sheet, the Commonwealth is declared internally self-governing and is expressly "required" for twenty-five years to restrict (thereafter it "may" restrict) acquisition of real property to persons of Northern Marianas descent, effectively barring outsiders from owning land. In addition it is guaranteed $8.25 million annually as operating expenses for at least the first seven years, approximately $40 million for capital improvement and economic development over the same period, and a one-time rental payment of $19.5 million for land rights surrendered. When augmented to adjust for inflation, as contemplated by the Covenant, this equaled nearly $10,000 for each man, woman, and child in the Marianas.

The Covenant also called for the holding of a Marianas Constitutional Convention, whose product would require approval by the people of the Northern Marianas and certification by the President of the United States. It directed the government so established to be republican in form, with separate executive, legislative, and judicial branches, and with provisions for a popularly elected governor and a bicameral legislature. Each municipality, irrespective of population size, must be assured equal representation in one chamber. More generally, the Marianas constitution must be consistent with the Covenant and the U.S. Constitution, treaties, and laws applicable to the Northern Marianas.[11]

During the whole period of the Marianas negotiations, and almost up to their conclusion, it was assumed by all parties that the siting of a $300 to $400 million joint Air Force, Navy, and Marine "airfield/logistic facility" on Tinian and rehabilitation of its harbor waited only on their conclusion. Environmental impact studies, although provoking the ire of Tinian residents who at first faced being dispossessed from their village, offered to them the promise of extensive welfare services and economic benefits to be shared by all of the Marianas once the facility was functioning.[12] Antagonism of U.S. Congressmen to acquiring the Marianas presaged strong opposition, and indefinite postponement of the base construction was later announced. Greater confidence of the military in its ability to retain advance facilities on foreign soil in East and Southeast Asia undoubtedly was an important factor.

On March 17, 1975, by a 47 to 39 vote in the U.S. Senate, demonstrating strong reservations,

$1.5 million was appropriated for funding the various transition costs in converting the Northern Marianas to a commonwealth. The Secretary of Interior could now take the steps necessary to place the Covenant before the people of the district for their approval. With the Micronesian Constitutional Convention set for July 12, and a Territory-wide referendum on all forms of future status mandated to be held before then, there was relatively little time left for first squeezing in the Marianas' definitive expression on their own commonwealth Covenant.

The May 15 issue of the Trust Territory's *Highlights* carried details of the Secretary of Interior's proclamation calling a plebiscite on the Marianas Covenant for June 17.[13] The same Secretarial Order created the position of Plebiscite Commissioner, assisted him with an advisory committee, outlined the plebiscite educational program to be carried out, detailed voter qualifications, and authorized a special plebiscite appellate court. After arriving on Saipan, Erwin D. Canham, the Washington-appointed Commissioner, oversaw all the election preparations. Under his direction both proponents and opponents were assured access to the public radio station. The Covenant and its supporting materials were translated into the Marianas' two vernacular languages.[14] His published explanations on the pertinent terms of commonwealth satisfied a public need, and proved impartial except for a tendency to accept without questioning the position of the American chief negotiator on constitutional issues inherent in the Covenant, which will remain doubtful until judicially tested. A massive educational campaign mounted by supporters of commonwealth, and the less ambitious program of opponents, the latter mainly financed by funds derived from the "unity" appropriation of the Congress of Micronesia, acquainted the voters with the major issues through speeches, rallies, posters, advertisements, and painted graffiti. Hastily, the District Legislature adopted a law requiring a five-year "domicile" to vote in the plebiscite, and in a small way helped to obtain the overwhelming approval of the Covenant by disenfranchising as many as 350 potentially opposed Micronesians born outside the Marianas but working at the Trust Territory Headquarters. Those who could vote were given the single option of casting a ballot for or against the Covenant, with a "no" vote equated with favoring the future of the Marianas be tied inexorably with that of the rest of Micronesia.[15] A little under seven-tenths of the Marianas eligible voters (and 78.9 percent of those voting) supported commonwealth status. A perilous confrontation between the Mariana District's two major cultural groups was avoided although undoubtedly the negative vote was heavily Carolinian. United Nations observation confirmed the freedom of the choice, but there is no gainsaying that the United States had helped engineer a situation in which the election results were a foregone conclusion.

At the time of the signing of the Covenant, Ambassador Williams outlined seriatim the nine additional steps remaining: ratification by the Marianas Legislature, plebiscite, issuance of a Secretarial Order to separate the administration of the Marianas, approval by the U.S. Congress, the writing of a Marianas constitution, a referendum to ratify the constitution, its approval by the United States, installation of the commonwealth government, and finally, possible in 1980 or 1981, the formalizing of the political union with the ending of the Trusteeship. He obviously contemplated that by the time of the Micronesian Constitutional Convention in July of 1975, or no later than during its course, the Trust Territory would be split, and just as when only the Marianas were under the Navy, there would be two distinct administrations. Implicitly, if sufficient speed were mustered, the Marianas could even be severed before any Territory-wide referendum on status ordered by the Congress of Micronesia, obviating the potential embarrassment of the district's citizens recording their status preferences when afforded a number of alternatives. Upon reconsideration, the unexpected negativism encountered in the U.S. Senate suggested greater discretion, and that the better strategy would be to defer separation of the Marianas before affirmative action by the Federal Congress. The order of steps was accordingly modified, and after the vote in June, the Marianas Covenant was submitted to the solons in Washington. The House of Representatives, by voice vote on July 23, quickly endorsed the Marianas union. In the Senate, the Covenant received a stormy hearing before the Committee on Interior. Although in October this Committee finally recommended acceptance of the Covenant, for month after month thereafter, the Senate Foreign Relations and the Senate Armed Services Committees delayed definitive action.[16] Anti-annexationists, fiscal conservatives, and constitutionalists all raised objections. Meanwhile, the Micronesian Constitutional Convention was now meeting on Saipan.

During the concluding phase of the Marianas negotiations, the question of whether the Marianas delegates should attend the Micronesian Constitutional Convention was hotly debated both within and outside the ranks of the Marianas people. By the end of 1974 it was certain that a commonwealth Covenant would be signed, and it was anticipated that the later separation of the district from the rest of the Trust Territory for administrative purposes would make further argument moot. With the order of planned steps to commonwealth altered, however, the Marianas delegates were each faced with the necessity of having to make his own choice. Even assuming the plebiscite affirmed the Covenant, there was no guarantee that the U.S. Congress would concur. Should the Marianas then have to remain with the rest of Micronesia, it could be under a constitution whose terms were disadvantageous to the district if its delegates did not participate in their formulation. Before the vote on the Covenant, the Marianas delegates publicly declared that if commonwealth were approved, they would not attend the Micronesian Convention. The Congress of Micronesia's Pre-Convention Committee countered by letter, formally inviting them to take part, notwithstanding the plebiscite. Up to the very assembling of the Convention it remained uncertain whether or not the Marianas delegates would attend. Given the vocal opposition in the U.S. Senate to commonwealth, most reversed their public stand. Indeed, one who had traveled to Washington to testify in favor of the Covenant, on returning to Saipan took his seat in the Convention. Once the Constitutional Convention was underway, each daily session was to pose the same unspoken question of whether affirmative action in the U.S. Senate would now be followed by the abrupt departure of the Marianas delegation from the Convention hall.

The negotiators on future status from the Congress of Micronesia early recognized that Marianas sentiment would not necessarily coincide with that of the rest of the Trust Territory. While some Congressmen may have accepted the inevitability of the Marianas District eventually hiving off from the rest of Micronesia, others adamantly rejected this breach. The latter sentiment was to prevail as late as the 62nd day of the Constitutional Convention, when eight delegates signed a resolution (Res. No. 30) voicing opposition to separate status for the Marianas.

In tactical terms, the Congress of Micronesia rejected the right of anyone but the representatives of the Congress to carry on negotiations with the United States for any part of Micronesia. Time and again objections were heard in the Congress to the illegality of the Marianas negotiations. Recognizing that a district may "eventually go its separate way" the Report on the Seventh Round of negotiations claimed the existence of an obligation "to give the people of that district treatment equal to that afforded to those of other districts, a chance to accept or reject a compact and constitution."[17] Until late in the negotiations on the Micronesian compact, the Joint Committee insisted upon the fiction that it was representing all of the Trust Territory's districts. Even after the overwhelming Marianas vote of approval for commonwealth, Micronesian leaders still held to the hope that a successful Micronesian Constitutional Convention might phrase so attractive a document as to convince the Marianas of the wisdom of reversing its decision to unite with the United States. Throughout all of the preparations leading up to the holding of the Micronesian Convention, and even to the final ninetieth day when the delegates were called upon to affix their signatures to the completed document, the ambiguity of the Marianas position continued to contribute near disastrous uncertainty to the conduct of the Convention.

Marshall Islands District. The Marshallese are a distinctive people in Micronesia, whose language, relationship to their atolls, and the dominant role of their hereditary leaders set them apart. The *iroij laplap* (paramount chiefs) own title to all lands, and the *kajur* (commoners) work it at the *iroij*'s sufferance. In turn, the *iroij* owe obligations of care. Their former arbitrary powers of life and death have been curtailed during the century of externally-imposed metropolitan rule, and today the *kajur* is recognized as having user rights to land which the courts will protect against unreasonable *iroij* action. Traditionally, each *iroij* exercised sovereignty over all or part of an island, or of several, his fortunes rising

and falling through warfare. The emergence of
the area as a single political entity may be directly traced to contact with the West. The Germans
in the late 1800s signed a protective treaty with
Iroij Kabua, who controlled Jaluit, a large atoll
in the Ralik (western) chain of the Marshall Islands, and affixed to him both the title "Great
Chieftan" and nominal authority over the whole
western group. During the Japanese era, the paralleling Radak (eastern) chain of the Marshalls was
similarly placed under a titular head, now called
"village chief." In actuality, time had materially
eroded the authority of these two _iroij laplap_
and of all others, and the limited powers retained
stemmed mainly from their ownership of the land
and their community role in the settlement of disputes. The final development under the Americans
saw the centralizing of but a single administrative
structure for all of the Marshalls, sans _iroij_
serving by ascriptive right, and with each[18] of
the atolls having its own municipal government.
The Trust Territory introduced the substitution
of election by the ballot box for hereditary selection, supplying a nonviolent means for operationa-
lizing the growing contest between modernized _kajur_
and _iroij_ supporter for dominance in the introduced
government. To those knowledgeable of Marshallese
society, the confronting forces which threatened
to split the Marshalls District asunder could be
epitomized by Amata Kabua, spokesman for the most
powerful of the _iroij_ and their adherents, and
by the politically active members of the Heine
family, representing the "anti-Kabua" sentiment.
Eventually, the very organizing of the Micronesian
Constitutional Convention was to turn on this cleavage, as was the whole issue of future Micronesian
unity.

Amata Kabua was born during the end of the
Japanese period, of a _leiroj_ (female _iroij laplap_)
mother married to a traditionally powerful _iroij
laplap_ holding extensive land parcels on Kwajalein
and elsewhere along the Ralik chain of atolls.
Due to the Marshallese matrilineal inheritance
pattern, although of _iroij_ blood Amata possibly
would not be recognized as a paramount chief.
However, through influence over "King" Lejellan
Kabua--for so his father was designated by his
name plate--and leadership of the _iroij_ faction
of which Kabua-related _iroij_ and their supporters
comprised key members, Amata Kabua has played a
major, if not controlling, role in Marshallese

politics. Educated for several years at a private college in Hawaii, he was initially employed in the district's education department. He early became active in Marshallese politics, and while reputedly personally wealthy, has had an undistinguished career in business. One journalist reported that "he has, from time to time, accepted government aid in rescuing his business interests from financial ruin."[19] Starting with the second annual meeting of the appointive Inter-district Advisory Council of Micronesia in 1956, he represented the Marshalls. The creation of the Congress saw him elected as a Senator, and quadrennially returned to office. Although it was a number of years since Amata Kabua had been a member of the Marshallese District Legislature (Nitijela), the angry charge of a co-chairman of the Joint Status Commission in 1973 that it was "a rubber stamp for Senator Kabua's wishes"[20] only reiterated the common belief held both within and outside the Marshalls.

The members of the Heine family are descendants of a German sailor turned missionary who established residence in the Marshalls, and his indigenous wife. During World War II, both he and his son were beheaded by the Japanese. His grandson, Dwight Heine, for a while served as chief counterpoise to the Kabua faction. Under the early Navy administration, Dwight had been the first trainer of school teachers, this before the founding of the Pacific Islands Teacher Training School (PITTS). After returning to the Marshalls with a bachelor's degree from the University of Hawaii, Dwight moved up the administrative ladder in the education department, and also entered local politics as a member of the Nitijela. He preceded Amata Kabua by a year in appointment to the (first) Inter-district Advisory Council of Micronesia. Like Amata, he was elected to the initial Congress of Micronesia, but to the lower house, which chose him as its Speaker. Resigning the office, he was appointed as District Administrator of the Marshalls, the first Micronesian to serve in so high an administrative post in the Territory. Later, when he became an assistant to the High Commissioner on Saipan, relatives, both consanguineous and marital, took up the cudgels in the Marshalls for democratization of the Marshallese society.

Two elections held in 1974 well illustrated the place of the Heine family in the polarization of the Marshalls. In November, when it appeared Amata Kabua would be returned to the Senate unopposed, Carl Heine contested the seat. Except for the election which established the Congress, when four candidates had filed for the district's two senatorial seats, Kabua's place had always been secure. While Carl, the cousin of Dwight, campaigned on the platform of "Carl vs. Amata," and pointedly disclaimed a "Heine vs. Kabua" fight, his late entry into the race, and the long history of the Heine family's role could not but have been so interpreted. Carl lost. Earlier, in June of the same year, after the Nitijela and the *iroij* faction boycotted the Constitutional Convention election, four of the six announced candidates who won seats as delegates were members of the Heine group. This placed the minority Heine family in position to speak for the entire district in the drafting of the Micronesian Constitution. These two elections were but part of a series of events which, much like Greek tragedy, inexorably unfold to some preordained conclusion.

Contacts with American missionaries in the Marshalls date back over a century, so that with the end of World War II, Marshallese attitudes were strongly favorable to the United States and its administration of Micronesia. Over time this inclination had been offset by antagonisms fanned by United States land acquisitions and the multiform negative effects of nuclear and missile testing in the Marshalls. There also had developed the belief that under the American Administration the district had been neglected in favor of other areas, and this conviction had only been exacerbated since the founding of the Congress of Micronesia. The Marshalls produce the most copra of any district, and long accounted for the largest portion of the Territory's copra export tax. When the Congress of Micronesia imposed an income tax, a majority of the revenues came from the Marshalls District, mostly, it ought be added, from expatriate workers on Kwajalein atoll. At the edge of the Trust Territory, financially contributing heavily but feeling discriminated against, a sense of frustration arose in the district which fed the agitation for a separate status for the Marshalls. Its antecedents could be traced back as far as 1953, when Marshallese spokesmen had told a U.N. Visiting Mission that they did not wish to lose their identity in an amalgamation with other Micronesians.

At the 1972 session of the Congress of Micronesia, the Marshallese demanded that half of the income tax revenues should be returned to the districts from which they had been collected. The copra export tax served as model. It was only just that the Marshallese, who bore the most destructive consequences of the U.S. military presence in Micronesia after World War II, should receive the greatest benefit indirectly derived from the military. The Congress responded unsympathetically to the Marshallese position.

At the same session of the Congress, after inaction on the tax legislation, the Marshallese sponsor introduced another measure authorizing each district to establish its own future status commission. The message it carried was obvious. It, too, died in committee. Shortly thereafter, the Marshallese Nitijela considered but did not enact legislation setting up a political status commission for the district.

At the 1973 regular session of the Congress, a 50 percent tax rebate bill was again defeated. In protest, some of the Marshallese Congressmen staged a temporary walkout. At this point, the Nitijela reentered the fight. In March of 1973, by resolution, it admonished the Congress of Micronesia that if the rebate bill were not passed at the 1974 regular session, the Nitijela would "promptly commence separate negotiations with the United States on the future political status of the Marshall Islands."[21] In April at the same 1973 session, the Nitijela adopted legislation setting up a status commission to make studies, and with the approval of the district legislature, to negotiate with the United States. However, in line with its resolution, the Nitijela delayed activating the Marshall Islands commission until the following year.

Many of the Congressmen regarded the action of the Nitijela as a form of blackmail, calculated to undermine the status negotiations ongoing with the United States. It did not help matters that about this time, use of Territorial funds transferred to the Nitijela by the Congress for the meeting of district expenses was being investigated; although no audit report was ever released, rumor had the Marshall District Legislators reprimanded. And to add reality to the fictive picture of the world collapsing around their heads, the District Legislators had to abandon their chambers on top of the three-story MIECO Building when the latter's roof caved in. As President of the Marshallese Import and Export Company, Senator Kabua had erected the cement building, and encouraged the Nitijela's move to these facilities.

At its 1974 regular session, the Congress of Micronesia again failed to adopt a tax-sharing bill and the Marshallese solons once more walked out in protest. A compromise offer--reputedly 25 percent--had been made, but the Marshallese Congressional delegation refused to consider it adequate. Territorial receptivity to the district's position had hardly been softened by the communication delivered by the Marshallese Congressmen that the Nitijela was now calling not just for a 50 percent income tax rebate, but for permission of the district to handle the marketing of its own copra, for refund of the Marshalls' share in the Trust Territory copra stabilization fund, and for cancellation of the general territorial franchise over external ocean transport. In the event these were not met, the Nitijela repeated it would have no alternative but to proceed with activation of the Marshallese status commission and to open separate negotiations with the United States.

This was not an empty threat. While Amata Kabua was outside of the Trust Territory, in the name of economy, the Nitijela reduced the size of the Marshallese political status commission, and took appropriate steps to have it get underway. Upon his return to the district, Senator Kabua was named chairman of the commission. The Nitijela also adopted a resolution to the United Nations advising that body the Marshalls were "unwilling or unable to be a member of the political family of Micronesia after the termination of the Trusteeship agreement" and that they desired to negotiate separately with the United States. The resolution welcomed "any advise it [the U.N.] might render to Nitijela *if requested by members of the Marshall Islands Nitijela*" (emphasis added).[22] To the day the Constitutional Convention met, the United Nations had never been so requested, nor had the Marshallese approached the United States to inaugurate separate status negotiations.

At the time the 1974 Congress of Micronesia adopted the enabling legislation calling the Constitutional Convention, the Marshallese, as well as the Palauan delegation, left no question but that a loose confederation with broad district autonomy would be the only form of government their constituents would tolerate. As for the Nitijela, angered by the failure to secure tax rebate legislation, it passed a resolution[23] declaring opposition to all Marshallese participation in the Constitutional Convention, including the election of delegates to that Convention. The same resolution carried comparable objection to further Marshallese attendance at the Congress of Micronesia. Reportedly, during this session of the Nitijela, members made the veiled threat that those Marshallese who took part in the Constitutional Convention would be considered no longer Marshallese, and did not have to return. More explicit intimidation was alleged later: "Prior to the election ... some people went on the radio and announced that any Marshallese who submitted his name as a candidate for election to the ConCon, and anybody who went to the polls, would be kicked out of his land."[24] There matters stood, and no investigation ensued. As for the boycotting of the Congress of Micronesia, Marshallese attendance continued, although whether with the approval of, or in spite of, the leadership of the Nitijela was never clarified.

Reinforcing the position of the Nitijela, an *iroij* proclamation was read from the church pulpits in the Marshalls endorsing the stand of the Nitijela and calling for a boycott of both the Constitutional Convention delegate elections and of the Convention itself. Later, the Nitijela resolution and *iroij* proclamation of boycott were collectively to prove stumbling blocks in efforts to organize the Marshallese delegation for participation in the Convention.

Back in 1973, when it became apparent that dysfunctional lines of difference were developing, Ambassador Haydn Williams had announced to a conference of district administrators in Majuro that "the question of political unity ... is basically one which the Micronesians must resolve for themselves. However, the United States has pursued the future status negotiations ... in the hope and expectation a common stance will be forthcoming for the Marshalls and the Carolines." The following year, after the Nitijela had taken its defiant action, the American position was reaffirmed[25] as the Marshallese debated whether to participate in the Constitutional Convention. To the trained negotiator, however, the United States had not taken an adamant stand foreclosing separate Marshallese talks such as were already underway with the people of the Marianas. Also, as a matter of more than passing interest, the Ambassador had reassuringly indicated that no constitution would be imposed upon the Marshallese against their will, this notwithstanding that until the very last minute, the language of the enabling legislation calling the Convention could have had precisely that legal effect.

Spurred by the hostility expressed in the Marshalls, the Congress of Micronesia at its 1974 Special Session finally adopted a 20 percent income tax rebate bill, but not to be first administered until the following year. Its terms did not satisfy the Marshallese Congressional delegation however, for a 50 percent rebate had now become a sine qua non to any compromise. At the same special session an amendment was proposed to the Convention enabling legislation allowing any district by a two-thirds' vote to reject its incorporation under the constitution, but was vetoed by the High Commissioner because of the measure's other contents. Bills to provide traditional leaders voting privileges at the Constitutional Convention, and declaring void the elections held in the Marshalls for constitutional delegates were introduced but failed of passage. The rationale for all of these measures lay in the attempt to head off the growing Marshallese opposition and its accretion of ever more justifications for suspending the Constitutional Convention. So serious was the threat to become that by the Regular Session of 1975, in one form or another all of these changes were to be enacted.

The anti-Kabua faction in the Marshalls might take comfort in the fact that the actions of the Nitijela and of the _iroij_ had not been unanimous, since internal opposition had been expressed, in the ranks of both. However, the June 4, 1974, special election for delegates to the Constitutional Convention dramatically displayed the strength of the growing resistance in the Marshalls to Micronesian unity. Of the nine delegate districts, in only two were there contests between candidates, and in each of four districts but a single candidate filed for election. The only woman delegate, Mary Lanwi,[26] the sister of Dwight Heine, and her doctor husband ran unopposed. At best, about 15 percent of the potential voters in the Marshalls even went to the polls. Given the lack of any declared candidates in three districts, the Constitutional Credentials Committee held a person with twenty write-in votes in one district, and another with only eight, as qualified for seating as delegates at the Convention. In the interim before the fall balloting for Congressmen, Senator Kabua was to comment that the Marshallese Convention election was probably legal, but that the results caused problems of true representation; eventually, even the legality was questioned.

Emotions ran high at the Congress of Micronesia elections in November of 1974. It was rumored Amata Kabua's life was threatened, and a guard was placed around his house. The largest vote-getter among the delegates elected to the Constitutional Convention, Carl Heine, garnered 36.5 percent of the tallies in his race against Kabua for Senator. Presciently, this was to prove an accurate measure of the proportion of Marshallese voters unwilling to follow the leadership of the *iroij* allied with the Nitijela. As further evidence of the depth of Marshallese feeling, in the House of Representative races the "traditionalists" almost carried the day. Incumbent John Heine, a brother of Dwight Heine, was defeated by a Kabua-faction endorsed candidate, Carman Milne Bigler. She was the first woman ever to be elected to the Congress, and had campaigned upon the slogan of "Marshalls Mokta" (Marshalls First). John Heine had accepted the 20 percent revenue sharing compromise of the Congress, although he prophesied to do so was "political suicide."[27]

The 1975 Regular Session of the Congress of Micronesia provided the opportunity for what was to be the final Marshallese effort at seeking redress. It also witnessed a greater show of compromise on the part of the Congressmen from the other districts. At a meeting of *iroij* and Marshallese Congressmen in Majuro, it was agreed to send four *leiroj* (female *iroij*) to Saipan, two from each chain of the Marshall Islands. The statement offered on behalf of the *leiroj* declared the use of a woman for seeking compromise to be the last resort possible in Marshallese culture. By implication, their presence represented the final straw. The plea was for at least a 50 percent tax rebate, invalidation of the Marshallese Convention election, and the adoption of a series of suggestions for the naming of the *iroij* delegate members. As by this time opinion in the Congress had swung around in favor of allowing a vote to the traditional leaders of each district in the Constitutional Convention, this last portion of the Marshallese request was easily accommodated. By a sleight-of-hand device, which permitted districts to add an extra 1 percent[28] to the Territorial income tax of 3 percent (of which the districts received one-third), in effect the Congress proposed to make it possible for the Marshalls to obtain rebate of a full one-half of the amount collected. Additionally, somewhat with tongue in cheek, the Congress tackled the question of nullifying the Marshallese election.

In the words of Senator Kabua, the Constitutional Convention law was "erroneous, improper, and embarrassing to the Marshallese people."[29] Senator Kendall, his Marshallese colleague, claimed that the various islands were novelly grouped into districts so that Radak/Ralik cultural factors were violated.[30] According to Representative Bigler, Marshallese refrained from participating in the election for delegates because, in part, there was confusion over whether they would be voting for a particular future status. As summed up by Representative Basilius of Palau, eligible voters stayed away from the polls because it was contrary to Marshallese custom for their chiefs not to be entitled to vote in every decision-making body; redistricting included some of the islands of the Radak chain among those of the Ralik; and there was improper dissemination of information on the conduct of the voting. Probably the most telling argument for the passage of legislation nullifying the Marshallese election was the Senate Committee's report, "... the unity of Micronesia will not stand or fall on legal arguments, but rather on the actions of the Congress.... Simply stated, the Constitution of Micronesia is far too important a document, to be drafted without the full participation of the people of one district."[31]

But did the Congress really intend to void the election of the Marshallese Convention delegates? Incongruously, the same Senate Committee report[32] also included all of the basic arguments on illegality of such corrective legislation which the House of Representatives, at the 1974 Special Session, had employed to defeat the proposed nullification. Then, too, an unsuccessful bill of this

Sixth Congress would have permitted the District Administrator of the Marshalls and the Speaker of the Nitijela to name the missing two traditional leaders and a Congressman to complement with appointed menbers the elected membership of the Marshallese Constitutional delegation. The intent was explained on the Senate floor as enabling a full Marshallese delegation to attend the Convention, should the High Commissioner veto the attempt at vitiating the results of the Marshallese election.[33] In fact, the High Commissioner did disapprove the nullification bill as being contrary to the democratic process. He argued that if the election were improper, the remedy was to appeal to the Constitutional Convention, for it was declared the sole judge of elections, returns, and qualifications, and the Congress was without power to act. As both the High Commissioner's special assistant for legislative affairs and his head of public affairs had previously recommended a veto, while enigmatically the attorney general submitted no comment at all, there are speculative grounds for believing that the Congressmen had engaged in a bit of playacting at Marshallese expense, knowing all along that the measure would not become law.

From the organizing of the arrangements-making Pre-Convention Committee in mid-1974 to the day on which the delegates formally assembled on Saipan the following year, the Committee members kept attempting to promote the attendance of a full Marshallese delegation at the Convention. Publicly, they maintained the posture that there were no differences between the Marshalls and the rest of the Trust Territory which could not be resolved to the end of enabling full Marshallese cooperation. In September of 1974, as part of its swing through the districts in preparation for the holding of the Convention, the Pre-Convention Committee met with the Nitijela. Reiterated to the Committee was that body's opposition to the Convention until all objections it had registered were corrected. A meeting was also scheduled with the _iroij_, but it was cancelled when only three of the more than fifteen traditional leaders on Majuro attended. As one Pre-Convention Committee member wryly commented, its visit to Majuro was "not quite as welcome or as warm [as elsewhere]."[34] Later, at the end of May 1975, a conference of Convention top staff with most of the Marshallese delegates-elect failed to disclose any thawing in the Marshallese chill.[35] A month thereafter, and again on Majuro, a confidential meeting was arranged between representatives of the *iroij*-Nitijela faction and some of the delegates-elect. It collapsed when it proved impossible to formulate a compromise which both allowed the Nitijela and *iroij* to save face, given their declared positions, and at the same time permitted delegates from the Marshalls to attend the Convention in other than observer status. Indeed, the potential utility of the observer device for breaking the logjam provided the rationale for some of the unsuccessful legislation which was hurriedly drafted by the Convention staff for consideration at the Special Session in 1975, just prior to the Constitutional Convention.

In 1974, Senator Kabua had announced he planned to introduce an amendment to the constitutional enabling legislation which would require each district to adopt the constitution by majority vote, in effect preventing the Marshalls from being forced to accept it. This safeguard, and a special election to rechoose delegates for the Marshalls, would be the basis for Marshallese participation. In the following year, although not simultaneously, the Congress of Micronesia acted affirmatively upon both preconditions. First, at the 1975 Regular Session, it nullified the Marshallese election, only to have its bill vetoed. Then, in the Special Session at mid-year, it adopted amendatory legislation which would preclude any district, including the Marshalls, from being brought under the constitution against its will. Now, as the convening date approached, would two traditional chiefs from the Marshalls be named to sit in the Convention and a Congressman be officially designated to head the Marshallese delegates? Reputedly, Congressman Ataji Balos had been the unofficial choice of the Marshallese Congressmen, but no official notice had ever been communicated. Without his formal assumption as delegation head, would the Marshallese delegates be able to organize? Conversely, what would happen should the Nitijela by resolution, backed by the supporting *iroij*, peremptorily demand that all Marshallese withdraw from the Convention? Would any Marshallese dare appear, and if they did, would they remain throughout and sign the constitution?

Palau District. If the peoples of Micronesia are placed along a theoretical continuum, with the soft-spoken, usually retiring Marshallese at one extreme by virtue of their non-competitiveness and the resulting sense of disadvantage which many share, the Palauans would be stereotyped as clustering at the opposite pole. Borrowing from John Adams on the New Englanders of his time, Palauans hold a profound conviction that: "The morals of our people are much better; their manners are more polite and agreeable, they are purer ...; our language is better, our taste is better, our persons are handsomer; our spirit is greater, our laws are wider, our religion is superior, our education is better."[36]

A recent observer characterized the Palauans as "confident, proud, aggressive, energetic and comparatively well educated."[37] He might have added, as well, that although these qualities brought them to the top posts of the Trust Territory government, they also tended to cause the Palauans to be a source of friction wherever they settled in other districts. "Palau for the Palauans," the slogan of the Modogkne--a religious movement in Palau, with cargo cult parallelisms--could as well be applied to the driving force motivating most all Palauan leaders.

Identification of Palau at the status talks in 1971 as one of the three districts in which the military desired to maintain a presence in Micronesia drew mixed reaction. Some Palauans were utterly opposed. Others who initially disapproved of military bases and the conducting of maneuvers over Babelthaup's terrain were later partially mollified by the United States' offer of the return of public lands to the districts prior to the conclusion of the status talks and the termination of the Trusteeship. In any event, there was yet to be negotiated the terms for assuring military access to some thirty-two thousand acres on Babelthaup for ground force training, availability of limited littoral land for the navy, and joint civilian-military use of an airport.[38] Most important, the Palauans recognized that as one of the "have" districts at the periphery, they now possessed greater leverage for bargaining with the United States than any of the three central districts of the Trusteeship. While in order of priority the military might rank the district's importance below that of the Marshalls or the Marianas, the latter's opening of separate talks with the United States suggested the Palauans might consider also striking out on their own.

In the spring of 1973, the Palau District Legislature directed one of its committees to study and report on the prospects of Palau entering into separate status talks with the United States. In the fall of the same year, the Legislature ordered a political education campaign be instituted to ascertain the Palauans' future political aspirations. By the spring of 1974, the Speaker of the Palau Legislature was to point out that the course of action taken by the people of the Marianas and the Marshalls made the possibility of unity in Micronesia more remote. Palau should reevaluate its position with respect to future status and its association with the other districts. Shortly thereafter, the Palau Legislature adopted a bill calling a Constitutional Convention for Palau to "prepare alternate draft constitutions providing for the government of Palau in a loose federation with other districts of Micronesia and in free association with the United States of America, or for the government of the future self-governing or independent state of Palau or for any other form of government which the delegates shall desire."[39] Since the members of the Palau delegation to the Micronesian Constitutional Convention were to sit and participate fully in the Palau Convention, its deliberations could not but prove material to later events on Saipan. Almost a year would elapse before Palau's first efforts at constitution drafting would be concluded. By then, a Palauan variation in the Micronesian unity dance, in the form of a district counterstep, would have been introduced.

In late spring 1975, the Palau District Legislature created its own political status commission. After organizing, the latter immediately communicated to Ambassador Williams its desire to "establish a formal dialogue with the United States government to consider a future political-status agreement between the people of Palau and the United States similar in nature to that of the Northern Mariana Islands."[40] No reciprocating response was officially forthcoming from the Americans, but as the Micronesian Constitutional Convention drew near, the Palauans had now established an alternative to joinder with the rest of the Trust Territory in drafting a Micronesian Constitution.

During the same period preceding the gathering of delegates in convention on Saipan, another factor was adding its own confusing contributions to the Palauan scene. Late in 1974, a report issued privately in Washington identified four optimum locations in the world for the building of mammoth oil importation, refining, and storage facilities. Three were in Europe, and Palau constituted the fourth. Japan required a reserve to reduce the trauma of potential Mid-Eastern oil embargoes. In addition, economies of size foreshadowed the use of huge five-hundred-thousand-ton-plus tankers, larger than the capacity of Japan's ports to handle even if the risk of augmented air pollution were discounted. With the big tankers barred from plying the Malacca Straits, Palau was on Japan's Mid-Eastern oil route, and offered several commodious harbors and space for oil storage. The pollution of the petrochemical industry would be blown out to sea, far from the shores of Japan. As news of the mammoth project filtered into the Trust Territory, and one of the authors of the study commenced promoting the Palau oil superport, the prospect of hundreds of millions if not billions of dollars to be spent in Palau promised to furnish a new economic base upon which the Palauans might erect their own future political status. Specifics remained secret, but many Palauans were generally disturbed by the threat it posed to their traditional culture; only after the conclusion of the Micronesian Constitutional Convention was more complete information to be made public, disclosing the need of extensive feasibility studies prior to the formation of a consortium of Iranian, Japanese, and United States interests. Meanwhile, a number of Palau's most influential politicians were privy to each new project development as it occurred, and foremost among them was Senator Lazarus E. Salii, architect of the Micronesian option for free association status.[41]

It appeared possible to reach only one conclusion from all of these perplexing elements: Palau, like the Marshalls, was keeping its options open. And here, the guidance of Senator Roman Tmetuchl could be comparable to that of Senator Kabua in the Trusteeship's easternmost district. One of the two major forces within Palau's Liberal Party (the other faction led by Senator Salii), his influence in his home district tended to be exerted covertly, and in that sense had been likened to that of the "Godfather" in the then currently popular films about the American Mafia. Except for one term, he had served either as a Senator or Representative in the Congress of Micronesia since its founding. His strength depended more on skills of political maneuver than on personal popularity which garnered large voter majorities, and his base of support derived from the Liberal Party's long control of the Palauan District Legislature.

During the near decade of Micronesian status negotiations, Senator Tmetuchl had been reported at one time or another as favoring practically each of the alternatives but statehood with the United States. In the spring of 1975, with the Congress of Micronesia then in session on Saipan, he was conspicuous as the only non-Marianas member who appeared at the signing of the Marianas Covenant. As Co-chairman of the Palau Select Committee on Development he had helped prepare the groundwork for holding the Palauan Constitutional Convention, and later, as its President, justified its existence by the adage of "Not putting all eggs in one basket." If the Micronesian Constitutional Convention did not succeed, Palau would at least have its own constitution. Finally, as Chairman of the Palau Status Commission, when he called for negotiations with the United States on the premise of commonwealth, he is said to have replied enigmatically to a request for explanation that one never negotiates by stating what is desired. Rather, start with an extreme position, and then it is always possible to compromise on one less radical.

When the first Palauan Constitutional Convention adjourned in May of 1975, after seventy-four days of session, it produced two divergent constitutions. Although not publicized, one contemplated complete independence for Palau and reinstitution of large components of Palauan traditional government. The other, more conventional in content, was compatible with Palau becoming part of a larger Micronesian entity. Reputedly, the former was the handiwork of supporters of Senator Tmetuchl, and incorporated the philosophy of anthropologist Dr. Thomas Gladwin, serving as a consultant. A deputy legislative counsel of the Congress of Micronesia, working under directions of Senator Salii, drafted the latter. Unable to reach agreement on one, or compromise by combining features of both documents as was authorized by the enabling legislation, the Palauan Convention consigned the two constitutions to the decision of the voters at some unspecified future date. There matters stood. Meanwhile, they provided an ambiguous platform upon which the Palauans might take their stand at the Micronesian Constitutional Convention. Eventually, both Palauan documents were to be relegated to complete oblivion, and new drafts to be prepared and to compete for public support.

As plans for the holding of Micronesia's Constitutional Convention progressed, the uncertainty surrounding the Palauan delegation increased. What was the significance of the proposed constitution which set Palau apart as an independent entity? Were the Palauan voters to be asked to go to the polls and endorse it? Would the Palauan Status Commission commence negotiations with the United States for commonwealth status? Mirroring the situation in the Marshalls, would the district's delegates even appear on Saipan, let alone wholeheartedly engage in the give and take of writing a constitution for all of Micronesia? A telex message received by the Pre-Convention Committee from the chairman of the Palauan Convention delegation in June, less than a month before the convening, prolonged the suspense: "...strong support people of Palau for Micro Con Con as organized and scheduled at least as means to reassess political elements and aspects of unity of Micronesia."

The uncertainty with respect to the Palauan delegation merely compounded the doubts and fears surrounding the Marianas and Marshall contingents. In the long weeks which led up to the fateful date of July 12, 1975, the portent of each day's events was examined like the entrails of a sacrificial animal. Did they augur the Convention would mount a quorum so as to be able to organize itself? More fundamentally, what light did they shed on the prospects of future unity for all of Micronesia?

Once embarked upon the constitutional convention route, the question of unity would not be answered definitively until the people of Micronesia voted on the adoption of rejection of their constitution, assuming, of course, that one were drafted so that stage could be reached. Now it became a matter of "first things first," and initially crucial for the Micronesian Constitutional Convention's success was the appearance on Saipan of a sufficient number of delegates committed to the writing of a constitution. As an aid to their efforts, and wholly in an advisory way, the Congress of Micronesia asked the voters to express their views on unity at the General Referendum it had directed to be held throughout the Territory. Delayed by the High Commissioner until July 8, 1975, after the people of the Marianas District would have an opportunity to approve a separate commonwealth, the referendum returns were not available in time to influence the attendance of the delegates on Saipan for the opening of the Convention. When published, they confirmed that the Marianas had definitively opted out of a unified Micronesia and that the Marshallese boycott was still running strong, with not even half of the voters from the latter district who did go to the polls favoring unity (48.8 percent). In Palau, a larger proportion of votes were cast for Micronesian unity, and only in a minor way trailed the cumulative affirmation expressed in all five districts (excluding the Marianas) of 76.1 percent.[42]

By the time the returns from the referendum were counted and announced, the Micronesian Convention was under way, with delegates from both the marshalls and Palau present. Irrespective of their districts' tallies, the delegates in attendance from the Marshalls were wholeheartedly to support a unified Micronesia, while the issues raised by the Palau delegation would prove near-devastatingly disruptive. A year earlier, at the 1974 Special Session of the Congress, Representative Timothy Olkeriil from Palau had recounted a possible "daydream": the "Palau delegates walk out [of the Convention] when the remaining districts refuse to accede to their demands for local control."[43] Was he really dreaming, or was he a clairvoyant?

---

1. If further parallelism between the Caribbean and the Pacific experiences be desired, upon Trinidad's withdrawal from the Federation, American funds were also forthcoming to finance capital improvements for the Caribbean island. Amita Etzioni, _Political_ _Unification_ (New York: Holt, Rinehart and Winston, 1965), p. 164.

2. Referred to in John Mordecai, _The_ _West_ _Indies_ (London: George Allen and Unwin, 1968), p. 47.

3. _Micronesian_ _Independent_ 5:38 (November 26, 1974), p. 3; responding to ESG, _Dialogue for Micronesia_, Program No. 15, November 20, 1974.

4. _Tia_ _Belau_ II:8 (July 1974), p. 5.

5. Chairman Edward D.L.G. Pangelinan, Marianas Status Commission, at the signing of the Northern Marianas Covenant on February 15, 1975 (<u>Marianas Political Status Negotiations</u>, Fifth and Final Session, February 4-15, 1975, p. 10).

6. Resolution No. 30-1971, Third Marianas District Legislature, Fourth Regular Session, February 19, 1971. The following day, arson extensively damaged the buildings occupied by the Congress of Micronesia on Saipan.

7. See note 15, <u>infra</u>. As the United States had taken less than a supportive stand for Australia in the Trusteeship Council when the latter joined New Guinea with Papua in an administrative union, it was in poor position to sponsor any administrative linkage of the Northern Marianas with Guam by virtue of the commonality of Chamorro culture, let alone administratively combining the whole of the Trust Territory with Guam. On the other hand, separating the Northern Marianas from the rest of Micronesia, and then integrating these islands with Guam, would have been to proceed against the view strongly prevailing in the Trusteeship Council that the Trusteeship had to be treated as a single unit and terminated at one time.

8. The United States position consistently has been that it was not the American but the Marianas negotiators who asked for separate negotiations. U.S. Congress, House Committee on Interior and Insular Affairs, <u>To Approve ... on HJR 549</u>, 94th Cong., 1st Sess., July 14, 1975, p. 401. See also, Resolution 1-1972, Third Mariana Islands District Legislature, 1st Special Session, 1972.

9. <u>Report of the United Nations Visiting Mission to the Trust Territory of the Pacific Islands, 1973</u>, T/1741, par. 166, p. 39.

10. It remains to be determined whether this "integration" will meet with the concurrence of the Security Council. United Nations Resolution 1541 (1960) declares that as one of the three valid means of achieving self-government [the other two: "independence" and "free association"], integration with an independent state "must be on the basis of complete equality of political status, including representation and participation at all levels of government" (<u>Official Records</u>: Fifteenth Session, Supplement No. 16 [A/4684], p. 29). The

Northern Marianas will not enjoy such representation and participation at the national level of the American government. According to the testimony of Ambassador Williams, despite being called a commonwealth, the Northern Marianas will "be an unincorporated territory of the United States the same as Guam and the same as our other territories. The only real distinction between the Northern Marianas and Guam would be that ... the people in the Northern Marianas will be given an opportunity to draw their own constitution" (U.S. Congress, Senate, Subcommittee on General Legislation, Committee on Armed Services "...on HJR 549," 94th Cong., 1st Sess., November 17, 1975, pp. 58-59). Since the Williams statement, even that difference has disappeared with Guam's empowerment to draft its own constitution.

11. Constitutionally questionable are the attempt in the Marianas Covenant to impose limitations on subsequent U.S. Congresses to legislate for the Commonwealth and some of the provisions to be incorporated in the Marianas Constitution which on their face appear to deny due process and equal protection. For treatment of this, and of the entire negotiations, see Paul M. Leary, The Northern Marianas Covenant and American Territorial Relations (Institute of Governmental Studies Research Report 80-1, Berkeley, Calif: 1980).

12. "In addition to the monies paid for land and improvements, the tangible fringe benefits of civilian employment, local purchases and military payrolls will contribute to your economy. Moreover, the associated infrastructure will likewise benefit local residents--that is, roads, docks, dredging, etc., etc." Statement of Ambassador Franklin H. Williams at the "Opening Round of the Marianas Political Status Negotiations," December 13, 1972, p. 11.

13. Highlights, May 15, 1975, p. 4.

14. The Covenant was translated into Chamorro and Carolinian, but the latter so closely to the time of the plebiscite that it received limited distribution. The accompanying supportive materials were never translated into Carolinian, but only Chamorro.

15. The International League of Human Rights objected to the Marianas Covenant vote on the basis

that other alternatives could not be considered at the same time. This objection appeared laid by the miniscule turnout of Marianas voters in July at the General Referendum ordered by the Congress of Micronesia. Compare the 1975 Marianas Covenant vote with the previous plebiscite held there on November 9, 1969. Then, only 65 percent of the registered voters went to the polls, and they divided as follows: 1,942 for "reintegration" with Guam; 1,166 for "free association" with the United States; 107 for "unincorporated territory;" and a scattering of 9 votes, <u>of which 1 was for "commonwealth.</u>"

16. Technically, the Marianas Covenant Resolution was only sent "for informational hearings" to the Armed Services and Foreign Relations Committees, and their approval was not a requisite for placing the Covenant before the whole Senate. Practically, their concurrence had to be won. The U.S. Senate did not act on the Resolution until February 1976, and it was not signed until late March, four months after the conclusion of the Micronesian Constitutional Convention.

17. <u>Report to the Congress of Micronesia on the Seventh Round of Negotiations</u>, January, 1974, p. 119.

18. There are two municipal governments on Majuro.

19. <u>Micronesian Reporter</u> 16:4 (1968), p. 27.

20. Statement of Representative Ekpap Silk, <u>Dateline</u>, April 6, 1973, pp. 1, 21.

21. Marshall Islands Nitijela, 20th Regular Session, March 1973.

22. Marshall Islands Nitijela, Resolution 18, 21st Regular Session, March 19, 1974. Precedent for this language is found in SJR No. 100, Congress of Micronesia, 3rd Reg. Session, 1970 (3rd "Resolve" clause).

23. Marshall Islands Nitijela, Resolution 57, 21st Regular Session, 2nd Sp. Session, April 25, 1974.

24. Congress of Micronesia, <u>House Journal</u>, Fifth Congress, First Special Session, 1974, p. 150.

25. See <u>Honolulu</u> <u>Advertiser</u>, May 16, 1973, p. A-14; <u>Micronesian Independent</u> 5:10 (March 25, 1974), p. 3.

26. The only other woman candidate in the Trust Territory was defeated.

27. Congress of Micronesia, <u>House</u> <u>Journal</u>, Fifth Congress, First Special Session, 1974, p. 150.

28. On December 9, 1975, a month after the Convention, Secretary of the Interior Kleppe placed a 3 percent ceiling on taxes which could be levied on U.S. activities, which nullified the attempt of the Congress of Micronesia to accommodate the Marshalls District through permitting an extra levy on Kwajalein.

29. Congress of Micronesia, <u>Senate</u> <u>Journal</u>, Sixth Congress, First Session, 1975, p. 134.

30. Congress of Micronesia, Senate S.C.R. No. 6-297, <u>Senate</u> <u>Journal</u>, Fifth Congress, First Special Session, 1974, p. 171.

31. Congress of Micronesia, Senate S.C.R. No. 6-44, <u>Senate</u> <u>Journal</u>, Sixth Congress, First Session, 1975, p. 431.

32. <u>Ibid</u>.

33. Congress of Micronesia, <u>Senate</u> <u>Journal</u>, Sixth Congress, First Session, 1975, p. 299.

34. Minutes of the Pre-Convention Committee, September 19, 1974, p. 23.

35. Senator Kabua was away from home, "fishing." The hope of compromise was still held out by the prospect of the <u>iroij</u> relenting and sending representatives to the Palauan "unity" meeting (see p. 126, <u>infra</u>).

36. <u>Works</u>, 2:395, quoted in Merrill Jensen, <u>The Articles of Confederation</u> (Madison, Wisc.: University of Wisconsin Press, 1966), p. 118.

37. David I. Hitchcock, "Information and Education for Self-Government in Micronesia," Sixteenth Session Senior Seminar in Foreign Policy, Department of State, 1974, p. 5.

38. Much later, the 1972 specifications of land for military usage in Palau were expanded, as see the Angaur Airfield defense site in Annex D of the "Agreement Regarding the Military Use and Operating Rights of the United States in Palau" concluded as part of the Compact of Free Association between Palau and the United States and initialed November 17, 1980.

39. Sec. 1, Public Law 5-6-16, Fifth Palau District Legislature, approved June 4, 1974.

40. Letter of Senator Roman Tmetuchl, as chairman of the Palau Political Status Commission, dated May 29, 1981. See *Tia Belau* III:2 (July 1-15, 1975).

41. See letter of Senator Lazarus Salii to Speaker of Palau District Legislature and District Administrator in *Tia Belau*, op. cit.; also Roger Gale, "Palau's Place in Japanese Oil Strategy," *Far Eastern Economic Review*, October 3, 1975, pp. 50-52; and letter to editor in response to Senator Salii, *Far Eastern Review*, December 5, 1975, p. 6.

42. In a letter to the Micronesian Constitutional Convention, dated July 22, 1975, Speaker Itelbang Luli of the Palau District Legislature wrote: "There may be a reliance on the part of other delegations that the last general referendum in Micronesia reflects the desires of the people of Micronesia toward Micronesian unity. But the number of votes cast in the referendum does not represent even half of the registered voters in Micronesia, and should not be taken as an expression of the wishes of the people of Micronesia in the formation of the future Micronesian Government." *CCM Journal* Vol. II, p. 947.

43. Congress of Micronesia, *House Journal*, Fifth Congress, First Special Session, 1974, p. 98.

PART II. SCENARIO AND CHARACTERS

The parties to the Micronesian Constitutional Convention appeared on scene without a prepared script, although their lines frequently echoed the spirit if not the words of earlier political dramas. As substitute, elaborate stage directions in the form of Convention rules provided order to the movements of the large cast of characters on the boards, and cued their impromptu contributions. Ultimately, it was to be on the experience of the players, and their competence to improvise, that success of the production would depend.

Chapter 5. Confusion Compounded

Great Britain and New Zealand, in severing ties with their Pacific colonies, have not hesitated to become active partners in formulating the charters of the new island governments. In Micronesia, once status as a territory of the United States was rejected, all parties accepted the premise that the Micronesians would write their own constitution. Conceivably, the responsibility could have been discharged by the Congress of Micronesia sitting as a constituent assembly. Direct Congressional involvement would have run counter to American practice, however, and most everyone in the negotiations early proceeded on the basis that delegates would be separately chosen. Once, while the enabling legislation for the calling of the Convention was undergoing critical buffeting, it was proposed calling on the Joint Committee on Future Status to draft a constitution. If this had been the course pursued, it would have been the Congress, through a select group of solons, performing the task. A plea of the co-chairman from the House that "in all fairness to your Joint Committee ..., this is asking too much"[1] helped discourage the novel approach. Instead, after a year and a half of indecision, the Congressmen finally concurred on the preliminary outlines of a constitutional convention--"preliminary" because they kept amending the legislation almost up to the very day delegates assembled.

The Fifth Round of status negotiations terminated on August 1, 1972, with Ambassador Williams' concluding statement anticipating a proposal by the Joint Committee of legislation calling a constitutional convention: "... [W]e wish you well in this endeavor as you begin to lay down your plans for your future government."[2] One day after the Ponape Special Session of the Congress opened in mid-August, Co-chairman Lazarus Salii introduced such a bill sponsored by the Joint Committee. However, it was not until over a year and a half later, in the spring of 1974, that the proposed measure, replete with additions and modifications, surmounted the final legislative hurdle in the closing hours of the Fifth Congress' Second Regular Session.

Initially, the delay in enacting legislation was allegedly due to a lack of necessary funding. The appropriation of $450,000 for this purpose from the U.S. Congress as part of the Trust Territory's grant erased the convenience of this explanation. In truth, the Convention was to cost nearly triple that sum, so that it is doubtful that money, alone, explained the procrastination. Rather, every fear, doubt, and conflict surrounding future status that could be entertained was invoked by the definitive act of calling a constitutional convention to establish a new governnment for Micronesia. Eventually it was concluded, as reported on the bill by the Senate Committee, "All opinion seems to be in agreement with the idea that a constitutional convention must be authorized, so that the convention can meet as quickly as possible and resolve some of the large questions that have proved stumbling blocks in our drive toward self-government. In this respect, this bill is probably the most important measure that the Congress has yet considered in the course of its existence, since upon the results of the convention hangs the very future of our government."[3]

Act 5-60 of 1974, as finally adopted, called for sixty delegates to meet on Saipan to write a constitution for Micronesia. To reach agreement on that Congressional direction required innumerable compromises and the deferring of important "details" to the delegates. Expressly among the latter was determination of the date on which they would meet, and implicitly the proposal of a decision on the future status of Micronesia. Dear to all politicians' hearts are questions turning on systems of representation and their formulas of apportionment, and the enabling legislation purported to resolve both. Originally incorporated in the bill was provision for two delegates to be elected from each of the Territory's twenty-one representative districts, and one additional delegate coopted from and by the membership of each of the six Congressional delegations. During the course of committee deliberations, Congressional districts were abandoned for not fitting with the Territory's current population distribution. Instead, forty-two new districts were delineated "to ensure the representation of identifiable ethnic and geographic minorities, and at the same time preserving geographical unity within each district."[4] The boundaries of these districts, as they became final, and the total number of delegates agreed upon, patently revealed that equality of population ranked lower in importance than recognition of municipal identity and the preservation of other criteria. This modification of the decade-old boundaries of Congressional districts, and the combining of areas which did not consider themselves culturally linked, was to undergird some of the opposition in the Marshalls to the holding of the Convention.

As the smallest administrative district, Yap was allocated three elected delegates, the Marianas four, Palau five, both the Marshalls and Ponape nine each, and Truk, as the largest, twelve elected delegates. In addition, the Convention membership was increased by twelve chiefly delegates to represent the Trusteeship's traditional leaders. As first proposed, each district legislature would have designated two. Several sessions of the Congress and many corrective amendments later, it was agreed that they were to be selected directly by the traditional leaders from among their own ranks. To accommodate the absence of chiefs in the Marianas, its District Administrator would name one "chiefly" delegate and the Legislature the other. Presumably, this would bring at least one Carolinian into the Convention.[5]

The constraints placed upon the activities of the Convention were of a two-fold nature. Some were spelled out in the procedural requirements to be observed by the Convention. Others arose out of the phraseology adopted by the Congress in granting powers to the Convention and charging it with specific duties. The last, in practice, proved minimally hampering:

> The Convention shall draft a Constitution for the future government of the state of Micronesia. Such Constitution shall make adequate provision for the exercise of legislative, judicial, and executive functions, and shall guarantee to all the citizens of Micronesia a form of government which permits the free democratic expression of their views.[6]

Conspicuously absent was any other direction to write a constitution whose express terms or underlying philosophy corresponded with those of the tentative free association compact so laboriously amalgamated in the long negotiations on future status.

The Convention was authorized to adopt its own rules of procedure, subject to the limitations that they could not be inconsistent with the enabling legislation. What appeared at first as a pro forma statutory direction upon reexamination proved to be of crucial importance. Until the very day the delegates convened, they faced the risk that requirements specified in the Congressional act would preclude the Convention from being competent to function.

A goodly part of the enabling legislation established eligibility of both electors and delegates, and the procedures to be observed in carrying out the elections. Significant to the events to occur over the ensuing year, was the declaration that "the Convention shall be the sole judge of the elections, returns, and qualifications of delegates."[1] As supplemented by its ability to declare vacancies, the leadership of the Convention was able to employ these powers to counter the uncertainty of delegate attendance.

The Congress of Micronesia labored long in adopting the enabling legislation, and once passed, kept on amending it, but always in the background was the possibility that the Congress would endeavor to reshape the Convention's handiwork. The original bill had called for certification of the completed constitution to the Congress for the addition of any changes it thought necessary before submission to the electorate, but this intermediate step had been deleted. Nevertheless, the delegates retained doubts over Congressional abstinence, and one of the first internal studies completed by Convention research staff plumbed the question. No categorical opinion could be expressed, for the answer turned on the Convention's legal premise: once activated, was the Convention an expression of the sovereignty of the Micronesian people, or was it merely an amanuensis of the Congress of Micronesia, the latter itself exercising law-making powers delegated by the United States? Shades of the quarrels over theoretical sovereignty, which underlay the status negotiations, now transmogrified as pragmatically relevant to the Convention! Before the completion of the constitution, the issue of sovereignty was to reappear in other forms.

Long after the enactment of the enabling legislation and the election of delegates, the Congress appended an expanded referendum procedure for adoption of the completed constitution. As provided in the original legislation, the High Commissioner would set the date for the election, presumably shortly after he had the constitution translated into various island vernaculars. It was silent on the minimum vote requisite for approval of the constitution. At the 1975 Regular Session, the Congress amended the enabling act by specifying a Territory-wide majority vote necessary for ratification and that it be supported by receipt of a majority in at least two-thirds of the districts both then existing and newly created. Later, at the 1975 Special Session, immediately before the Convention, this was reduced to a bare majority of the district voting at the time of the referendum. In effect, the Congress had eased the popular adoption of the constitution, and anticipating the possible divorce of the Marianas as a separate commonwealth, had prevented that event from negatively influencing the results of the election. Similarly, as a result of the 1975 Regular Session legislation, at least two-thirds of a district's voters would have had to indicate disapproval for the district to be excluded from the constitution. Then, at the Special Session, the Congress lowered the fraction to but a majority. One of the objections early raised by Senator Kabua was now met; perhaps at this late hour, the reluctance of the Marshalls and any of the other districts to participate in the Convention would be dispelled. The scaling down of the vote mandatory for popular approval stands as testimony to the Congress' realistic assessment of the difficulties anticipated in drafting and ratifying the constitution. Left unspecified were the options available for any district which elected to reject the document.

As the enabling act was adopted, the traditional leaders who were to sit in Convention enjoyed the privilege of debating, but not the right of balloting. Defenders of this Congressional treatment of the chiefs argued it both afforded them consideration befitting their rank and spared them the embarrassment of having to vote and being publicly defeated. Critics charged that the Congress was itself shaping the constitution, for the chiefs were being written off in favor of a new democratic government. Objections to the traditional leaders' limited role flowed into the Congress from various delegations. Partly because of it, the Marshalls refused to cooperate in the holding of the Convention. Responding to the pressure, the Congress of Micronesia at its Regular Session in the spring of 1975 removed all limitations on the participative powers of chiefs. This in turn triggered need for technical modifications in other parts of the enabling legislation, changing the Convention quorum and the vote requisite for formal actions. The consequent amendments, however, when read through a lawyer's lenses, proved only to heighten the rigidity of the Congressional directions. It became essential that they be relaxed if the Convention were not to flounder on the detail of its prescribed procedures.

Initially, the Congress had fixed the minimum quorum at thirty-six, three-fourths of the forty-eight voting delegates. With the addition of the twelve traditional leaders to the voting delegate ranks, the quorum was increased, but only to forty. The latter figure in fact represented two-thirds of the total membership, and was deemed "sufficiently low to prevent the work of the Convention from being disrupted...."[8] Concurrently, the minimum requirement for the Convention to take action was raised from two-thirds to three-fourths of the delegates present, in an attempt to compromise with the Palauan demand for delegations to vote by unit rule. In no event could a proposal be adopted by the Convention without support from at least three districts. The rationale was sound, but the continued use of a numerical quorum and garbled language in the amendatory legislation cumulatively presented a nightmarish prospect.

Given the uncertainty surrounding the attendance of the Marianas, Marshalls, and Palau delegations, continuously looming in the background was the spector of inability to muster forty delegates, so as to organize the Convention and keep it in session. Next, if this number were somehow induced to appear and remain, the literal reading of the enabling legislation's restriction would have required each question to secure an affirmative three-quarters vote. In parliamentary practice, this would have necessitated everything coming up for decision, no matter how minor or routine, to obtain an extraordinary majority of "yeas." A minority of one-quarter of the quorum could have deadlocked the Convention on the most trivial of issues. An even more disturbing problem was posed by the same amendments in their treatment of delegates present, but not voting, when determining the base upon which to compute the three-fourths poll. Again read literally, with a quorum of forty present, and all but four delegates remaining silent on roll call, three affirmative votes would be sufficient to adopt any motion, including the constitution, itself. Such a charade hardly coincided with Congressional intent, so corrective amendments would need be sought. The plans for holding the Convention had to proceed in anticipation of a sympathetic Congress removing the minimum of forty in fixing the quorum size and making other clarifying corrections. Meanwhile, preliminary rules would have to be prepared and procedures discussed with delegates in such a manner as both to cover the existing law as well as the requested changes which would be before the Congress only days before the Convention was scheduled to meet.

  <u>Matters Organizational</u>. To facilitate the work of the Convention and, not so incidentally, resolve deferred issues, the Congress made provision in the enabling legislation for a Pre-Convention Committee. Its grant of powers was sufficiently amorphous as to permit the Committee to take most any action it deemed appropriate. However, one of its charges was crucially specific: to the Committee was delegated the duty of fixing the date on which the Convention would assemble.

  The President of the Senate, Tosiwo Nakayama of Truk, was designated in the enabling act to head the "Pre-Con Committee," the name by which it quickly became popularly known. The delegates of each administrative district were charged with selecting a chairman from among their membership, who became that district's representative on the Committee. While the prescience of the Congress placed in the Committee chairmanship the man whom the Convention was later to elect as its President, the Congress signally failed to anticipate that the district delegations might be unable to organize, and no Pre-Convention Committee formed. The creaky machinery erected in the enabling legislation for organizing each district's delegates depended upon its Congressmen burying their differences and choosing one of their members to serve in the Convention, and he, in turn, calling a meeting of all delegates. Fortunately for the Convention, in all but the Marshalls the Congressmen were able to coopt members from their ranks to join their respective districts' delegates, and all delegations then agreed upon chairmen.[9] As part of the district boycott, the Marshalls' Congressmen did not follow suit, so the Pre-convention Committee invited the largest vote-getter in the district, Carl Heine, to participate in Committee deliberations. Thereafter, he continued to serve as "acting head" of the Marshallese delegates, and technically the Marshallese delegation remained unorganized during the life of the Convention.

In Palau, after the district's Senator Salii brought its delegates together, their predominantly Progressive Party affiliation led to the selection of John Ngiraked as chairman. He had served in the upper house of the first Congress of Micronesia, and as a Progressive Party standard bearer had unsuccessfully sought to return to the Congress. Senior Senator Petrus Tun of Yap was named to head that district's delegation. The delegates in Truk chose former Chutomu Nimwes, who had left the lower house of the first Congress to direct the district's education system. The Ponape choice was Leo Falcam, its District Administrator, who previously had been the Executive Officer at the Trust Territory Headquarters on Saipan. Lorenzo L.G. Cabrera was selected by the Marianas delegation; unlike his fellow Committee members, Cabrera had never held political office but was active in community affairs. In most of the districts, designation as delegation chairman carried no more than presiding authority and responsibility for tending to administrative details, without recognition of leadership over policy.

Of all the contentious issues the Pre-Convention Committee faced, the most difficult concerned the setting of the date and fixing of the site for the holding of the Convention. As introduced, the enabling legislation had designated Palau as the district in which the delegates would convene. Later, "Saipan was chosen for reasons of economy and convenience in terms of staff support and proximity of Trust Territory Headquarters. Logistical support to a Convention away from Saipan ... would overtax the resources which the Congress ..." provided.[10] With the separation of the Northern Marianas looming, however, the wisdom of the decision became ever more questionable, and strong sentiment persisted in the Congress to have the constitution physically written within the future state of Micronesia. Only on the last day of the 1975 Regular Session of the Sixth Congress was an amendment defeated to change the Convention situs to Palau. Later, at the Special Session in June of the same year, the Congress was to empower the Convention of its own volition to move to another island, should conditions on Saipan not prove conducive to its work.

Troubling the members of the Pre-Convention Committee as they deliberated was the worrisome question of whether the people of the Trust Territory were ready for the drafting of a constitution. Had they sufficient political education? If not, would the crash Education for Self-Government program underway curb the inadequacy? Did they have the "mental, psychological attitude" requisite for the Convention to be successful? More fundamentally, ought the Pre-Convention Committee under its mandate to "facilitate the work of the Convention" seek to arrange the political compromises necessary to enable the writing of a preliminary draft which could guide the work of the delegates? Consensus lay only in leaving to each district's delegates the task of determining the views of their constituents, and formulating the district proposals to be brought to the Convention. The Pre-Convention Committee would itself not undertake to coalesce popular opinion around any form of political regime, specific institution, or constitutional detail. It would hold meetings across the Territory to make sure the timing of the Convention would not "be in conflict with events or important matters in the district[s] that may be going on at that time...."[11] Not so incidentally, as it fully appreciated, an opportunity would be afforded to answer objections before they grew and festered, and thereby it could build diffuse support for the Convention. Thus, in response to the opposition which it encountered to the presence of delegates from the Northern Marianas in the Convention, given the district's separate status negotiations, it could explain the uncertainty surrounding the district's position and the Committee's desire to encourage its remaining with the rest of the Trust Territory.

Matters temporal. The Fifth Congress may not have been able to reach agreement on when to start the Convention, but somehow it was more certain in its appraisal that the Convention could complete its work within a ninety-day period. Both temporal matters were to trouble the Pre-Convention Committee. In Administration publications it was publicly surmised that the Convention would probably be held between August 1, 1974, and July 30, 1975. With the election of delegates delayed until June 4, and the Committee first meeting in August, the necessary arrangements could not be completed before late fall 1974, or the spring of 1975, at the earliest. Both periods were impossible, for Congress of Micronesia elections were scheduled by law for November, and the Congressional session to open in January. Convening would have to be postponed until at least adjournment of the Congress, in order that the Congressman-delegates could attend. But then the Convention might have to be cut short, for as originally appropriated, the money to fund the Convention was available only until June 30, 1975.

There were further temporal complications. At the 1974 Special Session, the Congress directed the Committee to appoint elected delegates to a credentials committee to scrutinize election returns and hear all contests prior to the Convention. The special committee was already being set up when the High Commissioner vetoed the bill. The possibility that lengthy challenges to delegates might cause the Convention to mark time, using up its allotted life span, dictated that this procedural requirement be handled with dispatch. Now activation of the special committee would have to wait until after the Regular Session of 1975, and its adoption of an amended measure meeting the High Commissioner's expressed reservations. But with the election for delegates having occurred in June of 1974, how much longer could the Convention be delayed?

In a radio program on October 3, 1974, the chairman of the Palau delegation, John Ngiraked, opined that all of the year 1975 should be totally dedicated to an intensive political education program, and the Constitutional Convention should be scheduled only after its completion. He did not attend the meeting of the Pre-Convention Committee held the following month on Truk, so did not vote on its decision to set July 12, 1975, Micronesian Day, as the convening date. A national holiday commemorating the founding of the Congress of Micronesia, its symbolism for unity was obvious. Lorenzo Cabrera from the Marianas had suggested further postponement, but the other members of the Committee felt constrained to resolve the matter once and for all, to which he concurred. Only later did it become know that the elections for the Palau District Legislature would be held in the fall of 1975, right in the middle of the period scheduled for the Convention. The Palau delegates to the Convention regarded these elections as crucial to the fortunes of the Progressive Party; eventually, the work of the Convention was to turn around accommodating their absence.

Notwithstanding the fixing of the convening date by the Committee, the Sixth Congress which met in Regular Session early in 1975 almost postponed the Convention for a further year. It mustered good reasons: the plebiscite on the Marianas Commonwealth Covenant might not occur until after July 12, the latest date which the High Commissioner could set for the Marianas and the rest of the Trust Territory to vote on the future status referendum just enacted by the Congress. A bill nullifying the Marshalls District delegate elections had been adopted and was before the High Commissioner for signature, and an amended credentials' committee bill similarly awaited executive approval. Delaying the Convention would afford a longer interim within which to hold a special election in the Marshalls, examine credentials, and hear protests. Deferral was not defeated until the last days of the Session, influenced by the probability of lawsuit for breach of contracts already entered into by the Pre-Convention Committee in anticipation of holding the Convention in July.

Despite the rejection of the move for further delay in the Congress, uncertainty still remained high. On the agenda of the April 2 meeting of the Pre-Convention Committee was an item on postponement. However, once Delegate Carl Heine had reiterated the reasons, stressing the lack of time to rehold elections in the Marshalls and prepare delegates for participation, arrangements for holding the Convention continued unslackened, and July 12 drew closer. But even this was not to be the end of the matter. Still impending was the Special Session of Congress slated for June. An augmented case for Congressional postponement of the Convention could now be made: the confusion attendant on the Secretary of Interior's delay in issuing his Order withdrawing the Marianas from the Trust Territory government; the failure of the Marshalls delegation to organize and its traditional chiefs to choose their representatives to the Convention; and the very recent call by the Palau status commission for separate district talks with the United States. The Research and Drafting Section of the Convention, staff now having been employed, concluded that legal basis for Congressional intervention might exist. Senator Salii, co-chairman of the Joint Committee on Future Status, informally met with the Pre-Convention Committee to canvas the possibility of Convention postponement. A debacle at the Convention would so discredit the Congress as to threaten its further legitimacy. As consultant to the Committee, I argued that desperate as the breakup of Territorial unity might appear, it was possible to salvage at least the minimum, a weak confederation, conceivable on the model of the American Articles. The alternative of additional delay held greater risk of complete Territorial disintegration. Although the decision remained with the Pre-Convention Committee, in retrospect, by what right had I, an American, intruded into the Micronesians' political future? The inexorable momentum of events, originally set in motion with the choice of Micronesia Day, 1975, for convening, convinced the Committee to carry on. Even then, backlash against the failure to defer the Convention almost defeated the supplemental legislation requested of the Congress at its 1975 Special Session. Its adoption was crucial, if the procedural restrictions were to be relaxed and the Constitutional Convention properly equipped to begin, not alone successfully complete, its task.

The second matter of temporal importance to the holding of the Convention concerned the ninety-day limitation on its life. The fixing of a period of less than three months for the delegates to meet, organize, and write the charter of a new polity, one which inevitably would have to eclectically select from both Micronesian and foreign experience, imposed a constraint of substantial proportions. Originally a length of 120 days had been proposed. Apparently it was feared that without a fixed term, the Convention would be under no pressure to reach any consensus. It was estimated that the money available would permit financing only a ninety-day session; thereafter, request would have to be made of the Congress for extension, but how this might be accomplished with the Congress not in session was never explicated. Much later, during the Convention, when its Administration Committee returned to the same theme, knowledgeable Senators among the delegates pointed to the dearth of funds for financing another special session of the Congress, let alone continuing the life of the Convention.

In employing "calendar days" for measuring the Convention's length, the enabling act in effect shortened the period further by every Saturday and Sunday within the ninety day period on which the Convention did not meet, as well as by any recess the delegates might declare. A statutory adoption of "working days" would have conveniently avoided this construction. When late in the spring of 1975, the Chairman of the Palau delegation, John Ngiraked, casually remarked to Convention staff that his delegation planned to return home from Saipan for the district's legislative elections, the necessity for greater time-period elasticity became overwhelming. With the participation of the Marianas and the Marshalls delegations enigmatic, the absence of the Palauans would probably result in failure to muster a quorum. Moreover, the convention committees' deliberations could hardly be completed before the proposed return to Palau would occur, so the delegates remaining on Saipan would have to mark time. The Convention faced failure unless some means could be evolved for extending its working life.

Buried in the records of the Pre-Convention Committee will be found a query from the Palau chairman inquiring whether the enabling legislation ought not be amended to permit the calling of recesses.[12] Whatever its rationale, in the context of the forthcoming Palau district elections, the need to make provision for absences was not incontestable. At the last possible moment, the Congress in its 1975 Special Session was prevailed upon to countenance up to thirty days of recess. Moreover, as it provided extra funds for the delegates' interim travel and the Convention's expenses, in effect it was authorizing work to continue on informally during this period, in effect an extension by one third of the Convention's life.

Matters physical. The decision to hold the Convention on Saipan had been reached by the Congress without first confirming the existence there of adequate facilities. Requisite would be a meeting hall large enough to accommodate sixty delegates, an indefinite number of interpreters, pages and floor staff, and the visitors attracted to observe the daily proceedings. Adjoining would have to be quarters for officers, secretaries, record keepers, account clerks, information personnel, attorneys and researchers, and a convention library. Later, it was to be discovered that overlooked had been the need for committee meeting rooms. The Pre-Convention Committee could find no public building on Saipan suitable to house the Convention, and tentatively decided to rent the Continental Hotel's main dining room for plenary sessions and rooms above it for supporting staff. Negotiations broke down over assuring the Convention exclusive and continuous use of the premises, and a comparable lease was then signed with the South Seas Corporation, owner of the White Sands Hotel. The latter hotel was under construction, but the Committee was assured that it would be ready for occupancy well before the convening date of July 12. The change in plans appeared fortuitous, with more commodious accommodations afforded at lower cost; as frequently happens, the bargain price concealed a hidden flaw. The White Sands hotel was the subject of a lawsuit which became ever more acrimonious, and all further building was halted. For many years after the conclusion of the Convention, it was still to register its first guest.

All parties to the lawsuit initially entered into a stipulation honoring the agreement with the Pre-Convention Committee. By early May, the main hotel building and adjacent lodges were completed, and Convention staff commenced moving into the quarters they were to occupy as offices for the next six months. Legal charges and countercharges continued to be hurled around their heads, and the Committee daily faced the prospect of being physically dispossessed. The electric power and air conditioning systems of the central building were not tested until July; without them, it was impossible for the Convention to meet in plenary session. Last minute withholding of fuel for the hotel's generator, so as to force a resolution of the legal suit, necessitated moving the workshop which preceded the Convention. On the following day, the noise and fumes of unexpected asphalt paving in the hotel driveway drove the delegates away. When the Convention finally opened on July 12, housed in the facilities planned, desks and equipment in place, it represented a feat which had appeared impossible just a few days previously. Even then, continuation in the hotel quarters remained on sufferance of the legal contestants. At any moment a new courtroom stratagem might force the Convention to seek temporary quarters elsewhere, this against the knowledge that any substitute available on Saipan was inadequate. Throughout the life of the Convention, paralleling the drama being played on the boards of the Plenary Session was the action of the staff as "property men" in the wings, figuratively holding the set intact.

Neither prior to the opening of the Convention, all during its 120-day life, nor up to the time its staff surrendered the hotel premises on winding up its affairs were any rental moneys paid. The Convention at all times was willing to perform its contractual obligations, but the litigants could not agree upon a custodian to receive the funds. When the staff first moved onto the premises, the hotel's construction contractor provided the essential custodial servicing and supplies, albeit under threat of their imminent termination. When he finally refused to continue unilaterally, another of the parties to the suit assumed responsibility for maintaining the premises occupied by the Convention. This, too, proved a tenuous arrangement. However, the surmounting of the repetitive crises eventually produced a state of numbness, immune to all further threat of disruption. With the Convention once ensconced and functioning, the political repercussions which would have flowed from dispossession probably assured that all litigants, despite their mutual antipathies, would somehow countenance its remaining in possession. None of this stress was apparent to the occasional visitor, who undoubtedly marveled at the cooperation of the hotel's management epitomized in the maintaining of a "free" coffee bar. In the camaraderie surrounding the signing of the original contract, this had been one of the conditions agreed upon. Once the impasse over fueling the hotel's generators had been resolved, so that electric lights and air conditioning became accepted normalcy, fluctuations in the adequacy of the coffee service continued as the staff's measure for anticipating the next onslaught of trouble. Only in the last week of the Convention, when hot *soba* (Japanese coarse noodles) was provided to all frequenters of the coffee bar as a demonstration of the management's "appreciation," was it certain that the Convention's siting was secure.

Matters monetary. At the 1973 Regular Session
of the Congress, the Senate Ways and Means Committee
estimated that the total expense of holding a four-
month convention, including submission of the constitution to popular vote, would approximate
$750,000.[13] The following year, the House of Repre-
sentatives fixed the costs at $550,000 for a ninety-
day convention, including $90,000 to cover both
the prior election of delegates and the subsequent
referendum on the draft constitution.[14] Since
$450,000 had now been added for this purpose to
the Trust Territory's grant from the Federal Treasury, only $100,000 more needed to be appropriated
by the Congress of Micronesia. In fact, at every
session thereafter, and up to the meeting of the
Convention, the Congress was to provide supplemental
funds, until over $600,000 of the moneys under
Congressional control were to be allocated in aid
of the Convention and the work of its district
delegations. Hidden subsidies, as in the form
of salaries of delegates and staff carried on Congressional and Administration payrolls, swelled
the actual cost of the Convention by some $200,000
more.[15] The total cost of the undertaking had
been sorely misjudged by the Congress, nor had
the monetary appetites of some of the district
delegations been appreciated.

The delegates were elected under a law which
promised them necessary travel expenses, standard
per diem, and $25 a day during the Convention.
They could not be "employed for gain or profit
while serving as delegates," but excepted were
the six coopted Congressmen, who would continue
to draw their regular Congressional salaries.
But was it just that the Congressmen elected as
delegates, as distinguished from those coopted
for service, receive only a stipend of $25 a day?
And what about the delegates in governmental service
whose regular salaries, when prorated, exceeded
that daily figure? To be more equitable, the Administration proposed raising the daily stipend of
all delegates to $32.85, the figure "the Congres-
sional salary works out to [,] approximately."[16]
The Congress embellished the Administration's suggestion, and amended the enabling legislation to
allow all governmental employees administrative
leaves with pay when serving as delegates, supplementing their salaries as necessary to assure every
delegate's receipt of at least $32.85 a day.

Fortunately for the Pre-Convention Committee,
and its successor, the Administration Committee

of the Convention, sufficient funds were appropriated in toto to permit them to staff and equip the Convention most adequately. But matters of money remained controversial throughout the Convention's life, and some delegates and politically selected staff individually continued to urge special consideration to their own advantage. All of the monetary pressure was not applied unidirectionally from the districts onto the Convention leadership, however, and the latter's reference to applicable financial restrictions helped keep the district delegations' pre-Convention preparations on course. In addition, a safeguard in the original legislation, which remained unchanged, declared that a delegate's stipend, travel expenses, and per diem were payable only "while on the business of the Convention or a committee thereof."[17] This the leadership found particularly useful as a potential sanction against those delegates inclined to absent themselves from the Convention on personal affairs.

<u>District delegations</u>. The enabling legislation passed at the Regular Session of 1974 specifically assigned only one collective role to delegates of each district before they met on Saipan: organize so that their respective chairmen could comprise the Pre-Convention Committee. Part of the opposition voiced to the holding of the Convention lay in the failure to "build into the legislation some provision for careful preparation at the district level before moving on to the major convention itself."[18] The Special Session of the Congress in 1974 countered this objection by appropriating money to fund the travel of each delegation throughout its district.[19] Delegates were to discuss issues with the people, better inform them about the Convention, and "to gauge the views of their constituents and otherwise to prepare themselves for the upcoming Micronesia Constitutional Convention...."[20]

Originally, daily pay was not provided for any delegation duties that preceded the Convention. Amendatory legislation encompassed the rendering of services prior to and during recesses of the Convention. Only the total of funds available furnished a practical restriction on delegation activities. Staff was hired by each delegation, although by necessity of modest size. To guard against profligacy, all equipment, supplies, and other property purchased by a delegation were to revert to the Congress of Micronesia upon completion of the delegation's tasks. Nevertheless, the remodeling at Convention expense of a Quonset hut on Koror to become the Palau delegation's office hardly constituted such a transferable asset. Moreover, it did have the dubious merit of eventually subjecting the Pre-Convention Committee to a lawsuit, when the heavily Progressive Party delegation refused to pay the billed charges as excessive. As an added dimension to the dispute, the construction company it had engaged reputedly was owned by the Liberal Party's Senator Roman Tmetuchl.

In the original appropriation, geographical distances were alleged to have been the basis for the differential amounts apportioned to the six districts. Subsequent funds were provided on need, as communicated by the districts. In all, $120,000 was directly appropriated to the delegations for their activities outside of the Convention. Much of the Marshallese share lapsed by virtue of that delegation's failure to organize. When it was disclosed that out of the initial appropriation, the Palau district chairman had allocated $1,000 to each delegate without any requirement for accounting, the Congress of Micronesia added the safeguards that delegation funds could no longer be expended without the concurrence of a two-thirds majority of each district's delegation plus receipt of approval from the Pre-Convention Committee's chairman.

Between September of 1974, when funds first became available, and the meeting of the Convention in July of the following year, delegations traveled extensively in their districts on fact-finding trips. The Ponape delegation as a group visited every municipality on all of the islands, many several times; held meetings with government employees, business groups, religious leaders, and the district legislature; and thoroughly canvassed its district. Unquestionably, these delegation visitations materially helped in educating the people to the significance of drafting a constitution for Micronesia. Less certain is the extent to which constituents, in return, influenced the delegates' views, as distinguished from remaining passive or minimally reacting to positions expressed by individual delegates or entire delegations. Through questionnaires, one thousand of which were distributed for individual answer on Yap proper, and which served as schedules for evoking group responses at meetings on the outer islands, the Yap delegation obtained numerically-weighted reactions to some thirty-six items it considered pertinent to the writing of the constitution. In contrast, the Truk delegation carried with it a draft constitution, based on that of the United States, which it used as a guideline for conducting discussions in each local gathering. The Palau delegation, after formulating the general policy of a loose federation of autonomous and largely sovereign states for Micronesia, reported that in its travels to nearly every village in Palau this position engendered strong support.

Notwithstanding the variety of effort aimed at sounding out public opinion which proceeded simultaneously with its structuring, the district delegations never succeeded in pushing much beyond the realm of generalities. They displayed little concern for the wide range of more specific matters with which a modern constitution must deal, and particularly, delegates were not prepared to initiate or debate many of the critical details. The Yap delegation in its preparations commenced auspiciously, but the actions of its members at the plenary sessions of the Convention did little to reveal that the questionnaire responses received from its constituents had equipped them for such a participative role. Despite the impression given by events later to transpire in the Convention, not even the Palau delegation arrived on Saipan with a comprehensive view fully articulating Micronesia's future constitution.

Unity efforts. As preparations for the Micronesian Convention gradually took shape, the majority of the Congressmen became ever more conscious of the vexatious disintegration of Micronesian solidarity. A successful Convention held out promise of binding the Territory together, but the Congress concluded that other efforts to the same end were necessary. A special subcommittee of the Joint Committee on Future Status in 1972 had recommended a Commission on National Unity be established, with "ombudsmanic" powers to ensure that governmental policies were conducive to uniform district treatment and encouragement of unity.[21] Provision for inclusion of representatives of the Administration on the Commission contributed to rejection of the proposed legislation, but its equating of uniformity with unity undoubtedly helped defeat it. Activity of the chiefs on Ponape pointed to another means by which the Congress might achieve its purpose of promoting Micronesian unity.

In April of 1974, the <u>nanmarkis</u> and the <u>nanikins</u> of Ponape invited all of the traditional leaders of Micronesia to meet with them over a ten-day period to discuss such matters as Micronesian unity, future political status, the constitution of a self-governing Micronesia, and the place of the traditional leaders in Micronesia's government. Only a few chiefs from Truk responded to the call. Lack of advance planning and problems of financing contributed to the failure of leaders from Yap and Palau to attend. The Marshalls, moreover, had now embarked upon its boycott, and Iroij Lejellan Kabua publicly rebuffed the invitation. If the Ponapean chiefs wished to speak with their counterparts in the Marshalls, let them come to the Marshalls. Despite the failure to secure Territory-wide representation, the chiefs now saw the Convention in the light of advantage to traditional status. In addition, a new avenue for unity had been opened, and the Congress was quick to seize upon it.

The Special Session of 1974 appropriated $60,000 to meet "the crucial need for an increased awareness of national unity among Micronesians."[22] The funds could be spent, among other purposes, for arranging seminars and cooperating with citizens' organizations and institutions. Soon, $12,000 helped finance a traditional leaders conference on Truk in the fall of 1974. This second meeting attracted "chiefs" from all districts, including an observer group of commoners from the Marshalls, and at least one senior citizen from the Marianas, accommodating the absence of traditional leaders in that district. While the Truk meeting consumed considerable time in organizing itself, it did adopt a number of resolutions: one supported unity, another requested financing for further conventions of traditional chiefs, and a third endorsed amendment of the constitutional enabling legislation so as to give voting rights at the Convention to Micronesian traditional leaders.[23]

In February of 1975, under the aegis of the Ibedul and Reklai, Palau's two paramount chiefs, a unity conference was called on Palau which the High Commissioner and most Congressional delegations attended. This meeting was Palau's response to the previous year's conferences on Ponape and Truk. With the theme "Let Unity Abide," a temporary feeling of euphoria prevailed. To the politically initiated, it also cloaked a byplay between Palau's two political parties, with the Progressive Party momentarily jockeying for position of advantage on the local political scene.

In the effort to counteract the disintegration of Micronesia, the Congress had seized upon the support of the Territory's traditional leaders for the shoring of Territorial unity. Only later were the full dimensions of their involvement to become apparent in the form of a demand for greater sharing in the governance of Micronesia. When the Congress so effusively responded to the invitation from Palau, it unwittingly was also setting forces in motion which were to compound the difficulty of drafting the Micronesian constitution. Whether or not unity was furthered by the Palau meeting, the local political gambit apparently aided the partisan fortunes of the Progressive Party within the district, and complicated the bringing of the Constitutional Convention to successful conclusion.

----
1. Congress of Micronesia, House Journal, Fifth Congress, First Session, 1973, p. 309.

2. Office of Micronesian Status Negotiations, "The Future Political Status of the Trust Territory," Proceedings of the Fifth Round Micronesian Status Negotiations, Washington, D.C., July 12-August 1, 1972, p. 17.

3. Congress of Micronesia, Senate SCR No. 56, Senate Journal, Fifth Congress, First Session, 1973, pp. 445-46.

4. Idem, p. 446.

5. The District Administration initially appointed Dr. Francisco T. Palacios upon the endorsement submitted on his behalf by the Sanol (paramount chief) and Reipi (traditional leaders) of the local Carolinian group called the Repaguluos. (See also Chapter 6, note 10.)

6. Public Law No. 5-60, Sec. 8.

7. Idem, Sec. 3 (8).

8. Congress of Micronesia, Senate SCR No. 6-1, Senate Journal, Sixth Congress, First Session 1975, p. 398.

9. District delegation chairmen were to be chosen by July 31, 1974. The Marianas delegates waited until the very last possible day to organize, reflecting the ambivalent position of the district.

10. Congress of Micronesia, House SCR No. 292, House Journal, Fifth Congress, 2nd Session, 1974, p. 480.

11. Minutes of the public meeting held by the Pre-Convention committee on Truk on September 19, 1974, p. 2.

12. Ibid., p. 14.

13. Congress of Micronesia, Senate SCR No. 90, Senate Journal, Fifth Congress, First Session, 1973, p. 496.

14. Congress of Micronesia, House SCR No. 292, House Journal, Fifth Congress, Second Session, 1974, pp. 479-80.

15. A further source of Convention funding was the not inconsiderable interest earned on the Federal Treasury grant, which upon receipt was placed in 9.5 percent time certificates.

16. Congress of Micronesia, HICOM Com/No. 131, Senate Journal, Fifth Congress, First Special Session, 1974, p. 206.

17. P.L. No. 5-60, Sec. 10.

18. Palau Representative Timothy Olkeriil, House Journal, Fifth Congress, First Special Session, 1974, p. 19.

19. P.L. No. 5-92, Sec. 1.

20. Ibid. The act also carried a proviso allowing all of Palau's share to be used to help defray the cost of that district's constitutional convention.

21. Congress of Micronesia, Senate SCR No. 233, Senate Journal, Fourth Congress, Second Special Session, 1972, p. 156.

22. Congress of Micronesia, Senate SCR No. 279, *Senate Journal*, Fifth Congress, First Special Session, 1974, p. 153.

23. Second Annual Micronesian Traditional Chiefs Conference, "Unity of Micronesia," November 11-15, 1974, Truk, 1974.

Chapter 6. Delegates and Delegations

The Congress of Micronesia either did not trust the election process to choose delegates both fully representative of all the people as well as competent to draft a constituent document fitting for Micronesia, or believed the collective legitimacy of elected delegates would be insufficient to assure acceptance of their handiwork. Thus the voters of Micronesia who went to the polls on June 4, 1974, elected only a little over two-thirds (42) of the Convention's membership. The balance would be selected by the Congressional delegations from their own ranks (6), and coopted by the traditional leaders (12). Even after the elections, the proper ratio of elected to appointed members continued to be disputed. At the Special Session of 1974, bills were defeated to add two more delegates for Kusaie, another two for the southern islands of Palau, and an additional pair of delegates for every district. Time was to show that respective numbers of elected members never became a matter of significance, as measured by bloc contribution, but that the difference in method of selection assured the consideration of matters which might never have arisen in the Convention.

The original decision on the number of delegates to elect was premised upon the 1971 Trust Territory census. While not an official count, it was believed to be reasonably accurate. This alignment of district population with delegation size kept deviation to no greater that 5 percent from the norm. The one-man-one-vote principle followed by the Supreme Court of the United States might not have the same binding effect on the Trust Territory, but nevertheless, too great a disparity might be attacked as a deprivation of fundamental poltical rights. During the following year, more accurate census data became available, and the apportionment was revised.

In the original allocation, Ponape appeared to be most disproportionately under-represented, by about 5 percent. In addition, Kusaie had to share its representation with other outer islands of the Ponape District. Relying upon the new census data, one of the Marianas' seats was transferred to Ponape, which eliminated the "discrimination" against Ponape as well as now allowing Kusaie to elect two delegates of its own. With Kusaie slated to become a separate district, it was obvious to all that its voice must be heard in the Convention through representatives of its own choosing.

In attempting to be equitable, the Congress of Micronesia only created a greater malapportionment. Now, with four delegates, the Marianas District markedly deviated from the norm by a minus 15.4 percent. The Marianas solons fully appreciated the impact of the change, but as Senator Edward D.L.G. Pangelinan remarked, "...[W]e recognize the fact that that constitution bill is so important to the people of Micronesia that we were willing to overlook that oversight."[1] Hindsight reveals that the entire difficulty could have been obviated through increasing the total number of elected delegates to forty-three. By the expedient of adding just one more member to the Ponape delegation, and retaining all other delegations unchanged, the disparity of the Marianas delegation would have been avoided. By this time, however, the Marianas Congressmen had probably realistically concluded that their district's future was not to be determined by the constitution which would govern the rest of Micronesia, so representation of their district at the Convention seemed a matter of minor import to them. Apparently the other Congressmen were also of the same mind, and so gave their attention to reducing total deviation for the other five districts. (See Table 3.)

The constitutional enabling legislation prohibited nomination papers and ballots from containing reference to party or the political affiliation of any candidate. Nevertheless, in Palau the Liberal and Progressive Parties took an active part in the picking of candidates and the running of their campaigns, so that they were well identified. Reportedly, Senator Lazarus Salii instructed his Liberal Party "to shy away from those candidates who (sic) he considered 'uncontrollable.'"[2] Progressive Party candidates, who polled only 18 percent of the total votes cast, won three of the five Palauan delegate seats! The defeat of the Liberal Party's candidates was attributed in part to the lacklustre people it fielded, but also

Table 3. Apportionment of Elected Delegates (original and revised)

Original apportionment (107,054)

	delegates	average	deviation from norm
Marianas	5	2615.2	-2.6%
Marshalls	9	2574.0	-0.9%
Palau	5	2537.2	+0.4%
Ponape	8	2677.9	-5.0%
Truk	12	2444.5	+4.0%
Yap	3	2456.3	+3.6%
Total	42	2548.9	16.5%

Revised apportionment (112,558)

	delegates	average	deviation from norm
Marianas	4	3,094	-15.4%
Marshalls	9	2,676	+ 0.1%
Palau	5	2,608	+ 2.7%
Ponape	9	2,633	+ 1.8%
Truk	12	2,643	+ 1.4%
Yap	3	2,550	+ 4.9%
Total	42	2,680	26.3%

Source: SCR No. 56, Senate Journal, 5th Congress, 1st Session, 1973, p. 446.
SCR no. 292, House Journal, 5th Congress, 2nd Session, 1974, p. 478.

to an alleged rigging of district boundaries which placed a disproportionate number of the voters for delegates in one of the three districts, the only one to elect Liberal Party candidates.

At the Special Session of 1974, Senator Salii introduced a bill to nullify the election for delegates in two of the Palau election districts. With both Palau Senators members of the Liberal Party, they convinced their colleagues in the Senate to adopt the measure and send it to the House. The Senate Committee on Judiciary and Governmental Operations, in recommending the bill, reported that:

> Simply stated, it was the intention of the Congress to provide for equal representation within a district, and to this end we employed "home area" figures for purposes of apportionment of delegate districts. Unfortunately, the definition of that term does not have equal application throughout the Trust Territory. In Palau, for example, if a person's clan is traditionally associated with X village, he will list his "home area" as X village regardless of the question of whether he lives there or ever in fact did live there, or ever intended to return there .... Thus, the "home area" population can be seen as arbitrary....[3]

The same committee report charged that neither the Chairman of the House Committee "who represents Palau, nor any members of the Palau delegation" took this factor into account. Not so, replied Representative Polycarp Basilius for himself and his Progressive Party colleagues when the bill reached the House of Representatives. Befitting the tenor of Palauan politics, the House Committee on Judiciary and Governmental Relations, which he chaired, reported that "The arguments supporting ... [the Senate Bill] reek with infirmities and judgments that cannot be defended."[4] Representative Basilius, himself, moved that the Senate Bill be filed in the House. So ended one phase of Palauan political parochialism, only to have another appear in the Convention associated with elections for the Palau District Legislature.

Despite the intrusion of party politics into the constitutional elections in Palau, this did not dampen the ardor of candidates who could not obtain party endorsement. They, and others, ran as independents, so every delegate seat in Palau was contested by more than two aspirants. Almost the same supernumerary situation, sans party labels, held for Ponape and the Marianas. At the other extreme, one seat in Ponape was not contested, nor was one in Truk. The Marshalls, facing the boycott, had four contests in each of which only one candidate filed, and in three others, in the absence of any person declaring himself a candidate, the delegate seats were won by write-ins.

Excluding the nine seats in the Marshalls where the boycott materially reduced participation, all but one of the elected delegates came to the Convention with mandates from sizable pluralities if not absolute majorities of their constituents. The exception was the election district in Yap where the vote was so scattered among multiple candidates that the winner tallied less than one-third of the votes cast. Of the remainder, eighteen of the elected candidates each garnered about 50 percent or more of the votes in their respective contests, and another fourteen fell within the credible total of one-third to one-half.

As originally introduced, the constitutional enabling legislation had declared Congressmen ineligible for election as delegates. In the House of Representatives, Representative Luke Tman successfully proposed the deletion of this limitation. Later, he was to be elected as a delegate from Yap, as were Senator Tosiwo Nakayama and Representative Sasauo Haruo from Truk. Two other incumbent Congressmen unsuccessfully sought to enjoy the fruits of this amendment (Chiro Albert and Lambert Aafin, both of Truk). However, with Senator Andon Amaraich not being returned to the Congress, his designation by the Truk Congressional delegation as the legislator from the district to serve in the Convention lapsed, and Representative Albert was appointed to fill the vacant post.[5]

In all, nine incumbent members of the Congress of Micronesia sat as delegates in the Convention--beside Nakayama, Senators Olympio Borja, Wilfred Kendall, Bailey Olter, Lazarus Salii, and Petrus Tun from, respectively, the Marianas, Marshalls, Ponape, Palau, and Yap, and Representatives Albert, Haruo, and Tman. Fourteen more had at one time been members of the Congress: John Heine and Dr.

Isaac Lanwi from the Marshalls; Heinrich Iriarte, Max Iriarte, Dr. Hirosi Ismael, and Daro Weital of Ponape; Soukichi Fritz, Chutomu Nimwes, and Hans Wiliander of Truk; John Ngiraked and Jacob Sawaichi of Palau; and Jose R. Cruz, Ben Manglona, and Dr. Francisco T. Palacios of the Marianas. When to their number are added the two delegates who had service as Clerks in the Congress, Carl Heine and Strik Yoma, and the delegates aided by interpreters with Congressional experience (given the direct and covert input of interpreters into the Convention's deliberations), nearly half of the delegates brought Congress-linked knowledge of government into the Convention hall. Augmented by incumbent and former district legislators, and those whose governmental posts closely associated them with the day-to-day functioning of these bodies, two-thirds of the Convention membership was familiar with legislative procedures and the role of committees as the mainstay of the legislative process. This background enabled delegates both to comprehend the Convention's process while at the same time adjusting to its deliberately slower tempo.

Some of the incumbent Congressmen became central figures in the leadership of the Convention, others played a less formal but none the less salient role, while a few remained peripheral in the wings. Several Congressmen absented themselves from the Convention for over half of its duration on personal and official duties. However, of all groups sharing a single characteristic, that of having service with the Congress of Micronesia identified the delegates who contributed most to the carrying on of the Convention's daily work. Paradoxically, from this same group arose nearly all of the basic issues causing cleavages which threatened to engulf the Convention.

On the opening day of the Convention, High Commissioner Edward E. Johnston addressed the assembled delegates:

> ... the voters throughout our six districts have chosen wisely from among your best minds and strongest leaders to join together in this First Constitutional Convention. Included among the 60 (sic) delegates to this Convention are teachers, farmers, businessmen, lawyers doctors, policemen, along with elect-

> ed, appointed and traditional leaders from the various eschelons of your present government. Forty-three have attended institutions of higher learning outside the Trust Territory, including 28 who are College graduates (nine of whom have pursued additional graduate studies)....6

As repetitively demonstrated in the staffing of the other political posts in Micronesia, education was deemed an important criterion in the selecting of delegates. And so did it figure in the designation of the some fourteen7 interpreters who during the course of the Convention aided the ten delegates who, at least nominally, required their assistance. The latter comprised the bulk of the "over 45" age cohort (14) of the Convention, and as children had received a limited education under the Japanese rule. Despite Micronesia's being a region where age has customarily legitimated leadership, a full two-thirds of the delegates who would determine the future government of the region were but young men between thirty and forty-five. In the new political institutions introduced under the American aegis, school-imparted knowledge had supplanted in primacy the sagacity traditionally attributed to age.

The youthful efforts of the four delegates under thirty received unanticipated supplementation from the Convention's interpreters, half of whom had not reached that age. The latter's contribution would prove to be far more than merely acting as the interface between two languages. Interpreters had their own points of view, and as advocates frequently brought them to the attention of their principals. Outside of the meeting times of the Convention, they spent long hours with their delegates paraphrasing proposals and committee reports into the vernacular, preparing their principals for the positions to be taken at the sessions of the next day, and assisting them in writing their speeches. During this interaction, they helped shape the delegates' policy positions which might be formally translated at a future time. Some interpreters even substituted for their principals at committee hearings. The interpreters so served as the alter egos of their delegates that one was indirectly rebuked for voting in the absence of his principal during a formal roll call of the Convention. In retrospect, when considering the relative input of education and age into the constitutional product, the conservatism which might normally be assumed associated with the older delegates of limited education was tempered by association with their younger and more worldly interpreters.

Unlike the first Congress of Micronesia and many of the early district legislatures with their heavy components of educators, employment as school teacher had prepared only about a third of the delegates for the performance of their duties in the Convention. Broader service within the executive branch of government and experience gained in the conduct of private business contributed a more diversified background upon which the delegates could rely. Although lines were drawn and redrawn, except for a group of traditional leaders coalesced around the protection of custom, it was to be difficult to detect any bloc of delegates whose consistency could be traced to common socialization of shared economic experiences. Rather, the distinctive configuration of district delegations loomed larger.

In composition there was little to distinguish one district delegation from another. Palau had relatively fewer delegates in government employ, and more businessmen. If anything, their level of education was a trifle higher. Unlike the other delegations with appointed traditional leaders (median age for all chiefs, 55), it included High Chief Ibedul Y. Gibbons, a young man who had been recalled from service with the United States army in Germany to assume the title. Among the elected members of the Truk delegation was an *itang*, one skilled in the esoteric language and lore of traditional statecraft. Delegates with medical training were to be found in a number of the delegations.[8] Quotations from Plato, Goethe, William James and others occasionally lent a scholarly cast to the work of the Yap delegation. But all of this was overshadowed by the internal coherence of the delegations, and the extent to which they functioned as units or their membership divided so as not to present a unified front to the Convention.

The Yapese delegation remained closely knit, supportive of its Congressman Luke Tman, who served as Floor Leader of the Convention, and of Senator Petrus Tun on whom fell the responsibility for proposing the future political status of Micronesia, as Chairman of the Committee on General Provisions.

The Palau delegation appeared monolithic, fiercely defensive of its district, and publicly all members speaking with a single voice. Careful scrutiny of their actions, however, would reveal that this "papered over" internal divisions of both opinion and leadership.[9] In contrast to the Palauans' seeming unanimity, differences over policy were to find members of both the Ponape and Truk delegations openly challenging their district colleagues on the Convention floor. Some of these disagreements were so acrimonious as to threaten the delegates' positions of employment upon returning home. Sharp as these schisms within the two delegations might be, they raised no difficulties commensurate with those evident to all in the Marshalls and Marianas delegations. A few of the members in both had to be inveigled to attend Convention sessions, and their participation never extended to joining with district colleagues in developing consistency in delegation position. The resignation of seated delegates and the failure of others to even show up in the Convention further contributed to undermining delegation solidarity. Only rarely, and that on an issue peculiarly appealing to the distinctiveness of district identity, was a sense of cohesion ever kindled in each one of the delegations.

Upon the conclusion of the procedures for delegate selection, in a number of districts the legitimacy of those chosen was questioned. The Trust Territory Administration recommended to the Congress that it provide for a Credentials Committee which could tentatively resolve all contests prior to the meeting of the Convention. Veto of the original legislation submitted by the Administration, after it was extensively amended by the Congress, delayed the setting up of the Committee until the spring of 1975. On April 2, and in anticipation of the High Commissioner's signing of the revised draft, the Pre-Convention Committee named Delegate Hilary Tacheliol of Yap, Dr. Francisco T. Palacios[10] of the Marianas, and Judge Soukichi Fritz of Truk to the Credentials Committee, the last designated as chairman. There was no known challenge to the credentials of any of the three.

Under the time limits fixed by the law creating it, all work of the Credentials Committee had to be completed by May 15. This necessitated the Committee act at breakneck speed. Within five days after the Committee issued its news release, credentials had to be filed. On the submission deadline, the Committee had in its possession evidence of credentials for all delegates but three from the Marshalls (the two traditional leaders and the Congressional delegation selection). On May 10, two weeks and three days later, the period designated to accommodate any protest mailed within the two weeks specified by law, the Committee had not received any objection to the delegates' credentials, and after examining the evidence in its possession, recommended the seating of fifty-six delegates and of Representative Albert as the Truk replacement for former Senator Amaraich. Credentials for Albert had arrived late, but in the absence of complaint, the Committee decided that the delay did not impair the validity of the Congressional selection. The Pre-Convention Committee accepted and forwarded the report on to the Convention, which later adopted it, with minor exceptions.[11]

It remains dubious that enough time had been allowed for mounting a successful challenge to the seating of any delegate. Given the Credential Committee's designation of April 23 as the last day for filing credentials, the law both specifying fourteen days thereafter for objections and also requiring five days' notice to appear to answer them, it is also extremely doubtful that sufficient time was permitted to perform the Committee's duties if there had been a challenge. Persons in Palau, the Marshalls, or the Marianas intent upon wrecking the Convention could have seized upon all of these inadequate time periods, and the details specified for appeal, to entangle the Convention in procedural snarls which would have long delyaed turning attention to the primary function of writing a constitution. Being of a mind to facilitate the organizing of the Convention, the Committee carried out its duties within the strict letter of the applicable law, and succeeded in its purpose. Later, a Special Credentials Committee, with two of the same delegates serving, was assigned the further duties of considering the credentials of persons named to fill vacancies in the Convention's ranks, and similarly responded with dispatch.

The judicial challenge filed in the trial division of the High Court alleging inadequate representation of the southwest outer islands of Palau[12] was ignored by the Credentials Committee as not constituting an "objection." Rather, the suit ran to the validity of the very law under which the Committee was acting, and it considered itself empowered only to make decisions based upon adherence to that law. Later, the suit was to be dismissed by the Court, and never became an issue before the Convention.

After the time for filing protests had elapsed, a petition was received objecting to the manner in which the traditional chiefs had been chosen in the Truk District. The Pre-Convention Committee deemed it filed in an untimely manner and the matter died without further comment. Background to the protest was the aggressiveness of Popuisom (Chief) Fichita Bossy, one of the two selected, who, while having traditionally correct claim to his title, was believed by some not to disport himself so as to command the respect desired of a chief. With the Convention underway, inquiry was raised by some of the seated Truk delegates about the identity of the protestors, but details by then had slipped into obscurity.

Prior to the adoption of the Credential Committee's report, the Chairman of the Palau delegation, John Ngiraked, informed the Convention that the illness of the High Chief Reklai Lomisang prevented his appearance, and in his place the Acting Reklai Eusevio Termeteet had been chosen as one of the Palauan traditional leaders. Similarly, Carl Heine as de facto Chairman of the Marshallese delegates, placed the name of Senator Wilfred Kendall before the Convention as the member of the Marshalls Congressional delegation to sit as Convention delegate. This nomination was justified by the concurrence of three of the six deadlocked Congressmen from the Marshalls, including the Senator's own vote. The Special Credentials Committee reported affirmatively upon the seating of both.

With the credentials of fifty-eight delegates passing muster, and with fifty[13] in attendance on opening day, much to many persons' surprise the Convention was in position to formally organize itself. Back in July 1969, the Future Political Status Commission had recommended the holding of "a Constitutional Convention including leaders from throughout the Territory, representative of all the disparate cultural, ethnic, social and commercial interests which comprise today's Micronesia...."[14] Although the Convention which met six years later was hardly a cross-section of the Trust Territory's population, being disproportionately weighted toward Western-style education and governmental experience, it reasonably incorporated the representation of Micronesia's disparity early enjoined by the first Congressional body established to chart Micronesia's future political status. About as well prepared a group of Micronesians as could be drawn from the whole Trust Territory through any combination of direct and indirect methods of selecting delegates now turned to the task of writing a constitution for Micronesia.

----

1. Congress of Micronesia, <u>Senate Journal</u>, Fifth Congress, First Special Session, 1974, p. 89.

2. <u>Tia Belau</u> 11:8 (July 1974), p. 17.

3. Congress of Micronesia, Senate SCR No. 296, <u>Senate Journal</u>, Fifth Congress, First Special Session, 1974, p. 169.

4. Congress of Micronesia, House SCR No. 325, <u>House Journal</u>, Fifth Congress, First Special Session, 1974, p. 194.

5. Later, Senator Andon Amaraich was to serve as an attorney on the staff of the Convention's Research and Drafting Section.

6. <u>Journal of the Micronesian Constitutional Convention of 1975</u>, Vol. I, p. 4 (hereafter referred to as <u>CCM Journal</u>). The figure of twenty-nine college graduates may be a little exaggerated, as four years of college was not always capped with the awarding of a baccalaureate degree.

7. In the Palau and Ponape delegations some delegates had more than one interpreter during the course of the Convention. Political intrigue explains the substitutions for Palau, and personality clashes, alleged incompetence, and sometimes both, in the case of Ponape. The workday of an interpreter for a truly non-English speaking delegate covered far more than the latter's waking hours.

8. Dr. Hirosi Ismael, as a Senator from Ponape, is credited with beginning the movement which eventually led to the Micronesian status negotiations with the United States (<u>Dialogue for Micronesia</u>, No. 38, August 13, 1981).

9. As when the Palau delegation split in 6 of the 36 recorded roll calls on Committee Proposals. However, rather than recording a contrary "yes" or "no," in each such case a Palauan member not voting "yes" with his delegation would "abstain." Under the rules, the abstention was in effect a negative vote in meeting the minimal requirement for passage.

10. The vacancy of Dr. Palacios' seat was declared on the 52nd day of the Convention, just moments after he had appeared for the first time in the Convention hall, prepared to introduce a resolution declaring that by popular mandate of the people of the Marianas all of the delegate seats from the Marianas had been dissolved (<u>CCM</u> <u>Journal</u>, Vol. I, p. 228).

11. See <u>CCM</u> <u>Journal</u>, Vol. II, Appendix A, pp. 1079ff.

12. Palau's southwest islands of Sonsoral, Tobi, and Puliana, some 137 voters strong, claimed denial of representation in the Convention when combined in a single delegate district with the approximately 424 voters of Angaur and Pelelieu, their nearest geographical neighbors who as Palauans are ethnically different. The inhabitants of the southwest islands are of mid-Carolinian descent and do not speak the Palauan language nor observe Palauan customs. See <u>CCM</u> <u>Journal</u>, Vol. II, p. 1082.

13. Eight delegates--Jose R. Cruz*†, Benjamin T. Manglona*, Dr. Francisco T. Palacios†, and Joaquin I. Pangelinan† from the Marianas; John Heine, Hemos A. Jack*†, and Wilfred Kendal* from the Marshalls; and Lazarus E. Salii from Palau--did not answer the first roll call of the Convention (*absence excused; †subsequently resigned). Fidel Mendiola, named by the Mariana District Legislature, submitted a letter of resignation before the Credentials Committee had been appointed, and the Legislature then named a substitute. The seat of Dr. Palacios was filled by the District Administrator's appointment of Alonzo Igisomar as a traditional leader of the Carolinians on Saipan, upon the recommendation of the United Carolinian Association of Saipan. Joaquin Pangelinan was replaced by Alfonso C. Rasa, for under PL 5-60, Sec. 4, vacancies for an elected delegate were to be filled by the runner-up. When Jose R. Cruz resigned, effective on the 67th day of Convention, it was

expected that he would be succeeded by Alfonso's brother, Representative Oscar C. Rasa, as receiver of the next highest number of votes, but the latter refused to serve. Similarly, it proved impossible to fill the post of Hemos A. Jack, when his seat was declared vacant on the 25th day; a letter sent to Namu Hermios, the runner-up, write-in candidate aligned with the *iroij*-Kabua faction, requesting the submission of credentials, was denounced by him. Previously Jack had cabled he could not attend the Convention for "Marshallese reasons," and this was interpreted as a resignation. Upon the action of the Convention, Jack denied he had resigned but "was merely unable to attend because the Marshallese Con Con delegation is not legally organized...." The declaration of vacancy continued to stand.

14. *Report of the Future Political Status Commission*, July 1969, p. 42.

Chapter 7. Confusion Confounded

As agreed, a tentative set of rules--based on the procedures of past conventions in the states of Hawaii, Michigan, New Jersey, and Tennessee--awaited me when I arrived on Saipan in the spring of 1975. They were the handiwork of Kaleb Udui, Legislative Counsel for the Congress of Micronesia, who served as unofficial attorney for the Pre-Convention Committee until staff could be assembled. Previously, I had proposed to the Committee that within the constraints of the enabling legislation, an "open" Convention be maintained. The delegates, working through separate committees, would attempt for themselves, piecemeal, to construct a constitution for Micronesia in the style long observed by state conventions in the United States. The alternative course of action would be the advance formulation of a draft whose contents the assembled delegates would then review and modify, snipping and patching until they arrived at a version satisfactory to the requisite majority. Although I well appreciated that the Convention's authorized life of but ninety days represented an exceedingly short period to undertake this gamble of incremental decision-making, I had concluded that the presentation to the delegates of a complete document, no matter how "preliminary" it was labeled, invoked greater countervailing risk. The members of the Pre-Convention Committee were of the same opinion, in part I suspect because they wished to avoid all appearance of American direction to the Micronesian effort.

The United States had encouraged the holding of the Convention and financed a major share of its costs. The technical staff of the Convention was to be overwhelmingly American. Many Micronesians believed that because of this influence, what would emerge would be an American-dictated constitution.[1] Given the three decades of experience with American principles of governance, and the political socialization which most delegates had undergone through the course of their education, there was a strong likelihood that many of those principles would appear embodied in the "unique, all-Micronesian constitution" which the delegates professed to want. However, any decision to incorporate American concepts, forms, and practices must patently be that of the Convention. Everything short of free delegate selection between competing alternatives which they, themselves, had posed, most certainly would draw the charge of a "rigged" Convention. And even if such a constitution succeeded of ratification, its future viability would remain questionable. Instead of a "ready-made American drafted constitution, as many Micronesians feared,"[2] the delegates would have to erect their own, despite the apparent absurdity of "building from the roof down."[3]

Another unspoken reason underlying the decision to assemble the constitution incrementally was to avoid the danger of having the Convention captured before it convened, not by Americans, but by a minority faction among the Micronesian delegates. A draft prepared in advance could so establish the position of one district as to polarize most of the Convention debate around the issues it raised, and under those circumstances, to ignore most others. An open, unstructured Convention could best be achieved by approaching the convening date without an advance draft narrowing delegation action. Future events demonstrated that pre-convention effort at preparing an entire tentative constitution for consideration by the delegates when they assembled would most likely have had to include either the Palauan delegates' position, or a series of compromises with them reached <u>in camera</u>.

The same rationale held for the committee structure proposed to the Convention. Committees should not be so delineated as to prejudge the decisions yet to be made. Creating a substantive committee with jurisdiction limited to the legislature of the central government, and another on its executive branch, would have subsumed the Convention's adoption of the American separation of powers doctrine. On the other hand, the extant problems of Micronesia indicated the advantage of establishing committees with scope broad enough to permit their deliberations arriving at tentative solutions to the Territory's major disagreements. In the latter category fell the area of public finance which was at the core of much of the current divisive feeling. To a second committee was assigned the broad gamut of future United States-Micronesian relationships, and all details of transition necessary to the ending of the Trusteeship. Civil liberties and traditional rights were bound to be major matters cleaving the Convention, and they fitted neatly within the obvious orbit of a third committee. Everything else was divided between the remaining two subject-matter committees: to the Functions Committee went the entire range of functions to be performed by government (including their allocation to the appropriate level of government), and to the Structure Committee was delegated full responsibility for outlining the form of the governmental units which ought to be prescribed or delimited in the constitution. Although this separation of structure from function appeared to defy structural-functional theory, it had as its objective the centering of each committee's attention upon a different, although admittedly related, set of issues, and then reconciling the incongruences which might emerge out of their combined recommendations. With all district delegations included in the membership of these two major committees, and overlapping committee membership prohibited by the rules, so long as the Convention adhered to its procedures, the writing of the constitution would have to proceed piecemeal. The danger was that the process might be so attenuated that the Convention's ninety-day life would expire before a constitution could be limned and agreed upon.

General experience in the mounting of constitutional conventions in the United States has taught the value of including a Style and Arrangements Committee to point up internal inconsistencies, and to assure the fit and to polish the syntax of the provisions destined for the completed constituent document. Personal experience has demonstrated the utility of allowing all delegates to introduce proposals, but after duplication and distribution, shunting them off to subject-matter committees where they eventually die. Convention consideration is then limited to committee proposals which embody and reconcile the substance of a number of these delegate submissions, a process which, not so incidentally, short-circuits the petty pride of delegate authorship. As a safeguard, with the consent of the Convention any delegate was still free to withdraw his proposal and have it treated by the Convention as a committee proposal. Little did I realize the importance which this provision was to assume when I suggested its inclusion in the rules.

Affording the widest opportunity for debate, and the narrowest of restriction on the introduction of amendments--all within the necessity of completing Convention business within its brief allotted life span--I proposed additions to the Convention rules curtailing guillotine motions ("previous question" and "indefinite postponement") along with the use of the Committee of the Whole device to facilitate informality of floor action. The Pre-Convention Committee members approved the encouraging of discussion, and directed fixing at five minutes the maximum length of time for which a delegate could hold the Convention floor before surrendering it. Double that time was allowed those addressing the Convention through interpreters. Rather than strictures rigorously enforced, these, too, were safeguards, but of the Convention against egregious abuses by delegates.

The last few years of the Congress, and the experience of many district legislatures in the Trust Territory, had disclosed the distressing tendency to delay final passage of bills until the final days of the session, and then to rush through the legislative logjam with minimal floor consideration and inadequate attention to statutory detail. While rules could not per se prevent this practice from being replicated in the Convention, they could attempt to anticipate and counter its negative aspects by slowing down procedures so as to allow all delegates adequate notice on action to be taken, and by spreading the adopting of proposals over a number of days, with full opportunity in each to debate changes. For a while the rules even required each committee adversely reporting on a delegate proposal to give its sponsor at least twenty-four hours' prior notice, permitting him to meet with the committee to remonstrate, but it proved too onerous a technical task, and eventually was deleted.

Upon a committee report and proposal being delivered to the Convention, the latter would receive nominal First Reading, and no sooner than the following day, go to the Committee of the Whole. Securing approval there by majority vote, the proposal would next receive the attention of the Style Committee, which in turn would report upon it, together with any amendments believed required. At this stage, the Convention now in the more formal Plenary Session, would consider the proposal, and a three-quarters vote would be requisite for passage on Second Reading. This hurdle past, once again the proposal would be referred to the Style Committee, including all amendments which might have been added, there to be held and incorporated into a complete draft with all other proposals so received. The ultimate act would be the resubmission of the whole constitution to the Plenary Session for formal adoption. Admittedly, the rules provided a circuitous procedure to follow, but it assured each delegate ample opportunity for careful scrutiny and the expression of his views. Not to be forgotten was that a constitution for the future governance of Micronesia was being written.

A few minor embellishments to the rules were later to enable the Convention to overcome internal problems with high political saliency. At the discretion of the Convention President, complex delegate proposals might be split among appropriate subject-matter committees. Minority reports on committee proposals would be treated as amendments or substitutes, and come up automatically for consideration on the Convention floor. Roll calls could not be demanded in the Committee of the Whole, so that divisions on the most delicate of issues could be approached without the dampening effect of a recorded vote. And seemingly most petty of all, delegates absent from the Convention without leave of their delegation chairmen could not receive compensation for the days lost.

The elaborateness of this procedure for conducting the work of the Convention hardly squared with the characteristic informality of Micronesian ways. However, on the one hand, it so resembled the normal legislative process with which most delegates were acquainted as not to be unfamiliar; and on the other, it introduced enough novelty to help counter the initial advantage enjoyed by the most politically experienced among the delegates. The use of a small number of committees with broad jurisdictions was a familiar practice in all legislatures of Micronesia. To assure that the Convention would not become entangled in its own procedures, while recognizing that deliberate parliamentary maneuver to such end could not be forestalled, I supported the Convention's selection of a Floor Leader as one of its principal officers.

The various Micronesia legislatures had long adapted this office to the making of the routine motions which contribute to the orderly and speedy conduct of business and, as necessary, to acting as floor manager in aid of the adoption of proposals. Under the experienced hand of Luke Tman, Floor Leader of the House of Representatives of the Congress of Micronesia, this office was to prove its utility in the Convention.

The next step was to acquaint the delegates with the physical and monetary arrangements being made for their stay on Saipan, to distribute copies of the tentative rules for their consideration and reaction, and to obtain their approval for the scheduling of a workshop to precede the opening of the Convention. My unannounced purpose for the urging of the workshop was to gain a few extra days for the Convention by speeding its organization.

Previously, once the Pre-Convention Committee had entered on its assigned tasks in 1974, it had begun planning the administrative structure necessary for servicing the delegates and supporting the day-to-day work of the Convention.[4] While the Convention retained final authority to make its own decisions on administrative organization, it was accurately foreseen that it would ratify the preparatory actions taken on its behalf, particularly since the chairmen of the district delegations collectively were making the preliminary arrangements. Approximately 150 applications for staff positions were reviewed. Victorio Uherbelau was early engaged as Executive Director of the Pre-Convention Committee, and later aided by Asterio R. Takesy, the two became, respectively, Convention Secretary and Assistant Convention Secretary. A complement of ten assisted the Secretaries in the Office of the President as sergeant-at-arms, journal clerks, and in performing Convention floor duties. A separate Administrative Section maintained the Convention records, duplicated its mountains of paper, supervised the disbursement of its funds, and otherwise tended to the myriad of tasks essential to facilitate the attendance of delegates and to keep the daily flow of work unbroken. At its peak, some eighteen persons were employed in this Section. A small Public Information Section of but four handled the release of public information on the activities of the Convention, and occasionally ghost-wrote the speeches

of some delegates, which later appeared in the
Convention Journal. The largest section by far,
with some twenty-six persons at one time or another
on staff, was the Research and Drafting Section,
which, belying its name, tended to all of the affairs of the Convention. Assisting me were to
be some seven attorneys, six law clerks interning
in the Trust Territory from the University of California at Los Angeles, two specialized consultants--
one on public finance, the other on style and phraseology--who could attend the Convention for only
part of its life, a supporting complement of research assistants and typists, and the librarian
for the Section's small working collection of reference materials. A heavy infusion of district patronage entered into the selection of a number of
the Micronesian members on staff, particularly
evident in the fifteen pages for the Convention
who were nominally listed as employees under the
Office of the President, the fourteen interpreters
similarly shown under the Public Information Section, and the seven immediate aides to the district
delegations, euphemistically classed as "assistant
sergeant-at-arms." From personal observation,
I was to witness the dedicated commitment of numerous staff members to the purposes of the Convention
in the overcoming of what appeared at times to
be insurmountable difficulties.[5] But most of this
staff was added as the Convention's opening drew
nearer, and only the key personnel had been assembled when I arrived on Saipan.

Starting late in May, less than two months
before the convening date, a team composed of the
three Section heads of the Convention staff met
seriatim with the delegations at the five district
centers outside of Saipan. On Majuro in the Marshalls, not all of the delegates-elect appeared,
an even smaller proportion assembled on Koror in
Palau, and no preparatory meeting at all was scheduled for the Marianas delegation. There seemed
little purpose in attempting the last, as the Marianas delegation had publicly stated it would withdraw from the Convention upon the June 17 plebiscite approving the commonwealth covenant. Not
until July 1 did it reverse itself, and by this
time delegates could individually consult with
Convention staff.

The tentative rules for the Convention as
distributed were too long and detailed to engender
an immediate response from the delegates. One

traditional leader on Ponape voiced the observation that the Convention ought follow Micronesian customary ways, but did not elucidate when pressed as to what he had in mind, given the lack of a single all-Micronesian tradition. If he intended the chiefs, as delegates, to direct the course of the Convention's deliberations, he was to be at least partially clairvoyant. Inchoately sensing my incapacity as an American to deal competently with Micronesian values, I pressed the different delegations for instructions on how to seat the traditional leaders. Nothing ressembling consensus was forthcoming as to physical arrangements nor anything revealing more covert attitudes toward including recognition of chiefly status in the Convention's direction, procedures, or product. The solicitation of delegation and individual delegate requests for the advance drafting of proposals brought disappointingly few responses, but sufficient indication of general delegate interest in constitutional content to give guidance to the staff for the preparation of a number of general research studies for distribution as background material to all delegates.[6] The proposal for a workshop met a favorable reception, which was undoubtedly reinforced when letters confirming the workshop advised the delegates that salary and per diem for attendance would be borne out of the Convention's appropriation.

The notice of the workshop also carried information on the five subject-matter committees and the Style Committee now incorporated into the proposed rules. (A second non-substantive committee which I had originally proposed--to oversee the Convention's public relations and assume responsibility for post-Convention "selling" of the Constitution--had been eliminated.) Each delegate was requested to acquaint staff with his first and alternative choices for committee assignments, so that all replies could be assembled for use when the Convention organized. Delegates were also informed that no specific way was favored for arranging Convention seating, or no single structure preferred for the leadership of the Convention. Both would be matters discussed at the workshop.

As requests for hotel reservations commenced arriving on Saipan, and forms expressing committee preferences were returned, it gradually became manifest that most all delegates were planning to participate in the workshop and remain at least for the opening of the Convention. The uncertainty of delegate attendance, which for so long had hung like an ominous cloud over Convention planning, was now lifting. Still remaining were the more immediate, in-house difficulties surrounding the use of the White Sands Hotel premises, and the acquisition and assembling of all of the equipment essential for the holding of the Convention.

The workshop opened precariously on the afternoon of Tuesday, July 8. Without fuel for the generators to power the hotel's air conditioning, its lighting, and the public address systems just being installed, the delegates met in the hotel's open-air foyer. Virginally new hotel chairs, commandeered for the purpose, started collapsing under the weight of delegates even before the workshop was called to order. (By the end of the Convention, chairs with broken arms and legs were to be piled high like corpses in one of the anterooms.) The plans for the initial meeting were abruptly cancelled as the Chairman of the Palauan delegation, echoed by a few of the other delegates, disgruntled over per diem payments and arrangements made for renting cars and reserving hotel rooms, angrily commanded that these matters be immediately rectified. The procedures to be established for conducting the Constitutional Convention would have to wait upon the more pressing demand of accommodating the personal needs of delegates and their interpreters.

Over the balance of the week, both in general workshop sessions and through individual meetings, the many problems attendant upon the presence of nearly seventy delegates, interpreters, and delegation staff members assembled on Saipan were resolved. Simultaneously, through Herculean efforts, the Convention facilities took shape. Tentative style manuals were finalized, routing directions charted, and the bureaucratic accouterments normal to any complex organization mushroomed. Administrative systems were improvised for servicing the unexpected requirements of both delegates and a functioning Convention. Concurrently, as described by a critical reporter, the assembled delegates were led "though four days of grueling workshop --too much like school, too little like the democratic process."[1] The actions of the recently concluded Special Session of the Congress of Micronesia amending the Constitutional Convention enabling legislation, and providing extra funds, were explained to the delegates. The attorneys of the Research and Drafting Section, with whom the delegates would intimately work for the next three months, were introduced. In turn, they discussed the general aspects of the subjects which they foresaw might be brought up for consideration by the committees to which they had been tentatively assigned. Emphasized was the role of staff as supportive but subordinate, precluded from initiating or recommending policy. Above all, to forestall a paralyzing impasse over the future status of Micronesia, which might leave the delegates no time for attention to anything else, I stressed that it was possible to draft a constitution without first reaching a decision on status: like clay in the potter's hands, the shape of future political status would emerge as the powers and structures of the new Micronesian government were decided upon and the polity took shape. Throughout the whole workshop, the underlying objective was to develop a momentum of purpose in which the delegates would be caught up and wholeheartedly share. Once understanding the process by which it was proposed to build the constitution, it was hoped that this spirit of involvement would carry over into the Convention, and sustain the delegates through the tedious months ahead until agreement upon a constitution could be reached.

As soon as it proved possible to occupy the hotel's dining room, which was slated to become the site for holding the Plenary and Committee-of-the-Whole Sessions of the Convention, delegates were faced with the problem of allocating seats. In the absence of any discernible consensus, recourse was to drawing names by lot, and arbitrarily assigning desks. This order of names continued to be used of all roll calls during the remainder of the Convention, but as could be anticipated, proved dysfunctional for floor action. Once the Convention was underway, and at the suggestion of the Palau members, one or more rows were assigned to each delegation, the smallest delegation at the front of the Convention hall, the largest arranged toward the rear as the expanding semi-circles of desks more adequately handled their numbers. To each delegation was left the task of deciding how it wished to place its traditional leaders. What had appeared as an unresolvable problem, when first planning for the Convention, proved to be of little consequence. Commoners and traditional chiefs sat together, apparently without status dictating their placement. Nor were the rules to give any recognition to their traditional position. Hindsight now reveals that if the traditional leaders had indeed been grouped and placed apart, the symbolism of their collectivity might well have added weight to their later efforts at shaping the constitution.

The stated rationale for holding the workshop was to review the suggested procedures for the governing of the Convention, and particularly, to agree upon the officers to be chosen and the manner in which they should be selected. An underlying purpose, which most delegates appreciated, was to afford the opportunity for them to size up the leadership capabilities of delegates not personally known to them. To the end of achieving both objectives, delegates were randomly assigned to five work groups, each of which coopted its own spokesman. The groups then separately examined the tentative rules, and communicated back their recommendation to the workshop. This effort was not an idle gesture, as a number of major changes were proposed in Convention structure. In place of a single Vice-President, each district delegation would nominate one or more of its delegates for Vice-President. After selection of the President by secret ballot, one Vice-President from each district would then be chosen. Given the multiple vice-presidency, the duties and powers of the office would be rotated daily. In addition to the regular standing committees, provision was also made for a Special Conference Committee to consist of two delegates from each district. (A month later, due to the pressure from chiefs in the Ponape District, this was amended so as to allow each district the opportunity of appointing a traditional leader, but was never exercised.) It was declared to be the function of the Committee "to consider and recommend solutions to such fundamental jurisdictional and substantive questions as are referred to it by the President or by the Convention."[8] As proposed, it was intended that this committee would be used for resolving basic issues which otherwise might disasterously split the Convention. Time was to show that after an undistinguished beginning, the Special Conference Committee never fulfilled that potential, and ad hoc committees were to serve the purpose. Nevertheless, inclusion of this committee within the Convention structure early gave each district delegation the assurance that it would have equal voice in a body to which could be referred the most important of issues.

The workshop did not propose any change in that part of the tentative rules which called for the President of the Convention to name the members of the various committees. Nor did it call for any modification in the power of each committee to select a chairman from its own ranks. Even the just-created Special Conference Committee would be peopled by appointees of the President, although here he was enjoined "to the extent possible, [to] accommodate distinguishable political, cultural, and geographical factors within the respective districts"[9] when making his appointments. The inability to promise appointment to key committee chairmanships removed the most valuable currency by which support for presidential candidacy might have been purchased. On the other hand, with committee posting delegated to the President, political sensitivity as an attribute of the candidate chosen to occupy the office became a *sine qua non*.

The balance of the workshop was devoted to formalities pertinent to the convening ceremonies of the Convention. Time of day, dress, dignitaries to be invited, order of precedence in the opening-day program, all were considered and concurrence received to the Pre-Convention Committee's recommendations. Insufficient time remained for formal caucusing preparatory to the election of officers, but electioneering had been covertly underway all during the course of the workshop, and the competence of potential presidential candidates appraised.

At one forty-five on the afternoon of July 12, 1975, as the rest of the Trust Territory celebrated Micronesia Day, a public holiday, the Micronesian Constitutional Convention was called to order. The first day's ceremonies included an invocation by a Catholic Father and a benediction by a Baptist minister, followed by the remarks of Senate President Nakayama as Acting President of the Convention, Mayor Vicente D. Sablan of Saipan, and High Commissioner Edward E. Johnston. Until the last day of the Convention, there was no further recognition of sectarianism; instead, each day commenced with a minute of silent prayer, a procedure imported into the Territory from Hawaiian legislative practice via the Congress of Micronesia. Invitations had been sent broadside to dignitaries in Washington and the United Nations, and within the Trust Territory all District Administrators had also been invited to attend. As anticipated, only local officials on Saipan appeared. Not even the new Director of Territories, Fred M. Zeder, who was visiting the Yap District, deemed it important enough to fly to the Marianas for the ceremonies. In truth, if all the persons to whom communications were sent had responded, it would have proved embarrassing for there was inadequate space to accommodate them properly. The opening ceremonies completed, a group photograph of the fifty delegates in attendance taken, the members returned to the hall, and turned to organizing the Convention.

The utility of holding the Convention workshop was now demonstrated. The procedures previously agreed upon at the workshop were quickly adopted as the Convention's "temporary" rules. With the floor opened for nominations for the office of President, the name of Leo Falcam was placed before the Convention by Heinrich Iriarte of Ponape. An elected delegate, Iriarte was of a chiefly clan, and regarded as a supporter of traditionalism in Micronesia. The nomination of John Ngiraked by Jacob Sawaichi, his colleague from the Palau delegation, followed. Both delegates proposed chairmen of their respective delegations. The third person to be placed in nomination was Acting President Tosiwo Nakayama, and it was a member of the Marianas delegation, Luis Limes, who advanced Nakayama's name. History was repeating itself. Ten years before, at the Congress of Micronesia, Ngiraked had been the apparent choice of the caucus preceding the organizing of its upper house, only to be opposed and defeated by Nakayama when the House of Delegates (name later changed to Senate) formally convened. At that time, too, Nakayama's name had been proposed by the Marianas District.[10] The only variation, now, was that the inclusion of Leo Falcam made the race a three-way contest.

The secret ballot held pursuant to the amended rules brought Senator Nakayama victory by an absolute majority of thirty-two votes. The twelve tallies amassed by Delegate Falcam corresponded with the number of members in his district's delegation; the six votes recorded for nominee John Ngiraked fell one short of the members of the Palau delegation present. Inquiry revealed that while

both Delegates Falcam and Ngiraked had been active
candidates, Nakayama reluctantly had allowed his
name to be placed for nomination, and then only
when told it would be written in on the ballot
regardless of his expressed desire to remain outside of the Presidential race. A number of the
delegates believed Falcam's long term of duty at
the apex of the Trust Territory Administration,
close to the High Commissioner, disqualified him
from occupying the symbolic post of Convention
President. Others had been antagonized by the
conduct of Delegate Ngiraked during the workshop.
A year earlier, when interviewed, Ngiraked had
opined that the Constitutional Convention "could
well break apart over its first official act--
the election of a Convention chairman."[11] Whether
this was a veiled threat, and whether the events
which followed in the Convention flowed from the
poor showing of the Palauan candidate--particularly
when linked with the failure of the Yap delegation
to support him, so that Palau as a small district
appeared isolated--must remain a matter of conjec-
ture.

The selection of the remaining Convention
officers proceeded without incident. Each of the
delegations nominated its chairman as the Vice-
President from its respective district. In the
absence of competing candidates, the rules were
suspended and all were elected by acclamation.
Similarly, Delegate Luke Tman from Yap was chosen
Floor Leader of the Convention without opposition.
The adoption of the temporary rules as the permanent rules of procedure for the Convention completed the organization, and delegates adjourned
for a reception jointly hosted by the Convention
and the Congress of Micronesia. At least in this
offering of food to the assemblage, Micronesian
tradition was being recognized, even though it
was in the modern guise of cocktails and accompanying canapes. Significantly, at this very early
juncture, two incumbent Congressmen occupied the
key offices of President and Floor Leader, and
in total, five delegates with experience in the
Congress of Micronesia had been chosen for the
Convention's eight highest posts.

With the second day of the Convention falling
on July 13, a Sunday, appointments to standing
committees waited until the following Monday.
The third day opened with the introduction of the
Convention Secretary and Sergeant-at-arms. Next,

after a recess to allow delegations further time to discuss committee assignments among themselves, tentative membership of committees, as selected by the officers of the Convention, was announced. For the most part, those delegates who had indicated their choices in advance of the Convention's organizing received their first or second preferences, and sometimes both. Of the forty-two making their desires known, thirty-three were so accommodated. Only nine might consider themselves as having been discriminated against by being placed on committees against their expressed priorities. However, after the committees coopted their own chairmen and vice-chairmen, three of these nine appeared in leadership posts, so that the number of delegates who might have cause for disgruntlement was even further reduced.

A review of committee membership revealed several anomalies. Great care had been taken to assure each delegation's participation on all of the committees, but some committees appeared weighted. For example, the Civil Liberties Committee numbered six traditional leaders among its twelve members. Of the eight delegates named to the Convention by their fellow chiefs, these six had designated this Committee as their first preference. Assignment to it could be treated as nothing more than affording them the courtesy befitting their station, but it also carried sharp warning of the disputes over traditional rights which were bound to arise.

Excepting delegates serving solely on the Governmental Functions or Structure Committees, the rules anticipated that all others would have posts on two subject-matter committees. A suggested meeting schedule, with designated committees assembling before and others subsequent to the Plenary Sessions of the Convention, proposed to maximize committee working time and eliminate conflicting assignments, but the system never fully functioned as intended. Instead, most committees initially met in the afternoons and conflicting overlaps in timing precluded full committee attendance. Eventually, it was decided by the Administration Committee that the mornings would normally be reserved for the Structure, Functions, and Public Finance Committees, while the afternoons would be assigned to General Provisions and Civil Liberties. This revised schedule was not always adhered to because few delegates were early risers. The daily, intensive attention desired of both Structure and Functions Committees never developed, which negated the underlying rationale for limiting a delegate's service to only one of them. Ultimately, the Structure Committee was to fall behind in its allotted tasks, compelling the Convention to slow its pace waiting for the Committee's recommendations on the building of the new government of Micronesia.

The fourth day of the Convention saw an amendment of the rules to add provision for an Assistant Convention Secretary. On the same day, the persons who had been designated by the President to convene the various committees announced the names of the latters' presiding officers. In the Civil Liberties Committee, Carl Heine of the Marshalls was elected as its permanent chairman, and Iskia Sony from Truk, its vice-chairman. Delegate Tun rose to state that the General Provisions Committee had elected Tosiwo Nakamura from Palau as chairman, only to have him later submit his resignation. Similarly, acting chairman Johnson Toribiong for the Committee on Style and Arrangement announced that Hans Wiliander of Truk had been chosen its chairman and that he, himself, had been elected as vice-chairman, but had submitted his resignation. Apparently no delegate from Palau would serve as a committee officer. The delegates glanced at each other with alarm! Was this the portent of the Palauan delegation's walkout from the Convention?

Delegates who had been members of the Second Congress of Micronesia might have recalled that after Lazarus E. Salii lost his bid for Speakership in the House of Representatives, all Palauan Representatives refused to hold any leadership post in that Session. Could this not be a repetition of the same tactic, a display of Palauan resentment over the decisive defeat of John Ngiraked in his bid for the Convention presidency? A few days later, this explanation was to prove inadequate, for while the resignations might have been triggered by mere pique, they were tied to a far more encompassing ploy designed to make the Convention turn around the axis of the Palau delegation.

As finally organized, Bailey Olter of Ponape served as chairman of the Public Finance Committee. During the latter's repeated absences from the Convention on Congressional business, the vice-chairman from Truk, Delegate Tatasy Wainit, was to lead the Committee through most of its preparatory studies. Dr. Hirosi Ismael of the Ponape delegation, recognized by all as a spokesman of the yet-to-be created district of Kusaie (later known as Kosrae), became chairman of the Governmental Functions Committee, with Sam Falanruw of Yap as its vice-chairman. The latter also was chosen chairman of the Executive and Judiciary Subcommittee of the parent committee. Heinrich Iriarte of Ponape was made chairman of the Governmental Structure Committee. Delegate Hilary Tacheliol of Yap served as his vice-chairman, and when the Structure Committee divided its work among subcommittees, headed its Executive Subcommittee. Judge Soukichi Fritz from Truk chaired its Judiciary Subcommittee. To complete the roster of committee chairmen, Delegate Petrus Tun of Yap led the General Provisions Committee, assisted by Daro Weital of Ponape, and Dr. Isaac Lanwi from the Marshalls played a similar supportive role to chairman Wiliander of the Style Committee.

On the tenth day of the Convention, the President announced the membership of the Special Conference Committee which had been added to the rules for the express purpose of resolving fundamentally divisive questions as they arose in the Convention. As the convener he designated Jacob Sawaichi from Palau, who had not been his delegation's choice for inclusion on that committee. When it met, the Conference Committee quickly proceeded to elect Delegate Sawaichi as chairman. President Nakayama had not forgotten it was Sawaichi who had placed the name of Delegate Ngiraked in nomination for the presidency, nor did he fail to remind some of the committee members of this before they chose their chairman.

In the interim between the withdrawal of the Palau delegates from all leadership positions on committees and the acceptance by Delegate Sawaichi of the chairmanship, the Palau District position had publicly taken shape. There was no longer any advantage to be achieved by refusal of the Palau delegates to so serve. In terms of maneuver, further rebuffs of the Convention would be dysfunctional. Overlooked in the shock which followed the initial confrontation was the fact that a number of Palauan delegates had later been designated as chairmen of subcommittees, and had not declined. Both the Governmental Functions and Structure Committees and the General Provisions Committee had divided into subcommittees to facilitate the consideration of delegate proposals, and to prepare reports and committee proposals for full membership approval. Johnson Toribiong was not willing to head the Legislative Subcommittee established by Functions, and Tosiwo Nakamura the Subcommittee No. 3 of General Provisions. Delegate Ngiraked assumed responsibility for Structure's Legislative Subcommittee. But not to be lost sight of was the conspicuous absence of one name from this reappearance of Palauan delegates in Convention posts, that of Lazarus Salii, acknowledgedly the most politically adroit member of the delegation.

A review of the committee structure reconfirmed the now apparent consensus of the Convention to assign its leadership roles to delegates familiar with Congressional procedure. Delegate Sawaichi had been a Congressman, and a majority of the other delegates appointed with him to what promised to be the key Convention committee had Congressional service. Chairmen of five of the other six standing committees either were presently, or had been Congressmen. It had been the members of each of these committees who had chosen their respective chairmen, without any prior caucus of the Convention allocating the posts. Of the thirteen-membered Administration Committee, composed of the Convention officers and standing committee chairmen, ten were either incumbent or at one time had been Congressmen. As the Convention got underway, this group of delegates with Congressional experience was in position to direct its course. And ready to assist them were a former Clerk of the Senate, now serving as Convention Secretary, the Chief Clerk of the House of Representatives, now acting as his understudy, journal clerks for the Congress sitting at the Secretary's table and maintaining the Convention's daily record, and in the wings a whole corps of persons borrowed from the Congressional staff. The head of the Convention's Public Information Section, Dr. P. Fred Kluge, had once served the Congress in a comparable capacity, and even my antecedents, as consultant to the Convention, stretched back to the setting up of the original Congress of Micronesia.

With the Convention formally organized, the Administration Committee, chaired by the President, assumed responsibility for supervising all matters of internal administration. Previously its work had to wait upon the selection of chairmen by the other committees, and a number of problems remained unresolved for the first few days of the Convention, creating a pervading undercurrent of disgruntlement. Once underway, monetary matters initially consumed much of the Committee's attention. The petition of the chiefs asking that their interpreters receive a per diem, over and above the daily pay and housing allowance originally agreed to, was compromised. The same $10 per day benefit also went to the staff members whom the delegations had brought to Saipan. Special arrangements had to be made for delegates hospitalized due to illness, and those facing emergency problems in their home areas. The question of Convention supplementation of delegates' governmental salaries particularly exacerbated tensions until an appropriate weekly formula could be devised. For these and other comparably sensitive problems, the procedure normally followed was for the Convention Secretary to work out the details, and then bring a recommendation to the Administration Committee for approval or rejection. Run of the mill matters were handled by the Administrative staff, under the Convention Secretary's supervision, without recourse to the Committee.

Over the course of the Convention, relatively little pressure from individual constituents or organized interest groups was brought to bear upon delegates on Saipan. Committees might schedule public hearings, but frequently the persons testifying were not self-volunteered but invited to appear. A few communications, addressed to the Convention, commented upon action proposed to be taken or protested decisions already made. Delegates relied heavily on staff for the developing of background data and the delineation of alternative courses of action. Many of the delegates brought with them a broad understanding of the workings of government in the Trust Territory and a general comprehension of the matters to be encompassed within the constitution, and received little prompting or direction from outside the Convention to aid them in completing the details.

In part, the minimal inflow of communication to the Convention reflected the inability of the average Micronesian to comprehend many of the technicalities with which the delegates had to grapple. Unfortunately, it was also attributable to the limited amount of information on total delegate activities which was being disseminated, a matter not corrected until midway in the life of the Convention.[12] By that time, most proposals had already been put into at least preliminary form so that input from without the Convention would have narrowly circumscribed impact on the range of possible constitutional decisions. In retrospect, the average constituent's contribution to the writing of the Micronesian constitution was probably long since made at the time district delegations met with him prior to the organizing of the Convention, and at best was reinforced at the recess.

The Micronesians do not take congenially to the making of hard, conceptual decisions. I knew from past association that culturally they are conditioned to avoid them whenever possible, to temporize, and only when absolutely necessary, to respond with definitive action. Faced with the prospect of writing Micronesia's own constituent law or eventually having one imposed, there appeared little option to the Congress of Micronesia other than to establish an all-Trust Territory body to perform the drafting task, an institution wholly foreign to island tradition. Somehow, through the interplay of ideas and the interaction of delegates there was to emerge agreement on the future governance of Micronesia. And into all of this I had interjected myself, sponsoring the procedural means by which this was to be accomplished, and standing ready to supply the data and analyses essential for the delegates to accomplish their task. The Convention was now functioning, fully structured, its parts meshed, its staff assembled and engaged. Each individual delegate to greater or lesser degree was ready to range broadly and dispose narrowly on the future constitution of Micronesia, as he both submitted his own ideas on many subjects in the form of delegate proposals and as a committee member helped shape the particular area of the constitution within his committee's purview. The pitfalls which threatened to prevent the constitution from even organizing had been surmounted, although admittedly its continuance daily remained highly conjectural. The gamble I had counseled was apparently being won.

I realize now that through all of this, when as consultant I helped the delegates on their appointed tasks, unconsciously, I was violating the strictures which I had set upon my own participation. I considered myself to be mechanically facilitative, committed to the success of the Convention but leaving solely to the delegates the making of decisions within their own frame of values.[13] Actually, every suggestion on the conduct of the Convention, notwithstanding the intention to aid aseptically, was also inherently deliminating, and all data were necessarily furnished within conceptual frames which carried their own constrictive boundaries. I could not serve but from within my own cultural conditioning, and the very logic which I employed, even the sensual feelings which governed relationships with my fellow man, were culturally so circumscribed. Unwittingly, I had contrived a <u>deus ex machina</u>, and in reaching solutions the delegates would be asked to order the world of reality through my eyes.[14] If the modernizing processes to which Micronesia had long been subject in varying degree had not already modified their <u>weltanschauung</u> so as to be congruent with mine, imperceptibly they were to be influenced to adopt it by the very situation which now prevailed. Long preceding Western contact, the discrete islands of the Marshalls comprised complete polities unto themselves. The Santeleurs governed an empire from behind prismatic volcanic rock walls on their man-made Venice in the shallows of Ponape. Yapese hegemony stretched six hundred miles east over the low islands of the Ngek, supported by the black magic of Yapese sorcerers. Divisions formed and reformed in the Palaus before the Melekeiok and Koror confederations of more recent day emerged. None of this comprised part of my cultural comprehension except as a viewer of history, an outsider. The delegates would continue to contribute their lines, but on the stage I had helped set, and within the confines of the conceptual views I was supplying.

---

1. "Although non-Micronesian personnel may assist the Convention in specialized technical matters, the basic work of the Convention (i.e., development and approval of a Constitution) must be the duty of Micronesians...." (<u>Report of the Future Political Status Commission</u>, July 1969, p. 42). For those, both Micronesians and American sympathizers, inclined to see hidden intrigue in Micronesian-American relations, there was a more devious American plot: funding supplied from the Federal Government and repeated encouragement by the United States for the holding of the Convention (see <u>Highlights</u>, November 1, 1973, p. 1) anticipated eventual

collapse of the Micronesian effort in abject failure, allowing the United States to "pick off" each district, one by one, at its own price. As consultant to the Convention, I thus was either conspirator or simpleton. (The later revelation that CIA surveillance had been conducted in Micronesia during 1975 may have reinforced the former surmise.) With respect to the latter, I already knew when I arrived on Saipan that American administrative personnel "on the hill" (Trust Territory Headquarters) were wagering that the Convention would not succeed.

2. Honolulu Advertiser, July 24, 1975, p. A-13.

3. Drawing up a constitution before first working out the future status for Micronesia had been critically likened to "building a house from the roof down." See Hitchcock, "Information and ...," op. cit., p. 12.

4. The Pre-Convention Committee originally planned on a staff of about thirty-three, including pages but excluding borrowed personnel. See minutes of Pre-Convention Committee Meeting held on Truk, September 19, 1974, p. 20.

5. May I be permitted the pleasure of here publicly calling attention to and acknowledging the contribution of the various members of the Research and Drafting Section staff who truly worked "over and above the call of duty" in their zeal to achieve a successful Convention.

6. In all, twenty-six General Research Studies and a comprehensive manual on the constitutional aspects of government finance were issued. In their preparation, all show of erudition was deliberately avoided, concepts were expressed in simple English, examples of practices outside the United States encouraged (particularly in other Pacific Island areas), and a conscious effort made to present information in a value-free form. Given the staff's American legal training, judicial precedents from the United States figured prominently; in part to offset this, the delegates were supplied with a study of "Legal Systems: Modern and Traditional" in which non-common law systems were discussed (GRS No. 8). Sometimes studies requested by individual delegates were, with their permission or at their direction distributed to all delegates as General Research Studies, which explains the

issuance of "Limiting Powers of Government to Protect Economic Freedom" (GRS No. 18) before the more complete study of "Constitutional Provisions for Economic Systems" (GRS No. 21).

7. Honolulu Advertiser, July 21, 1975, p. B-7.

8. Rules of Procedure, Micronesian Constitutional Convention of 1975, Rule 26a (CCM Journal, Vol. II, p. 961).

9. Ibid.

10. See Meller, The Congress ..., op. cit., pp. 318-19. Note that the ancestors of the Carolinians resident on Saipan emigrated from the outer island area of the Truk District from which Senator Nakayama hails.

11. Hitchcock, op. cit., p. 13.

12. At an interview on August 21, 1975, conducted by the Education for Self-Government Task Force (ESG), President Nakayama stated that the information coming out about the Convention "was not correct." It covered only about 10 percent of what was going on. Unreported was the careful and conscientious work occurring in committee.

13. In honesty, the statement in the text should be qualified by the admission that I believe it to be in the best interests of the Micronesians in the modern world that they achieve unity as a single political entity. The reasons for this conclusion were cerebral, and based on Western logic--my cultural logic.

14. To be sure, there is a degree of hyperbole in this text, for there were a goodly number of persons on the Research and Drafting Section staff, and many had contact with delegates. However, they were all committed to "value-free" service, and to assure this (and for other, more technical reasons) I reviewed all research studies, practically all draft proposals, and most all committee reports until the concluding days of the Convention when it became humanly impossible.

Delegates to the Micronesian Constitutional Convention.

A relaxed moment on the Convention floor.

Yap chiefs flanked by their interpreters.

Style Committee at work.

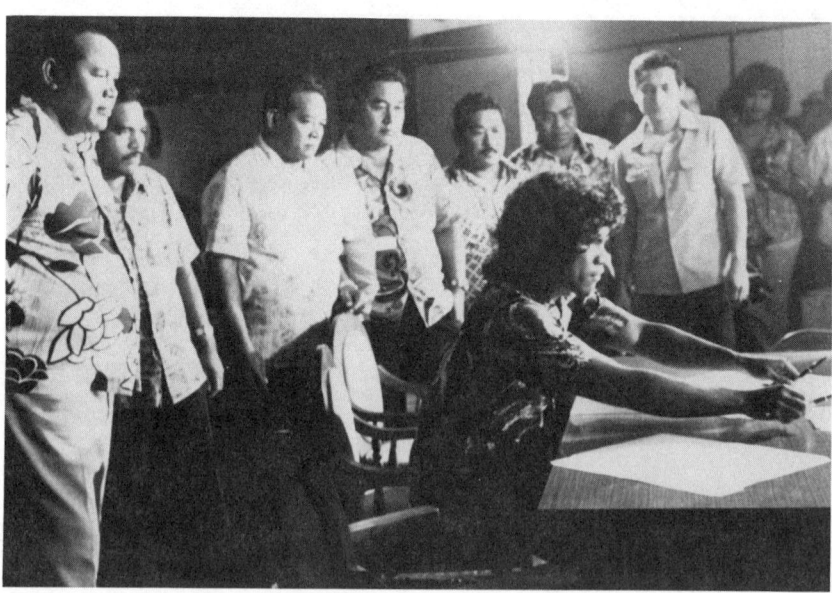
Truk delegates signing constitution.

Palauan delegates signing constitution.

Ponapean delegates signing constitution.

Officers presenting constitution to High Commissioner.

Inauguration of Tosiwo Nakayama as F.S.M. President.

PART III. ACT I

The scene has been set with suspense, the principal actors have tried out their roles, and the curtains are now fully open. The unfolding of the drama begins. Is that the cadaver of a unified Micronesia in the shadow of the wings?

Chapter 8. The Palauan Ploy

On the 7th day of the Micronesian Constitutional Convention, with but a handful of delegate proposals introduced, the Palauan delegation submitted its seven non-negotiable demands.[1] In the words of Delegate Salii, "We believe that it is in the interest of this Convention to know exactly the conditions under which Palau will accept Micronesian unity. If the Convention dismisses any of these conditions, then we tell this Convention this morning that Palau will not consider joining the other districts."[2]

In a doctoral dissertation written fifteen years before, anthropologist Robert McKnight had described how Palauans traditionally have been educated in the use of seven classical forms of political maneuver. "Like zen or the yogi disciplines, they require intimate tutoring, demonstration, and practice."[3] The Micronesian Constitutional Convention was to offer ample opportunity for the use of these arcane skills. Befitting the multi-member composition of the Palauan delegation reflected in its leadership, as many as three of these classical forms may have been deliberately or unconsciously employed during the course of the Convention.[4]

The essence of _Tuich el Kululau_ (firebrand politics) is the successful threat. This technique may involve display of anger, and in refined use, it utilizes veiled threat, soft rather than harsh words, quiet confidence rather than open bragging. Senator Salii's observed behavior over the years in the Congress of Micronesia and with the status negotiations had tended to identify him as a skilled practitioner of this approach. More popular is _Ideuekl chemaidechedui_ (the concealment of the lizard), which involves tactics designed to surprise, confuse the opposition, and to keep the opponent off balance. This strategy maximizes the unexpected and the variable, and ideally the objective is secured before the plan is discovered. The behavior of the chairman of the Palauan delegation on the opening day of the workshop, and some of his statements during the course of the Convention nicely fitted within the dimensions of this maneuver. Up to the very end of the Convention, a few of the Palau delegates apparently were seeking subordinate ends through indirection, using the threat of Palauan secession as concealment. There is also the suspicion that incorporating the demand for the Micronesian capital to be placed within Palau was an illustration of <u>Mengar ma Mecherochr</u> (to taste the bitterness of salt). This third approach is characterized by a determination to accomplish the near impossible.[5] Or perhaps it too was but a concealment, its inclusion as the last of the Palauan demands was deliberately designed to wreck the Convention.

Palauans of varying political persuasion had long declared they supported a loose federation of autonomous and largely sovereign states. The central government would be relegated to the furnishing of essential services. Some, reminiscent of the period of the United States under the Articles of the Confederation, but narrowing even further the powers of the confederal government, contemplated that these states might each be responsible for its own relations with foreign powers, foreign trade, and issuing its own currency. Palau's Congressmen in both houses had reiterated the theme that no district could dominate the government of the new nation, and this had been fully endorsed by a resolution adopted by the 1974 Palau District Legislature.[6] The speaker of that legislature had even bluntly stated that Palau would secede from Micronesia unless a loose federation, with weak central government, were formed. All this had given ample warning that the Micronesian Constitutional Convention would be stormy, should other delegates dare cross this strongly-expressed position of the Palauans.

The uncertainties surrounding the holding of the Palau Constitutional Convention further contributed to the general uneasiness of all delegates. Although the enabling legislation was approved in mid-1974, sessions of the Palau Convention did not open until March of the following year, and did not conclude until about a month before the Convention on Saipan. There matters rested. The contents of the two proposed constitutions it had sponsored were not publicized outside of Palau, but the intent of the Palau convention was declared to "ascertain the desires and wishes of the people in Palau in contemplation of formulating a platform of the Palau Delegation to the Micronesian Convention."[7] Most of the delegates on Saipan undoubtedly knew that the more recently created Palau Political Status Commission was charged with the responsibilities of reviewing both the draft Palau constitutions and whatever might be forthcoming from the Micronesian Constitutional Convention, all as part of Palau's conducting separate negotiations on its own future political status. At the very least, the Palau delegates on Saipan could be expected to support a loose federation position, and to do so with firm conviction. But the tactics adopted were far to exceed mere argumentative persuasion, and to all delegates not privy to the Palauan ploy, they carried the risk of playing a variant of Russian roulette.

The initial refusal of Palauans to hold committee chairmen posts had been the signal that some Palauan move was imminent. A few more days were necessary for the Palauans to ready their "seven demands." As presented, "the Palau Delegation to the Micronesian Constitutional Convention will support the Unity of Micronesia *if and only if* the following terms and conditions are incorporated in the final draft constitution of Micronesia..." (emphasis included).[8] When briefly summarized by Delegate Ngiraked several months later, they did not appear as intemperate as did the claimed non-negotiability of their initial details, and the take-it-or-leave-it manner in which the ultimatum was delivered to the Convention.

> The seven points are: 1) The central government would have only those powers given to it by the constitution, and the districts would have all others. 2) A unicameral (single house) legislature with equal representation from each district. 3) The district controls ownership and use of land. 4) Foreign aid would be divided and shared equally by the districts and the national government. 5) The districts would contribute equally to the central government. 6) Each district would have the right to withdraw from the union for a certain period of years, and 7) The seat of government would be in Palau.[9]

While many of the delegates might find some or even most of these general provisions acceptable, their contents, which were not elaborated on by him, plus the Palauan aggressiveness proved less palatable.

The delegates from Palau had arrived on Saipan without any express formulation of the stand they would take in the Convention. General attitudes had already hardened, however, and the conditions in the Palauan "petition" were alleged to have "evolved especially from the experience Palau ... had in the Congress of Micronesia and the manner in which we have treated each other in the Congress."[10] During the first few days of the Convention, the Palau delegates met informally with Palauan leaders resident on Saipan and after much discussion settled upon the language finally incorporated. Even then, ratification by leaders in Palau was considered necessary, and one of the delegates, bearing a draft, hurriedly returned to Palau to obtain the endorsement of the Palau District Legislature. In a formal communication to the Convention, Speaker Luii of the Legislature, as chairman of its Executive Committee, went on record "that we fully support the conditions raised by our Delegates to the Micronesian Constitutional Convention and if they are not met, the Palau District may not join the future Micronesian Government."[11]

The Palauans proposed to create a central government limited to powers specifically delegated in the constitution, with all "reserve of residual and implied powers"[12] reposing in the districts. Jurisdiction of the central government would include only those matters which are of common concern and mutual interest to all of Micronesia, necessarily "limited to international, inter-district and kindred matters." So far no major difficulty, but the remaining specifics could fall outside the confines of any existing consensus. A unicameral legislature would have equal district representation, and funds received from external sources would "be divided and shared equally by all districts of Micronesia with the central government."[13] Of course, restrictions on distribution and use as contained in the terms of externally-generated funds would need to be adhered to. The central government's taxing power would be confined to business transactions and services falling within its authority, and would exclude the imposition of a personal income tax; beyond these limited fiscal powers, the central government would derive additional revenues from the district governments, and each would contribute equally to the national treasury. Not alone would the latter "have full authority over the ownership and use of land," but the central government could exercise the power of eminent domain only with the district's approval. Even more pointedly, both "ownership and use of land by foreign governments, corporations, nationals, or international organizations ... [were to] be the responsibility of the district governments."[14] Here appeared to be revealed the fulcrum upon which Palau could raise itself in preparation for the unilateral secession which its sixth point would permit. The ability to negotiate with the United States over military use of Palauan lands, and with foreign corporations to erect the oil "superport" about which rumors were now rampant, could provide the economic base for sustaining Palauan independence. The last of the seven points --locating the seat of the central government in Palau--was regarded by many delegates as merely the insulting slap of the glove across the face after being pommeled by the Palauan fist. Almost lost sight of in the consideration of the Palauan seven points was the addendum which declared that the Palauan delegation supported keeping Micronesia's options open with respect to future political status and relations with the United States.[15]

The Palauan petition ended with the rather enigmatic declaration that "in the event the Convention will not incorporate any of the above terms and conditions in any of the proposed draft constitutions, the Palau Delegation will put together an Alternative Draft Constitution incorporating all of the above terms and conditions and shall present the same to the Convention and, hopefully, to all the Micronesian voters for final consideration and approval."[16] Probably, the very recent experience of Palau in concluding its own constitutional labors with the production of unreconcilable drafts had led the Palau delegates to assume the same fate might befall the Micronesian Convention. The preparation of an "ALTERNATIVE DRAFT CONSTITUTION" (it was so capitalized in the "petition") constituted the ultimate threat of formal action to be taken within the Convention, just as the Palau delegation's implied willingness to walk out if crossed in its purposes represented the quintessence of informal finality.

On the 11th day of the Convention, after the Palauan "petition" had been duplicated and referred to the Functions Committee, the latter's chairman requested it be split up by subject matter, and parts also re-referred to three other standing committees. The Palauan thrust had been temporarily parried, but not for long.

In 1951, the first United Nations Mission visiting the Trust Territory received a petition to establish the capital on Koror. At that time, Trust Territory headquarters were not even within Micronesia. Much earlier, the German administrative center had been on Koror, the closest port to the German governor headquartered in New Guinea. The Japanese, too, after six and a half years of navy rule, conducted its civil administration from Koror. While the reasons were unstated, most likely economic and strategic considerations dictated the Japanese decision. During its existence, the Council of Micronesia raised the question of where the Trust Territory headquarters should be located, and came to no conclusion. Thereafter, the Congress of Micronesia wrestled with the problem. The report of a Joint Committee on Program and Budget Planning in 1972 pointedly failed to recommend Koror, but agreed upon no single site if the Marianas did not remain with the rest of the Trust Territory.[17] Finally, in 1975, the Congress of Micronesia by joint resolution directed the Territorial Planner to look into the moving of the Micronesian capital to Ponape "or an alternative site," and report his findings to the Congress in 1976.[18] Against this background, inclusion within the "non-negotiable" items of the demand that the capital be in Palau could easily be interpreted as at least an attempt to goad the delegates from the other districts, and more likely as the excuse for a show of outraged feelings behind which the Palauan delegates might eventually quit the Convention.

There is another, less Machiavellian and more mundane explanation for the Palauan incorporation of such a controversial provision within their petition. A number of influential Palauans resided on Saipan, and occupied leading positions in the Trust Territory bureaucracy. It is claimed that some strongly urged the capital be moved to Koror so that they would be living in their home district should Palau later secede. In the informal Palauan discussions on Saipan which preceded the "petition," opposition had been expressed to the strategy of demanding this point because of its vulnerability. Reportedly it was Senator Salii who insisted upon its retention, which perhaps explains his vehemence during the Convention when this potential Achilles' heel in the Palauan position was mocked by Representative Tman in humorously proposing Yap as the capital site.[19]

Coincidentally, on the same day on which the Palauans first voiced their seven points, the chairman of the Functions Committee introduced a resolution "unanimously" agreed upon by his committee, whose title read, "Declaring a consensus ... that a federation of autonomous states be established as the sovereign government of Micronesia."[20] Its intent was to have the Convention direct all of its standing committees to conduct their affairs on the premise of creating a federation of autonomous states, a central government limited to expressly delegated functions, and the several districts reserving the right to withdraw from the federation "by constitutional process." As so phrased, this resolution probably represented the inchoate views of a majority of the delegates.[21] But the Palauan demands for equality in representation and division of funds, and for the capital to be sited in their district, had interjected disturbingly new elements and now stasis ensued. A week later, the chairman and six members of the Functions Committee presented another resolution, differing diametrically from the first, declaring a "consensus ... that a unitary strong central government be established in Micronesia...."[22] The Palauan delegates angrily spluttered, and thereby revealed their underlying strategy: "The individual delegates must decide what they want to try to achieve in this Convention. Then, from that, each delegation must determine what their position is with respect to the future government."[23] It was to be delegation against delegation. The other delegates in the Convention did what Micronesians know best. They temporized. The first resolution (No. 1) was referred to the Special Committee chaired by Palauan Delegate Sawaichi, and there it remained until after the recess when it was reported out favorably and eventually filed. The latter (No. 6) was shunted back to the Functions Committee to die.

For the next two and a half weeks, while the demands of the Palauan petition were before the various standing committees to which they had been

assigned, individual delegates continued to submit
their own proposals at an increasing pace. The
content of a number of them varied sharply from
the Palauan position. The committees, left to
their own discretion, proceeded to weigh them all.
Reportedly angered by the Convention's failure
to respond to the Palauan points, not alone express
concurrence, on the 27th day of the Convention
the entire Palauan delegation introduced Delegate
Proposal No. 100, to be known as the "Palauan Constitution." Here was "the second phase of the
Palau position,... the implementation ... in more
specific terms. Mr. President, the Palau position
is not leaving any room for compromise...."[24]
Apparently this was the embodiment of the threat
contained in the concluding words of the original
Palauan "petition," the alternative constitution
to be submitted to the people of Micronesia. No
delegate or delegation was to offer as comparably
complete a proposal. Thereafter, much of the Palauan maneuver in the Convention was to be directed
toward bringing its Delegate Proposal No. 100 before
the delegates. While the other delegations had
no objections to its contents being evaluated by
the standing committees among which it was divided,
the fate which had befallen the previous "petition,"
they assiduously sought to prevent the entire document from being debated as a single unit on the
Convention floor.

The constitution offered by the Palauans fleshed out their initial seven demands. The Palauan
"petition" had left large areas of constitutional
content unspecified, and many of these were now
supplied, raising the spector of additional disagreement. The initial task of drafting the "Palauan Constitution," and filling in these hiatuses,
primarily was delegated to a staff attorney of
the Congress of Micronesia. Previously he had
been instrumental in preparing a shadowy document
for the Joint Committee on Future Status which
came to be called the "Warnecke draft" constitution. One of the two drafts considered by the
district convention in Palau was also his handiwork. As to be expected, Delegate Proposal No. 100
traced some of its contents to these prior constitutional documents. Then, too, its preliminary formulation had been reviewed at the meetings of the
Palauans on Saipan, and subjected to style revisions
from many sources, so that as introduced its parentage was multiple. Nevertheless, the "Palauan
Constitution" contained a number of provisions

whose antecedents still remained evident, as illustrated in its Preamble:

Delegate Proposal No. 100	"Warnecke Draft"
We, THE PEOPLE OF MICRONESIA, in exercise of our inherent sovereignty, do hereby adopt this Constitution of Micronesia.	The Micronesian people, in the exercise of our inherent sovereignty hereby adopt this Constitution.
With this Constitution, we affirm our common wish to live together in peace and harmony, to preserve the heritage of the past and to protect the promise of the future.	We do so in order to achieve a unity of purpose that will permit us and our descendants to develop in freedom while preserving the cultural diversity entrusted to us by our ancestors. In finding their home in the land and surrounding waters of Micronesia, our ancestors displaced no other people. None, therefore has prior or competing claim.
We make one nation of many islands. We respect the diversity of our cultures. Our differences enrich us. The seas bring us together, they do not divide us. Our islands sustain us, our island nation enlarges us and makes us stronger. Our ancestors, who found their homes on these islands, displaced no other people. We who remain, wish no other home than this. Having known war, we hope for peace. Having been divided, we wish unity. Having been ruled, we seek freedom.	
We extend to all nations, what we seek from each: Peace, friendship, cooperation, and the recognition of our humanity....	We extend to all countries what we expect from each, friendship, cooperation, and recognition of our common humanity....

Possibly because of major divisions within the Palauan community living on Saipan, or the

Palauan delegation itself, agreement could not be reached on the composition of the national legislature. Alternative forms had to be included, although steadfast to the Palauan seven points, equal district membership was an element found in both. For the first time, a crack in the Palauan solidarity was publicly disclosed.

Delegate Proposal No. 100 called for the election of a president by the national legislature from among its membership. Ambivalently, it also assigned veto powers to him, so that it was unclear whether or not it intended to embody the American separation of powers' doctrine. All of this was of great significance, for until the last days of the Convention the nature of the national legislature and chief executive remained in dispute, as did their relationship. The Palauan position assumed particular import, since the compromise to be reached would have to accommodate it.

Another provision of the Palauan Constitution opened a brief window on the hidden agenda which might be underlying the whole Palauan strategy. Originally, one of the "non-negotiable" points had declared it to be the right of a state, for a limited time, to withdraw from the Federated States. Delegate Proposal No. 100 pinpointed this period to begin at the end of eight years following the effective date of the constitution, and to continue for five years. All delegates knew that the terms of the proposed compact with the United States would not permit unilateral termination before a fifteen-year period had run its course. Why a right of secession before such determination, and then for only an interim of five years?

For the delegates who pondered this question, the answer probably lay in Palau's becoming the site for the proposed oil superport. It was general knowledge that money was still being sought to finance an intensive multi-million-dollar feasibility study which might require as long as a year to complete. Final decision, and then erection of the mammoth facility could take as much as a decade. Here would be a source of income which eventually could allow the Palauans to break completely from the rest of Micronesia. A few delegates recognized the almost perfect parallelism with the Bougainvillians of Papua New Guinea: as Papua New Guinea moved to independence, the immensely profitable copper mine at Kieta on Bougainville enabled them to mount demands for separate political status. Palau would remain with the rest of Micronesia until the central terminal station was constructed; once self-supporting, the five-year secession clause could be exercised. Meanwhile, the economic benefits from the oil development would begin redounding to the advantage of Palau, for Delegate Proposal No. 100 denied the central government of Micronesia any taxing power over trade and commerce between foreign nations and a single state, or upon foreign corporations doing business in a single state. In each case, "single state" could just as well have been read as "Palau." No wonder, then, that the delegates at the Micronesian Constitutional Convention had to proceed warily in dealing with the Palauans and their "non-negotiable" demands.

To the average delegate, the Palauans undoubtedly appeared to occupy an impregnable position, and had little need for the rest of Micronesia. However, at the same time Micronesia was anticipating the setting up of a central terminal in Palau, negotiations were near conclusion between Japan, Indonesia, and Saudi Arabia for constructing a $1.4 billion depot to be erected on Lombok Island in Indonesia. Then, too, proponents of the Palau site were stressing its political stability within an American Trusteeship. Prior to any decision to locate the superport in Palau, some assurance would be required that it would remain under the protection of the United States. Apart from the ecological, engineering, and financial hurdles, local cultural opposition also would have to be surmounted, so that in reality the Palau project was highly problematic. As in the case of the Marshalls, Palau was in fact keeping all of its options open, but rather than by boycotting, it was through the provisions it demanded be part of the Micronesian constitution.

A few days before the convening of the delegates on Saipan, members of the Pre-Convention Committee had met with Senator Lazarus E. Salii as co-chairman of the Joint Committee on Future Status to discuss whether the provisions of the compact must be considered a limitation on the scope of the Convention's deliberations.[25] He had surprisingly, although not strongly, argued against the holding of the Convention, that its possibility of failure held too great a danger of causing a breakup of Micronesian unity. In fact, with all of the preparations for the Convention underway for almost a year, practicalities countered postponement. It was then that I referred to the American experience with the Articles of Confederation, and opined that at the very least the Convention should be able to formulate a comparable minimal agreement. Delegate Proposal No. 100 proved to be concerned with the same basic issues of representation, taxation, land, and the shape and power of the central government as the American Articles,[26] and in many ways adopted similar solutions. States would have equal votes in the Congress, regardless of size of delegation, and extraordinary majorities would be required for the taking of major actions. Although the Micronesian central government would be granted a minimal taxing power, for the most part it, too, would have to rely upon the states for locally collected revenues. The states would retain their lands, so land matters would be within the purview of the states. True, the Palauan proposal would create a more elaborate central governmental structure, and allot it a larger grant of powers, but this would still be extremely limited in today's world of expanded government. In spirit, the "Palauan Constitution" was aligned with the American Articles rephrased in modern political metier. Unbeknownst to me, about five years before, Senator Salii had met with a group of professors at the University of California at Berkeley who had rejected a highly decentralized confederal system, on the grounds that there has been no successful confederation in modern history.[27]

    Once the Palauan proposal was spelled out, the other delegations again responded in a characteristically Micronesian way. Not only did they not submit district proposals of their own for a Micronesian constitution, and thus avoided confrontation within the Convention of adamantly declared district positions, but mutually encouraged each other to reply moderately when the Palauans resorted to intemporate address. Action in Convention committees, and discussions behind the scenes, probed to determine exactly how far the Palau position would bend, if not break. To watchers of the long continuing status talks, "non-negotiable" has had a more flexible meaning in Micronesia than implied in any dictionary. Delegate Salii was to protest: "The Palau Delegation came to this Convention prepared. We had positions. We told you about them. We had drafted a Constitution.

We told you what we required of you if Palau was to be part of you. Out of all the Delegations here, none has responded to us. Out of all the Delegates here, I know of only three individual responses."[28] All to no avail. The Convention was to recess without the Palau delegation able to maneuver the other districts to play their roles in the manner desired.

On the 57th day of the Convention, one day before the October 2 deadline beyond which committees were enjoined to commence reporting out their Committee Proposals, the chairman of the Palau delegation objected that the "Palau Proposed Draft Constitution ... was, to our dismay butchered into pieces and assigned to the various committees of the Convention, where its fate was a dishonorable burial under piles of committee reports and proposals.

"Mr. President, I do not know whether such action on Delegate Proposal No. 100 was triggered by design or simple unthoughtfulness, but it is clear to us that it would have been a clever way to do away with the seven minimum requirements....

"Mr. President,... it becomes incumbent upon the Palau Delegation to exhume all the parts of the Palau Proposed Draft Constitution from their various committee burial grounds, assemble them into one document, and resubmit it to this Convention for serious and good faith consideration.... [O]ther parts of Delegate Proposal No. 100 may be improved and comprised [sic], but let me repeat myself that the seven minimum requirements remain as they have been--a 50-50 compromise."[29]

It was not that the Palauan demands had been ignored. Rather, in the words of Delegate Hans Wiliander, committee discussions had "been acutely aware, painfully aware, of the Palauan position." Previously, he prefaced the use of this phrase by referring to the Convention rules as expressly calling for the assignment of a complex proposal to a number of committees. "We all knew that Delegate Proposals were to go into Committee, be considered with all other Delegate Proposals and other ideas, and then each Committee was to report out its best judgment.... We all understood we were not going to line up a whole Truk Proposed Constitution against a Palau Proposed Constitution, and both of them against a third Yapese Proposed Constitution. As Delegates we came to consult, and discuss, and in Micronesian style arrive at a consensus on the various points of view....There was <u>no</u> trickery, <u>no</u> 'unthoughtfulness'"[30] in the division of Delegate Proposal No. 100.

By this time some portions of the "Palauan Constitution" had been adopted by the Convention, others were on their way to be recommended by committee, and there had been no definitive vote openly challenging the Palauans on their non-negotiable points. After a flurry of parliamentary action, Delegate Proposal No. 100 was withdrawn from committee, with the understanding that the Palau delegation "would leave it up to the officers of the Convention to decide what to do when the Proposal is passed on First Reading."[31] The language employed by the Palauan delegates was, surprisingly, almost pleadingly placating. Something was afoot.

To further confuse the situation, Delegate Leo Falcam had called for his proposal No. 120, and another of Delegate Soiter Mwety, to be similarly withdrawn, on the basis that they were "comprehensive and also set a framework,"[32] the formula used by the Palauans to justify the treatment of Delegate Proposal No. 100 as a single unit. They, too, passed First Reading. This occurring, all three were immediately referred to a special committee of the Administration Committee, composed of the Standing Committee chairman and headed by Delegate Falcam. Later it became obvious that for purposes of home district politics, the Palau delegation had been making a record to show it had forced the Convention to act on its proposal, the "Palauan Constitution." Once this was achieved by having the nominal First Reading, the delegation was more than willing to allow it to languish in the special committee, secure in the knowledge that all of its contents were still receiving piecemeal attention elsewhere.

But the Palauan threat was not yet dissipated. As late as November 1, one week before the end of the Convention, when Floor Leader Luke Tman was publicly reported as saying on PEACESAT--in a discussion with students in Hawaii on the Convention's work--that the Palauan non-negotiable demands were mostly strategy rather than a "very serious demand," the leadership of the Convention held its collective breath. The risk yet remained that responding emotionally the Palau delegation would take umbrage and quit the Convention.

1. <u>CCM Journal</u>, Vol. I, pp. 28-30.

2. <u>Ibid</u>., p. 31.

3. Robert McKnight, "Competition in Palau," Ph.D. Dissertation, Ohio State University, 1960, p. 83.

4. All identifications of individuals with Palauan traditional tactics are appraisals made by the author.

5. <u>Ibid</u>., pp. 93-96.

6. Congress of Micronesia, <u>Senate Journal</u>, Fifth Congress, 3rd Regular Session, 1974, p. 80.

7. Sec. 7, Public Law 5-6-16, Fifth Palau District Legislature, approved June 4, 1974.

8. <u>CCM Journal</u>, Vol. I, p. 29. For the full statement see Appendix C.

9. Summary of ESG interview with John Ngiraked, <u>Dialogue for Micronesia</u>, Program No. 49, October 14, 1975, p. 1.

10. <u>CCM Journal</u>, Vol. I, p. 31.

11. Miscellaneous Communication No. 9, dated July 22, 1975, <u>CCM Journal</u>, Vol. II, pp. 946-47.

12. Students of American constitutional law are aware of how drastically the United States government would be curtailed if limited narrowly to "expressly delegated" powers, without augmentation by necessary and proper "implied powers" or the exercise of the "residual powers" of a sovereign nation.

13. This ambiguous portion would later be clarified, so that each district and the central government would receive an equal share.

14. <u>CCM Journal</u>, Vol. I, pp. 29-30.

15. Proponents of Palau as a site for an oil superport stressed its being a "politically stabilized place--within an American trusteeship" (<u>Marianas Variety</u>, March 28, 1975, p. 5). For any decision to locate the facility in Palau, it would seem necessary there be some assurance that it would

remain under the protection of the United States, hence, apparently, the need to keep the status options open.

16. CCM Journal, Vol. I, p. 130.

17. Congress of Micronesia, "Study of Permanent Site of the Capital of Micronesia," Joint Committee on Program and Budget Planning, 1972.

18. Senate Joint Resolution 6-41, Sixth Congress, First Session, 1975.

19. CCM Journal, Vol. I, pp. 57-58; and see Delegate Salii's response, p. 64.

20. Resolution No. 1, CCM Journal, Vol. I, p. 31.

21. Delegates were acutely aware of the possibility of secession. In the swing through the districts prior to the workshop, when I raised questions regarding matters to be researched, instructions received were not to issue a general report on secession: "If you touch upon this right now, and if you know the mentality of Micronesians, we are always looking for the loopholes."

22. Resolution No. 6, CCM Journal, Vol. I, p. 57.

23. Delegate Lazarus E. Salii, CCM Journal, Vol. I, p. 64.

24. Delegate John Ngiraked, CCM Journal, Vol. I, p. 100.

25. The terms of the compact were not considered to be limiting, as the Congress had not agreed to its provisions.

26. See Merrill Jensen, The Articles of Confederation (Madison: Univ. of Wisconsin Press, 1973); Arthur E. Sunderland, Constitutionalism in America (New York: Blaisdell Publishing Company, 1965).

27. Letter of Dr. Eugene Mihaly to Congress of Micronesia (circa 1971), in papers of Professor J.W. Davidson, MS6106, Box 18, File 28, Australian National Library, Canberra.

28. Delegate Lazarus E. Salii, CCM Journal, Vol. I, p. 173 (part of this statement was also quoted in the Prologue, supra, pp. 1ff).

29. Delegate John Ngiraked, <u>CCM</u> <u>Journal</u>, Vol. I, p. 258.

30. Delegate Hans Wiliander, <u>CCM</u> <u>Journal</u>, Vol. I, p. 274. See full statement, pp. 273-75, for allocation of the various portions of the Palauan constitution to committees, and their action thereon up to the 59th day.

31. Delegate Lazarus E. Salii, <u>CCM</u> <u>Journal</u>, Vol. I, p. 264.

32. Delegate Leo Falcam, <u>CCM</u> <u>Journal</u>, Vol. I, p. 265.

Chapter 9. The Issues Take Shape

In the fall of 1974, when the Pre-Convention Committee was sounding out public opinion across the Trust Territory, it met with a group of Micronesian students attending the University of Guam. The transcript records that John Ngiraked commented, "The task of drafting a constitution is not such a difficult job. It's not very difficult to put together the mechanics ... that concern[s] paperwork --it is not that difficult. It is what you want to put in that constitution.... We have the benefit of having before us many, many nations and many constitutions. You can take one of them and just change a few words and declare it to be our constitution. But the difficulty is to be sure that we intend to say them and intend to go through and carry them out to protect them...."[1] Instead of following the path of adapting another country's constitution, numerous ideas were to be brought to the attention of the Convention, and the delegates would pick and choose among them. Most were incorporated in the 163 proposals which the delegates, themselves, introduced; some of them owed their origin to witnesses who appeared at the public hearings scheduled by the committees during the first four weeks of the Convention. Much of the detail completing the total constitution was derived from staff work which had identified potential constitutional content for committee consideration and decision.

Initially, delegates had to adjust to working with each other, as well as overcoming the disinclination of the average Micronesian to take positions in a positive manner. The chairmen of the Functions, Structure, and General Provisions Committees had to learn the nuances of coordinating with their subcommittee chairmen, just as the latter needed to become familiar with the styles of their committees' leaders. In most cases it was to be the coopted chairmen who set the pace of committee action, but all were dependent upon developing consensus within their groups, so as to assure an affirmative Convention reception of their committees' proposals. Devoid of an internal power structure cutting across the delegations and committed to a particular policy program, this was an open Convention. Primary reliance would be upon the reasonableness of the committees' proposals, the strength of the committees' commitment to their respective positions, and the stature and probity of the participants who argued the pros and cons within the Convention.

A committee pushed by its chairman to concur with his favored policy decisions might desert him on the floor, and in part this is what occurred with the chiefs sitting on the Civil Liberties Committee. On the other hand, it was incumbent upon each chairman to maintain a sense of pressure within his committee to assure the members would conclude their allotted task in sufficient time to permit the Convention to adopt a completed constitution. Both policy leadership and the undertaking of administrative chores were his responsibilities, and he shirked either at the peril of the entire Convention's success.

Discernible differences of style distinguished the various committee chairmen. Some, like Delegate Carl Heine of the Civil Liberties Committee, would introduce proposals to be referred to their committees just to assure a full range of subjects would be before them for consideration. At the other extreme, Delegate Heinrich Iriarte not alone appeared to be proceeding on the premise that his Governmental Structure Committee could not push beyond the subject matter of proposals expressly referred to it, but continued to wait for them until after it had long become apparent that the committee must initiate some of its own. With the jurisdiction of the Functions Committee overlapping those of all others, Dr. Hirosi Ismael deliberately steered his committee's discussions into subject areas which he believed were not receiving consideration by the committees charged with more specific assignments. Serving the various committees, their chairman and sub-chairmen, the staff members assigned could prepare background studies and arrange agendas for committee discussions, but proceeded no faster than they were instructed. Sometimes this meant they marked time until the committee leadership matured into a positive force setting the directions of committee deliberations.

Little overt show of decision-making was to be expected in the first few weeks. Committee procedures once established, members had to become conversant with the general scope of their committees' subject matter responsibilities. Here staff working with the committees could assist in assuring members they were alerted to the full range of matters with which they might deal. Silence of the constitution upon a particular subject would not be a matter of oversight, but positive declination to take action. At the same time, staff attempted to eschew even the appearance of advocating committee adoption or rejection of any proposal.

Comparable to bill drafting for legislatures, the specific language of most proposals was phrased by the staff of the R. & D. Section so as to accomplish the expressed objectives of the delegates. The subordinate elaborations were frequently supplied by the draftsman. Depending upon the attention with which a committee examined a particular delegate proposal referred to it, or concerned itself with subjects brought before it by the study agenda it had set for itself, committee proposals, too, might originally owe much of their detail to the handiwork of the staff. Wherever initiated, however, until very late in the Convention, when it was under pressure of time, the committees would generally not adopt any specifics until they had fully considered them, exploring all anticipated effects flowing from their application. And under these circumstances, past events within Micronesia particularly helped shape and prune committee proposals as they became part of the emerging constitutional document, assuring that the new government aborning would profit from the experience of that functioning within the Trust Territory.

An example of this adaptation was furnished by Secretarial Order No. 2882 creating the Congress of Micronesia, which declared a convicted felon ineligible to sit in the Congress.[2] The Order also contained an exception: a pardon restoring civil rights removes the disqualification.[3] Edgar Edwards of Truk had been elected in 1974 to the House of Representatives, even though not qualified to sit because of a felony conviction. On January 20, 1975, one day before the House credentials committee was to report, the High Commissioner granted him a pardon. The delegates were fully conversant with this incident, and in the language prepared for the part of the constitution dealing with the proposed new Congress, included a comparable provision holding a felon ineligible.⁴ Rather than giving to the executive the power to waive the limitation, however, it would now be left to the Congress by statute to determine whether the constitutional disqualification may be modified or additional qualifications added. The Structure Committee declared itself "wary of the executive pardon power."⁵

All Convention actions occurred within a constraining paradigm of language and law which most delegates could vaguely sense, but about which I was acutely aware and could do little. Everything formally said and written was in English, the official language of the Convention, as was all personal intercommunication between delegates not hailing from the same district. Interpreters labored to bridge the gap between the vernaculars of their principals and the complex English within which ideas frequently took shape, try as staff might to simplify the language employed. But there was a problem beyond interpretation or minimizing the use of "legalism," for all of the English terminology employed was technical in the sense that it depended upon a warp and woof of historical concept and legal experience with which few of the delegates were adequately conversant, regardless of their English-speaking abilities.

To give specificity to the words employed, and being trained in American law, the staff referred to American practice and judicial construction of meanings. As a matter of course, they shaped delegate and committee proposals, as well as the supporting rationale contained in committee reports, within the general conceptual frame of a common law jurisprudence. Thus, unless accompanied by delimiting strictures, "murder" as it might be used in any proposal or prepared explanation would carry the meaning generally attributed to the term found in any English language dictionary. Both unmentioned and excluded would be all varieties of legal killings permitted, excused, or considered lesser acts and not within the concept of "murder."

What other course could the staff have followed in an area which for over three decades had been and was yet being administered under the usages of the English language as embodied in American legal practice? Even when Delegate Proposal No. 140 would have the constitution declare that "judicial decisions rendered prior to the effective date of this constitution shall not constitute precedents which must be observed by the courts of Micronesia," the intention being "to limit future judges to ... [base] their decisions only on the Constitution and laws enacted thereunder, our own Micronesian customs ... and ... relevant aspects of our Micronesian lifestyles,"[6] the constitution would remain expressed in the English language, and the general meaning of its provisions would continue to be so circumscribed. There was no sure way out of this short of prohibiting a Micronesian judge from applying to a provision of the constitution any meaning ever attributed to comparable language by a judge in any other polity![7] The solution eventually adopted by the Convention was to declare court decisions must be consistent with Micronesian customs and traditions, and the area's social and geographical configuration.[8] This language would enable the courts to avoid the rule of stare decisis, and permit expanding the scope of the underlying law so that it would not be confined to that recognized in the United States. But it would not remove Micronesia from inclusion among those jurisdictions which observe a common law approach, nor would it necessarily preclude the use of American principles of constitutional interpretation.

Viewed from even broader perspective, why the adoption of brevity as the mode for expressing the contents of the Micronesian constitution, consisting mainly of generalities and specific only when deemed essential, as in delineating skeletal government, or when politically necessary, as in incorporating political compromise? Here, too, American practice was unconsciously being replicated, just as more fundamentally it was in the very act of concretizing the constitution in a single document, a normal process for new polities founded since the United States was formed.

A reading of the constitution drawn in London for the independent Commonwealth of Fiji, or in Apia by the Western Samoans for themselves, or similarly in Port Moresby by and for the Papua New Guineans, reveals a different stylistic approach to the same type of undertaking. In the documents named, the declaration of a general right will be found followed immediately by a long list of qualifying exceptions and described applications. The American inclination, on the other hand, is to rely upon the courts or the legislatures for the furnishing of these addenda, and to stop with the expression of a broader statement of principle in the constituent document. The constitution drafted for Micronesia was premised upon an undeclared but clearly implicit assumption: its form was to permit comparable malleability, just so long as the means countenanced by the constitution were employed to that end.

Delegates, staff, and the general public fully understood the sensitivity of the future political status issue. The Committee on General Provisions early began holding hearings to determine the positions of delegates on the political future of Micronesia, but everyone appreciated that this would not become the subject of one of the first committee proposals to be reported to the Convention. Similarly, it could be anticipated that questions touching upon land would require the most delicate of handling. On the other hand, the potential contents of a Bill of Rights for the constitution not alone engendered a considerable number of delegate proposals, but also the expression of numerous supporting and opposing statements at "public hearings on issues as wide ranging as capital punishment, women's equality, eminent domain, [and] the traditional leadership...."[9] Many of these and comparable other subjects pertinent to a Bill of Rights were to be embodied in committee proposals released early by the Civil Rights Committee, only to meet with basic conflict on the floor touching the quick of Convention emotions regarding the primacy of traditional rights over the civil liberties more recently introduced into Micronesia. Related to this, but only beginning to gather the divisive momentum which later was sharply to split the Convention, was the issue of providing a functional role for traditional leaders in the new government being planned. In turn, such inclusion of the traditional leaders was to be but one dimension of an issue of broader scope facing the delegates, namely, the form of government for all of Micronesia capable of maintaining both the existing districts and their cultural differences.

Political science texts are fond of differentiating between unitary and federal systems. In the latter, in theory at least, political powers are divided between the central government of the whole country and the "equally autonomous" governments of the parts so that each tier is legally independent within its own sphere. In actuality, although the political system is labeled "federal," little individuality may be allowed the regional governments, while conversely, laboring under a unitary system does not foreclose the enjoyment of considerable territorial autonomy. The distinction between the two systems in action in fact turns on the nature and degree of central control exercised. Widespread sentiment in Micronesia opposed instituting a system of government which failed to both recognize and accommodate the heterogeneity of the districts, so that a fully unitary system would not have been tolerated. But there was less unanimity over the degree of centralization which ought be countenanced.[10]

The initial voicing of the Palauan demands opened the vista of nearly independent states, separate and equal, joined for mutual convenience and primarily for the narrow objective of achieving a common external position, with at best only a minimal central government, and it a creature of the states and serving their convenience. It mattered little what particular label might be attached, as etymologically, "there is little to distinguish between 'federal' and 'confederal,' or between 'federation' and 'confederation' or 'confederacy'...."[11]

Delegate Proposal No. 100, when introduced by the Palauans, went far to discard the co-equal individuality of the respective regional governments loosely tied for cooperative ends. In this sense, Delegate Falcam's Proposal No. 120, which was also withdrawn from committee during the later developments of the "Palauan Ploy," displayed greater emphasis upon the principle of equality. In it, both executive and judicial branches contained structural assurances for the maintenance of state parity. Nevertheless, both delegate proposals in fact abandoned the implementing of a narrowly drawn confederal form of government. Consequently, the Convention faced a different type of problem: rather than disputing over the dimensions of a confederation of cooperating equal states, the delegates would be asked to apply a slide rule in allocating public duties and responsibilities between the central and regional entities of a system of government in which one was not permanently subordinate to the other.

Decentralization may be secured by affording the regional governments a very large part in deciding which functions are to be performed, or by allocating to them a major role in the administration of centrally adopted laws, or by utilizing both. While a federal system, the Swiss have attempted to achieve decentralization by relying heavily upon the cantonal governments for the execution of federal laws, this in addition to their administering the enactments adopted under cantonal powers. Papua New Guinea, whose constitution denies it is a federal nation, proposes to divide the potential functions of government between the national government and the provinces, and also to have officials of the latter responsible for the administration of various central programs and governmental activities within the provinces. Despite the different labels appended to their political systems, both nations illustrate the adoption of the same means to achieve decentralized government. Most of the delegates came to the Micronesian Constitutional Convention antagonistic to the centralization of the existing Trust Territory structure, and they early demonstrated that imprinting of the "dual-federalism" of the American political system had led them to assume that decentralization was to be achieved only by providing for two distinctive, separate systems of government, with the central government denied many functions inside the geographical limits of Micronesia.[12] Perhaps they never fully grasped the potential of the alternative which would have seen regional units within Micronesia implementing nationally determined policy.

Once the Convention appeared positioned within the frame of federalism, pertinent experiences from around the world were brought to bear upon Micronesia's paralleling problems. The issue of freedom of personal movement could be examined in the ill-fated Caribbean federation; its postponement was one of the factors contributing to that federation's lack of success.[13] The apparently insurmountable barrier of Palau's demand to be the site for the capital of Micronesia could be placed within a different perspective: this was not novel, and had plagued other federal nations. By its 1956 constitution, Pakistan's National Assembly rotated meetings between Karachi, the federal capital, and Dacca, and the same applied to sittings of the Supreme Court. In the 1962 constitution, the central government was located both in Islamabad and Dacca. With the status compact of the United States very much in the minds of most delegates, its approval and implementation would need be articulated with the Micronesian constitution. But even this had its instructive echoes from elsewhere. As in the United States, some federalisms in Asia gave to the central government the authority to implement treaties, even on subjects exclusively within regional powers. Others in Africa, however, required the expressed consent of the regional governments. There was reassuring precedent for requiring state consent to the compact as yet in limbo, but which it was anticipated would delegate the major functions of national defense and foreign affairs to the United States.

In the effort to erect structural ties between the district governments and the central, at first impression dual membership in the regional and national legislatures appeared a logical vehicle. Here, the negative experiences of India, Nigeria, and Pakistan countered its repetition in Micronesia. Counseling in its favor were the difficulties suffered by the West Indies, where in the absence of such a link, most competent politicians proved unwilling to relinquish their regional positions for the uncertainty of sharing national powers.

"Of all federal problems, the financial relation between the Center and the units are the most difficult."[14] Given the apparent intransigence of the Palauan position, there was solace in the knowledge that Micronesia had company elsewhere. However, it is doubtful that any comparable euphoria in these other federalisms underlay their assumptions of future governmental income. Somehow, probably from the United States as the _quid pro quo_ for Micronesia's contribution to American national security, the new government would receive funds adequate for the performance of those services believed necessary. Rather than the problem faced being one of whether sufficient revenues would be available to support viable government, it was transliterated in Micronesia into an exercise of costing the services which would have to be performed.

Bandied around the Convention was a very rough estimate that the annual expenses of a central government, once a federal form was installed, could be contained within a little over $17 million dollars.[15] The largest single component was to be $3 million dollars for that portion of the foreign affairs function not surrendered by Micronesia, followed closely by $2.9 million for education, and $2.1 million estimated to cover the regulation of shipping, communications, and commerce. Health services would approximate $1.8 million, the expenses of the national legislature were fixed at $1.7 million, and legal affairs would need $1.5 million. Tax collection, immigration, social security, postal service, the courts, and agricultural and marine resources all wore price tags varying from over $100,000 to $600,000, each. As a catch-all, apparently, general administration would account for $2 million more. Little of this would cover district and field services currently being performed by the Trust Territory; the new states' budgets would have to shoulder that burden. Contemporaneously, it had been estimated that once all of the planned Micronesian facilities and improvements were in place, it would cost about $50 million dollars each year to operate and maintain those facilities and meet the operating expenses of all government in Micronesia, central and regional.

During the 1946-48 period, as a safeguard against concentrating central authority which might fall into the hands of the Chinese, it was the Malays who insisted upon land being left under the control of the states in the federal constitution of Malaya being drafted. Three decades later, it was not fear of an ethnic minority but of an entrenched, impersonal bureaucracy within government which divided the delegates of Micronesia when facing the question of how to place the regulation of land within a constitutional context. The Islanders' difference of viewpoint turned around whether or not eminent domain powers were to be recognized at all in the constitution, and if granted, were the central government's condemnation powers to be conditioned upon receipt of permission from the new states. Secretarial Order 2969 which transferred control over public lands to the Trust Territory had declared that the eminent domain power was reserved in the central government, and on return of the lands to the districts, could also be exercised by them. The subject of land went to the very heart of the island cultures, and this, together with the sharpness of the cleavage, quickly negated any easy transfer ability of example from elsewhere. Complicating the problem, the dimensions of governmental land use extended to more than just the exercise of eminent domain. Private lands leased to the Trust Territory government were also in issue. Early, when the Pre-Convention Committee had made its swing through the districts, in Truk inquiry pointedly asked if the constitution could not direct the returning of leased private lands. As a further aspect of the land problem, the constitution would have to deal with the question of whether non-citizens were to be prohibited from owning land, but here, if the experience of the other Pacific Islands was to be any measure, less difficulty was to be encountered, and this only over the ease of naturalization.

Use of a plural head at the apex of the executive branch of government is rarely encountered on the American scene. The single chief executive, enforcing the laws and responsible for the administration of government, whether he be president, governor, or mayor is the more familiar mode. None of the colonial powers which had preceded the Americans in Micronesia had introduced the concept of a plural executive by the example of the administration they had practiced. The interim under American military government, and then the Trust Territory with its High Commissioner appointed from Washington, only continued the symbolism of the all-powerful chief colonial administrator. Perhaps because of this long imposed government, there existed a somewhat amorphous uneasiness throughout the Trust Territory over the prospect of a single chief executive heading any new government proposed for Micronesia.

Fundamental support for instituting a plural executive could be found in its capacity for bridging the cultural differences which separate the various regions of Micronesia. With representatives from each on a multi-membered executive body, policy-making and implementation could be kept attuned to the pluralism of Micronesia, rather than running the risk of being pressed into a procrustean pattern by an executive head familiar with only one of those cultures. The Truk District constitutional delegation, when contacting its constituents, discovered opinion divided over whether to install a six-member council or a single chief executive. The Yap delegation's questionnaire reflected a similar difference of views, but with a six-membered council favored by a majority response. Much earlier, the 1970 status delegation report had recommended the creation of an Executive Council "to exercise final decisionmaking power in the executive branch of the Trust Territory Government."[16] But it, and unsuccessful Senate Joint Resolution No. 26 of 1971 which proposed to give Congress of Micronesia backing, could be attributed to Micronesians' desire to share executive power with the High Commissioner during the transition period prior to termination of the Trusteeship.[17] More currently, the unofficial "Warneke" Constitution had proposed an Executive Committee whose members would be selected from each of Micronesia's six districts. The issue was bound to come before the Convention, if for no other reason than that a plural executive permitted opportunity for reaching a politically viable compromise between the districts.

After concluding its hearings, the Governmental Structure Committee in its report to the Convention recommended a plural executive "... to promote unity and to provide an executive branch representing the widest possible Micronesian experience."[18] Background research covering the Swiss government furnished ample evidence that a plural executive could function in a non-parliamentary, federal system. More immediately poignant, the Convention's opting for six vice-presidents had demonstrated the political value of equal district participation within the executive. But notwithstanding all of this, the delegates bore the imprint of long association with the American executive form, and eventually it was to prove to be the controlling factor.

Conspicuously absent in the Convention was the manifestation of intent to introduce revolutionary change, to cut the pattern of Micronesian government to any radical ideology,[19] or even to establish the measures of the "good" society by which the new government was to conduct itself. If anything, the institutionalizing of democracy as against the perpetuation of Micronesia's stratification represented the apex of delegate idealism. There was no expression of an underlying thrust such as inspired the constitution-writing efforts of Papua New Guinea to reduce inequality, prevent favoritism, and minimize economic class distinction. Nor was there a comparable effort to curtail the evils flowing from access to governmental power through a public leadership code and a requirement of asset and income disclosure by governmental officials.[20] About all which might be singled out for attention within such philosophic rubric is the "radicalism of restoration." In part this took the form of reducing the preeminence of the central government in the Trust Territory so that the cultures of the districts might be better reflected through their own laws and administration. It also was concerned with the erosion of traditional leadership and of the role of custom in the ordering of Micronesian life. Eventually, "restoration" became one of the predominant issues, on which the Convention was nearly to founder. Early this was presaged by the Palauans in Delegate Proposal No. 100 incorporating alternative provisions for the national legislature, one of which would have increased its size so as to include two traditional leaders from each state in its membership. However, in reality the effort at "restoration" in the Convention belied its etymology, for the championed details aimed at appending new functions to the traditional leaders, now fitted into an introduced government of Western derivation, rather than reestablishing their customary roles within a traditional setting.

Few delegates came to Saipan ready with a predetermined list of proposals for inclusion in the constitution. The first week of the Convention saw the introduction of only five delegate proposals, each very short and not covering the single sheet of paper on which it was written. Delegate Carl Heine's proposal prohibiting sexual discrimination, eventually destined for inclusion in the equal protection of the laws section of the constitution, had the distinction of being the first filed. The second week closed with the submission of 25 more delegate proposals, and by the 21st Convention day, an additional 43 had been introduced. For a week thereafter, this rate of delegate sponsorship held on almost a plateau (39 more delegate proposals by the 28th Convention day), and then it appeared that the delegates had begun to run out of ideas. Prior to the recess on the 42nd day of the Convention, 244 xeroxed pages (representing 144 delegate proposals) of the total 264 pages which were to embody the delegates' individual suggestions (163 delegate proposals) were placed in the delegates' files and referred to the subject-matter committees for their action.[21]

Once committees commenced their deliberations, they proceeded at a slow pace, and with caution. There were delegates who despaired over whether a committee proposal on any subject would ever be forthcoming.[22] The delegates were apprehensive, and needed to feel sufficiently secure in their own judgments, or their reliance on those to whom they could look for leadership, before the first definitive steps could be taken. Everyone knew that the future political status of Micronesia was at the foundation of the government to be built, but few wanted to tackle it headlong. Even the "Palauan Constitution" straddled that issue. Then, too, confronting the Palauans on any of their seven demands raised the spector of Convention dissolution, so all were discretely skirted until the total dimensions of the constitution could take shape. Committees such as Public Finance and Governmental Functions might instruct their staffs to prepare detailed analyses and evaluations of the Palauan position, but beyond that stage their members hesitated, and looked forward to the coming recess as a means to avoid testing the adamancy of the Palauans. While some committees were "working on complete packages to present to the full Convention rather than approving and recommending individual proposals,"[23] the subjects for consideration before other committees required, or at least permitted, their submission to the Convention in single sections.

On August 4, the 24th day of the Convention, Floor Leader Luke Tman proposed to the Administration Committee that one of the standing committees report out some non-controversial matter as a committee proposal. This would enable the Convention fully to test its rules at least once before going into recess. It would permit determining whether the planned procedure of an initial debate in the Committee of the Whole, followed by Style Committee refinement and final adoption in Plenary Session could work smoothly, or if the procedures would require modification so as to accommodate the volume of work bound to reach the Convention floor once all the committees started reporting out the bulk of the constitutional provisions for Convention deliberation. Notwithstanding the stated rationale, there were other reasons for urging the release of at least one committee proposal. Over a quarter of the Convention's life was now spent with no definitive action yet taken. There was the fear that the Convention was losing momentum and only failure would be its final product. The delegates ought to return home at the recess with the Convention having the adoption of at least one constitutional provision to its credit.

The suggestion of the Floor Leader had the immediate effect of encouraging a number of committees to release short provisions in the form of committee proposals for Convention action, rather than withholding their substance until a total article could be agreed upon and a lengthy proposal submitted. Chairman Carl Heine of the Civil Liberties Committee advised his colleagues on the Administration Committee that a "non-controversial" provision destined for the Bill of Rights was in about complete form, and on August 11,[24] Committee Proposal No. 1 on Freedom of Speech and Press received first reading by the Convention. On August 14, his Committee's Proposal No. 2 also passed First Reading.[25] The other committees were not to be outdone, and before the recess on August 22, six committee proposals were to be delivered to the Convention Secretary by four out of the five subject-matter committees. Only the Finance Committee failed to rise to the challenge.

These six initial committee proposals revealed how "acutely aware, painfully aware"--again to refer to Delegate Hans Wiliander's observation[26]-- the other delegates were of the Palau delegation's demands and their elaboration in Delegate Proposal No. 100. Only one proposal was not on a subject touched upon in the "Palauan Constitution;" the other five either used identical terminology or were consonant with if somewhat broader than its language.[27] Committee Proposal No. 2, as introduced, spelled out the protections encompassed under freedom of petition and to peaceably assemble, but when it came before the Committee of the Whole, Chairman Heine moved its amendment so that it read the same as the parallel portion in the Palauan Bill of Rights.[28] Committee Proposal No. 5 from General Provisions presented the most inescapable evidence of reliance upon "The Palauan Constitution," for the contents faithfully duplicated, word for word, the entire Preamable in Delegate Proposal No. 100.

Unfortunately for the Floor Leader's plans, Committee Proposal No. 1 on Freedom of Expression did not prove to be as non-controversial as Chairman Heine anticipated. No objection was registered to the guarantee in the abstract, but as soon as the proposal was debated in the Committee of the Whole, it immediately brought to the surface the fundamental schism between traditional and introduced rights in Micronesia. A later submission by the Civil Liberties Committee of Proposal No. 4, providing for the preservation of local customs, in no sense satisfied the champions of tradition, and was only to be the preliminary scrimmage of the major fight later to erupt in the Convention.[29] While Committee Proposal No. 2, and then Nos. 1 and 4, were to be passed by the Committee of the Whole and referred to the Style Committee, the latter decided to defer action on all until after the delegates returned from the recess, and there was opportunity for further deliberation.[30] The other committee proposals either were introduced too late, or passed the Committee of the Whole too soon before the recess was scheduled to start, to allow Style Committee consideration. Thus not one proposal had been approved by the Convention in Plenary Session when it recessed on its 42nd day, nor had there even been a full-scale test of the Convention's procedures for adopting the constitution as the delegates left Saipan for their home districts.

Unintentionally, Floor Leader Tman's thwarted effort did have the salutary effect of underscoring the key role to be played by the Committee on Style and Arrangement. Its first report, "a progress report" on Committee Proposals Nos. 1, 2, and 4, put the Convention on notice that it proposed to rewrite provisions so as to "use language which is easy to understand, and equally easy to translate." Subject matter committees were admonished to eschew technical expressions, and in order to avoid any ambiguity which might flow from that course, their accompanying committee reports should make clear the meaning intended by the language used in the proposal.[31] In effect, the Style Committee refused to be stampeded until problems of intent could be resolved, uniform style adopted, and related provisions articulated. It was to hold to these high standards so long as it could, but eventually the late date at which some committee proposals reached the Convention floor, and the delaying of fundamental compromises to the last few days of the Convention, subjected the Style Committee to near-impossible time constraints.

These early meetings of the Style Committee also provided Dr. Isaac Lanwi with an excellent forum to sharpen his fine sense of humor. Dealing as it did with the niceties of language, the Style Committee afforded ready openings. The meaning of "abridge" as contained in the protection of freedom of speech in Committee Proposal No. 1.? Obviously, the connecting of two points. For the significance of "redress of grievances" as used in Committee Proposal No. 2, Delegate Lanwi also had a ready explanation. When the Israelites were under bondage in Egypt, they dressed themselves in sackcloth and ashes, and petitioned the Pharoah that their many onerous burdens be lifted. This once completed, they bathed to remove the ashes, and redressed. Thus the "redress of grievances." The internal life of the Style Committee was always harmonious, so Delegate Lanwi's recourse to humor remained wholly extracurricular; on the Convention floor, however, his sallies were frequently aimed at aiding the delegates to regain a sense of perspective on the occasion when feelings ran high.

Although the prospect was far from bright when the delegates recessed on August 22, all was not lost. Much of the preliminary work by the standing committees had been concluded, and their members were ready to apply themselves to examining definitive specifics of committee proposals then in the course of being drafted. For another thing, not appreciated was the significance of a seemingly innocuous event which had just occurred. Early in the life of the Convention, Chairman Ismael of the Functions Committee had attempted unsuccessfully to obtain directions from the Convention over whether it desired a centralized or decentralized government to be erected.[32] With the Convention sidestepping by shunting his resolutions off, just before the recess he presented a "working paper" for delegate study summarizing to that point of time his committee's internal decisions on the allocation of specific powers between levels of government. Avoided were all abstract labels and potentially inflammatory delineations. And that is how the constitution eventually was to be assembled by committees, each incrementally making its own decisions without instructions from any preliminary draft or Convention declaration charting a substantive course for all committees to follow.

----
1. Transcript of meeting of the Pre-Convention Committee, University of Guam, 1974, p. 12.

2. Secretarial Order No. 2882, Sec. 7. At the convening of the first Congress, it was determined this prohibition did not run to felony convictions in state courts.

3. *Ibid.*

4. The Federated States of Micronesia (hereafter referred to as FSM) Constitution (Art. IX, Sec. 9) also includes state felony convictions, covering the situation referred to in note 2, above.

5. SCRep. No. 36, October 14, 1975, *CCM Journal*, Vol. II, p. 845.

6. Misc. Com. No. 22, October 10, 1975, *CCM Journal*, Vol. II, p. 952.

7. The delegates voicing the preceding protest gave notice that later in the Convention, they would "make a motion to strike from all records of this Convention all reference to U.S. common law" (*idem*, p. 953). See Appendix C.

8. FSM Constitution, Art. XI, Sec. 11.

9. *ESG Notes*, No. 28, August 1, 1975, p. 2.

10. See statement of Senator Petrus Tun before Congress of Micronsia declaring that not everyone in Micronesia favored a decentralized government (Congress of Micronesia, *Senate Journal*, Fifth Congress, Second Reg. Session, 1975, pp. 318-20).

11. R.L. Watts, *New Federations--Experiments in the Commonwealth* (London: Oxford University Press, 1966), p. 9.

12. See Watts, *op. cit.*, pp. 11ff.

13. The constitution of Kiribati permits a restriction on the freedom of movement of people for "environmental conservation" (*The Kiribate Independence Order 1979*, Chap. II, Sec. 14). It is believed that this will also include the protection of social as well as physical environment.

14. K. Santhanam, in Watts, *op. cit.*, p. 192.

15. Summary of ESG Interview with Dr. Hirosi Ismael, *Dialogue for Micronesia*, No. 48,(October 9, 1975), pp. 2-3.

16. *Report of the Political Status Delegation of the Congress of Micronesia*, Third Congress, Third Regular Session, 1970, p. 50.

17. Congress of Micronesia, Senate SCR No. 10, *Senate Journal*, Third Congress, Third Regular Session, 1971, p. 125. The use of an executive council also represented the advice of Professor J.W. Davidson, consultant to the Status Delegation, who brought personal experience with the functioning of parliamentary systems within the Pacific ("Report to the Future Political Status Commission," March 1969, in papers of Professor J.W. Davidson, MS 5105, Box 18, File 28, Australia National Library, Canberra). The "Berkeley constitution" proposed by a group of professors at the University of California at Berkeley to Senator Salii had advocated an executive council or cabinet, with each district to have at least one and not more than two seats (in papers of Professor Davidson).

18. Delegate Hilary Tacheliol, *Dialogue for Micronesia*, No. 52, October 22, 1975.

19. Not that there was total lack of interest in the hustings for incorporating economic constraints of a "radical" nature. Some of the leaders of the outer islands urged the Truk delegation "that a constitution be drafted to fit a socialist type of government which would restrict individuals from owning big businesses or private vessels, etc..." (*Marianas Variety*, March 14, 1975, p. 2). The responses to the Yap delegation questionnaire demonstrated relatively little support for private enterprise to wholly conduct transportation, communication or utilities, and favored governmental control of business (author's analysis). Constitutional modification of a capitalistic system was a subject raised and discussed with several delegations on the staff's pre-Convention swing through the Territory.

20. See John Golding, *The Constitution of Papua New Guinea* (Sydney: The Law Book Company Limited, 1978), pp. 189ff. The one exception is the language in the FSM Constitution, Article IX, Sec. 13, aimed at Congressmen: they are disqualified for three years after the end of their terms from being elected or appointed to offices or employment created by statute during their terms of office nor may sitting Congressmen engage in activities

which conflict with the proper discharge of their duties.

21. See Appendix B.

22. The introduction of committee proposals followed an almost inverse chronology to that of delegate proposals. As to be expected, their presentation was delayed and the mode occurred late. Almost all committee proposals were reported out from committee after the recess, and this continued right through the 13th week of the Convention. See Appendix C.

23. Delegate Dr. Hirosi Ismael, *Dialogue for Micronesia*, No. 38, August 13, 1975.

24. *CCM Journal*, Vol. I, p. 112.

25. *Idem*, p. 121.

26. *Supra*, p. 182.

27. A minority report in Committee Proposal No. 3 would apparently have been in conflict with the Palauan position (SCRep. No. 4 [A], *CCM Journal*, Vol. II, p. 772).

28. *CCM Journal*, Vol. II, p. 636.

29. See Chapter 13, *infra*.

30. The members of the Style Committee were also aware that enough controversy over the subject matter of the proposals had been engendered as to question the possibility of obtaining the three-fourths' vote requisite on Second Reading, should it have returned the resolutions to the Plenary Session.

31. SCRep. No. 8, *CCM Journal*, Vol. II, p. 775.

32. See *supra*, p. 177.

PART IV. ENTR'ACTE

The tension is suspended as the curtain falls on Act I, and the delegates disperse to their home districts. The plot has now taken shape, the principal characters have been identified, and as in all plays, some form of resolution is awaited in the concluding Act to follow. But unlike other plays, the intermission is to become an integral part of the action.

Chapter 10. Crises at the Recess

At the very last moment, the Congress of Micronesia in Special Session had permitted the Convention to extend its life by recessing, and had allotted it the extra money necessary for the splitting of its deliberations. Given the uncertainties surrounding the holding of a Convention in the Marianas, and, indeed the continued availability of the very premises in which the Convention planned to meet, the Congress had also included authorization in the enabling legislation to transfer the Convention to another island. As a safeguard against hasty action, two-thirds of the delegates would have to concur in such a move. When to start the recess caused little problem, how long to recess even less, but where to reconvene sharply divided the Convention. Thereafter, the events which transpired during the recess interim were materially to influence the shape of the constitution, and the possibility of its adoption at popular referendum in the indefinite future.

A conspiracy of silence with respect to the recess enveloped the Convention. No one publicly commented, let alone complained, that the calling of a recess was solely for the convenience of the Palau delegation. The public press carried no reference to the overriding desire of the Palau members to return home to participate in the campaign for their district legislature. With the elections scheduled for September 2, the only matter to be resolved was the day in August on which to commence the recess. Perhaps all this merely represented the willingness of politicians the world round to oblige their colleagues, once all engage in joint undertaking. Or perhaps confrontation with the Palauan seven "non-negotiable" demands had so unnerved the other delegations that they all welcomed an opportunity to leave Saipan and renew their resolve by consulting with their constituents back home.

Toward the end of July, the subject of calling a recess was brought up at a meeting of the Administration Committee. Each of the vice-presidents, having previously ascertained the views of his delegation, replied affirmatively, although it was also indicated that the Marianas and Yap districts held no strong views either pro or con. Delegate Ngiraked from Palau then proposed a recess beginning August 15, and extending for twenty days. Apprehension was voiced over whether the delegates would have anything "substantial to take back to the people," and the date of the recess was delayed a week to August 22. The recess would extend through September 14, twenty-three days in all. After an unsuccessful attempt by the Palauans in the Committee of the Whole to defer this decision, they concurred with the other delegates in unanimously adopting the recess resolution, but their desire to return home earlier had not been laid. A week after the vote, the question of paying delegates absent from the Convention was considered by the Administration Committee. Its decision left no doubt that any delegate leaving Saipan before the recess to campaign in Palau would do so to his own economic disadvantage.

The recess resolution, as introduced, called for the delegates to return to their districts "for the purposes of consulting with their constituents regarding proposals introduced in the Convention, as well as submitting their views of the Convention."[1] It also "urged" the delegates to return "within eight days prior to the reconvening date." Presumably this earlier return would facilitate the drafting of additional proposals as well as permit the delegates to attend pre-convening committee meetings. The delegates responded unfavorably to this implied limitation on their freedom of movement, and the Convention deleted it.[2] Notwithstanding, the Chairman of the Finance Committee later bravely informed the Administration Committee that a sub-committee of his would remain on Saipan during the recess to carry on the work of the full committee. They never did formally meet. Further illustration of how unrealistic was the hope that delegates would arrive back from the recess early, primed for work, was the failure of the Convention to muster a quorum on the date it was scheduled to reconvene, even though the meeting hour continued to be postponed until after nine o'clock in the evening. There was no alternative other than to delay reopening proceedings until the following day.

The recess resolution adopted on August 1 deliberately left the place of reconvening to separate Convention action. It was assumed the expense of moving the Convention staff and its supplies and equipment off Saipan would be so prohibitively high that only an emergency could warrant its consideration. Much to the surprise of everyone, and the consternation of many, the head of the Administrative Section reported that savings from $44,000 to $61,000 could be realized, most from the cancellation of the Saipan hotel rental agreement. The expense factor removed as a deterrent, the educational benefit to be gained from writing the constitution close to the people who would be governed under it, together with the rhetoric of doing so on "Micronesian soil," carried the day in the Administration Committee. Delegate Ngiraked withdrew Palau as a possible site, cautioning that feelings would be running high there due to the legislative elections. Besides, there was the competing need of the district legislature for the meeting halls and offices which the Convention would have to occupy. Ponape thus became the choice of the Committee's majority.

When the matter of relocating the Convention site reached the Convention floor, it met hostile objection, and fully two-thirds of the delegates voted to defeat the resolution. An alternative, specifically directing the Convention to reconvene on Saipan, at the White Sands Hotel, then easily passed. Rather than concluding the matter, it only added further complications. The very tenuous tenure of the Convention in its quarters made it imperative that the Convention's officers be impowered to move the site during the recess, "should it prove necessary," whether on or off Saipan, and this had now been foreclosed by the substitute resolution. The delegates remained suspicious of any attempt to reopen the issue. Only with great difficulty was a "fail-safe" resolution finally adopted.

The public press reacted negatively to the scheduling of a recess. The <u>Guam Pacific Daily News</u> headlined its story "Recess Decision ConCon Biggest Step in Three Weeks."[3] The delegates were sensitive to the snide asides that they were all to enjoy a paid vacation. Response on the floor of the Convention stressed the virtues of cautious consideration of proposals, as well as the right of constituents to be consulted on many crucial issues posed. Nevertheless, the delegates were troubled, for they knew the timing of the recess was ill-advised, and that when they went home they could not report any definitive action on the new constitution. Rationalize as they might, they could not justify it as anything but an accommodation by the Convention of the political needs of the Palau delegation. Little did they realize that when they reconvened, political events in Palau were to add a distinctive torque to the actions of the Palau delegation within the Convention.

For their part, the Palauan delegates must have been particularly conscious of the unspoken animus of the Convention as the date of the recess drew near. All during the first part of the Convention they had emphasized the adamancy of their position. When they described their proposal as a compromise, a "50-50 compromise between Palau and the rest of Micronesia,"[4] it was to be lampooned as "50% for them and 50% for the rest of Micronesia!"[5] The inability of the Convention to adopt even the "non-controversial" proposals of the Civil Liberties Committee only added to the tension. On Friday, August 22, the last day the delegates would meet for the next three weeks, Delegate Salii's wrath boiled over.

"In forty days we have accomplished a great deal of nothing," he exploded in cold fury. Delegates and delegations came in for his censure. The rules of the Convention and members of its staff particularly were targets of his scathing criticism. The only way to avoid failure was to abolish all the standing committees, create a single drafting committee, and utilize the "Palauan Constitution" as the vehicle around which to prepare a full constitution. In addition, staff should be purged. Draconian efforts were required, and the recess afforded the opportunity. "Unless these steps are taken, Mr. President, you and the rest of us might as well forget it."[6] The "it" in his concluding sentence undoubtedly referred to the chances of writing a constitution for Micronesia. Given the failure of Senator Salii to either seek or occupy a major leadership post in the Convention, completely atypical behavior for him as viewed by his tenure in the Congress of Micronesia, it was confidently thought by some delegates that this was his swan song. Next would come his resignation, and when the delegates reconvened, he would not be among them.

At the ensuing meeting of the Administration Committee, the Convention Secretary tendered his verbal resignation, which was declined. I offered mine, if the Administration Committee was dissatisfied with the consultation provided them or my direction over the Convention's research and drafting. Vice-President Ngiraked, head of the Palauan delegation, disassociated the remarks of Senator Salii from the delegation's position. The Senator's observations on the Convention personnel were his personal opinion, "uncalled for,"[7] and not to be used as a basis for any staff resignation. The Administration Committee then proceeded to ignore the Salii speech, and the Convention rules remained unchanged. When the delegates returned, it would be to a Convention structured as they left it, and with the constitution still to be fitted together as the product of their joint efforts. For the record, when interviewed, the leaders of the Convention expressed satisfaction with the way its work was proceeding. Considerable groundwork had been completed, and they professed not to be particularly disturbed that there was yet little to show for all of the effort. Privately, though, they were worried, for there was no gainsaying the Convention was behind in its work. Senator Salii's objections could carry the portent of the Convention's downfall.

How valid were the charges? The delegation of sifting and drafting chores to subject-matter committees was not an innovation, nor novel to Micronesia. About two-thirds of the delegates were intimately familiar with the procedures of legislative bodies, and well understood the function of their standing committees. Long before the delegates had been elected, the ESG Task Force in its broadcasts had been anticipating their use. "Once the Committees have completed their work, they will all come together again and begin the all-important task of putting their work together into one document which will then become the draft constitution."[8] However, there was substance to the protest that it was impossible to obtain a complete picture of the evolving constitution from the piecemeal work ongoing in committee. The individual parts of the mosaic were being cut and polished without the total design having yet taken discernable shape. But the other districts fully appreciated that the continued use of standing committees provided them with an effective buffer against the Palauan thrust until it could be contained in the eclectic constitution abuilding.

Several other delegates had also voiced dissatisfaction with the slow speed at which the Convention was proceeding. To Delegate Tipne Philippo of the Marshalls "it appeared as if the <u>Standing Committees</u> are really <u>sitting committees</u> ... sitting on delegate proposals" assigned to them for consideration.[9] According to Delegate Jose R. Cruz of the Northern Marianas, the Convention's procedures were too complex, and instead, the "Micronesian way of having open discussion unrestrained by rules" ought be employed.[10] These objections apparently sought to bring all matters to the Convention floor for informal discussion until a consensus evolved. In reality, Senator Salii's complaint that there was just talk, without decision, ran diametrically counter to any such adoption of Micronesian consensus debate. While the procedural rules of the Convention were but variants of the legislative procedures with which most of the delegates were familiar, they had been materially bent to reflect Micronesian custom through embodiment in the Committee of the Whole of a delegate's unlimited opportunity to debate and the prohibition against use of the "previous question" motion. However, if at any time the Convention desired to move with dispatch, it could telescope the entire Committee of the Whole step, debate any proposal under a limited time rule, and the Convention was then free to push immediately on to decision. Unquestionably there was disgruntlement among the delegates, but the Convention format and its rules of procedure were being made the scapegoat. Issues of the most fundamental character were before the Convention, and their resolution would consume the total life span of the Convention no matter what its structure or how it went about its business. So, at least, ran the rationale justifying the Administration Committee's failure to respond publicly to the criticisms raised.

There was no lack of work for the Research and Drafting Section during the brief recess period. Digests were prepared of all delegate proposals and, as well, a subject-matter index published so delegates and staff alike could find their way through the pile of paper amassing. Staff assigned to committees completed the background research remaining unfinished and prepared memoranda on items not yet resolved within their committees. Final drafts of committee proposals, and committee reports to accompany committee decisions already tentatively made, were readied in anticipation of the delegates reconvening in September. Areas of committee overlap were identified--and whether duplicating, congruent or conflicting--in the attempt to head off the potential of dysfunctional competition between committees. And probably most important of all, opportunity was afforded to begin a mockup of the constitution taking shape and to identify the regions of constitutional turf to which greater attention would have to be turned if the government which the constitution apparently proposed to establish were to be viable.

Simultaneously the rest of the Convention staff was also putting the recess to very good use. The Administration Section took advantage of the respite to catch up on backlogged accounting and to prepare a revised budget, its approval awaiting the return of the Administration Committee to Saipan. The Public Information staff turned its attention to the preparation of releases on the major issues before the Convention. While I and everyone else was thus busily engaged during the recess interim, down deep inside me there remained a gnawing, disturbing uncertainty over the Convention's future, triggered by the parting blast of Delegate Salii. Would the Convention collapse in its own efforts?

The September legislative elections in Palau caused havoc to the control long exercised by the Liberal Party. In place of a majority, it now held about twelve seats in the District Legislature. The Progressive Party increased its membership in the Legislature to at least eight, and, alleging support by the six nominal independents, claimed victory at the polls. Among the legislators-elect were Constitutional Convention Delegates Nakamura, Ngiraked, and Sawaichi, all Progressive Party members. Delegate Johnson Toribiong, aligned with the Liberal Party, also was successful. As the two chiefs in the Palau Constitutional delegation served ex-officio as members of the District assembly, three-fourths of the Palau delegation to the Constitutional Convention were slated to take office at the new Legislature's first sitting.

Reportedly on the evening of September 14, the day on which the delegates were slated to reconvene on Saipan, leaders of the victorious Progressive Party met in Palau, intent on capitalizing upon the momentum of their election success. The following day, dispatches signed by the "Palau Delegation to Micro Congress" arrived on Saipan, purporting to remove Senator Salii as a delegate to the Convention and to replace him by Congressman Kuniwo Nakamura, brother of Delegate Tosiwo Nakamura.[11] Later, correspondence and telephone messages were to confirm that three members of the Palau delegation in the Congress of Micronesia, constituting a majority, had indeed sent the message. As the constitutional enabling legislation expressly declared that "no appointment as a delegate to the convention may be revoked by the appointing authority,"[12] the legal basis of the Palau Congressional delegation's action was very dubious.[13] Its rationale was reputedly Senator Salii's having demeaned the importance of his representation of Palau in the Congress because he had filed and than withdrawn as a candidate for a seat in the District Legislature; his being a disruptive force in the Micronesian Constitutional Convention; the Senator's action in the Convention abasing the Palauan delegation there; and for good measure, a miscellany of minor matters.

The timing of the attempt to remove Senator Salii as Congressional delegate to the Convention lent credence to the suspicions that the show of Progressive Party strength was designed to politically embarrass him in his 1976 campaign for reelection as Senator. He had just gone to Japan to receive delivery of a fishing boat under a grant from the Trust Territory Development Fund, so would not be present in the Territory to answer the charges personally. President Nakayama's response to Palau, that the purported removal was ineffective, negated any need for such action by the Senator on his own behalf. Rumor has it that at a meeting of his Palauan backers on Saipan, it was decided that the Senator should be encouraged to remain in the Convention and take a more active role, supportive of the constitutional effort. Whether or not the meeting did occur, the tenor of the delegate's remarks during the second part of the Convention were to be in sharp contrast to his perfomance during its initial weeks. The logic of his arguments on the floor of the Convention and his ability in parliamentary maneuver were frequently to aid in the adoption of conten-

tious proposals. Although he continued to stand
firm with his district's delegation in its championing of the "Palau Constitution," he no longer
seemed to be patterning himself on the biblical
Samson, bent on bringing down the Constitutional
Convention around his head. One of the Convention's crises had been met and passed.

Unnoticed in this flurry of Palauan politics
was another aspect of the Progressive Party's win,
and its relation to the Convention. Without publicity, a shift in patronage occurred within the
delegation during the recess. Upon reconvening,
the interpreter of the Ibedul was replaced by Delegate Ngiraked's wife. A comparable move to remove
Senator Salii's sister from her staff post with
the Palau delegation was attempted, but proved
not as successful, and eventually was abandoned.

The Palauan-induced recess was not yet laid.
Those successful in their quest for seats in the
Palau District Legislature were to plead the necessity for the entire Palau delegation[14] to be excused
from the Convention on October 8 to return home.
They asserted it was essential that they attend
the organizational meeting of the new district
assembly. The familiar spector of the Palauans'
absence causing the lack of a quorum, and bringing
the Convention's business to a halt, again took
shape. President Nakayama's request to the Acting
High Commissioner for his intercession by postponing
the meeting of the Palau Legislature neatly truncated this threat, which could have seen the Convention
running out of time before it had written a constitution.

The tempest in Palau, at the westernmost periphery of the Trust Territory, was geographically
balanced during the recess by another crisis of
different character arising in the district at
Micronesia's eastern border. After the long period
of boycott, and denouncement of the Marshalls delegation to the Convention as not properly organized,
through an unusual combination of events two Iroij
came forward to be seated as representatives of
the traditional leaders of the Marshalls. What
to do?

Just prior to the recess of the Convention,
the traditional leaders from Ponape introduced
a resolution, inviting the participation of the
Marshallese chiefs.[15] After Delegate Carl Heine

returned to the Marshalls, he referred over the district radio to the contents of the resolution. He also broadcast the statement of Delegate John Heine, who had appealed at the Convention, "The chiefs of Ponape are asking their brother chiefs from the Marshalls to join them at this Convention. They want the Marshalls chiefs to join ... [naming the seated chiefs] so that together they can protect and defend our Micronesian traditions at this Convention."[16] In response, two younger Marshallese chiefs, Iroij Litokwa Tomeing and Iroij Jeltan Lanki, volunteered themselves to attend the Convention. Since they had not been nominated as traditional leaders, for no meeting of the Iroij had ever been called for that purpose, according them the status of delegates would be highly questionable, and in very close votes on the Convention floor, might later open its actions to judicial challenge.

From the Marshalls, Delegate Carl Heine sent a dispatch to the Convention advising that the two Iroij were coming to attend "as full fledged participating members." Somehow, during the course of the transmission, another portion of the message, which requested the withholding of a news release pending their formal seating, was deleted. The ensuing publicity engendered a veritable storm in the Marshalls. Some of the Marshallese delegation to the Convention objected to Delegate Carl Heine's action, alleging that it was taken without consultation.[17] The faction in the Marshalls opposing the Convention was outraged that two minor chiefs "were unilaterally selected by Carl Heine without any notice to a single Marshallese paramount chief or to [the] Nitijela." Seven Iroij Laplap signed the cable of protest. Not to be outdone, a letter supporting the appointment of Litokwa and Jeltan as delegates was sent to President Nakayama, signed by nine Iroij and Leiroj, and included among the signatories was the name of one who was listed as having signed the cable of protest.[18] It was evident to all in the Trust Territory that open division existed among the chiefs in the Marshalls. On the other hand, there was now the threat that once drafted, rejection of the Micronesian constitution in the Marshalls would automatically follow: "If Con Con continues to approve seating of Marshallese illegally or irregularly selected..., all chances of district approval of final con con documents will be irreparably damaged."[19]

For obvious reasons, the views of the Iroij somehow had to be included in the deliberations of the Convention, but these particular volunteers not seated as official delegates. The adoption of Resolution No. 28 upon the reconvening of the Convention provided the vehicle for resolving the dilemma. It recited that the two had expressed "their willingness to come to Saipan and give of their counsel in aid of the drafting of the Micronesian constitution," and then invited them to take part as "participant observers, so that the delegates of the Convention can have the benefit of the views of these traditional leaders of the Marshall Islands...."[20] They were formally welcomed, and given desks on the floor of the Convention and committee assignments. Each was free to speak in debate, and both were prominently present in the meetings of the traditional leaders which significantly influenced the final language included in the constitution. Each day on convening, the names of the two Iroij were included at the end of the roll call, but at no time was their presence counted to satisfy the requirements either of quorum or minimum vote in any formal Convention decision. What effect their presence in the Convention would have on opinion in the Marshalls, when at some future day the constitution would be presented to the district for ratification, could only be conjectured. Meanwhile, this crisis had been passed, at least for the life of the Convention.

When the delegates returned home during the recess, many learned that misinformation about the Convention within their districts had assumed near critical proportions. Those constituents who had knowledge about the Convention at all had heard only of its more sensational aspects, and believed it near collapse. They lacked information about the Convention's more routinized, normal activities, upon which the constitution was being built.

Part of this skewing stemmed from a misunderstanding over the function of the Convention's Public Information Section. It gave primary emphasis in daily coverage to Plenary Sessions, slightly less attention to Committee-of-the-Whole proceedings, and only selective coverage of individual committees. Much as the mass media in searching for newsworthy items provide fuller coverage of the controversial and the exceptional, so had the releases from the Section tended to give prominence to the Palauan demands and the other confrontational aspects of the Convention. The bulk of work underway, which was occurring in committees, as diffuse, preliminary, and hypothetical was deemphasized. Each afternoon when the Convention met, the information officer would prepare a short highlight of the day, and this would be duplicated, distributed to the Micronesian News Service (MNS) of the Trust Territory Administration and the private press representatives, and broadcast on Saipan. The MNS would in turn send the release to all districts, but whether it would then be broadcast, either in English or the vernacular, would be at the discretion of the District Administrator and his staff.

The Education for Self-Government Task Force (ESG) also disseminated news releases prepared in greater depth, and taped interviews with delegates on constitutional issues for broadcast on the district radio stations. Once the Convention was organized, it heavily concentrated its printed materials and oral interviews on the Convention. It, too, was at the mercy of the programming decisions made by the district personnel, and the delegates returning home reported ESG materials badly backlogged, so that when distributed or broadcast, frequently they were out-of-date.[21]

When the Convention officers became aware that complete information on the Convention was not being disseminated in the district centers, they sought the assistance of the Trust Territory Administration to rectify this inadequacy. Arrangements were made to bring a number of reporters from the district radio stations to Saipan to prepare English language and vernacular programs to be relayed daily via telephone for direct broadcast to their home areas. The Deputy High Commissioner "requested" each District Administrator to "personally ensure that all news items and other information related to Con Con be aired as soon as received...."[22] During the concluding portion of the Convention, for the first time it became possible for Micronesians within range of the district broadcasts to obtain reasonably complete accounts of each day's events on Saipan. In order of priority, newsworthiness was subordinated to voter education.

The recess afforded me a respite from my near dawn to late dark contact with delegates, which had allowed little opportunity to assay committee progress. In the area of civil liberties, members in the committee of the same name had about reached formal agreement on the nature of the protective rights to be placed in the constitution, and only the newer, "affirmative" rights were yet to be discussed. The Functions Committee had well in hand the identification of duties and responsibilities of government and their allocation to levels of governmental structure. Although it might take several weeks more after reconvening before the Committee presented its final draft to the Convention, there was little danger in this area. The Structure Committee's lack of progress gave cause for alarm. Its work had been proceeding through subcommittees, with inadequate attention to correlation of their probable recommendations. The subcommittees, in turn, had devoted much of their time to minor detail, and had ignored the basics which would serve as the supporting foundation for their recommendations. A highly specific judiciary article, much along the lines of the Trust Territory's existing court system, was still before subcommittee in tentative form. Two drafts, one of a unicameral and the other of a bicameral Congress, were being submitted to the full Structure Committee from its legislative subcommittee. The executive subcommittee was only at the preliminary stages of considering a plural executive. Most important of all, the role of traditional leaders in government remained completely unresolved.

A review of the work of the Finance Committee revealed as little progress. Except for import duties which were to be imposed by the central government, little concurrence had been reached by the members of the Committee over matters of taxation. A direction for central budgeting had received tentative agreement, and there was committee accord on placing a public auditor in the central government. Beyond this, a great deal of groundwork remained before committee proposals could even be formulated.

The General Provisions Committee, which was responsible for a hodgepodge of matters, had considered a wide variety of subjects and had reached preliminary agreement on most. In addition, its members were being systematically supplied with full information on the problems of transition and post-Convention requirements. Drafts of provisions on amendments, national territory, admission of new states, and comparable other subjects within its scope were being circulated among committee members during the recess. Unless an unforeseen disagreement erupted, like the Functions Committee, it could be expected that the General Provisions Committee would meet its commitments to the Convention within several weeks of the latter's reconvening.

Although I did not find the total picture particularly encouraging, it was not sufficiently bleak as to register yet another crisis. It would be incumbent upon the Convention officers to exert stronger leadership, and particularly to prod the lagging committees, and so I informed them. This non-traditional role was apparently distasteful and instead, the Administration Committee eventually set collective deadlines.

There was no assurance that agreement would be reached over the Palauan "non-negotiable" demands either within committee or on the Convention floor, and there was always the prospect of their becoming nonretractable road blocks, causing further drafting of the constitution to come to a halt. But most of what was being discussed in committee, and could be anticipated as next coming before the Convention in the form of Committee Proposals, was outside the scope of the demands, so decision on these Proposals did not need to be delayed. Of course, if the Palauans were to insist upon the adoption of every detail in their "Palauan Constitution," this would cast an entirely different light upon the future of the Convention. It could then well prove impossible to bridge the gap between the Palauan position and that of delegates from the other districts. The language of the constitutional provisions brought before the Committee of the Whole during the first part of the Convention had been identical with or had embraced that proposed by the Palauan delegation, and so had presented no obstacle. Having to accept an entire "Palauan Constitution" would prove to be a much more difficult hurdle.

A very provisional outline of what might be anticipated as destined for inclusion in a Micronesian constitution, as disclosed by the state of committee discussions to the time of recess, was next prepared. Its import was not so much in the substance of its contents as in its demonstration that considerable work was near completion and still more was actively ongoing, this despite the absence of publicity either within or outside the Convention halls. Its purpose was to provide a psychological prop to support the resolve of the Convention's top leaders. They were advised that it was not impossible, improbable as it might then seem, for the Convention yet to succeed in preparing its own constitution through the cooperative participation of all the delegates. Once the latter accepted the reality that there was no longer time for the shirking of the routine or avoidance of the fundamental, nor could the task be assigned to anyone else, all of the necessary elements were now in place for assembling a constitution based upon a Micronesian consensus.

The long dependence of Micronesians upon the American Administration as a father-figure, serving conveniently both as object of complaint but also always available to furnish succor in times of difficulty, was drawing to an end. Fred M. Zeder, Director of Territorial Affairs in the Department of Interior, had written to President Nakayama during the Convention recess, "We in Washington ... have not taken any part in the [Convention] proceedings, feeling rather that the work you are doing toward the formation of a future Micronesian government is a matter for the people and leaders of Micronesia themselves."[23] The second part of the Convention would determine whether or not the elected representatives and selected traditional leaders of the people of Micronesia, assembled for the purpose, would be able to evolve such a constituent document.

----

1. Resolution No. 9, CCM Journal, Vol. II, p. 989.

2. CCM Journal, Vol. II, p. 606.

3. Guam Pacific Daily News, August 3, 1975, p. 3.

4. Delegate Santos Olikong, CCM Journal, Vol. I, p. 124.

5. Delegate Samuel Falanruw, CCM Journal, Vol. I, p. 167.

6. Delegate Lazarus Salii, *CCM Journal*, Vol. I, pp. 173-74. A more extensive quotation from this statement is carried in the Prologue.

7. *Marianas Variety*, August 29, 1975, p. 12.

8. *ESG* radio script number 8, June 3, 1974.

9. Delegate Tipne Philippo, *CCM Journal*, Vol. I, p. 131.

10. Delegate Jose R. Cruz, *CCM Journal*, Vol. I, p. 150.

11. At the same time a dispatch was sent to Tosiwo Nakayama as President of the Senate purporting to remove Senator Salii from the Joint Committee on Future Status and to replace him by Congressman Polycarp Basilius as one of the members representing the Palau District.

12. P.L. 5-60, Sec. 4(5), as amended. Later the constitutionality of the restriction in the enabling legislation was to be questioned, but never legally challenged. The threat was made that an opinion from the Trust Territory Attorney General would be sought. At the time, brothers of both Senator Salii and Representative Nakamura were serving on the Attorney General's staff, so that it could be anticipated full deliberation would precede the issuance of any opinion, and its appearance would not be until late in the life of the Convention, if by then.

13. Doubtful, also, was the attempted removal of Senator Salii from the Joint Committee on Future Status, as its members and their replacements were appointed by the presiding officers of the two houses of the Congress of Micronesia (HJR No. 102, S.D. 1, Third Congress, 3rd Session, First Resolve Clause).

14. All members of the Palauan delegation were in one way or another personally involved with the internal organizing of the new Legislature and its choice of officers. Summary Record Administration Committee, October 6, 1975.

15. As amended, Resolution No. 20 was expanded to ask that the traditional leadership of the Marianas also be represented, referring to represen-

tation of the district's minority Carolinian population (CCM Journal, Vol. II, p. 993).

16. CCM Journal, Vol. I, p. 156.

17. Micronesian Independent 6:33 (September 19, 1975), p. 1.

18. An Iroij claimed his signature was affixed to the original cable without his consent (ibid.).

19. Constitutional Convention of Micronesia filed records.

20. Resolution No. 28, CCM Journal, Vol. II, p. 1002.

21. The ESG printed materials were also sent to Micronesian students outside of the Trust Territory, in the effort to reach as wide an audience as possible.

22. CCM Journal, Vol. II, p. 944.

23. CCM Journal, Vol. II, p. 949.

PART V. ACT II

The players take their positions on stage, cued to resume where they left off. Carefully skirting obstacles already raised, and fully aware of the growing bitterness of the gulf in their midst between tradition and modernity, they direct their steps and weave their collective dialogue into a slowly emerging, holistic pattern for governance. But the pace is slow, and the fall of the curtain certain, so that their effort may be for naught, and the name of the play be tragedy. Or is there a Micronesian style of leadership which transcends all and can bring the Convention to successful conclusion?

Chapter 11.
The Shape of the Government to Come

On September 15, with only thirty-six delegates responding to the roll call, the absence of a quorum[1] forced formal resumption of the Convention after the recess to be postponed until the following day. When they did get down to business, the delegates now had the distinction of planning for self-government in the world's last trust territory, for Australia and the United Nations had just terminated their trusteeship agreement for New Guinea, and a combined Papua New Guinea had become a fully independent nation. Whether the Micronesian delegates would also opt for a comparable status was as yet undetermined.

Prior to the workshop on Saipan preceding the Convention, when briefing the staff members of the R & D Section, I had opined that a constitution for Micronesia could be drafted with a "status hinge," a constituent document sufficiently flexible to accommodate independence, free association, or most any other relationship with a sovereign nation which might later be contracted. The almost universal response counseled avoidance of any mention of such possibility: the Congress of Micronesia and many Micronesian leaders outside its membership were desperately looking to the Convention to resolve the issue of future status and point the way for concluding the stalled status negotiations. If offered such an easy way of equivocating, the delegates would eagerly seize upon it and fail to provide the definitive direction sought. Responding, during the workshop I deliberately avoided any mention of incorporating a "hinge," and, instead, employed the analogy of clay on the potter's wheel, and a decision on future status emerging out of the sum total of the Convention's incremental decisions.[2]

As of the time of the recess, the Committee on General Provisions had detected no clear consensus in the testimony it had heard on the desired political future of Micronesia. Some witnesses individually supported associated state status, others complete independence, and in at least one case, a delegate testified that his delegation had declared no district position. The returns from the Territory-wide plebiscite on status ordered by the Congress of Micronesia had provided little assistance. Early in August, Chairman Tun of the Committee in a radio interview reported that "it is hard to tell if we are going towards independence of free association at this time."[3] However, by the recess the Committee was considering a draft proposal on the subject, and less than two weeks after the delegates reconvened, reported it out as Committee Proposal No. 11, supported by an explanatory Committee report.[4]

In the phraseology adopted by the Committee, C.P. No. 11 stated the supremacy of the constitution and recognized the sovereign and independent state of Micronesia. As the supreme law of Micronesia, all treaties (including any status compact with the United States) would need be in compliance with its terms, and specifically identified were inalienable rights of the Micronesian people which could not be delegated or "prejudiced." The text of the accompanying committee report ran into objection from Delegate Cabrera in the Plenary Session due to its inclusion of his district as an example of subordination, but after the offending language was removed, the report was accepted and C.P. No. 11 passed its pro forma First Reading.[5] Surprisingly, the Proposal next cleared the Committee of the Whole without discussion,[6] and only when up for adoption on definitive Second Reading in the form polished by the Style Committee did the delegates fully appreciate the magnitude of the decision they were being called upon to make. Repeatedly they deferred action. The Convention then materially trimmed the contents of the Proposal upon the premise that the excised material would be covered by that in other proposals already reported out or soon to be before the Convention. In effect, the tilt of the language toward independence was deleted. With only one section remaining, and that declaring the supremacy of the constitution, the delegates still hesitated.

Delegate Olter, who as a Senator also served on the Status Commission, pointed up the issue:

> ...If we are going to declare this place a country, we are going to also have a Constitution as the supreme guideline

> to be abided by every citizen, every policy
> and every move we make in the country.
> The United States cannot pray to its own
> Constitution as the supreme law of its
> land and country and turn around and tell
> us that our Constitution is going to be
> secondary to a Compact....I think that
> if we are going to draft a Constitution,
> that [it] is going to be supreme. Whatever
> comes must be subservient.... Since there
> is no Constitution at present, in our
> negotiation with the U.S. we are sort
> of flapping left and right, not knowing
> whether to accept the Compact or the Con-
> stitution when there is no Constitu-
> tion....[7]

With the ayes and noes called, the Convention Hall grew tensely silent as two delegates voted in the negative, and gradually were joined by nine others who abstained. This opposition was disbursed across the delegations and scattered throughout the roll call. The thirty-seven affirmatives garnered were barely sufficient to provide the three-fourths' vote necessary to adopt the Proposal.[8]

Later, on November 1, in a PEACESAT broadcast with Micronesian students in Hawaii, Delegate Ismael stated that the supremacy clause added to the constitution (as its Article II) would provide as much self-government as possible, but did not rule out a free associated state relationship with the United States. Delegate Wiliander, long considered one of the spokesmen for Micronesian independence, concurred: "Should there be a compact..., it must be in conformity with the Constitution."

Early in its deliberations, the Functions Committee had determined that "ratification of treaties involving a delegation of basic functions of government, such as foreign affairs or national defense, (political status related treaties) shall be by approval of two-thirds of district legislatures."[9] Under its sponsorship, in modified form this became part of the constitution (Art. IX, Sec. 4). As the net result of the combined Convention actions, the delegates in effect had written a "status hinge" into the constitution, defusing the explosive subject of future status, and successfully sidetracking it from distracting the attention of the delegates from the many other issues facing them. Meanwhile, as the constitution continued to take shape, areas of potential conflict between constitution and compact gradually became apparent, but the delegates, having decided on adopting the supremacy clause, appeared bent on almost deliberately pushing these potentialities from their ken of attention. Events long after the Convention were to reveal how harsh the clash was to become between American and Micronesian negotiators over the scope of the Supremacy Article, and the significance of the treaty provision in enabling the reconciling of status compact and constitution.

It was Dr. Ismael, Chairman of the Governmental Functions Committee, who had offered the floor amendments trimming the language of the supremacy proposal. Indeed, during the course of the debate in the Plenary Session, a motion was made for the Proposal to be referred to his committee for further action, rather than back to General Provisions, but later was withdrawn as the delegates moved to definitive vote. All of this reflected both the jurisdictional overlap of the Functions Committee with the other subject-matter committees--for all were concerned with the permissable or prohibited actions of government--and also to a degree the leadership style of Delegate Ismael. Governmental Functions and Civil Liberties Committees held separate hearings on the power of eminent domain, and the dispute which simmered in the Convention for many weeks over the granting of this power could be traced in part to the difference of views developed within the two committees. Governmental Functions met with and attempted to work out a compromise with the Public Finance and Taxation Committee on fiscal provisions over which they contended on the floor of the Convention. But probably the provisions on courts and the judiciary system which were finally incorporated into the constitution illustrate the most pronounced and prolonged disagreement involving the Governmental Functions Committee and another committee protagonist.

At the July 24 meeting of the Administration Committee, Delegate Ismael had raised a question over the appropriate committee to which judicial proposals should be referred, and succeeded in having them jointly assigned to the Governmental Functions and Structure Committees. Later he indicated that while his committee recognized that Structure might propose some combination of the executive and legislature, the Functions Committee contemplated a separate and independent judiciary.[10] Meanwhile, Structure's Judiciary Subcommittee under the aegis of its chairman, Judge Soukichi Fritz, developed a proposal for a unitary Micronesian court system, premised upon common law, and modeled on that currently existing in the Trust Territory. Following the advice received from High Court Associate Judge Robert Hefner, the tentative judiciary article was drafted in relatively great detail so as to assure the independence of the judiciary. That Micronesia might be constituted as a federalism was held not to preclude the erecting of a unitary judicial system.[11] Executive appointment of judges, subject to legislative consent, was proposed, along with fixed terms of office so as to assure opportunity for periodic review of judicial performance. Part of the explanation for a single court system was the intent to assure that state and local courts would be adequately funded.[12]

Two weeks later, the Governmental Functions Committee reported out its Committee Proposal containing a complete Judiciary Article whose sections not only failed to coincide in many details with those of the Governmental Structure Committee's proposal, but in at least one respect, fundamentally clashed.[13] Functions proposed that the constitution provide for only a national system of courts, to be paralleled by separate court structures erected by the states, and with jurisdiction divided and the systems articulated, much as found in the United States.

Meetings between the two committees resulted in the reaching of a compromise in which Governmental Structure had the face-saving recognition of its Committee Proposal being retained as the vehicle for establishing the judiciary, but the contents were gutted so as to incorporate the Functions Committee's dual court system, and a number of minor matters such as life tenure for justices.[14] Following the model of the United States, the Supreme Court has original and exclusive jurisdiction in a limited number of cases--as disputes between states, and the Court will also share concurrent jurisdiction over a wider range of designated matters with inferior national courts, when they are established by statute. The state courts tend to the balance of litigation. The ultimate judicial interpretation of the constitution, federal laws, and treaties lies with the Supreme Court, whether a case arises in the national or state court systems, but the Court may exercise its discretion over whether it will undertake such review. Harkening back to the Structure Committee's favoring of a unitary court system, appeals from a state court on non-federal matters may also be entertained by the Supreme Court if the state constitution permits. And Structure's concern for adequate funding of the judicial function, particularly in the maintaining of local courts in the outlying islands, was met by incorporating a constitutional mandate that the national government contribute to the financial support of state judicial systems and by a constitutional authorization for furnishing other forms of assistance.

Probably best illustrative of how the give and take which takes place in a convention--as the delegates go about compromising their differences--closely corresponds with what occurs in the average legislature, the Structure Committee had favored a Supreme Court with at least four justices, including the Chief Justice, so that the Court could have both trial and appellate divisions, with three justices sitting to review matters without the trial justice being included in their midst. While also desiring the bifurcation of trial and appellate court business, and the disqualifying of a justice from hearing an appeal from his own decision, the Functions Committee wanted a five-man appeals panel; in addition, fearing "court packing" to influence decisions if the Congress had unfettered power to increase the size of the Court, it proposed a six-justice Court. The language included in the constitution sets the maximum size at six, but requires only a three-justice panel to hear appeals, which implies a minimum-sized Court of four.[15] Any veteran legislator would have been at ease in these negotiations.

The Governmental Structure Committee's proposal had contained the innovation of a separate land claims court in each State, with appeals limited to the State's highest court. In part, the land court was intended to forestall the recurrence of the backlog then existent in the Trust Territory High Court, and which was blamed on the great proportion of land matters before it.[16] More importantly, it would assure that each land case would be decided by a judiciary composed of indigenous judges, and within an environment most sensitive to the nuances of the land law applicable. While there was ample precedent for land and title courts elsewhere in the Pacific, the proposal did not engender wide support in the Convention, and with the abandonment of the unitary court system, reference to the land court also disappeared. However, a vestige of special provision for the handling of land adjudications remained, in the form of exception from the original and exclusive jurisdiction of the Supreme Court over cases "in which the national government is a party ... where an interest in land is at issue" (Art. XI, Sec. 6 [a]).[17] This elimination of land cases from the jurisdiction of the national judiciary was to have its companion in a far more divisive matter turning around whether the constitution would grant power to condemn land to any government.[18]

The same report of the Governmental Structure Committee which favored a unitary judicial system also specified that there should be three levels of government in Micronesia.[19] In addition to the national government, "States" would replace the districts of the Trust Territory, each with its own constitution embodying the form of government its people approved, just so long as it was democratic. The states would devolve some of their powers geographically on local governments of their choice. Not wanting to require the latter's creation solely for purposes of symmetry without regard to need, the states need not have local government in those areas where none existed on the effective date of the constitution. The delegates responded favorably to all of these structural recommendations, for they nicely expressed the consensus shaping up in the Convention.

Earlier, in considering the pre-recess resolution of the Governmental Functions Committee,[20] the Special Conference Committee had concluded that the federal form of government best coincided with the various views being voiced by the delegates.[21] Proceeding from this, the Functions Committee primarily took as its task the allocating of powers between the national and state governments within the rubric of federalism, while the General Provisions Committee tackled the delineation of the physical boundaries, and the fitting of the states within the geographical whole. The latter's work encountered far less controversy, for much of the groundwork had long been laid during the course of the protracted history of the United

Nations-sponsored Law of the Sea Conference, and the sharpening of the disagreement between the Micronesian delegation and that of the United States over the American position before the Conference.[22]

Concisely put, General Provisions proposed that what is the Trust Territory and also what could be claimed by historic right and custom to be part of Micronesia[23] would constitute the new Micronesian polity. Unless limited by treaty or its own act, included would be the integral waters connecting the islands of the archipelagos, and, in addition, jurisdiction would extend over two hundred miles of external waters and their seabed. Each state is comprised of the islands which formed its predecessor district, and marine boundaries are to be drawn equidistantly between them. National boundaries, of course, would be shrunk by any district failing to ratify the constitution. Conversely, they would be expanded by any territory added, which would be on approval of the national Congress; if the new area is to become part of an existing state, the state legislature would also have to concur (Art. I, Secs. 1-3). Anticipating difficulty over the sharing of natural resources located within the Micronesian marine space, it was compromised by only giving to the national government control over those found beyond 12 miles from the island baselines and also by dividing all net revenues derived from those ocean floor minerals equally between the national and appropriate state governments (Art. IX, Secs. 2[m], 6). While the economic feasibility of mineral exploitation as yet remains unproven, the delegates well understood that licensing the catch of pellagic fish held immediate promise of a considerable monetary return. The twelve-mile limit line emerging in the Law of the Sea Conference as the demarcation of sovereignty had been adapted by the delegates for internal use in splitting the ocean's bounty between central and state governments.

The Governmental Functions Committee, in identifying the powers to be allocated to the national government, and those to be shared with the states, proceeded with circumspection. Not to be forgotten was that the Palau delegation advocated a weak central government, and an unknown number of delegates from other districts shared a similar viewpoint. Carefully, the Committee distinguished between a "limited" and an impotent government:

While the powers of the national government are express, limited, and narrowly defined [and those of the states are "residual"], your Committee does not feel that the system of government herein proposed establishes a "weak" national government....[Rather] the responsibilities are limited, though not insufficient.²⁴

National defense and foreign affairs, regulation of foreign and interstate commerce, patents and copyrights, and issuance of currency are but a few of the many specific powers assigned to the national government, most familiar to the student of comparative politics as being exercised by the federal government of the United States. An unusual inclusion gives to the central government authority to define and punish major crimes--traceable to a latent fear of state impotence--this apart from the relevance of the crimes to any of the subject-matter areas placed within the jurisdiction of the central government.

The powers to be enjoyed by the national government are stated in broad grants, and as the Committee pointed out, each contains innumerable "incidental or implied powers," as the building of post offices and the issuance of stamps within the express authority "to provide for a national postal system." Complementing them is a separate category of "inherent" powers possessed by the national government,²⁵ intrinsically woven out of parts of the constitution, as the executive branch taking custody of a recalcitrant witness punished for contempt by the national Congress within the latter's exercise of its lawmaking functions. Finally, beside all specifically listed powers under the national Congress and executive, the Committee also included an all-embracing safeguard by assigning to the central government matters "of such an indisputably national character as to be beyond the power of a state to control...." (Art. VIII, Sec. 1). The Committee elaborated upon the great flexibility incorporated into this grant, just so long as the preconditions of indisputability and powerlessness are met,²⁶ and its interpretation remained unchallenged during the course of Convention debate.

To the states is allocated authority over everything not expressly delegated to the national government or prohibited to the states. The Committee cited as examples the enactment of marriage, divorce, adoption and inheritance laws, the regulation of corporations and other forms of business associations, and basic social welfare activities such as housing, consumer protection, liquor control, and food and drug regulation.[27]

Four areas are singled out in which the national and state governments are to share "concurrent" powers: promotion of education and health, establishing of public welfare and social security systems, appropriating public funds, and borrowing money (Art. IX, Sec. 3). To a person unfamiliar with constitutional law, it undoubtedly appears odd to give separate mention to the borrowing and appropriation of money, which are normal activities of governments the world round. The rationale becomes clear, however, when it is recalled that the Congress of the United States, under its appropriation power, has been able to direct federally raised funds to achieve ends which it could not constitutionally reach under its more expressly defined authority. Whether the money powers of the Micronesian central government will be similarly employed and then judicially sanctioned yet remains to be determined.

The influence of the Palauan "non-negotiable" demands was evident in the assigning of concurrent power over education and health, and congruent with this was the inclusion of welfare and social security within the same rubric. While the Committee's intent is for the national government to promote education and health, to fix appropriate standards, and to provide financial assistance, primary responsibility is to rest with the states. The national government is expected to continue the social security system created under the American administration of the Trust Territory, and if circumstances warrant, establish a public welfare system.[28] The constitution does not appear to preclude the central government from instituting welfare or health programs in a manner which preempts the field, leaving nothing for the states despite the authority being nominally shared concurrently by both.

The empowerment of the central government to act in the areas of education, health, and welfare is supplemented by a separate constitutional provision recommended by the Civil Liberties Committee which "recognizes the right of the people to education, health care, and legal services" (Art. XIII, Sec. 1). This might place Micronesia in the forefront of the welfare states but for the further direction to the national government that it "shall take every step reasonable and necessary to provide these services." The effect of this language is to offer an escape clause reducing the "right" to only a declaration of policy. The national authorities may use their best judgment in determining what portion of the costs, if any, the central government will bear.[29] These services, then, are to be regarded in the nature of privileges, at best bordering on the edge of inchoate rights, and to be distinguished from the "fundamental rights" which comprise Article IV of the constitution, and which are also the handiwork of the Civil Liberties Committee.

In the United States Constitution, the classic freedoms of speech, press, and assembly, and the various criminal protections are guaranteed against actions of the federal government, but have only incrementally been extended to the states by virtue of judicial construction which over time has read them into the due process and equal protection clauses of the 14th Amendment. Not so the constitution for Micronesia, for the rights expressed constitute limitations on all governments, whether national, state, or local. The Civil Liberties Committee took pains to recommend language that did more than just copy the Bill of Rights chapter of the Trust Territory Code with which most delegates were familiar. Instead, it sought terminology which more aptly expressed the additional meanings accreted elsewhere over time through court interpretation:[30] freedom of speech and press becomes "freedom of expression" and the right of association is expressly recognized (Art. IV, Sec. 1). Not only may no person "be denied the equal protection of the laws," but it is declared that "equal protection of the laws may not be ...impaired on account of sex, race, ancestry, national origin, language, or social status" (Art. IV, Secs. 4,5).[31] Some of these categories are found in the phraseology of Section 7 in the Code, but the Committee augmented them by inclusion of reference to ancestry, national origin, and social status.

The separation of church and state has raised cleavages within the Trust Territory which have cut deeply into Micronesian society. New religious organizations, particularly those of Protestant fundamentalists, of recent years have been challenging the more established faiths long ago introduced by the missionaries who converted the Micronesians from their traditional ways. The territorial Code has barred any attempt by government to ban the proselytizing of the competing religious groups or to regulate the gospel they preach. The requisite state neutrality also has precluded direct public support of parochial schools, this notwithstanding that they have educated most of today's Micronesian religious leadership. At the hearings of the Civil Liberties Committee, representatives of both the Catholic and Protestant faiths testified in support of freedom of religion. They also urged that government should be permitted to aid non-sectarian church activities.[32] The Reverend Mack Williams of the Community Church on Saipan--liaison to the Convention from the combined Congregationalists, General Baptists, and Liebenzells--felt strongly that government should not subsidize religious instruction, but knew that his views were not in concurrence with those of the Micronesian Protestant leadership.[33] As reported from committee, the "freedom of religion" clause contained no mention of parochial schools. On the floor of the Convention an amendment was offered permitting governmental aid to them for non-religious purposes, and it was accepted by the chairman of the Civil Liberties Committee without debate (Art. IV, Sec. 2).[34]

Another proposal prohibiting capital punishment aroused extended discussion in the Committee of the Whole. The Civil Liberties Committee's report claimed that the whole concept of punishment by death ran counter to Micronesian respect for the value of each individual member of society,[35] but this represented a bit of hyperbole. The Protestant coalition instructed the Reverend Williams to express its opposition to capital punishment,[36] and undoubtedly this was one of the factors helping to muster the three-fourths vote requisite for the Convention's adopting the constitutional ban on the death penalty (Art. IV, Sec. 9).

The Functions Committee proposed to empower the national executive with authority to suspend the civil rights guaranteed by the constitution upon the declaration of a national emergency in the event of threat of war or insurrection, civil disturbance, or national disaster. While recognizing that the ensuring of public safety and national security might require placing some form of emergency power in the hands of the executive, the delegates nevertheless feared that such suspension might unnecessarily run to all rights, and that the judicial and legislative safeguards proposed to be expressly written into the constitution would be inadequate to prevent excesses.[37] The compromise finally reached continues the grant of emergency power, but a civil right may be impaired only to the extent actually required for the preservation of the public peace, health, or safety. Meanwhile the courts are to continue functioning. During the first thirty days the declaration is to be free from judicial interference, but within the same period the national legislature is to convene. If not sooner revoked, or extended by the legislature, any declaration of emergency has a maximum life of but thirty days (Art. X, Sec. 9).

With but one exclusion, the Bill of Rights incorporated into the constitution applies to all persons, whether or not citizens. The exception is the freedom to travel and migrate, which refers only to citizens (Art. IV, Sec. 12).[38] The Convention rules did not assign responsibility for proposing the qualifications for citizenship and eligibility for naturalization to the Civil Liberties Committee, but to General Provisions. The latter addressed itself to the matter within a different frame of reference, for the whole subject of citizenship was contemporaneously before the Congress of Micronesia in the form of proposed amendments to the Trust Territory Code.[39] Here the Congressional membership of Chairman Tun and other delegates had direct linkage with Convention deliberations, and for a while was even reflected in the Committee's adoption of the Congressional concern for the plight of children found abandoned in the Territory.[40]

As finally agreed upon by the Convention, citizens of the Trust Territory who are domiciled in a district ratifying the constitution automatically receive citizenship in the new polity. Children born of mixed marriages, with one parent a Micronesian citizen, similarly are citizens. In cases of dual citizenship, failure to register intention to preserve Micronesian citizenship will cause a forfeiture, although status as a Micronesian national is retained. For an interim period, persons becoming nationals of the United States under the Northern Marianas Covenant, and domiciliaries of districts not ratifying the constitution may become citizens by initiating appropriate court action (Art. III).

The Committee had originally proposed to restrict naturalization to a few specific categories of people--spouses of Micronesian citizens, persons adopted under the age of eight by a Micronesian citizen, and Micronesian nationals. After seemingly minor objection, and with only minimal debate, the opposite tack was abruptly adopted, and the regulation of naturalization, immigration, and emigrations was assigned to the national legislature without specification of any qualifications on its exercise of power (Art. IX, Sec. 2[c]).[41] This reversal of the Committee's position represented a modification of major significance, as naturalization is integrally tied to a number of other sections in the constitution which give national suffrage to citizens eighteen years of age and over (Art. VI, Sec. 1),[42] restrict to citizens the holding of national legislative and chief executive offices (Art. IX, Sec. 9; Art. X, Sec. 4), and disqualify noncitizens and corporations not wholly owned by citizens from acquiring title to land (Art. XIII, Sec. 4). So acutely sensitive is the issue of reserving land to only Micronesians, and so pervasive the fear that control over it may be lost, as through the loophole of lax citizenship requirements, that it raised an insurmountable obstacle to working out a compromise on the terms of eligibility for naturalization to be included in the constitution, which helps explain the shunting of the whole matter over to the national Congress for later resolution.

While the Governmental Structure Committee debated long over the chief executive,[43] other dimensions of the executive branch were gradually taking shape without comparable travail, including those determined by positive decisions on what was not to be incorporated into the constitution. A number of delegate proposals would have had the constituent document specifically create executive departments with prescribed responsibilities, but the Committee opted for complete constitutional flexibility. Left to full legislative discretion are the number and authority of the departments to be structured into the executive branch of the central government (Art. X, Sec. 8). After hearing the testimony of the Trust Territory Director of Personnel, the Structure Committee approved of the merit principle undergirding the national public service system, but did not accept his recommendation that the states follow the policies and guidelines of the national system. This Committee view coincided with that of the Functions Committee, and by the latter's Committee Proposal No. 21 was incorporated into the constitution in the form of an express grant of power "to establish and regulate a national public service system" (Art. IX, Sec. 2[n]). "National" here refers only to employees of the central government, and to allied matters such as procedures for the appointment of public officers requiring the advice and consent of the national legislature.[44] Each state is free to set its own personnel policies for state officers and employees.

Fortified with an extensive manual on public finance prepared by a consultant, the Taxation and Public Finance Committee delved into the somewhat esoteric subjects of governmental budgeting, the structure of the national treasury, and the appropriation of public moneys. The central government would be administered under an annual budget plan prepared by the national executive which would attempt to balance income and out-flow, and would take precedence over individual proposals for public expenditures. The national treasury would contain both a general fund and special funds from which no moneys may be withdrawn except as authorized by statute. Overseeing the financial administration of the national government will be the Public Auditor with authority to inspect and audit accounts of all public agencies and nonprofit organizations receiving public funds from the central government. Although part of the national executive branch of government, and reporting annually to the legislature, the Auditor is to remain independent of administrative control (Art. XII, Secs. 1-3). None of these provisions evoked much argument; rather, it was on the more immediately acute decisions relative to the revenue raising powers of the central government, and the manner in which the states share in the public funds both internally and externally generated, that delegate attention centered. Here the specific demands of the Palauan Delegation had thrown down the gauntlet. The adoption of a constitution for Micronesia probably turned on how the challenge was to be met, and complicating the process was the fact that the Governmental Functions Committee, in addition to

Public Finance, also had turned its attention to delimiting the scope of the national revenue powers.

As the elements of the new government began to take shape, it appeared to me that its administration would be materially eased if the Micronesians could become familiar over time with its various dimensions by gradually learning to operate its institutions, rather than having at some future date to take control abruptly without prior preparation. With the tacit consent of the President, I attempted to sound out the attitude of the authorities in Washington toward facilitating parts of the new Micronesian government to become operative before termination of the Trusteeship. With even an unofficial sign of willingness to countenance this development, drafting of the constitution would need be phrased so that some of its provisions could be held in abeyance over an interim period. The conduit for contact was the representative of the State Department resident on Saipan. No positive response on this partial implementation was forthcoming. Instead, the impression gained was that this development was regarded as but one more trading element to be incorporated in the long-continuing status negotiations, and there the matter was allowed to drop.[45]

The Administration Committee was loathe to declare a cutoff date on the introduction of delegate proposals. They continued to trickle in, and some engaged the attention of the Standing Committees until near the end of the Convention.[46] On the other hand, the Administration Committee recognized the essentiality of providing the Standing Committees with a target date against which to pace their work. In mid-September, acting upon the optimistic assurances of committee chairmen, October 2 was designated for all of the Standing Committees to submit their proposals for consideration on the Convention floor. That date was in good part observed in the breach, and when on October 3 I made a report to the Administration Committee on the state of Convention progress, the submission date was postponed for a week.

The October 3 progress report, which had been presaged by the contents of a speech by Delegate Wiliander in the Plenary Session on the same day, supplied the delegates with their first outline of what appeared destined for inclusion in the Micronesian constitution. It incorporated subjects moving toward decision in committee, in proposals on the Convention floor, and the few provisions which had already been adopted:

State of the Constitution
(as of October 3)

<u>Preamble</u>   passed

Article 1   <u>Territorial Jurisdiction</u>
  National Territory;   -Com Prop 7
    District Territory
  Secession/Admission   -<u>Gen Provs.</u>
    of New Areas   working on

Article 2   <u>Sovereignty</u>
  Supremacy of Constitu-   -Com Prop 11
    tion/Future Status
  Nat'l Govt/District   -<u>Functions</u>
    Govt. Powers   working on

Article 3   <u>Civil Liberties</u>
  Freedom of Expression;   -Com Props. 1,2,4,9
    Freedom of Assembly;
    Freedom of Religion;
    Protection of Custom
  Balance of Bill of Rights   -<u>Civ Liberties</u>
                                signing Proposal
  Affirmative Rights   -<u>Civ Liberties</u>
                                  discussing

Articles 4-7   <u>Structure</u>
  Three Branches-passed
  Executive: structure   -<u>Structure</u> nearly
                                  completed with draft
            functions   -<u>Functions</u> completing
                                  hearings
  Legislature:structure   -<u>Structure</u> working
                                  on draft
            functions   -<u>Functions</u> completing
                                  hearings
  Judiciary   -<u>Structure</u> signing
                                  draft
  Independent Officers:
    public auditor   -Com Prop 12
    public defender, etc.   -<u>Structure</u> working
                                  on draft

Article 8   <u>Fiscal</u>
  Budget Process   -Com Prop introduced
                                  today
  Taxation: Public Debt   -<u>Finance</u> and <u>Functions</u>
                                  both working on

Article 9	*Citizenship*	–Com Prop 10
Article 10	*Amendment*	–Com Prop 8
Article 11	*Transition*	
Effective Date		–*Gen Provisions* signing final draft
Transition Provisions		–*Gen Provisions* working on

All detail was missing, and the final version of the constitution was to exhibit an extended and somewhat rearranged format. Nevertheless, the delegates now had before them both a pattern into which to fit the anticipated committee proposals yet being formulated and the tantalizing contours of a tangible product toward which they had long been laboring.

External to the Convention, and anticipating this outline, the Trust Territory Public Affairs Office on September 23 had widely distributed to the ESG district task forces a large wall chart to be displayed in public places. Its surface was divided into columns headed by the names of designated Articles into which it was believed the constitution would be apportioned. As each constitutional provision was adopted by the Convention, the ESG proposed to paste copies under the appropriate Article heading. In this way[47] the public could literally see the constitution taking shape. Within the Convention, the delegates tackled each committee proposal in the order of its procedural precedence without reference to any logic of constitutional content; so to the Style Committee and the staff of the R & D Section fell the burden of assuring that each new provision fully articulated with those the Convention had previously adopted. The concluding action of the Style Committee would be the transmission to the Convention for its final approval of the completed draft, its provisions harmonized, its terminology consistent, and its contents arrayed in rational sequence.

On October 13, about a fortnight after the tentative" constitutional outline was first unveiled to the Administration Committee, a much fuller "rough draft" of a Constitution of the Federated States of Micronesia was distributed to all delegates. It had been compiled by the staff at the request of the President and the Administration Committee "so that [in the words of Floor Leader

Tman] we will know where we stand now."[48] This expanded version of the emerging constitution carried full detail, and its inconsistencies mirrored the conflict between the proposals of Committees with overlapping responsibilities. The delegates were warned that it was "preliminary and subject to change," and that some of its contents were sure to be modified before final adoption. It also served to highlight the areas where agreement had yet to be reached, and thereby contributed to stoking the pressure building within the Convention to face up to the divisive issues still facing the delegates.

By another fortnight, I had become concerned that the leadership of the Convention did not fully appreciate there were a number of time-consuming necessities to concluding the Convention which had to be anticipated and for which ample provision should be made. On the Convention's 75th day, the Administration Committee was alerted that it should apportion the working days remaining to the Convention. Assuming that the immediate next seven Session days were devoted to debating and passing practically all of the remaining constitutional provisions, the last few days of October would be available for finishing up "tag" ends and allowing the Style Committee to conclude and duplicate a completely repolished draft. After several days' time allotted to the delegates for reading and studying the revision, November 3 through 6 could be earmarked for seriatim debate on all of the draft's provisions and the resolution of any inconsistency brought to the Convention's attention by the Style Committee. The Convention's penultimate day would then be fully occupied in double-checking all procedural actions supporting the contents of the final draft, and proofreading and reproducing the official copy of the constitution for signing on November 8, the nineteenth and very last day of the Convention. Privately, I anticipated that the November portion of the schedule would have to be contracted a little if the concluding compromises were protracted, and spilled over from October. The catalystic psychology of the "Thermidore" period of a constitutional convention differs little from that of an ordinary legislature, and I was confident that it would enable the handling of a quantity of work which under normal circumstances would appear near humanly impossible. I was not prepared, however, for the amorphousness of the "Micronesian Way" which continued to defer the crucial decisions from day to day and eventually compressed the final adoption of the constitution into the span of a few short hours.

Prior to the recess, when the delegates in the Committee of the Whole were debating over the initial contents to go into the constitution, Chairman Heine for the Civil Liberties Committee proposed that the language originally submitted by his Committee be amended so as to substitute the "freedom of expression" phraseology used in Delegate Proposal No. 100, the "Palauan Constitution."[49] When, on October 9, Delegate Ngiraked urged delay in the Convention's consideration of the name of "Federated States of Micronesia" as the designation for the new national government being formed, he was reminded that it was the name advanced in Delegate Proposal No. 100,[50] and the Convention then proceeded to adopt it.[51] A week later, the Plenary Session was opened with a reading of the Preamble to the Constitution, a practice which was followed on each remaining day of the Convention. The Preamble, too, had been originally copied word for word from the "Palauan Constitution," and with only a very minor change passed Second Reading. The daily repetition was intended to emphasize Micronesian unity which the Preamble proclaimed. But did these examples of bodily incorporation of the "Palauan Constitution" also signify, symbolically, that a constitution for all of Micronesia was to be possible only by recognizing the totality of the Palauan position? This had yet to be resolved as the final days of the Convention drew near.

---

1. The failure to achieve a quorum to permit reconvening was allegedly due to revised airplane schedules, which delayed the return of some delegates to Saipan. On one other occasion, Saturday, October 11, the absence of a quorum also compelled a recess of the Convention. CCM Journal, Vol. I, p. 314.

2. See supra, p. 154.

3. Dialogue for Micronesia, No. 36, August 7, 1975.

4. SCRep. No. 16, CCM Journal, Vol. II, p. 784.

5. <u>CCM Journal</u>, Vol. I, p. 239.

6. <u>CCM Journal</u>, Vol. II, p. 672. In this and all subsequent descriptions of actions occurring in Plenary Session and Committee of the Whole of a nature not reported in the formal record, primary reliance has been upon the extensive notes kept of the daily observations by my wife, Terza Meller.

7. <u>CCM Journal</u>, Vol. I, p. 347.

8. <u>CCM Journal</u>, Vol. I, p. 348.

9. Summary Record of Governmental Functions Committee (Unnumbered Meeting), August 6, 1975.

10. <u>Dialogue for Micronesia</u>, No. 38, August 13, 1975.

11. "Report of Subcommittee on Judiciary," Governmental Structure Committee, September 22, 1975, p. 3.

12. C.P. No. 24, <u>CCM Journal</u>, Vol. II, p. 918, at pp. 922ff; SCRep. No. 36, <u>Ibid.</u>, p. 823, at pp. 848ff.

13. C.P. No. 30, <u>CCM Journal</u>, Vol. II, p. 933; SCRep. No. 49, <u>Ibid.</u>, p. 876.

14. Technically, C.P. No. 24 was amended, and C.P. No. 30 filed; the explanation for all new material incorporated in this "Joint Amendment No. 10," and not found in either committee's report, are considered in SCRep. No. 58, <u>CCM Journal</u>, Vol. II, p. 885.

15. At least until there are retired justices, etc., who may be temporarily brought back to sit in the Supreme Court.

16. Summary Record of Governmental Structure Committee, 16th Meeting, September 25, 1975.

17. In explaining this language, Delegate Ismael said it meant the national government would not have jurisdiction over land matters (<u>CCP Journal</u>, Vol. I, p. 448), and this was later concurred in by Delegate Toribiong (<u>Ibid.</u>, p. 542).

18. Eminent domain is treated in chapter 12.

19. C.P. No. 24, *CCM* *Journal*, Vol. II, p. 918; SCRep. No. 36, *Ibid*., p. 835.

20. See *infra*, p. 205.

21. Special Conference Committee Report No. 4, *CCM* *Journal*, Vol. II, p. 940.

22. See Micronesian Delegation to the Law of the Sea Conference letter of April 23, 1975, addressed to Ambassador John R. Stevenson, Special Representative of the U.S. President for the Law of the Sea Conference, referring to foreign policy powers under the Micronesian status compact negotiations carrying control over the resources of the sea. The draft of the constitution dealing with the marine boundaries of Micronesia, and the rights within them, was reviewed by the consultant to the Micronesian Delegation, and amended in accordance with his recommendations.

23. The Congress of Micronesia had previously declared Enen-kio Atoll, shown on maps and charts as Wake Island, to be part of traditional Micronesia. HJR No. 3, Fifth Congress, 2nd Regular Session, 1974.

24. SCRep. No. 30, *CCM* *Journal*, Vol. II, pp. 813-14.

25. *Ibid*., p. 815. Initially, "the comprehensive draft Committee Proposal" distributed to the delegates prior to the recess, as part of the Governmental Functions Committee's "Working Paper No. 1," specifically declared that the central government had "all powers necessary and appropriate to carry out the powers and duties expressly delegated to the national government." (The antecedents of this clause in Article I, Section 8 of the U.S. Constitution are obvious.) This language was deleted from the final proposal submitted, so to the courts will fall the ultimate determination of whether the Committee intent, as expressed in its report, is to be read into the Micronesian constitution.

26. *Ibid*., pp. 815ff.

27. *Ibid*., p. 814.

28. *Ibid*., p. 820.

29. SCRep. No. 52, <u>CCM</u> <u>Journal</u>, Vol. II, p. 881; SCRep. No. 61, <u>Ibid</u>., p. 887; Committee of the Whole, October 31, 1975, <u>Ibid</u>., p. 730.

30. The obvious exceptions are the references to "bills of attainder" and "ex post facto laws" (Art. IV, Sec. 11). Defeat had to be admitted by the draftsmen, for no substitutes were found which in so short a compass expressed comparable meaning, including their historical overtones. On the other hand, the Style Committee deleted the phrase "interception of communication by any means" from the section granting protection to privacy on the grounds that it was necessarily included within the reference to privacy. See SCRep. No. 44, <u>CCM</u> <u>Journal</u>, Vol. II, p. 872.

31. Treatment of the basic conflict regarding the primacy of traditional rights over civil liberties will be found in Chapter 12, following.

32. Summary Record of Public Hearings, Committee on Civil Liberties, July 30, 1975.

33. Harold F. Nufer, <u>Micronesia</u> <u>Under</u> <u>American</u> <u>Rule</u> (Hicksville, N.Y.: Exposition Press, 1978), p. 172.

34. <u>CCM</u> <u>Journal</u>, Vol. I, pp. 463-64. Under existing Territorial law, limited aid could be extended to students of non-public schools. The amendment cut to the heart of the "separation" principle by directly designating assistance to parochial schools and, in addition, had the practical effect of permitting broader benefits than then possible.

35. SCRep. No. 23, <u>CCM</u> <u>Journal</u>, Vol. II, p. 803.

36. Nufer, <u>op</u>. <u>cit</u>.

37. See <u>CCM</u> <u>Journal</u>, Vol. I, pp. 374-78.

38. The Trust Territory Code, Section 8, refers to the movement of "inhabitants" of the Trust Territory. The constitutional right appears narrower, and it may be surmised, deliberately so.

39. See House SCR. No. 6-47 and SCR. No. 6-48, <u>House</u> <u>Journal</u>, Congress of Micronesia, Sixth Congress, 1st Session, pp. 554-56.

40. The separate provision on citizenship of abandoned children of unknown parentage was later deleted during the course of Convention deliberation.

41. CCM Journal, Vol. I, pp. 292-94. Citizenship is also included under Congressional regulatory power, but here the other constitutional provisions would set bounds to Congressional action.

42. The Congress may only raise residence and registration restrictions, and set disqualification for crime or mental incapacity. See SCRep. No. 31, CCM Journal, Vol. II, p. 811.

43. For a short period, after the "Palauan Constitution" and its two companion delegate proposals were referred to the special committee (see p. 184, supra), the Governmental Structure Committee deferred further consideration of the major subject areas included in those proposals. Only upon it becoming evident that referral was a superficial, politically face-saving gesture, did the Structure Committee return to deliberations on the chief executive and national legislature.

44. SCRep. No. 33, CCM Journal, Vol. II, p. 819.

45. Most of the informal response seemed bent on emphasizing that should the delegates persist in drawing up a constitution whose provisions potentially clashed with the tentative future status compact, the whole agreement would have to be reopened, and this could well lose some of the financial advantages the Micronesians had already gained --a risk they could not afford. Since the delegates were already aware of this possibility, and seemed convinced that come what may the United States would continue to provide the necessary support as the quid pro quo for strategic denial and military access, I did not view my function to be that of an unofficial conduit for negotiations on future political status in the guise of counseling reconsideration of Convention actions.

46. On the 82nd day of the Convention, the Governmental Functions Committee met to consider Delegate Mwety's proposal on eminent domain introduced on October 13. Summary Record of the Governmental Functions Committee, October 30, 1975.

47. Daily newspaper accounts, radio news broadcasts, interviews with delegates, and ESG Notes

were also now widely distributing news on the Convention. Unfortunately, some of these various accounts confused the fact a proposal had been adopted by the Committee of the Whole with its having hurdled its definitive passage on Second Reading, so that some of the information as disseminated did not coincide with the official records.

48. CCM Journal, Vol. I, p. 316. Floor Leader Tman was in error when he attributed the compiling of this preliminary draft to the Style Committee; it was wholly a staff enterprise.

49. CCM Journal, Vol. II, p. 641.

50. CCM Journal, Vol. I, p. 306.

51. SCRep. No. 26 listed seven other names which were submitted for consideration (CCM Journal, Vol. II, p. 805). Some formed acronyms with offensive meanings in the Micronesian languages, so were considered unsatisfactory.

Chapter 12.
Traditional Leaders and Customary Rights

"I know that all of us are born on this earth and we are the same. However, some of us are born to rule and some of us are born to serve. Mr. President, among us there are some people who were appointed by God by virtue of our birth and tradition." So the Journal of the Plenary Session for the 76th day of the Convention records Delegate Heinrich Iriarte.[1] Unlike Namwarki Max Iriarte, his delegate brother, delegate Heinrich Iriarte sat as an elected member, but was recognized as in line for high title on Ponape and an acknowledged spokesman for the preservation of Micronesian custom. This date of October 23 served to mark the zenith of the confrontation long abuilding between the supporters of Micronesian tradition and those delegates who for want of a better name might be called young modernists. It had become manifest in a number of guises, some substantive in the form of provisions to be incorporated into the constitution, others procedural which ascribed to the traditional leaders a distinctive place in the conduct of the Convention. The reference to God-given leaders served to coalesce the "modernists," so that while the constitution was to contain a number of ameliorating references to custom and tradition, the thrust of the traditional leaders was to be turned and they were not to gain guaranteed roles in the new government.

The amendment of the enabling legislation giving full voting rights in the Convention to delegates sitting as traditional leaders signified that the Convention would have to reckon with them, personally, and the pressures exerted by others under the rubric of preserving custom. The hyperbole supporting such a statutory change flowed easily:

> The traditional leaders of Micronesia occupy a very important place in our culture and traditions, and therefore, to

a certain extent, deny them the power to assist in the shaping of our future political destiny is to deny not only their great wisdom and insight, but in a certain sense, our own cultural heritage as well.[2]

Within the Convention, the ranks of the traditional leaders coopted by their peers to sit as delegates were augmented by elected delegates who had claims to traditional leadership roles based on Micronesian custom, and also by some delegates whose political power bases back home depended upon the support of traditionalists. As most chiefs in the Convention expressed themselves through interpreters, and with other delegates as well as the paid interpreters purporting to speak the chiefs' positions, it remained difficult to determine which of the arguments advanced in the name of preserving Micronesian custom actually should be attributed to them, or were even consonant with their privately held views. In addition, a traditional leader who might appear to be a bastion of conservatism on one issue might on another be in the forefront of change, as Namwarki Max Iriarte's introduction of a proposal to protect labor unions in Micronesia (D.P. No. 147).

In general, a body of diffuse sentiment favoring perpetuation of a Micronesian life-style was shared by all delegates, differ as they did over exactly what this was or how its preservation should be expressed in the constitution. All tacitly conceded that there might have to be some nod to custom and tradition. Even the delegates most adamant in their objections to recognition of the traditional leaders were reluctant to challenge them openly. For one thing, they had no desire to give personal offense; to even appear to be doing so ran deeply contrary to Micronesian mores. More poignant politically, they fully appreciated the necessity of abating chiefly opposition so as to obtain approval of the final draft within the Convention and thereafter help insure the adoption of the completed constitution by the voters at the polls.

The first show of cohesion among the traditional leaders took the form of a petition from them and the other delegates with interpreters, and dated back to the workshop preceding the Convention. In the request for additional expense money for the ten interpreters, it alleged the petitioners "know these demands are extremely reasonable and fair in light of the circumstances surrounding the Convention." Most delegates believed the interpreters were the major moving force behind the petition. The Administration Committee responded with a little show of irritation, noting that "it is important they [the petitioners] also know that satisfaction of such demands depends upon availability of funds."[3] The petition also ignored district delegation staffs, whose members would have to be accorded comparable treatment. Eventually, it was determined that all would be paid larger daily allowances, computed retroactively, but not as much as the petition sought. Face was saved in all quarters.

Next, the two traditional leaders from Ponape proposed that the Convention rules be amended to restructure the Special Conference Committee. One of the pair of delegates to which each district was entitled on the Committee would have to be a chief for those districts represented by them at the Convention. At the time it was believed that the issues of major moment would be assigned to the Committee, hence this interest in its composition. Lines dividing traditionalists and modernists had yet to be drawn in the Convention, and the amendment was quickly defeated with but ten hands raised in its support. However, the delegates apparently did not wish to give affront to the traditional leaders, and twenty-two failed to vote at all, almost as many as those who actively expressed either ayes or nays.[4]

On the 17th day of the Convention, July 28, the Chairman of the Governmental Structure Committee formally requested "all traditional leaders to meet with the Committee ...[on the following day] and this meeting will be closed door."[5] The eight chiefs from Palau, Ponape, Truk, and Yap attended the session. Delegate Heinrich Iriarte, speaking on behalf of the other eight members of his Committee present, after thanking them for appearing, informed them that the Structure Committee felt it was not proper for it to decide what role and power the chiefs should have in the future government. This was something for the traditional leaders to determine. After they responded with a spattering of comments, they stated the desire to consider this further in their own separate chiefs' meeting. Two of the Committee's members--

Dr. Isaac Lanwi from the Marshalls[6] and Luis Limes from the Marianas--were then designated by Chairman Iriarte to attend to represent the traditional interests of the two districts without chiefs at the Convention. In this manner, structure was provided to the amorphous traditional leadership group within the Convention. Soon, some of the chiefs found themselves being carried along on the current of views announced by the group's self-appointed spokesmen, not necessarily concurring but unwilling to appear publicly in opposition to their fellow traditional leaders.

When the chiefs first gathered, the problem of priority among equals[7] was resolved by President Nakayama chairing the meeting. His suggestion was adopted that the leaders take turns in presiding in the order that their names were drawn. Not infrequently this actually meant that the chiefs' interpreters conducted the meetings, raising questions, and actively guiding the course of discussion. Other delegates appeared from time to time, nominally representing absent traditional leaders or in lieu of their interpreters, and several elected delegates who strongly advocated the traditionalists' position unilaterally attached themselves. At the outset, meetings were infrequent, discourse proceeded inconclusively, and the consensus sought on various matters kept retreating until the Procrustean pressure of the Convention's limited life compelled decision irrespective of the readiness of all the chiefs.

The guarantee of civil liberties in the constitution publicly disclosed the Convention's deep divisions over Micronesian custom and tradition. The Governmental Functions Committee concluded as part of its internal deliberations that "the central government evolving should have the exclusive authority to regulate civil rights and liberties, but must give due recognition to local custom."[8] Contemporaneously, the Civil Liberties Committee was formulating an entire Bill of Rights, but in response to the call from the Convention's Administration Committee for a show of demonstrable action before the recess, reported out Committee Proposal No. 1, relating to freedom of speech and press. C.P. No. 2, protecting the right to petition and peaceably assemble, followed within a few days. Not until over a full week later did C.P. No. 4 appear, providing for preservation of local customs, and by that time the schism within the delegate ranks had so kindled emotions that the Convention was to recess without any definitive decision possible.

Was freedom of speech and press to be extended if it violated the custom of a particular district? No, according to an amendment offered in the Committee of the Whole by Delegate Falcam, which would hold every person responsible for abuses "including violations of Micronesian customs, traditions, and standards of morality protected by District legislation." Adopt the amendment and it was "tantamount to creating a police state out of Micronesia" declared Delegate Carl Heine of the Civil Liberties Committee. After further exchanges, "Delegate Eperiam [of Ponape] stated that he may be out of order, but moved that the Convention let God draft the articles on speech and press for the Micronesian people." Dr. Lanwi seconded the motion, but "did not agree that his God would descend to draft the proposal, that they would have to go up to Mt. Sinai to draft it." Delegate Toribiong of Palau noted that "customs and traditions have been spoken of in the abstract, and he asked that certain customs and traditions be identified for the benefit of the Delegates so that they could deliberate on the proposed amendments with information and full understanding." The Chairman of the Committee of the Whole again indicated his desire to invite the legal staff to provide expert opinion on the question, and again met with objection. "Delegate Falcam stated ... he did not come here to be lectured on terms and technicalities...." And so the debate waxed hot over "whether the provisions of our Constitution with respect to freedom of speech and press must completely and totally subscribe to that principle without regard to our customary laws and traditions, or whether the concept, the basic tenets of freedom of speech and press, must be accepted or be incorporated in our Constitutional provisions with modifications to recognize our customary laws and traditions." Floor Leader Tman, who phrased this analysis, recommended the whole matter be referred to the Special Conference Committee "to come up with a procedural recommendation as to should we include customary laws and traditions when every bill of rights comes to the floor, or whether we should keep the traditional and customary question entirely separate as part of the Bill of Rights."[9] The Plenary Session endorsed the suggestion, and the whole problem was temporarily shunted over to the Special

Conference Committee under instructions to resolve the procedural matter.

While many of its members kept returning to the substantive issue in its internal debates, the Special Committee attempted to hold to its instructions, and eventually succeeded. In the Committee discussion, Delegate Ismael advocated that the Bill of Rights should contain language qualifying all freedoms in terms of local custom, and his view was widely endorsed.[10] The position of Dr. Ismael was fully in accord with the conclusion already reached in the Functions Committee which he chaired. The Special Committee report recommended that the Bill of Rights should contain a provision equal in rank with the others to protect and preserve Micronesian customs, traditional laws and morality. Once divorced, attention could concentrate upon it. Repetition of the same issue each time a new civil rights measure came before the delegates would be avoided, with the net result of speeding the Convention's business. To the Civil Liberties Committee was referred the task of drafting the separate section on custom.

No sooner was the Special Committee's report accepted by the Convention than Chairman Heine introduced Committee Proposal No. 4 from his Civil Liberties Committee. It purported to give the customary law of the various parts of Micronesia the full force and effect of the law, but only "so far as such customary law is not in conflict with the Constitution or the statutory law of Micronesia." The accompanying Standing Committee Report declared that the proposal's substantive content was already incorporated in the Trust Territory Code,[11] and so constituted no innovation. Delegate Falcam was far from mollified: "... this proposal dilutes quite extensively my amendment to Committee Proposal No. 1 and the intent of this report does not reflect the intent of my amendment."[12] There the matter temporarily rested in the Committee of the Whole, the calm before the anticipated storm when Committee Proposals Nos. 1 and 4 would once again be taken up for consideration. Meanwhile, somehow the Committee Proposal on freedom of assembly, association, and petition (C.P. No. 2) easily slipped through the Committee of the Whole. Apparently the attention of the delegates was so diverted by another tempest just brewing over the issue of eminent domain, or was so lulled by the anticipated debate on the other civil rights proposal that no objection was raised.

Freedom of speech and press in C.P. No. 1--now reworded to be freedom of expression--next came up before the Committee of the Whole. Protest as the traditionalists might over the separation of the substantive right from the recognition of custom, and give notice of their dissatisfaction over the phraseology of the section on preservation of tradition in C.P. No. 4 which would later be before them, the debate inexorably wore down to the taking of a vote. A secret ballot was called for, the first time it was ever used in Committee of the Whole and the tally disclosed 29 ayes and 15 noes (plus 2 void). This was sufficient for the Committee of the Whole to report passage, but foretold inability to obtain the necessary three-fourths vote for final adoption in Plenary Session.

On the following day, when the Committee of the Whole finally reached the Committee Proposal protecting customary law (C.P. No. 4), Delegate Carl Heine had a different version ready in the form of an amendment: legislation and administrative action could protect custom and tradition, and if challenged as violative of the introduced civil liberties, "the essentiality of the Micronesian tradition protected may be considered [by the courts] as a compelling social purpose warranting such governmental action." These were state of the art legalisms, words carefully weighed. Affirmative governmental intervention would first be requisite, and to the courts would fall responsibility for umpiring between custom and the introduced rights. Their standard for adjudging? "You must prove to the court that the social reasons you are bringing before the court are so important that the basic fundamental rights [in the constitution] can be curtailed."[13] The Committee of the Whole accepted Committee Proposal No. 4, as amended, but Delegate Falcam continued to express his opposition. Neither C.P. No. 4 nor the other proposals destined for the Bill of Rights were to be reported out from the Style Committee until long after the recess, and by that time the cleavage over custom and tradition had considerably expanded to engulf other issues. One of them was eminent domain, and as expressed by a traditional leader, "Micronesians need their land more than they need civil liberties."[14]

In its report to the Congress of Micronesia on the Seventh Round of Negotiations, the Joint Committee on Future Status stated its position to be that "the power of eminent domain should 'be severely curtailed in its exercise' ... [and additionally] the exercise of this power should be reserved to the several districts."[15] In expanding upon this, Senator Salii had added that the Joint Committee believed action by the Trust Territory Government itself should not be adequate to condemn property.[16] Underlying the Joint Committee's negotiating position was Micronesia's past experience under the Japanese Administration and the general dissatisfaction over the Trust Territory's handling of public lands and acquisition of private lands. The possibilities of losing their properties through public condemnation by the American Administration was believed to be the moving force for the owners agreeing to lease or sell them. The subject of eminent domain had been raised by delegates in nearly every meeting which the top staff of the Convention had held with the district delegations in the preliminary swing through the Trust Territory. The Convention consequently approached the issue with considerable caution, and some delegates displayed extreme emotional commitment. Traditionalists among those opposed saw in any grant of condemnation powers to government the potential eroding away of chiefly authority, for much of it traced to the usage of land.[17]

The Governmental Functions and the Civil Liberties Committees had eminent domain within their frames of reference, the former with respect to the grant of the power, and if so, the determination at what levels of government. Prohibition against the taking of property without due process brought the subject before the Civil Liberties Committee. Both held hearings, but the Functions Committee acted first. Its Committee Proposal No. 3, and supporting Committee Report No. 4, placed eminent domain in the states, with the central government having to request permission of the states to exercise it. Eminent domain "is said to be inherent in a sovereign government" and "is considered by your Committee to be an essential one...."[18] These declarations of the Committee were to haunt the Convention as the ramifications of the issue grew.

To Chairman Ismael of the Functions Committee, the taking of property with due compensation was a power necessary in a democratic government. Its locus should be in the states "in order to assure the best understanding of local custom and traditions as they relate to land values."[19] A minority of his Committee disagreed, and desired to allow both the central and state governments concurrent authority to acquire property. The Committee reported out a mid-position, which would not deny eminent domain to the central government, but only to be exercised with the consent of the state government concerned. As a nod in the other direction, national law would determine the manner in which approval would be granted. Unsatisfied, the minority submitted a dissenting report and under the Convention rules its position also came before the Committee of the Whole. But there were to be additional viewpoints, and the issue accreted complexity.

One delegate contended no land should be taken without tender of substitute property. Traditionalist Delegate Mwety from Truk objected to any exercise of the eminent domain power, but he was voted down. Popuisome Fichita Bossy from Truk offered an amendment solely limiting to state governments the power of condemnation, and requiring the land taken to revert to its original owners upon termination of the public purpose for which it was acquired. It failed to receive a majority vote. Floor Leader Tman proposed an amendment which would reserve the power to the states, but upon request a state legislature could grant the national government authority to exercise it. This variation of the Functions Committee's attempted compromise met with approval in the Committee of the Whole, notwithstanding that

> Chief Bossy reminded the Delegates that the draft Constitution would have to be ratified by the people, and that the people of one district might disapprove the draft Constitution because the Delegates failed to heed their views by including a contrary position.[20]

Brought back before the Plenary Session, the Proposal now in a form polished by the Style Committee, it became apparent that the debates in Committee of the Whole had so trifurcated the Convention that the requisite three-fourths majority for final passage could not be obtained. One small group of delegates objected, adamant in its demand that the central government must possess eminent domain powers. Traditionalists, whose views ranged from denial of all governmental exercise of eminent domain to the raising of narrow restrictions on its employment, constituted another opposition group. Only thirty-two affirmative votes could be mustered.[21] The delegates who disapproved of the Proposal or were silent were divided between the two minority camps. Interestingly, nowhere in all of the exchange of rhetoric was reference made to the central government's need to condemn land if it were to meet possible commitments to the United States under a future status compact.

"Killed," the eminent domain issue would not die. The report of the Governmental Functions Committee had already given notice that the power "is said to be inherent...," which could mean that if the Constitution remained silent, all governments in Micronesia would possess it, and this without limitation. Continued stalemate presented the delegates with the least desirable of all possible solutions. There was no alternative but to try again. C.P. No. 3 was reconsidered, and an amendment offered which declared simply that the condemnation power was vested in the states. During the debate which followed, some of the delegates announced changes of their stands, but nonetheless, when the vote was taken, the final tally remained identical.[22]

Thereafter the whole matter appeared to be pushed to the background, but the gnawing uncertainty over what might occur in the absence of any constitutional provision continued to trouble delegates. Attempting to break the standoff, Delegate Mwety introduced a proposal (D.P. No. 162) declaring the power of eminent domain remained reserved to the people of each state. It nicely supplemented this delegate's belief that eminent domain was unnecessary, for before modern government and the taking of property for compensation, Trukese were induced to dedicate land for communal purposes through appeal to their civic conscience and the prestige they would achieve. As the last serious delegate proposal to be introduced during the Convention, it was referred to the Governmental Functions Committee. Under the principles of interpretation recognized in American constitutional law, the language would deny any governmental authority to take property until authorized by constitutional amendment or comparable legal enablement. Even though committee work was now being replaced by long hours of Convention debate, the members of the Functions Committee met to ponder over the proposal and the dispute continued within their ranks. Some delegates objected that the new proposal could vest the power in the states while continuing to deny it to the central government.

On the Convention's penultimate day, and without the formality of committee proposal or report, the stage was set for what was to prove to be a last desperate move to resuscitate the proposal. The rules of the Convention were suspended, and eminent domain again placed on Second Reading. Under the aegis of the Functions Committee, Delegate Mwety's language was now substituted.[23] Although more delegates voted than ever before, still only thirty-two were tallied in the affirmative, and the proposal again failed of passage.[24]

Delegate Ngiraked from Palau, by his remarks on the significance of the vote, attempted to establish a record of constitutional "intent" to which the courts might later refer, only to be refuted by a fellow Palauan:

> **Delegate Ngiraked**: I think it is proper to take note of what has just happened here. By remaining silent we have left the power of eminent domain floating around and it is available at all levels of government and, possibly without intending to do so, we have delegated the decision to our future courts to decide.
> **Delegate Toribiong**: Point of privilege Mr. President. I wish to have the record reflect that it is my opinion that in considering all the proposals concerning land and concerning the delegation of powers, I conclude that the national government does not have the power of eminent domain.[25]

The specter of inherent powers of eminent domain had not been laid, and the issue yet remains to be resolved. Meanwhile the prohibition against the depriving of property without due process (Art. IV, Sec. 3) assured protection against arbitrary taking.

Governmental powers might conceptually be treated as distinct from governmental form, but all delegates understood that eminent domain and its placement were integrally related to the decisions which would be reached on shaping the government for Micronesia. Similarly, all of the principals sensed, if they did not fully comprehend, that the role to be given the chiefs within the new governmental structure was closely linked to the disagreement over civil liberties. During the early hearing of the Civil Liberties Committee, Namwarki Max Iriarte had opined that the traditional leaders should comprise a special body with veto powers over all developments relating to traditional rights. Popuisome Fichita Bossy testified in favor of affording the chiefs a fundamental role "so as to be able to protect all Micronesian traditions."[26] Apparently Chairman Heinrich Iriarte of the Structure Committee strongly held to the same view, but speaking for his Committee, at first committed it to wait upon the traditional leaders reaching a declared position. Interrelated as all these matters considered at the Chiefs' Meetings might be, their task was complicated by the fact that they were expected to move beyond vague generalizations and reach specific agreements, each individually linked with a particular proposal under consideration. In addition, some chiefs saw their responsibility not as staking out a chiefly position but, as appropriate to their traditional status, seeking consensus between the extremes expressed by traditionalists within their meeting and opposing views outside. Discussing subjects with which they were at best only generally conversant, and being called upon to act in a wholly unaccustomed manner, the work of the Chiefs' Meetings proceeded haltingly, and on a number of occasions the Convention was called upon to defer a proposal to allow time for the chiefs to confer further. Eventually, positions might be declared in their collective name, and go unrepudiated by the traditional leaders who stayed silent, but lack of cohesion remained within their ranks.

Irritation over the slowness of the Governmental Structure Committee to submit any part of a proposed skeletal outline for the future government gradually grew within the Convention. Its recommendations were central to the compromises which would have to be reached. By early October, Chairman Heinrich Iriarte was expressing his impatience with the chiefs in their failing to delineate their desired role.[27] Finally, the Committee concluded it could wait no longer on the chiefs to reach consensus, and concluded work on what proved to be the Convention's longest Committee Proposal accompanied by the lengthiest committee report submitted. It provided the entire framework of the central government and for the articulation of its parts. For good measure, it also included structural strictures applicable to the states. The portions of C.P. No. 24 applicable to the traditional leaders had been referred to the Chiefs' Meeting, and their suggestions adhered to in its final version. Within the Committee, the traditionalists had carried the day. To the chiefs were given roles both in the national and state governments, and for good measure it was declared that they were not to be considered disenfranchised, so could run for and hold any elected office. Special state courts would have jurisdiction over land and matters governed by traditional laws and customs, as provided for by state law. The states were also mandated to make provision "for an active, functioning role for the traditional leaders" within their governments, but each state would be free to exercise its own judgment when complying.

The Subcommittee on the Executive reported that to it had been referred at least five delegate proposals, plus a resolution, which would establish a federal council of traditional leaders. It, in turn, proposed to the full Structure Committee that there be a Chamber of Chiefs within the national executive. The parent body then proceeded to reject this by voting to give no formal role to the traditional leaders in the central government. Incensed, Chairman Heinrich Iriarte surrendered the chair to Vice-Chairman Tacheliol and announced that if the decision of his Committee remained unchanged, he would duly report it to the Convention, but then vote against it. The Committee reconsidered its action, and the matter was temporarily deferred until the further views of the Chiefs' committee could be ascertained.[28] Reported back was that the latter desired a position in the central government, but had failed to mention where. A Chamber of Chiefs--one from each state--was then reinstated in the draft of the Committee Proposal, vested with veto powers over all national legislation involving custom and tradition. To it would also be assigned advisory functions, mediation between the states, and other responsibilities relative to preservation of tradition. All of this occurred against the backdrop of a letter sent the previous month by Naniken Heinrich Stephen of Ponape to the Convention publicly recanting his support for a chamber of chiefs and advocating that "Micronesia's traditional leaders should assume an important and functional role at the District level rather than at the National level."²⁹

It soon became evident that few delegates within the Convention looked with favor upon the Structure Committee's massive effort to incorporate the traditional leaders within the national government. Eventually, Delegate Heinrich Iriarte was to salvage what he could, having the constitutional language amended so as merely to permit a Chamber of Chiefs, and leaving wholly to national legislation the delineation of the Chamber's functions, if, indeed, it were ever believed needed. Concomitantly, the states would no longer be mandated--but just authorized--to furnish a place for the traditional leaders in their governments (Art. V, Sec. 3). The state land court provisions disappeared, as previously related,³⁰ as also did the special assurance to the traditional leaders against their disenfranchisement. The last became unnecessary in the light of the proposal from the Civil Liberties Committee prohibiting discrimination on the basis of ancestry or social status (Art. IV, Sec. 4). All of these structural modifications occurred in the last few days of the Convention, postponed from day to day until after the settlement of the dispute over the anti-discrimination proposal of the Civil Liberties Committee, and the proviso attached to it declaring traditional roles and functions were unaffected by the constitution.³¹ Meanwhile, the center of attention had shifted to the phraseology of the Bill of Rights, and away from the specific details of formal governmental structure, and the Convention appeared to totter on the brink of collapse under the threat of chiefly boycott.

Over a month after reconvening, the Style Committee reported out a complete Bill of Rights for final Convention action. It contained the three ill-fated proposals which the Civil Liberties Committee had somewhat naively advanced in attempting to register Convention approval quickly on some issue before the delegates returned home, then only to run into unexpected objection. Also included were the other protections which the Civil Liberties Committee had endorsed in its later Proposal No. 14. The Style Committee materially rearranged and rephrased all of the language, and perhaps because of this cosmetic effort the section on "protection of traditions" originally contained in Proposal No. 4 now easily³² received the approval of the Convention, as did the portions on freedom of expression and assembly (C.P. Nos. 1 and 2). It was the protection against discrimination which became the focus of objection by the traditionalists, because it was subject to interpretation impugning custom, negating the making of special provision for traditional leaders, and precluding placement of the chiefs within the formal structure of government.

At the request of the Committe of the Whole, before which the anti-discrimination protection section was pending, the Committees of Civil Liberties, Governmental Structure, and Governmental Functions met with the traditional chiefs on October 17. In effect, about half of the Convention attended, but curiously absent were the delegates from Yap, including the area's two traditional leaders. Chairman Carl Heine from the Civil Liberties Committee recommended an amendment which would ensure the constitutional prohibition against discrimination did not "prohibit a State from establishing a council of traditional chiefs." Not alone was this narrowly directed to only one of the objections being raised, but it was so specific as to suggest truncating the entire thrust of the Structure Committee in its provision for the traditional leaders. A competing amendment, prepared in the names of all ten traditional chiefs at the Convention, declared that:

> ...nothing in the Constitution takes away a role or function of a traditional leader as recognized by custom and tradition, or prevents a traditional leader from being recognized, honored, and given formal or functional roles at any level of government as may be prescribed by this Constitution or by Statute (Art. V, Sec. 1).[33]

After oral legal opinions on the meaning of the competing amendments--for by now counsel of two of the committees had assumed the adversary stances of advocates--and considerable discussion, the consensus of the joint meeting endorsed the amendment proposed by the chiefs. Later, as a proviso tacked onto the prohibition against discrimination, this became part of the total Bill of Rights reported out from the Committee of the Whole.

On Thursday, October 23, with the delegates voting seriatim in Plenary Session on the various provisions in the proposed Bill of Rights, the section prohibiting discrimination, along with its attached "chiefs' provision," failed on Second Reading to secure the necessary three-fourths vote. It was during the course of this debate that Delegate Heinrich Iriarte referred to "some of us being born to rule and some of us ... to serve," the quotation with which this Chapter opened and that stiffened the adamancy of the modernists. A motion to reconsider promptly attempted to repair the seeming affront to the chiefs, but garnered only three more affirmative votes. Still two tallies shy, the section remained rejected. Rallied around the chiefs, the traditionalists would countenance an equal protection clause in the constitution only if accompanied with language safeguarding the traditional leaders and permitting them special treatment. The minority modernists had no fault to pick with the prohibition against discrimination, but were equally opposed to the "chiefs' proviso."[34] They would have no recognition, even indirectly, of the chiefs written into the structure of formal government. The daily Session ended with Delegate Ngiraked, "on behalf of the two traditional leaders of Palau," extending an invitation for "all traditional leaders, or those who consider themselves to be traditional leaders in the Convention" to meet in a room adjoining the Convention hall.[35]

The gathering of the traditional leaders and their supporters was by all accounts heated. Delegates Falcam and Ngiraked particularly waxed indignant, fanning the discontent of the chiefs.[36] The outcome informally announced was that the chiefs had decided to remain away from the Convention until after they met again on the following Monday, when they would then decide what next to do. Rumors were rife that some traditional leaders were acquiring airline tickets to return home.

When the confrontation between traditionalists and modernists began taking its final shape, Delegate Nimwes from Truk requested a resolution to be drafted declaring that the Convention had no desire to affect adversely the relationships which prevail between traditional leaders and the people of Micronesia. It in part recited:

> ...that it is the consensus of the Convention that all due honor and respect continue to be accorded the traditional leaders of Micronesia, and nothing in

the Constitution of the Federated States of Micronesia is intended in any way to detract from the role and function of traditional leaders in Micronesia or to deny them the full honor and respect which is rightfully theirs.[37]

The resolution was submitted to the Convention Secretary on the fateful day, October 23, but under the priority fixed by the Order of the Day, did not come up for introduction until after the defeat of the anti-discrimination section with its "chiefs' proviso," and in printed form would not be before the delegates until the following day.

On October 24, the day the Convention next met in Plenary Session, eight chiefs failed to answer to the roll call![38] Hurriedly the resolution was made a Special Order of Business, in the hope that its ameliorative language and the direction it carried that it "be included with all duplication of the Constitution so that the intent of the Delegates may be evident" would placate the traditional leaders. If the intent of the resolution was to deny the traditional leaders a place in the structure of the government, Delegate Falcam said he would vote against it. Floor Leader Tman was inclined to vote for the resolution for the basic reason that "I now subjugate myself to the proposition that there are some people that are born to rule. I am one of those who was born to serve." Delegate Ngiraked called the vote "an action to deliver a condolence to our chiefs, our traditional leaders, that they are necessary evils of our society. I am going to vote in support of this Resolution, but I will do so in comfort [sic] with all of our chiefs with us." After his unsuccessful attempt to postpone its consideration, the Convention adopted the resolution. Would the traditional leaders now return?

Delegate Eperiam of Ponape was worried:

> ...I beg leave of all non-traditional leader Delegates to this Convention, including myself, to make a request. On behalf of all the non-traditional leader Delegates to this Convention, I would like to request the President of this Convention to write a letter to all of the traditional leader Delegates to this Constitutional Convention to come and

join with us again beginning on Tuesday of next week.

President Nakayama responded that customs differed, and in Truk the use of a letter would be inappropriate; he preferred that each delegation approach their chiefs in the manner fitting with their customs. Delegate Olikong of Palau proposed that the President appoint a special committee to see the chiefs and request them to come back to the Convention, only for the motion to be defeated. In irony, Delegate Mwety mused: "I wonder why we just cannot give the airfares to the leaders to go back to their homes."[39]

Previously that day, when in Committee of the Whole the Executive Article was reached for discussion, Delegate Sawaichi from Palau was recognized on a point of privilege:

> We are considering one of the most important proposals that has been brought before this Convention, but I don't see most of the traditional leaders around to participate with us.... Although I understand that there is a quorum and under our Rules of Procedure we can proceed, I don't think that it is proper to take any action on this important one without the participation of our traditional leaders.[40]

The entire Article was deferred. The Convention might not follow the lead of the traditional leaders, but physically present and participating they must be.

Saturday, October 25, six chiefs were still absent. The President delayed the roll call until finally a quorum was present. Delegate Philippo from the Marshalls voiced the anxiety felt:

> ...I would like to request this Convention, regarding the long discussion on Committee Proposal No. 14, Section 4, "Prohibition on Discrimination," to let me offer my personal concern over the absence of our traditional chiefs in this Convention. The great concern I have in this respect is that, if I may, Mr. President, I would like to see the faces again of our traditional chiefs in this Convention. Because of differences in personal opinion, the

> absence of our traditional chiefs has resulted. In order to iron out these differences and to protect the genuine interest of this Convention, Mr. President, I would like to see that this happening not be released to the newspaper or any news media from this Convention. May I ask that this be silent.[41]

It was far too late to impose a news blackout; radio broadcasts already had widely disseminated information on the chiefs' walkout.

The Convention leaders pondered over ways to break the boycott and end the deadlock.[42] The answer was to be found in the ranks of the traditional leaders, themselves. There was no unanimity within any delegation in support of the walkout's purpose,[43] and by Monday only two traditional leaders failed to answer the roll call opening the Plenary Session.[44] Polarization within the Convention had failed to occur. The chiefs' threat of removing themselves proved mostly to be a show of pique on the part of a few, which was then manipulated to the end of achieving substantive goals. Nevertheless, public acceptance of the Convention's efforts, not to mention the future unity of Micronesia, could turn upon the endorsement of all Micronesia's traditional leaders. A disgruntled chief might still quit the Convention if some mollifying mechanism were not found to gloss over the interlude.

At the Plenary Session on Tuesday, October 28, after Delegate Ngiraked moved to place the Bill of Rights discrimination section back on the Order of Business, followed by a short recess, he announced:

> Mr. President, during the recess we have come to an understanding with the leadership. I think we can more efficiently dispose of the matter if I withdraw my motion.[45]

Observing the precedent earlier pointed out by the Special Conference Committee in the dispute over the protection of Micronesian custom, the Civil Liberties Committee arranged to sever the "chiefs' proviso" from the prohibition against discrimination with the understanding that the protective language would appear in another part of the constitution, outside of the Bill of Rights. This controversial section was then reconsidered and the surgery successfully conducted notwithstanding a statement by Delegate Heinrich Iriarte which tended to add confusion to the maneuver. The "safeguarding" clause was next separately adopted, but with difficulty and without a single affirmative vote to spare, this after the unusual procedure of the Convention Secretary twice calling the abstentions.[46]

Only then did Delegate Tun exercise the right he had previously reserved to explain the Yap delegations' vote:

"Mr. President, recently some Delegates decided not to attend this Convention, perhaps because of their disappointment and anger at the Convention's failure to pass a measure which recognizes the rights of chiefs, including the chiefs' right to participate at all levels of government.

"Mr. President, the Yap Delegates, including their traditional leaders were not among this group....

"Part of the reason is that Yap's traditional leaders do not believe that the defeated measure is so important to them. Other chiefs may disagree, but Yap's traditional leaders do not need to pass laws, cite cases, or count clauses when it comes to defending their role. They do not need to meet and lobby to protect themselves ... Yap's chiefs know their position and so do the people of Yap ... this hotly contested issue was irrelevant to Yap and unnecessary to our Constitution....

"Their [Yap chiefs'] instructions were that they did not want their roles, their powers, debated about and legislated upon. They did not want to occupy a corner of the national government.... Furthermore, our chiefs believed that equal treatment of all citizens in a Bill of Rights did not threaten their customary honor or power. Their conclusion was that they did not need--Yap did not need--the kind of dubious protection which is included in ... [the section adopted].

"In their wisdom, however, the chiefs added another instruction. They told us that, if the unity of Micronsia required it, we should compromise.... We voted for it because other districts think they need it ... and because maybe our yes votes will keep Micronesia together."[47]

All of the structural provisions originally designed to force the placement of the chiefs within the national and state governments were redirected. Full discretion on the formal accommodation of the traditional leaders is left to the new governments. Neither they nor the provisions in the constitution relating to legal recognition of custom and tradition are made self-executing; all will require positive legislative or constitutional action for effectuation. However, this did not signify that the role of the traditional leaders in writing the constitution was now eclipsed. They yet had an important part to play in concluding the work of the Convention, this one truly appropriate to their place in Micronesian custom.

---

1. CCM Journal, Vol. I, p. 398. Upon interviewing delegates and interpreters from Ponape, other than the principals, there appears to be some doubt over whether this part of the statement of Delegate Heinrich Iriarte was translated into English exactly as he had phrased it. However, the same informants indicated that the reference to God-given leaders was in harmony with his known views, and consonant with the full tenor of his remarks that tradition and democracy must be combined.

2. SCRep. No. 278, Senate Journal, Congress of Micronesia, Fifth Congress, 1st Special Session, 1974, p. 149. Note that the Senate Bill No. 278 which this report supported was not the vehicle by which the Congress of Micronesia ultimately was to grant voting powers in the Convention to traditional leaders sitting as delegates.

3. SCRep. No. 1, CCM Journal, Vol. II, p. 768; Ibid., Vol. I, p. 60.

4. CCM Journal, Vol. I, pp. 72-73. There was no recorded roll call which would permit reconstruction and analysis of the vote. The subsequent amendment proposed to Rule 26a, which made chiefly substitution discretionary with the district, was proposed with the joint sponsorship of elected delegates from Palau, Ponape, and Truk.

5. CCM Journal, Vol. I, p. 66.

6. When the two Iroij from the Marshalls joined the Convention after the recess, they sat as members of the ad hoc Chiefs' Meeting.

7. That the traditional leaders were all regarded as equals reflected more than the commonality of their statutory selection. Only by courtesy is a traditional leader's status recognized outside his district. The two Trust Territory meetings of traditional leaders held in 1974 (see p. 126, *supra*) functioned only by virtue of treating all chiefs as equals. It was thus proper for the same decorum to be observed within the Convention.

8. Summary Minutes of the Governmental Functions Committee, August 7, 1975.

9. All quotations are from the Summary Minutes of the Committee of the Whole for August 14, 1975, *passim*. See *CCM Journal*, Vol. II, pp. 625-32.

10. Summary Record of the Special Conference Committee, Third Meeting, August 15, 1975, p. 4.

11. SCRep. No. 5, *CCM Journal*, Vol. II, p. 773, at p. 774.

12. *CCM Journal*, Vol. I, p. 136.

13. Summary Minutes of the Committee of the Whole, August 19, 1975, *CCM Journal*, Vol. II, p. 649.

14. Office of Public Information, "Con-Con Special Report No. 1," August 29, 1975, p. 4.

15. *Report to the Congress of Micronesia on Seventh Round of Negotiations, January 1974*, pp. 29-30.

16. *Ibid.*, p. 38.

17. William A. McGrath and W. Scott Wilson believe the influence of the Iroij over land in the Marshalls has grown ever stronger after World War II "because of the prominent role the chiefs play as the main negotiators for the land-owning groups in dealing with the government, and in the settlement of disputes." See Ron Crocombe (ed.), *Land Tenure in the Pacific* (Melbourne: Oxford University Press, 1971), pp. 186-87.

18. SCRep. No. 4, *CCM Journal*, Vol. II, p. 771.

19. *Dialogue for Micronesia*, No. 38, August 13, 1975.

20. Summary Minutes of the Committee of the Whole, September 20, 1975, <u>CCM</u> <u>Journal</u>, Vol. II, p. 664.

21. <u>CCM</u> <u>Journal</u>, Vol. I, p. 226. (Here is an example of where the participation of the Marianas delegation in the Convention helped defeat a proposal, thus shaping a constitution under which its members did not believe they would be governed.)

22. <u>CCM</u> <u>Journal</u>, Vol. I, p. 235.

23. <u>CCM</u> <u>Journal</u>, Vol. I, p. 538. By now, delegates from the Marshalls were voicing opposition.

24. <u>CCM</u> <u>Journal</u>, Vol. I, p. 543.

25. <u>CCM</u> <u>Journal</u>, Vol. I, p. 544.

26. Summary Minutes of the Civil Liberties Committee for August 1, 1975, dated August 5, 1975.

27. <u>CCM</u> <u>Journal</u>, Vol. I, p. 288.

28. Summary Record of the Committee on Governmental Structure, 21st Meeting, October 3, 1975.

29. Misc. Com. No. 18, <u>CCM</u> <u>Journal</u>, Vol. II, p. 950.

30. The Subcommittee on Judiciary reported the consensus of traditional chiefs who testified before it was against setting up traditional courts or requiring them by constitutional provision. Rather, the states should be permitted to do so, in effect what the revised Judiciary Article now allows. See Summary Minutes of Subcommittee on Judiciary, September 22, 1975.

31. Summary Minutes of the Committee of the Whole, November 6, 1975, <u>CCM</u> <u>Journal</u>, Vol. II, pp. 758ff. However, as early as November 1, Chairman Heinrich Iriarte had proposed an amendment which would have eliminated the mandatory character of the Chamber of Chiefs (PEACESAT Broadcast, November 1, 1975).

32. "Easily" warrants qualification in two respects: several delegates protested it was unneces-

sary to legislate tradition (CCM Journal, Vol. I, p. 394). On another dimension, the delegates who had earlier protested may have been lulled into acquiescence.

Art. V, Sec. 2 of the FSM Constitution declares that "protection of Micronesian tradition shall be considered a compelling social purpose warranting" legislation which may be passed for that purpose. At first reading this appears to give the protected tradition superiority over any civil liberty. However, the Style Committee's intent in changing the language was only to signify that "the courts are commanded to take custom and tradition into account," not to impugn the courts' ability to balance the conflict between introduced rights and the protection of custom on a case by case basis. See SCRep. No. 44, CCM Journal, Vol. II, p. 872, at p. 874.

33. The language quoted in the text has been slightly altered so as to read as it appears in the final form of the Constitution. The Federated States of Micronesia Constitution's declared neutrality is highlighted by the incorporation into the "Palauan Constitution" of a provision preventing any governmental action in Palau revoking traditional rights of chiefs not inconsistent with the constitution as adopted by that entity in 1980.

34. See interview with the three "Devil's advocates"--Delegate Kikuo Apis of Ponape and Delegates Maketo Robert and Iskia Sony of Truk--in Dialogue for Micronesia, No. 52 [sic], October 24, 1975.

35. CCM Journal, Vol. I, p. 403.

36. It appeared to the observers that both Delegates Leo Falcam and John Ngiraked displayed unusual fervor. For the latter, the explanation may have lain in the fact he is a member of the Udes Clan of the High Chief Reklai, and potentially in line for the title; for the former, his conduct may have been reaction to the resistance which the proposed chamber of chiefs and the plural executive had met with that day in the Committee of the Whole.

37. As Resolution No. 32 it now appears appended to all duplicated copies of the Federated States of Micronesia Constitution.

38. Absent from the Plenary Session of the Convention on October 24 were the Ibedul and Reklai from Palau, the two Iriartes and Naniken Stephens from Ponape, and Chief Bossy from Truk. Also absent were Chief Hathay from Yap and Iroij Tomeing from the Marshalls. Chief Luktun (Yap), Iroij Lanki (Marshalls), and Chief Kintoky Joseph (Truk) were present. Later, it was determined that the Yapese traditional leaders, while not wishing to offend their "brother" chiefs, did not approve of the boycott, so characteristically took the course of splitting their attendance. It is possible that the same applied to the Iroij. The following day, on the opening of the Session, the four responded to the roll call. Chief Kintoky Joseph attended all session, observing the traditional role of the Trukese chief as one of mediation and resolution of conflict. He was on record pointing out there would be a true conflict over the role of the chief in the introduced government only if the constitution were to <u>deny</u> traditional leaders any ability to take part. <u>CCM Journal</u>, Vol. I, pp. 390-91.

39. All quoted references on October 24, the 77th day of the Convention, from <u>CCM Journal</u>, Vol. I, pp. 409-11.

40. Summary Minutes of the Committee of the Whole, October 24, 1975, <u>CCM Journal</u>, Vol. II, p. 707.

41. <u>CCM Journal</u>, Vol. I, p. 423.

42. A memorandum prepared for the President and Floor Leader by this author identified six issues involving "traditional rights and chiefly position--conceptually distinct subjects but actually intertwined in the process of drafting the Constitution.... For some of these issues there is [now] little or no controversy.... On some of these issues the majority view is known; while there may be one or more minority views, each is never capable of becoming a majority.... Some Delegates who are part of the majority with respect to one or more of the issues are also members of the minority as to others." An examination of the issues followed, indicating the positions prevailing on each and the logical alternatives--my logic--for reaching consensus.

43. Of all traditional leaders sitting as delegates by virtue of their being coopted by their

fellows, only in the Palau delegation did both consistently fail to appear in the Convention. It appears likely, however, that their absence was designed to be symbolic, rather than expressing personal commitment to the substantive position of the protesting chiefs, as witness the provisions of the "Palau Constitution," D.P. No. 100, which prohibited discrimination on the basis of ancestry or social status.

44. On October 27, Chief Luktun from Yap and Delegate Heinrich Iriarte from Ponape were excused. The statement of Delegate Tun in the text disclosed that Chief Luktun's absence was not related to the boycott. Rumor had Delegate Iriarte as being ill after the Ponape luau. (See Chapter 13, *infra*.)

45. CCM *Journal*, Vol. I, p. 439.

46. CCM *Journal*, Vol. I, p. 458.

47. CCM *Journal*, Vol. I, p. 459. See also statement of Floor Leader Tman in CCM *Journal*, Vol. I, p. 356.

Chapter 13. The Micronesian Way

Micronesians culturally sense what visitors to their islands only gradually come to understand: that the various regions each have their own styles of discourse, with the offering and partaking of food a common element. Avoidance of sharp confrontation and the maintenance of discussion to the reaching of what at least has the appearance of consensus characterize many of the areas. And delay and procrastination over difficult decisions are endemic. All were amply evident during the Micronesian Constitutional Convention of 1975.

The Congress of Micronesia opened the Convention with a formal reception, and before the recess the Marshallese community on Saipan presented a "brunch" for the delegates, embellished with the singing of the area's songs by the Marshallese women. On September 20, after reconvening, the Palauans on Saipan hosted a Palauan feast under the theme of "Let Union Abide,"[1] replete with Palauan food and entertainment. A month later, on October 25, at the apogee of the traditional leaders' crisis, the Ponape delegation held its scheduled reception, and all of the delegates attended, including the traditional leaders who had indignantly absented themselves from the Convention. For them not to have been present would have constituted an unconscionable affront.

The Ponapeans skillfully adapted their traditions to the occasion: a yam competition with the presentation of a mammoth tuber overshadowing all other offerings would have hardly been appropriate, but they served up two roast pigs, both bigger than the single animal at the "Palauan Evening." The table-sized cake with its replica in colorful icing of the Ponapean invitation theme, "In Unity There is Strength," was so large that it had to be baked on Guam and then flown to Saipan by plane with seats rearranged. It proved immaterial that a special air-freight load of mangrove crab and reef lobster had spoiled on its trip across the Trust Territory from Ponape, so that the Palauan coconut crab could not be bested; the Ponapean tables were so heavily piled with platters of reef fish, dishpan sized containers of breadfruit, taro, and tapioca, and other forms of food and drink that the absence went unnoticed. The double entendre of the entertainment did not escape attention, however. Dances and songs of all the other districts were offered, not just those of Ponape, with persons from those districts also participating. A week later, the reception held under Marianas' auspices was anti-climactic, no more than a polite display of courtesy required by the Convention's meeting on Saipan, in its way symbolizing the detachment of the Marianas' people which was soon to be legally formalized. In these and various other less organized ways, the gastronomic aspect of Micronesian discourse was amply evidenced.

Throughout its ninety days, the Convention Journal records the calling of numerous short recesses to sort out procedural tangles and bring the delegates back on course. Usually these recesses were taken at the instigation of Floor Leader Luke Tman. A careful reading of the Journal reveals that the major function of the recesses gradually shifted as the delegates became more conversant with the Convention rules. Ever more frequently, they served the purpose of forestalling the further flaring of emotions on the floor, and aiding in reconciling the differences of views expressed. Should substantive incompatibility be manifest, the recess at least provided opportunity for agreeing upon the procedural avenue to be followed, and avoiding an open, frontal clash. Mostly the nuances of the Convention rules were observed in the breach, the Floor Leader referring to them when necessary to move the work of the Convention along and deliberately remaining silent when it was apparently proceeding well enough by their being ignored. Appeals were made to the Standing Committees to settle their differences outside of the Plenary Session and Committee of the Whole, so that there would be no occasion for them to erupt upon the Convention floor. The "Micronesian Way" of discourse was to become most evident in two parliamentary maneuvers, with diametrically opposite goals, the Palauans' final attempt to sell their "non-negotiable" demands and the Convention's end game, in effect breaching the former and bringing the delegates to agreement through consensus technique.

When on October 22 the Special Committee reported on its study of Delegate Proposal No. 100 (the "Palauan Constitution") that "... practically all of the subjects included ... have been covered in the deliberations of the various subject matter committees, and with only minor exceptions are incorporated in Committee Proposals already before the Convention or now being introduced,"[2] it was referring only to consideration and not necessarily to Convention acceptance. However, as Delegate Ngiraked a few days earlier had remarked, in commenting upon the mock-up "staff constitution,"[3] it showed many parts of the Palauan position were being adopted as part of the Micronesian constitution.[4] Indeed, the reading of the Preamble at the start of each Session was a daily reminder to the delegates of their debt to the Palauan document. Other provisions recommended by the Standing Committees also owed at least their turn of phrase to the "Palauan Constitution," but a review of the various Committees' summary minutes reveals that this represented no expression of pliant subservience to the Palauan delegation. Rather, many delegates, including the Palauans, appeared as individuals before the Committees to argue their respective proposals, and extended evaluation went into the weighing of all alternatives. Only then, with the Committee members independently concluding that the approach embodied in the Palauan document best fitted within the framework of the limited central government preferred, might its terminology or intent[5] be accepted. This subtle flattery fully accorded with the desire to give the Palauans no opportunity for taking public offense. The first open confrontation on the Convention floor over the Palauan "non-negotiable" conditions did not occur until mid-October, when the constitution's public finance provisions were before the delegates, and in effect the Palauans then urged the Convention to resort to Micronesian informal discourse in resolving the issue.

The Committee on Public Finance faced the dual problem of drafting the constitutional sections governing the handling of grant funds originating external to Micronesia and also providing for internal taxation. The Palauan position on both permitted no misunderstanding: the national government should be narrowly limited to the raising of revenues from interstate and foreign commerce, and from foreign corporations doing business in two or more states. (Delegates interpreted the last as designed to exclude from national taxation all companies which the superport might bring to Palau.) Specifically denied to the central government would be power to levy taxes on personal income or wages, the major base for the revenues being raised by the Congress of Micronesia. To make up any shortfall for funding essential national functions, the central government could impose equal levies on the states, but given their disparities in size and resources, the practical efficacy of the power was regarded as minimal. Externally generated funds would also have to be divided equally, with the national and each of the state governments receiving identical amounts.

The Committee on Public Finance and Taxation considered these constraints as unfeasible, but debated long on how to exceed their limitations. Complicating the reaching of decisions was the overlapping jurisdiction of the Governmental Functions Committee with which it was unable to reach a compromise after a joint meeting. In the opinion of some of its members, "the taxing powers suggested by ... [the Functions] Committee were unrealistic in terms of the proposed governmental services which revenues from those taxes were to finance."[6] Eventually, the Functions Committee withdrew from the field, deliberately postponing the expression of its views on taxing powers until the Committee whose "primary concern" it was had reported.[7]

C.P. No. 15 as reported out by the Public Finance and Taxation Committee recommended that foreign aid be distributed "equitably" (not the Palauan's "equally"), with the exception of earmarked or conditional funds for which the directions of the donor would have to be observed. Referred to the Committee of the Whole, it was adopted by a show of hands after much discussion. The report from the Committee noted that the Palauans had objected to the "Palau Constitution's" provision "with respect to equal distribution of foreign aid" not being adequately accommodated.[8]

While this was transpiring, the Public Finance and Taxation Committee placed C.P. No. 26 on the Convention Secretary's desk.[9] It exclusively assigned the taxing of income--both personal and business--and imports to the national government, with the proviso that a minimum of 50 percent of the revenues realized must be paid to the state where collected. All other tax bases would be reserved to the states. The Committee was aiming to provide "wide fiscal latitude to the states while giving realistic revenue potential to the central government."[10] Inferentially, it was also seeking to end the long-festering quarrel in the Congress of Micronesia over the sharing of income tax revenues which had seen the gradual disengagement of the disgruntled Marshalls District.[11] The Palauan fiscal position had now been openly challenged on two fronts, and the two Palauan members of the Public Finance and Taxation Committee had not exercised their right to append minority statements to the Standing Committee Reports accompanying the Committee's Proposals.[12] The Convention awaited the Palau delegation's next move.

The Proposal governing equitable distribution of externally generated funds reached the Convention floor on October 18 bearing minor clarificatory changes suggested by the Style Committee. Delegate Ngiraked next urged the Convention to substitute the Palauan's "equal share" formula, but was defeated in a close vote. Rather than allowing the Proposal to go to definitive Second Reading, Delegate Ngiraked reminded the delegates that the taxation proposal was in the offing:

> ... We have come to the crossroad ... we are split between our commitment to our people [in Palau] and our love for Micronesia. Please be patient with us. We want to join Micronesia. So, I move, Mr. President that before we take one further step on this item, we defer action.

C.P. No. 15 was postponed until October 21, when the taxation proposal was scheduled to come before the Convention.[13] On that Thursday, ominously, the taxation measure passed the Committee of the Whole without discussion,[14] and temporarily was then detoured to the Style Committee for polishing of phraseology. Next on the agenda of the Plenary Session was C.P. No. 15, with its authorization for equitable distribution of externally generated funds.

Once again the Palauan mandatory "equal share" formula was offered as an alternative, but now augmented by an accompanying provision allowing the central government to levy assessments on the states for supporting essential national functions.

Equality would also be the measure for any levy. It appeared as if the Convention was at last facing the long-anticipated showdown. Before the vote could be called, Delegate Ngiraked left his desk and walked over to speak to Delegate Falcam. The latter then moved for a "brief recess," referring to the importance of the "very substantial amendment in intent as well as the impact on other matters." The delegate from Palau seconded the motion, and at the same time announced the Palauan delegation desired to meet immediately "with the Chairmen of all Delegations and all interested Chairmen of the Standing Committees." The "brief" recess lasted for a full hour as the Palauan delegates faced what in fact was the entire leadership of the Convention. On reconvening, action on C.P. No. 15 was deferred for an additional week, and during this interim the Convention officially marked time on the issue.[15]

All accounts of what transpired in the off-the-record meeting coincide: amicably, and without any show of threat, the Palauans defended the justice of their position, pointing to past inequities and logically mustering arguments not raised on the Convention floor. Devoid of the tension which accompanies the effort of making telling points in public debate, and lacking all confining strictures which adhere to the observance of parliamentary procedure, the delegates felt at ease within the informality of the unstructured discussion, all of which fostered a sense of shared community and a readiness to believe that a meeting of minds could somehow be reached. Capitalizing upon this, the Palauan delegation requested an opportunity to meet separately with each district delegation over cocktails, and the delay of a week ensued. The Palauans had decided upon the issue of State equality as the foundation of their position,[16] and were now bent on low-key persuasion to achieve it.

That evening the Palau and Marshalls delegates conferred over drinks. Although not committing themselves, the Marshallese delegates concurred that the Palauan position had strong, sustaining arguments. Next the Palauans attempted to apply their "cocktail diplomacy" to the Yapese. Privately, some of the latter had confided to me that as a small, and possibly the smallest, state, Yap stood most to benefit by the Palauan formula for distribution of foreign funds; however, they also feared it would spell impotence for any national government built wholly upon the "equality" principle. If they accepted the Palauan invitation, they knew it would be difficult to rebuff being importuned to support the Palauan position. Rather than having to appear to compromise in some way with their Palauan hosts, they refused to attend. From this point on, the Palauans' drive through informal discourse faltered, but they had succeeded in laying the groundwork for securing the Convention's grudging acceptance.

When the Convention again scheduled C.P. No. 15 on its agenda, the attitude of many delegates may have remained one of skepticism, but was no longer hostile. With the national government potentially slated by C.P. No. 26 to exercise greater taxing powers than contemplated by the "Palauan Constitution," there was no need for the Constitution to authorize levies on the states, whether equal or not, and this feature quickly disappeared. For the Palauan delegation, Johnson Toribiong pointed out that the national government with its control over international relations, had the inherent capacity to assure funding grants would be phrased conditionally, and so could avoid the equality principle whenever it wished to do so.[17] Delegate Sony of Truk concurred that the possibility of equal distribution was "a very remote possibility."[18] Confounding the members from the other districts, Delegate Nakamura defended "equal distribution" as assuring his home district of Palau would not selfishly benefit from foreign funds.[19] Delegate John Heine announced his stand behind the Palauan amendment because it was only fair that all districts share in money originally designated for just the Marshalls.[20] Delegate Ngiraked likened the resolution of the problem faced to the sharing which accompanies a happy marriage, and that the whole matter was simply one of basing unity on equality.[21] Senator Olter of Ponape was one of the few delegates converted by neither the congeniality nor logic of the Palauan delegation. He did not "believe that unity can be bought by threats nor with equal distribution of money."[22] Put to a vote, C.P. No. 15, amended as desired by the Palauans, received the three-fourths tally requisite for passage, but only after some delegates changed their abstentions to ayes, and then without one vote to spare. Delegate Olter remained indignant, and his amendment to delete the equal distribution of foreign aid provision was waiting when the proposal next came before the delegates on the Convention's 90th day, as the entire constitution was presented for final approval. Reluctantly, he was persuaded to abandon this parliamentary maneuver when an informal "nose count" by the Floor Leader disclosed it would not succeed. Still adamant in his opposition, Delegate Olter then abstained from voting on the adoption of the constitution, but later appended his signature to the document.[23]

With the equal distribution of foreign aid issue disposed of, the Convention awaited the events of the following day when C.P. No. 26, permitting the national government to levy an income tax, would come before the Convention for definitive vote. Since the Palauan delegation had allowed the measure to pass Committee of the Whole scrutiny without comment, its raising of objections now would be tantamount to a doublecross. All of this reasoning was premised upon assumption, however, for the Palauans had made no firm commitment tying the fate of the two proposals. Upon Second Reading, Delegate Toribiong, with the aid of his district colleagues, did attempt to amend the proposal so that a state might increase its income tax revenues by adding a surtax, but was defeated. Delegate Sony sought to fix the maximum (rather than minimum) of a state's share at 50 percent, and Delegate Ngiraked warned:

> Mr. President. I think about everybody in the Convention has settled down on the language as provided in the Proposal, and let us not open any field of disagreement....[24]

The Truk delegate's amendment was rejected. With one change--deleting the prohibition against the imposing of export taxes--the taxing proposal passed almost unanimously. Unheralded in the public information releases of the Convention was this first breach in the Palauans' "non-negotiable" position.[25]

The financial issues were not the only matters before the Convention when the delegates were called upon to debate their terms. Simultaneously, the delegates were considering the extensive report of the Governmental Structure Committee proposing the future shape of the national government. Some of its contents were closely linked with the financial decisions made, for state equality in lawmaking and execution would help assure their observance.

The Governmental Structure Committee had pondered interminably over what its recommendations ought be for national legislature and chief executive. The attempt by a majority of its members to include the traditional chiefs in the central government has already been related in Chapter 12. Its Legislative Subcommittee could not reach agreement, and so presented the full committee with two options, one for a unicameral and the other for a bicameral body. It had at least eliminated a third option, that of a tricameral body proposed by Naniken Stephen, delegate from Ponape (D.P. No. 135), which the subcommittee concluded was outside the area of delegate interests. The full Structure Committee settled on a bicameral legislature, copying the Congress of Micronesia in the composition of its two houses. A majority of the delegate Proposals considered by the Committee favored a plural chief executive, and this, too, was the choice of the full Committee. It was claimed that "in many ways, the plural Executive proposed ... is very similar to the Swiss Executive Structure,"[26] but the correspondence was somewhat tenuous. The particular form agreed upon would have had each state elect a Minister to sit on the Council of Ministers, with the Minister charged with the supervision of one or more executive departments in accordance with the directives of the Council. It would be collectively responsible for administration of the laws. The Council would coopt one of its members as Prime Minister, who would serve as head of state. In addition to performing the duties connoted by the title, the occupant of that post could also exercise veto powers over legislation, and with the concurrence of the Council (and Senate) make appointments to the nation's highest offices.

None of these structural recommendations was in harmony with the provisions of the "Palauan Constitution," and to propose the Congress of Micronesia as a model for the new national legislature directly challenged one of the Palauan "non-negotiable" demands. Much of the subordinate matter in the Structure Committee's proposal (C.P. No. 24) was to survive Convention review, but the plural executive and bicameral legislature did not gain the requisite support, just as the Committee's recommendation for a unitary judicial system failed to secure Convention endorsement. In retrospect, it can only be concluded that on basics the Governmental Structure Committee amassed a record of ineffectiveness.

There was widespread interest throughout the Trust Territory supporting a plural executive. The Yap questionnaire showed the people of the district favored a council over a single national executive, but divided over whether it should be elected directly. Delegate Tacheliol from Yap told the Governmental Structure Committee that he had no choice but "to go for the plural executive."[27] Debate in the Committee of the Whole and in Plenary Session demonstrated that the delegates fully comprehended the principles of separation of powers and checks and balances as exemplified by the American system of government, and wished to preserve them. They were less certain in their appraisals of a plural executive, how it would function and its relation to the same concepts, having experienced no other than a presidential system.[28] Some mistakenly assumed that the naming of a single chief executive through legislative selection, as called for in the "Palauan Constitution," automatically meant the creation of a parliamentary system.[29] But all understood that the electing of a president by popular vote raised questions of both practical politics and district separatism which could wreck the Convention. On the other hand, if choice of the executive was to be indirect, through the national legislature, then the structure and composition of that body became doubly important. The assuring of rotation and the procedures for the registering of choice for chief executive became matters of mere detail as compared with resolving the fundamental issue of the representation which each state was to be assured. The Structure Committee's proposal, which in essence would continue the Congress of Micronesia under new name, failed to satisfy.

On and on the debate continued, with attention alternating between the proposed executive and legislative Articles. Fairly early, an amendment substituted a popularly-elected chief executive for the council of ministers recommended by the Governmental Structure Committee, but that did not point to any consensus on either the national executive or the shape and apportionment of the national legislature. Round and round went the repetitive arguments over the relative merits of state equality versus representation based upon population. They were not unfamiliar to Micronesia, nor were those mustered in the dispute over unicameralism versus bicameralism, for the bicameral Congress of Micronesia had originally been instituted in 1965 over the objections of the American Administration, and then continued by decision of the Congress in 1969 when called upon by the Secretary of the Interior to reexamine its composition.[30] But equality of legislative representation having now accreted the support of a number of delegates from other districts than Palau, the retention of bicameralism would be more than just an affront to the Palauan position.

With the Convention's life running out, on November 3, its 85th day, a suggestion was "floated" before the Administration Committee that the Convention meet informally in closed session. In the words of Delegate Ngiraked in the Committee of the Whole:

> ...Let me take the liberty to announce to the floor a development, a decision, a consensus that was reached by the Administration Committee this morning. It has become very obvious that some Delegates are inhibited to speak in front of a large audience--and 50 people is large enough. If I may prevail upon the kindness and understanding of our public observers and guests in the gallery, it was decided that maybe we should sort out some of our differences in a closed door session. Then the Delegates could really express themselves in an open manner and candid manner.[31]

Here was a call for return to Micronesian ways of discussion, nominally providing a forum for those delegates who felt the urge to speak frankly, but actually allowing indirectness and vagueness to provide opportunity for shaping of consensus. The substantive contributions proved minimal: most speakers repeated what they had said already, and neither new arguments nor solutions were forthcoming. However, tension was reduced and the delegates placed in a frame of mind more conducive to compromise. On a number of occasions straw ballots were taken in the Executive Session, disclosing that a single executive was favored over a plural body, but not sufficiently to achieve the necessary three-fourths' majority. Comparable informal tally on unicameralism/bicameralism and equality/population representation revealed a nearly even bifurcation existed within the Convention. Notwithstanding, when the President voiced the opinion that it appeared the delegates had now reached the feared abyss, and agreement might be impossible, negative objections prevented the calling of any halt to the delegates' discourse.

From this off-the-record meeting emerged another device to reach consensus, a Special Committee comprised of two delegates from each district, selected not by the President but their respective delegations, to which the issues in dispute were to be referred.[32] One of each pair of delegates was nominally required to be a traditional leader, but in fact Committee membership fluctuated, with another district colleague occasionally sitting in as substitute for the chief as the Special Committee progressively attacked specific matters. Eventually, as many as seventeen delegates in all took part in these Committee deliberations. Since it was tacitly understood that Committee decision was to be reached through mutual concurrence, the amorphous membership fully accorded with Micronesian mores and their accommodating degree of slippage; strict limitation of participation to designated membership, while in harmony with the tidy concepts of introduced parliamentary procedure, would have carried the risk of hardening positions and making differences irreconcilable.

Traditionally, decisions were not achieved in Micronesia through formal debate or rhetoric; rather, weighing of the various social impacts and personally specific effects fed into a decisional process devoid of parliamentary dialectics. Recourse to the Special Committee in effect was the Convention's harkening back to this pre-contact frame. Indeed, the very inclusion of the traditional leaders helped cloak the Committee with an aura of capacity for resolving issues, for once theirs had been the function of enunciating, not debating, decisions.

In fact, the inclusion of the traditional leaders represented no casual happenstance. The ground had been laid carefully by a number of the Convention's leaders,[33] apparently some contemplating it would enable chiefs getting together and working out compromises whenever the delegates proved impossibly divided. Events were to demonstrate that this definitive role would not evolve. For one thing, the traditional leaders were insufficiently versed in the intricacies of the problems faced so were unable to assume such a crucial part. However, their presence during the days of negotiations did have a very positive salutary effect by serving as a dampener on the airing of strong emotions within the Committee. In respect to the chiefs, Committee discussions were conducted deferentially. Occasionally, when President Nakayama believed the exchange occurring between elected delegates was becoming dysfunctional, he would deliberately call upon a traditional leader to express his views. Befitting a chief's customary style, the latter might counsel patience, and the seeking of compromise. However, should he introduce a substantive element, it would be difficult for his companion district delegate to refute openly, and others would do so only with diffidence. In this way dialogue would be maintained and mounting adversarial clash would be periodically eased. Slowly, over the span of two days, the "executive or legislature" version of the classic "chicken and egg" conondrum proved amenable to resolution in a wholly Micronesian way.

Some of the Marshallese delegates had said on the Convention floor that they would not approve a constitution with only one house, but their objections seemed mainly directed to the failure to afford separate representation to all four subregions of the district. Several delegates from Truk had implied that they would not vote for a unicameral legislature but significantly this was not a delegation position. The Ponapean delegation was split. The Palauan delegates had declared a legislature with equal state membership absolutely essential, and this supported unicameralism. The Special Committee first addressed the unicameral-bicameral impasse. It rejected bicameralism, or any half-way measure, such as the temporary adoption of unicameralism and then allowing the voters, when ratifying the constitution, to opt for bicameralism.[34] Instead, the conferees settled four-square upon a single-house Congress. To reach this decision, it was incumbent upon them to dispose of the representation dilemma pitting equality versus population. Characteristically, they did so by seizing both horns, rather than favoring one or the other of the alternatives. To be enacted, legislation must successfully run the gauntlet of a two-thirds vote of members on initial reading, and two-thirds vote of the state delegations must concur on final passage (Art. IX, Sec. 20).[35] For actions by the national Congress other than the passing of legislation, membership vote suffices.

By the time C.P. No. 24 was placed before the Special Committee, it had been amended to include provision for a single chief executive. Starting with this premise, the conferees sought a means other than popular election to choose the officer, and seized upon indirect selection through the Congress. This method was already adumbrated in the provisions of the "Palauan Constitution." A number of amendments had previously been prepared for C.P. No. 24 which would have had two categories of representatives elected to a unicameral legislature, one from each state for longer, four-year, terms, and the others apportioned by population for two-year terms. During the deliberations of the Committee, this duality was adopted so as to serve the function of furnishing a pool of nominees, one from each state, from which the national Congress could name the President and Vice-President of the Federated States. Only legislators serving four-year terms would be eligible. Once chosen, these executive officers would vacate their Congressional seats (Art. X, Secs. 4,5), and serve much as their counterparts in the United States. Many of the delegates appreciated the method of selection did not vitiate the presidential system of government, having before them the naming of Vice-President Gerald Ford, and later his succession to the Presidency.[36] In this and all of its other solutions, the Committee displayed little innovation, but served only to facilitate the working out of compromises based upon proposals already before the Convention.

One final matter remained, the apportionment of the new Congress. Using the population estimates most readily available, and allotting to each state a total representation of approximately one member for each four thousand inhabitants, the Committee fixed the size of the first Congress at twenty-eight, of which six would be elected for four-year terms. This formula combining the two classes of members when apportioning state population was rejected by Palauan delegates when brought before the entire Committee of the Whole. Although a betrayal of the compromise, the delegates supporting it in Committee did not now defend it, but accepted the Palauan-offered substitute. The Congressmen elected on the basis of state equality would be regarded as a group apart, and a 6,000 to 1 ratio would be made applicable to the two-year members. This decreased the Marshalls and Ponape delegations by one member each, and that of Truk by two, while the total chamber size was reduced to twenty-four members (Art. XV, Sec. 6). At least every ten years the Congress must reapportion itself, which power is broad enough to include changing the size of the chamber, just so long as each state is afforded at least one member elected on the basis of population. To each state is assigned responsibility for dividing itself into single member Congressional districts, with each approximately equal in population after giving due regard to language, cultural, and geographic differences (Art. IX, Sec. 10). The major effect of this new formula for allotting members was to assure disproportionately greater representation for Kusaie, when it should break from Ponape and become a separate state, due to its minimal population of approximately four thousand persons.

At the time the Committee deliberated, the issue of traditional leaders' involvement in the central government had not yet been completely laid, and this is reflected in adding a provision permitting a state to have a chief occupy one of its two-year term seats in the Congress. If the right is exercised, the number of Congressional districts whose boundaries are drawn on the basis of population will be reduced and the state reapportioned accordingly. The Committee had anticipated that the traditional leaders would be elected at large,[37] but the Convention at Plenary Session left the manner of selection to the states (Art. IX, Sec. 11). While a concession to the traditional leaders in their effort to obtain formal role in government, the constitutional language is not self-executing, and depends upon state legislative action, the same deferring solution adopted with respect to other structural incorporations of the chiefs.

Only under the pressure of the fast approaching 90th and final day of the Convention's duration were these compromises pieced together. Some of the delegates most outspoken in their views had not served on the Special Committee, and found themselves confronted with accepting either the solutions reached or responsibility for the Convention's failure. The "Devil's Advocates" stated that for the sake of unity, the members of the "Club" would vote in favor of the executive compromise.[38] Chief Bossy, a strong advocate of custom and tradition, noted that "even though many of us are 100 percent against [the compromise], we accepted with pain only for the sake of unity."[39] On the 88th day, Delegate Mwety proposed modification of the vote necessary for adoption of legislation by the national Congress because "my sense of fairness tells me that I should make that motion," only after a short recess to add that "because of extreme pressure on me by my own delegation, I withdraw my motion."[40]

Into the compromises went elements compatible with the views held by various delegates. The Yap delegation knew that the district's questionnaire showed its people favored continuation of the method of selecting legislators followed in the Congress of Micronesia. A chief executive elected through the Congress, and state equality in the enacting of national legislation were in full accord with the "Palauan Constitution," although the compromise modified both to also include relative population weighting the decisional process. All in all, the delegates regarded the structural recommendations of the Special Committee as the best resolution of the impasse which could be reached under the time constraints faced, and one which they considered politically palatable. Events following the Convention were to provide measure for the adequacy of that judgment.

So pleased were the delegates with the mechanism of the Special Committee for coming to grips with the Convention's most divisive issues that they assigned it the last two "non-negotiable" demands of the Palauan delegation--right of unilateral secession and the situating of the national capital in Palau--which had been successively deferred up to the last days of the Convention.

The General Provisions Committee had met the withdrawal issue frontally by expressly denying the right of any state, once having joined the Federation, to secede (C.P. No. 27). Two members of the General Provisions Committee did not sign the supporting report. Upon the Committee Proposal coming before the Committee of the Whole, motion was made to adopt the Minority Proposal (C.P. No.

27a), which would allow any state for a period of five years, starting eight years after the effective date of the constitution, to withdraw. As rationale for the Palau position embodied in the Minority Proposal, Delegate Nakamura cited the possibility of a district's disapproving of the terms included in a future status compact, and so wishing to disengage from the Federation. The rebuttal was two-pronged: should the compact be negotiated before the vote on the constitution, any district not approving of its conditions could refuse to be bound by the constitution; on the other hand, should the compact be negotiated under the constitution, all delegations of major powers to the United States would have to secure approval of the State legislatures, so the states would have a share in the ratification of the compact. Reservation of a right of secession as a defensive measure was unnecessary.[41] Delegate Ngiraked requested deferral and there the issue hung suspended until referred to the Special Committee.

Minor signs outside of the formal debate in Plenary Session and Committee of the Whole all suggested that the Palauan delegation had changed strategy, and was no longer adamant in its stand on secession. Indeed, it now appeared to favor constitutional silence as the delegates from other districts began pressing for inclusion of a declaration positively denying any right of state withdrawal. The Special Committee's solution was to reject both positions, and substitute an amendment reading, "It is the solemn obligation of the national and state governments to uphold the provisions of this Constitution and to advance the principles of unity upon which this Constitution is founded" (Art. XIII, Sec. 3).[42] Delegate Nakamura then withdrew his Minority Proposal amendment, while indicating that his conscience still bothered him "due to the fact that this inalienable right should not be prohibited in this Constitution."[43]

The final action of the Committee of the Whole was on the capital site of the new nation. Early in the Convention, in the General Provisions Committee, Delegate Falcam had categorized this issue as one of secondary importance, which could be disposed of later in the Convention or assigned to the future national government. Delegate Ngiraked's response was that it was a matter of style, and "maybe the future Legislature could decide the issue but this body [the Committee ?]

is far better equipped to make the choice than the Congress of Micronesia."[44] The General Provisions Committee then proceeded to sidestep the demand that the national capital be placed within Palau by recommending the matter be referred to the new national Congress, which would make a decision within one year after the effective date of the constitution (C.P. No. 25). A minority report supported the Palauan claim for the national capital.

On the 88th day, the Committee of the Whole referred both to the Special Committee. When President Nakayama, as the officer who would chair its deliberations, requested "instructions as to how to treat this particular Proposal," Delegate Nakamura for the Committee of the Whole asked the Special Committee "to iron out the differences between the Committee Proposal and the Minority Proposal,"[45] no mean task. On the morning of the 89th day, the Special Committee did secure consensus by eliminating all mention of the capital from the constitution, this with the concurrence of its Palauan members. Later that day, the Administration Committee met with Chairman Ngiraked of the Palauan delegation at his request "to consider the possibility of introducing to this Convention an alternate course of action ... a resolution to effectuate that thinking."[46] As explained by Delegate Nimwes, a gentlemen's agreement was made to have the Convention recommend by resolution "that Palau be considered as one possible site,"[47] an innocuous direction. But Delegate Nimwes had not attended that meeting of the Administration Committee, and others who did remember only that the resolution desired by the Palau delegates was to call for the new government to choose a permanent site. Resolution No. 37 as introduced went far further than either recollection, and declared the Convention "recommended" the Palauan site!

At seven o'clock in the evening of the Convention's penultimate day the Plenary Session faced what appeared to be a desperate attempt by the Palauan delegation to salvage the last of its seven "non-negotiable" demands. Upon angry objection, Senator Salii, belying his conduct during the latter part of the Convention which had helped move action on the floor to agreement, again raised a veiled threat of opposing the constitution:

> Mr. President, I am a little bit confused as to what the amendment was in

the Committee....If the agreement, as
I understand it, has been violated, I
think it is a very serious violation with
the way we have proceeded to try to resolve
these problems, and it is going to have
a bearing on my action with respect to
this constitution.[48]

One hour and two recesses later, the Convention adopted a revised version of the Resolution, one which identified the Palauan offer of a site as the first to be considered when all are evaluated in selecting the location of the permanent capital. The Journal reads that the "Convention applauded" the passage of the Resolution.[49] The dangerous shoals of the Palauan "non-negotiable" demands had now been successfully navigated and conclusion of the Convention's work was at hand.

All during the long weeks of sparring over the major issues of the Convention, less inflammable matters were also being brought before the delegates and adopted without engendering extended controversy. "Radioactive, toxic chemical, or other harmful substances" are not to be "tested, stored, used, or disposed of" within Micronesia without the express approval of the national government (Art. XIII, Sec. 2), a provision destined to raise the hackles of the United States representatives at the future status negotiations.[50] Agreements for indefinite-term use of land are barred, and all existing agreements voided after five years (Art. XIII, Sec. 5).[51] The national government is directed to seek renegotiation of land use agreements to which the United States is a party (Art. XIII, Sec. 6). Amendment of the constitution can be by convention, popular initiative, or Congressional act, but ratification will require the extraordinary majority of a three-quarters vote in three-quarters of the states (Art. XIV).

A myriad of technical provisions covering the transition from the Trust Territory to the new political entity also needed to be spelled out to assure that rights were not lost, violators of existing criminal statutes did not go unpunished, governmental property was transferred, and inconsistencies between the existing government and the new constitutional prescripts could be tolerated until they were resolved (see Art. XV). By resolution a Transmission Commission was recommended to promote a smooth and orderly transfer of the

functions of government (Res. No. 33). This was
not a novel idea, having been a subject "considered
by the Congress on numerous occasions in the
past...."[52] More immediately, as the Convention
would have to account to the Congress of Micronesia
for its expenditures by June of 1976, it would
be incumbent to provide post-Convention staff to
conclude the paperwork and both figuratively and
literally tidy up after the Convention had adjourned
sine die.

Article XVI, the constitution's terminal section, fixed the effective date of the constitution
as one year after ratification, unless the Congress
of Micronesia specified an earlier date. Should
the latter occur, a "separation" clause temporarily
waived any part of the constitution which would
be in fundamental conflict with the United Nations
Charter or the Trusteeship Agreement. Resolution
No. 39, adopted after the Convention had approved
the constitution, requested the Congress of Micronesia to arrange for putting into effect those
portions of the constitution capable of being implemented prior to the termination of the Trusteeship
Agreement. The delegates were eager to have the
new government instituted at the earliest possible
moment. The enabling legislation under which the
Convention met charged the High Commissioner with
responsibility for designating the date on which
to hold the referendum on the constitution. As
the Convention drew to a close, all delegates confidently anticipated that this would be as soon as
the constituent document was translated into Micronesia's many languages and preparations were completed for educating the Micronesian voters on
the meaning of their affirming or rejecting the
constitution.[53]

While the last few hours of the Convention
were distinguished by a display of deliberate decorum, those which immediately preceded appeared close
to organized confusion. The final language of
the concluding compromises had to be drafted, and
then all of the various sections of the constitution
fitted together into one cohesive whole, with grammar, syntax, spelling, and consistency checked
and rechecked. The records were double-combed
to guarantee no constitutional detail upon which
the Convention had agreed was omitted from the
final version of the constitution. Even when it
was ready for presentation to the delegates at
12:50 a.m. on the Convention's 90th day, technical

errors were still being found and corrected orally for Journal recordation.

The rules called for the delegates to vote, Article by Article, on the completed constitutional draft. The Preamble passed on a vote of 45 affirmative votes, with no negatives or abstentions, and all delegations approving. For the first time along the tortuous path to this moment of decision, the delegates could be certain that they had succeeded in forging a consensus. Quickly, the Convention suspended its rules, and adopted the remainder of the constitution by a single vote, 43 ayes and 2 abstentions.[54] While the champagne was not to be drunk until later that evening, like an uncorked bottle the Convention's spirits bubbled over with a touch of bathos. Some delegates offered self-congratulatory speeches, others the sentiments contained in congratulatory messages received from constituents. Delegate Mary Lanwi, the only woman seated in the Convention, was designated to lead the delegates in singing the Micronesian Anthem, whose mid-stanza significantly reads:

> Now all join the chorus, let union abide,
> Across all Micronesia join hands on every side.
> Across all Micronesia join hands on every side.

In late afternoon, the Convention reassembled for the formal ceremonies of signing the engrossed constitution. After an invocation by a Catholic priest, delegation by delegation, starting with Yap as the smallest, trooped to the front of the hall for its members to affix their names to the document, each prefaced by the introductory remarks of its spokesman. An address by High Commissioner Edward E. Johnston followed,[55] and a benediction by a Protestant minister brought the convention to an end. Four delegates, who were not in attendance at the closing ceremonies, later added their signatures.

A month earlier, when the Convention was braced to face the many issues which appeared near irresolvable, I had received the following message from its chief strategist:

> Professor: In the event (I hope it won't happen) the Convention is unable

to come up with an agreed draft constitution by November 9th, could you give me your thoughts as to the next step we should take. You might also suggest what the Congress [of Micronesia] should do. I will discuss this with you further.

There the matter had rested until two weeks later. Then, faced with the traditional leaders threatening to boycott the Convention, I was asked by the Administration Committee if I had prepared the contingency plans. My response was in the affirmative, holding up a sealed envelope, to which I appended the suggestion that psychologically it did not appear wise to reveal them until absolutely necessary. Reassured that there were plans, no question was raised concerning their contents. Not until the signing of the constitution was all need for them abrogated.[56]

The delegates were caught up in the emotion of the concluding hours. Eyes misted and voices choked, and suspiciously some wore dark glasses despite the dim light of the Convention hall. Moved by the euphoria of the moment, one of the delegates from Ponape instructed the staff to use the expense money due him to purchase champagne for the entire Convention.[57] This and the spirits which flowed at the reception which followed left all of the delegates in a mellow mood. In the bonhomie which prevailed, all of the schisms which had beset the Convention seemed healed. However, I, for one, could not forget how the Convention had long teetered on indecision as it faced the apparent intransigence of the Palauan delegation.

In form, the Palauan delegation had succeeded in obtaining much of what had earlier been posited as "non-negotiable"; in substance, the Convention had denied some of its demands and had responded to others in ways which materially deleted from their content. A true federation was created, rather than the state being "recognized as the basic political unit of government." The powers delegated to the central government provided it with a far greater scope of authority than contemplated by the Palauan delegation's outline of its position. The Convention accepted the Palauan demand for a unicameral legislature, but only after the delegation's partial surrender of its companion provision requiring "equal district representation." The constitution expressly denied the ownership of land to non-citizens and to corporations not wholly owned by citizens, rather than leaving this to the responsibility of the states. As for state control over the exercise of eminent domain, that power was left in a condition of utter confusion. The greatest subject matter victory of the Palauan delegation was in having the equal distribution of foreign assistance expressly written into the constitution, although its own member pointed up the means by which it could easily be circumvented by the national government. The potential fiscal powers of the central government would be far more potent than originally intended by the Palauan delegation, obviating any need for inclusion in the constitution of provision for State contributions which had been part of the Palauan position. Right of state secession was completely eliminated, and rather than the gap being silent, the history of reaching this decision recorded in the Convention's intention that with the Federation once formed, unilateral state action was totally proscribed. Finally, Palau was not declared by the constitution as the seat of the national government of Micronesia, although the Convention did allow the Palauans the pallative resolution which made the area's consideration _primus inter pares_ when the decision on the capital was eventually made.[58] All in all, the Palauan delegation had called the tune, a compromise had been struck, and only time would tell if it would hold.

In an area of the world where magic and superstition still constitute important parts of the average man's life, one final program note before ringing down the curtain on the Micronesian Constitutional Convention of 1975. With the delegates leaving Saipan for their home districts, and the shutting down of the Convention premises imminent, the Convention Secretary cleaned out his office preparatory to its closing. Hidden away in the inner recesses of a desk drawer he found a half coconut shell, its meat partially charred, and with some brown liquid apparently poured over the small heap of leaves and grass placed within its concavity. No question but that it was magic, but was it "good" magic, assuring the success of the Convention, or "black" magic, symbolizing the stillborn death of the constitution at the hands of the voters?

----

1. The capitalization on the theme of the Palauan chiefs' meeting held late in the spring (see p. 126, *supra*) was obvious to all. It only served to add futher ambiguity to the Palauan intentions should their seven "non-negotiable" demands be rebuffed.

2. SCRep. No. 7, October 27, 1975, *CCM Journal*, Vol. II, p. 942.

3. See p. 247, *supra*.

4. *Dialogue for Micronesia*, No. 49, October 14, 1975, p. 3. Also see *Marianas Variety*, October 17, 1975, pp. 4, 10.

5. I.e., that health and education powers to be exercised concurrently under the FSM Constitution (Art. IX, Sec. 3), is in line with the Palauan delegates' expression before committee of the intent of the "Palauan Constitution." Summary Record, Governmental Functions Committee, September 26, 1981.

6. Summary Record, Public Finance and Taxation Committee, 29th Meeting, October 7, 1975.

7. SCRep. No. 33, *CCM Journal*, Vol. II, p. 813.

8. *CCM Journal*, Vol. I, p. 324.

9. On the previous day, the General Provisions Committee's proposing C.P. No. 25 to defer the decision on location of the national capital, instead of placing it in Palau, had been unveiled, heightening the building sense of a showdown with the Palauans. This particularly explosive issue was deferred (*CCM Journal*, Vol. II, p. 688), allowing public finance to occupy center stage. The site of the national capital again became critical as the Convention drew to a close.

10. Summary Record, Public Finance and Taxation Committee, 30th Meeting, October 8, 1975.

11. According to the statement of Delegate Wainit, the "fifty-fifty sharing formula" for internally raised revenues was incorporated to eliminate provision for concurrent taxing power (*CCM Journal*, Vol. I, p. 471).

12. Two delegates did not sign SCRep. No. 27 accompanying C.P. No. 15; three members signed as not concurring with SCRep. No. 38, the report supporting C.P. No. 26. The Journal does not record whether the non-signers or the non-concurrers were from Palau. (My concurrent field notes read that SCRep. No. 27 "had been signed by several Palauans on the Finance Committee!" However, see implication of Delegate Nakamura's remarks in CCM Journal, Vol. I, p. 370.)

13. CCM Journal, Vol. I, p. 360.

14. CCM Journal, Vol. II, p. 695.

15. All quotations are from the Journal of the 74th day (CCM Journal, Vol. I, pp. 370-71).

16. The other aspect of "equality" was the state's representation in the national legislature. Apportionment is treated subsequently.

17. CCM Journal, Vol. I, p. 441. With Palau out of the Federation, the remaining states agreed to ignore the constitutional mandate. Later, on the demand of Ponape, the revised formulae were included in the compact, but to protect against abrogation of the distribution agreement by the Federation--a different use of Delegate Toribiong's strategem.

18. CCM Journal, Vol. I, p. 445.

19. CCM Journal, Vol. I, p. 444.

20. CCM Journal, Vol. I, p. 445.

21. CCM Journal, Vol. I, p. 444.

22. CCM Journal, Vol. I, p. 442.

23. The other abstainer on final adoption of the constitution, Delegate Kendall from the Marshalls, also a Senator, likewise had an amendment to change the apportionment formula. Whether or not that was the reason for his abstaining, he like Delegate Olter, later signed the Constitution.

24. CCM Journal, Vol. I, p. 475.

25. On the day the Convention approved the provisions calling for equal distribution of foreign

aid, the Public Information Section issued a news release on the Palauan "apparent victory" (Con-Con Release No. 106, October 28, 1975). Delegate Ngiraked attempted to have the release withdrawn, expressing fear over the repercussions it might engender in the Convention, but it had already been released.

26. CCM Journal, Vol. I, p. 389.

27. Summary Record, Governmental Structure Committee, 26th Meeting, October 23, 1975.

28. The Japanese government, which Convention oldsters knew, most likely appeared to them as headed by a single chief executive (either the Emperor or the Head of the South Seas Administration in Micronesia), rather than as a parliamentary system. Most of the younger delegates who had gone outside of the United States for education were exposed to the presidential system of the Philippines. The opting of the Marshalls for a parliamentary system in 1979 must be attributed to a combination of unusual factors, chief among which was a centralization of political power unknown to the rest of Micronesia.

29. CCM Journal, Vol. II, p. 706.

30. See "The Congress of Micronesia after 1969, arguments for and against unicameralism and bicameralism," 1968 [Legislative Counsel, Saipan].

31. CCM Journal, Vol. II, p. 743.

32. CCM Journal, Vol. I, p. 489.

33. Or at least to the author these Convention leaders took personal credit for suggesting the inclusion of traditional leaders in the membership of the Special Committee.

34. The amendment to C.P. No. 24 originally proposed by Delegate Apis from Ponape.

35. A number of the delegates were fully aware that under the American Articles of Confederation each state had one vote in Congress, despite the size of its delegation.

36. Perhaps because of the American trauma over Watergate and the threatened impeachment of Presi-

dent Nixon, the FSM Constitution refers to impeachment and removal (Art. VII, Sec. 2[o]), but when specifying the grounds for removal lists only "treason, bribery, or conduct involving corruption in office" and provides for judicial review of the legislative decision (Art. VII, Sec. 7).

37. CCM Journal, Vol. II, p. 754.

38. CCM Journal, Vol. II, p. 745.

39. CCM Journal, Vol. II, p. 751.

40. CCM Journal, Vol. I, p. 522.

41. CCM Journal, Vol. II, pp. 732-33.

42. Quoted is the language as finally incorporated in Article XIII, Section 3, rather than as first presented. For original, see CCM Journal, Vol. II, pp. 765-66. (Given the history of this section, when preparing the final version of the FSM Constitution in the form to be adopted, the author believed it would be a travesty to have the section head Article XIII, so preceded it by two other provisions which appeared to have more substantive content.)

43. CCM Journal, Vol. II, p. 765.

44. Summary Record of the General Provisions Committee, Fourth Meeting, July 29, 1975, pp. 1-2.

45. CCM Journal, Vol. II, p. 766.

46. CCM Journal, Vol. II, p. 767.

47. CCM Journal, Vol. I, p. 548.

48. CCM Journal, Vol. I, p. 548.

49. CCM Journal, Vol. I, p. 550.

50. Resolution No. 36 also calls for the provisions in the compact on future political status to be renegotiated to conform to the constitution, a matter requiring post-Convention treatment (see Epilogue).

51. Here see Fischer's assertion that the indefinite lease, rather than the acquiring of full title, "is in full harmony with traditional and

present Trukese culture....is highly appreciated by the Trukese involved and admired as remarkably just by all" (John C. Fischer, "Native Land Tenure in the Truk District," in John deYoung [ed.], <u>Land Tenure Patterns</u>, <u>Trust Territory of the Pacific Islands</u> [Guam: Office of the High Commissioner, TTPI, 1958,] 1:191).

52. "Report to the Congress of Micronesia on Seventh Round of Negotiations, January, 1975," pp. 117-118.

53. The referendum on the constitution was not to be held for nearly three years (see Epilogue).

54. See note 23, <u>supra</u>.

55. The remarks of the High Commissioner Edward E. Johnston, which compared the Convention to the automobile industry, so outraged the sense of propriety of a reporter of the <u>Guam Daily News</u> covering the story that her account of the concluding day's proceedings omitted all reference to them.

56. The author's emergency plan, should the Convention have been unable to draft a constitution, as contained in his notes: "The constitution, to the extent drafted, goes to the Congress of Micronesia via resolution of the 'con-con.' The Congress, in joint session sitting as a constituent body (as Papua-New Guinea Assembly did), adopts a constitution in final form, after reconciling differences which appeared in the Convention, and filling in gaps. It is then submitted to popular vote (although not legally necessary)."

57. The ceremonies following the Convention's close completely erased from the delegate's memory all reference to his expense money having been used to purchase five cases of champagne, and on the following day he appeared at the staff offices to inquire about receiving the expense money due him. It should also be added that contributions of alcoholic beverages were received from other sources, so that many participated in the spirit of the occasion.

58. The order of detailing the Palauan demands follows that in the Palauan delegation's "Outline of Position." See Appendix E.

PART VI. EPILOGUE

   The play is over, but the curtain does not fall. The free association compact remains the backdrop of the stage and negotiations renew, featuring some of the same principals who had key roles during the Convention. Anomalously, the proposed Federated States of Micronesia Constitution is both part of and apart from the continuing drama.

Chapter 14. Farewell Micronesia, Fare Well

The signing of the Federated States of Micronesia Constitution immediately posed a host of questions, all interrelated, some of which are still unanswered. Would the United States countenance the submission of such a constitution to Micronesian approval, and if so, when? Given the opportunity, would a majority of the people in a majority of the districts ratify it? And if, indeed, the document's compromises were so confirmed, when would the new polity come into existence and the Trusteeship end?

All appreciated that as a practical matter the Trust Agreement would not be terminated until the United States succeeded in securing an agreement on future political status to its liking. As the constitution did not coincide with the provisions of the free association compact already tentatively outlined, how were the two to be reconciled? Assuming this objection were met, and further postulating that the voters approved the compact, additional obstacles would have to be surmounted. Concurrence of the United States Congress would next be in order, and then remaining would be the hurdle of the United Nations. Would the Trusteeship Council complacently accede? Could the threat of a veto in the Security Council be circumnavigated? Meanwhile, throughout this tortuous course, would Micronesia--<u>sans</u> the Northern Marianas--hold together? The last question was the first to be answered, and in the negative.

At the meeting of the Pre-Convention Committee with the traditional leaders of Truk back in September of 1974, Chief Kintoki Joseph, who was to serve as a member of the Truk delegation, inquired: "What is the relationship between the draft compact ... and the constitution that is proposed to be written? Can the delegation ... do something independent of that compact...?" Senator Tosiwo Nakayama replied that "it will be best to draft a constitution without knowing what is in the draft compact, because in working on the constitution, we are dealing with the interests of the people of Micronesia and we should not be concerned with trying to protect the interests of someone outside of Micronesia." Chief Kintoki Joseph was not fully satisfied: "What happens in case of a conflict between the two documents?" Marianas delegate Lorenzo Cabrera then volunteered: "Personally, I feel ... if certain provisions do not conform with the draft compact ... then we tell the Congress of Micronesia to negotiate again with those provisions that conflict with our constitution." Later, when meeting with Truk and Xavier High School students, and the same question being posed, the Committee elaborated: "[T]he compact is still a draft, not signed yet, still subject to negotiation so there is a possibility of having that particular language in the draft compact change[d]; perhaps at the conclusion of the negotiation[s] ... the constitution will be recognized as the supreme law of the nation."[1] And indeed the drafting of the constitution proceeded without declared effort to assure any specific provision fitted within the terms of the compact, although throughout the Convention's life, the delegates individually remained apprehensive about the constitution's traversing territory over which bargaining on future status had been conducted.

Once the constitution was signed, admittedly there were areas in which the two documents would have to be reconciled, particularly since Article II, Section 1, declared the constitution to be "the supreme law of the Federated States of Micronesia" and that "an act of government" in conflict was invalid. In the Style Committee's polishing of the Committee Proposals, this all-embracing phraseology had been preferred over that of a more specific listing of "treaties" and other matters. Despite this supremacy language, however, through the ability to delegate functions via the treaty power, for which express provision was made--albeit, obliquely, in Article IX, Section 4--a safeguard had been incorporated for dovetailing constitution and compact. Almost three years were to elapse before this means for alignment was to be acknowledged by the American negotiators.

It took Washington eight months to complete its examination of the draft constitution and officially to phrase its many objections. Earlier, Ambassador Haydn Williams had signalled the American rejection of the constitution: "Regretfully the

United States cannot agree with conclusions as
to the basic compatibility of the two draft documents.... Free Association as envisioned by the
compact is clearly inconsistent with the sovereign
independent status called for by the draft Constitution. We have futher concluded that mere revision
of the compact will not alter this basic fact."[2]
To this the Micronesian negotiators responded
that "while the Constitution may be inconsistent
with your interpretation of free association, it
is not inconsistent with ours."[3]

According to Ambassador Williams' assessment,
"Free Association ... is a free and voluntary and
terminable relationship between a self-governing
territory with a fully independent state. Free
Association by definition is not a relationship
between two independent states."[4] Apart from this
claim of general inconsistency, the United States
more specifically identified as conflicting the
constitution's claim of jurisdiction over ocean
waters (Art. I, Sec. 1). Another objection contested the power of the Federated States to acquire
new territories (Art. I, Sec. 3). The supremacy
clause of the constitution (Art. II, Sec. 1) also
was censured as contrary to comparable compact
language declaring the latter's dominancy. The
citizenship provisions (Art. III, Secs. 4 and 5)
were deemed to cause serious international complications. The limitation of the Federation Government to the powers delegated to it by the constitution (Art. VIII, Sec. 1) was faulted as potentially
reducing the national government's power to carry
out compact obligations. A number of detailed
powers granted to the Federation Government (in
Art. IX), such as foreign relations, postal, etc.,
were declared to be contrary to the relevant articles of the compact. A technician's nightmare
was conjured out of the approval process; instead
of a popular plebiscite as contemplated by the
compact, if the constitution were approved first,
it would then require compact ratification by the
Federation Congress and two-thirds of the state
legislatures. The jurisdiction of the national
courts was questioned insofar as it affected United
States responsibility for foreign affairs in Micronesia. In the latter part of the constitution,
but by no means least in order of importance, Washington opposed the document's general provisions
restricting the testing, storage, and use of toxic,
radioactive or other harmful substances within
Micronesia. Together with the prohibition of indef-

inite land leases and the demand for their renegotiation, these general provisions, particularly, appeared to fly in the face of the compact's raison d'etre, the United States military's access to and use of Micronesia's lands and waters.[5]

What to do? Ambassador Williams suggested that all conflict could be cured if inserted into the constitution were words comparable to those in the draft compact (Sec. 101) declaring that the constitution and laws of Micronesia were not to infringe upon the responsibilities and rights vested in the government of the United States by virtue of the compact's approval.[6] Such action assumed that the Congress of Micronesia enjoyed residual power to amend the constitution, a dubious legal matter once the Convention had concluded its work. Nevertheless, this interjecting of the Congress in some manner into rephrasing the language of the constitution as a means to break the impasse would not die. The Acting High Commissioner in his "State of the Territory" address at the beginning of 1977 urged the Congress to "examine 'every legal remedy' to insure that the draft Constitution be 'consistent' with the draft compact before it is submitted to the people for ratification."[7] Later, in mid-1977, when Ambassador Peter Rosenblatt, as President Carter's Personal Representative, took up the negotiation cudgels, he reiterated the American complaint about the "serious inconsistency" between constitution and compact. He did not advocate, however, that the Micronesians amend the constitution "because that would require convening the Convention, which would be a headache. Instead, he ... [wanted] the Congress of Micronesia to approve 'appropriate legislation' that would solve the problem."[8] Apparently he had in mind a "rider" to be attached to the constitutional referendum declaring the supremacy of the free association compact. Senate President Nakayama's response paralleled the fable of belling the cat, and its unspoken difficulties: it would be necessary first to clearly define "free association."[9]

For two years following the American denouncement of the proposed constitution, the United States' position continued to nourish the seeds of doubt first planted in the minds of the Micronesians by Ambassador Williams that to support the Federated Constitution was to favor "independence." Impliedly, the Micronesians would then be ineligible for United States economic assistance, other than possibly as foreign aid along with the myriad of Third World countries. The uncertainties so conjured troubled many Micronesians bent on obtaining at least an interim of American-financed self-government. The protagonists of Marshallese and Palauan separatism echoed the charge and fanned these fears. The end of the year 1977 found Senate President Nakayama complaining about Ambassador Rosenblatt still reiterating the refrain that "a yes vote on the Constitution would mean Micronesia would be independent.... [It] would actually mean nothing more than the people would be given the opportunity to form their own government."[10] This not so subtle attack on the constitution continued until barely three months before the constitutional referendum, when "the Carter Administration accepted the Constitution and pledged that if it is adopted, economic aid would not be unilaterally cut off."[11] As Senator Bailey Olter for the Commission on Future Political Status and Transition accurately observed, "[Now it] can be said that the theoretical argument over compatibility is over."[12] The "Compact of Free Association as negotiated hereafter will be submitted to the [treaty] processes ... of the Draft Constitution."[13]

When the Congress of Micronesia debated the holding of a Constitutional Convention, Senator Lazarus Salii proposed "... that the Constitution be drafted sometime during next year [1975], and that we suggest to the drafters ... that they put a clause in the Constitution calling for ratification ... one year after it is drafted[,] sometime in 1976." The following years would be a transition period for sections of the constitution to be implemented, and "... on July 12th, the anniversary of this Congress, 1981, the full Constitution can go into effect."[14] This scenario was modified during the passage of the enabling legislation, which mandated "the referendum be held on the date the High Commissioner shall specify."

Shortly after the Convention adjourned, its officers presented the High Commissioner with an enrolled copy of the constitution. Possibly caught up in the general euphoria prevailing in the Convention's wake, and not yet instructed by Washington, he expressed the desire to call the election in June 1976. The Convention leaders considered this too soon, for the constitution had yet to be translated into Micronesia's many languages, and there was also need of lead time to mount an educational campaign.[15] As an alternative, they suggested the referendum be held simultaneously with the Congress of Micronesia elections scheduled for five months later in November. Now it was the turn of the High Commissioner to demur, saying that the Congressional contests might distract the voters' attention from the fundamental issues faced; better to wait until after the Congressional elections. Months then stretched into years as the American negotiators in the status talks challenged the constitution, and the Trust Territory Administration accommodatingly delayed. Meanwhile, the fragile support for Micronesian unity underpinning the constitution's compromises eroded away.

The centrality of the Palauans to the Micronesian constitutional process--both substantively and procedurally--did not end with the adjournment of the Constitutional Convention on Saipan. No sooner had the Palauan delegates returned home than their proclivity to confrontational politics reasserted itself. The Progressive Party members, unable to control the organization of the District Legislature as they had anticipated, for week after week boycotted the daily sessions, denying them a quorum.[16] On Saipan, the Palauan delegation to the Congress warned the House of Representatives that secession of the district from the projected Federated States was imminent unless the Congress met its demand for locating the national capital in Palau. The House responded by postponing action.[17] Later in the year, two former delegates to the Convention sponsored a resolution in Palau's District Legislature reciting that the prospects for a "unified Micronesia" had grown ever more "dismal, and the trend appears to be irreversible, in light of, among other things ... the fundamental conflict between the draft Constitution of the Federated States of Micronesia and certain provisions of the draft compact of free association...." Direct negotiations between Palau and the United States were requested.[18] Finally, at the Special Session in the summer of 1976, the Congress faced up to the Palau challenge and designated Ponape as the seat of the national government, this over the protests of the Palauan Representatives who absented themselves from the House vote.[19] Had the decision located the capital in Palau, it would have materially altered subsequent events.

Up until his resignation in July of 1976,[20] and disregarding the growth of the separatist movements in the Marshalls and Palau, Ambassador Williams continued publicly to assert that the United States supported the unity of the Marshalls and the Carolines. "While there clearly are some fundamental inconsistencies between the Micronesian Constitution and the draft Compact of Free Association there is no difference--no conflict--between the two with respect to the ideal of a united Micronesia and of self-government based on the sovereign will of the Micronesian people."[21] Earlier he had stated, "The position of the United States has not changed. It continues to hope that out of the process of writing and ratifying a Constitution for Micronesia will come unity."[22] Nevertheless, separate status negotiations with the Marshalls and Palau were to be initiated before submission of the proposed constitution to popular referendum, and this undermining of unity was to be a further factor contributing to the rejection of the constitution by the Territory's two peripheral districts.

The United States negotiators found themselves in a discomforting situation, spokesmen for a world power unwilling to appear the tyrant and yet unable effectively to exert its superior position. Notwithstanding public declarations that the Trusteeship would shortly be terminated, the prospect of achieving this to the liking of the United States was ever receding. They recognized that a disintegrating Micronesia potentially posed numerous long-run disadvantages for the Americans: the more new polities the greater the administrative complexity in dealing with them, the larger the probably financial drain on the United States in contributing to their maintenance, and the more real the danger that the process of fragmentation would continue unabated along internal lines of traditional incompatibility. On the other hand, the draft constitution had raised serious doubts in Washington over whether the strategic requirements of the United States could be adequately secured. Conveniently, the direct appeals to the United Nations from the Marshalls and Palau for separate negotiations protected the flank of the United States against the hostile charges of the Soviets that the Americans were pursuing "divide and rule" tactics.[23] Apparently because of both the overriding dominance of the military considerations and the sheer inertial drag on further bargaining in the accustomed manner occasioned by the many specific objections raised to the constitution, the United States elected to follow what seemed to be the least trying course of action. Departing from the policy of three preceding presidents, the Carter Administration positioned itself to treat separately with the Marshallese and the Palauans.[24]

In March 1977, United States Secretary of State Cyrus Vance and Interior Secretary Cecil Andrus took the first overt steps to implement the change of policy, proposing that Micronesian legislative leaders from the various districts--and not just the spokesmen designated by the Congress of Micronesia--meet with a broad group of representatives from the various federal agencies interested in the Islands "for a full discussion of our relationship and of how we might best proceed with detailed negotiations on the future status of Micronesia."[25] The leadership of the Congress traveled to Honolulu armed with a long list of matters to raise, including fixing the date for holding the constitutional referendum. While the talks did aid in clearing some misconceptions and clarifying objections about the United States Micronesian policy, they also afforded opportunity for the Marshallese and Palauan status commissions adamantly to voice their separatist positions.[26] It soon became evident that the "roundtable" was just a transition, a face-saving device in the move toward changing the negotiating mode. The session concluded with Ambassador Philip W. Manhard, who headed the eighteen-member United States delegation, asking all assembled around the meeting table to join hands as an earnest of good will, a circle in which Palauan and Marshallese status representatives along with all other Micronesians present joined as equals of the negotiators from the Congress of Micronesia.

At our request, Professor Leonard Mason and I had met informally with the chief members of the Washington delegation late in the evening preceding the opening of the Honolulu discussions in the attempt to impress upon them the gravity of the situation. If the representatives of the Marshallese and Palauan status groups were formally recognized in any way before a Territory-wide vote on the constitution, Micronesian unity was certain to break, imperiling the future of the Federation. In retrospect, I am confident that Washington had already discounted as to the United States the possible negative effects arising from Micronesian territorial disintegration. The "joint communique" issued upon the conclusion of the talks read: "The participants engaged in forthright and constructive <u>multilateral and bilateral exchanges</u> of views on a number of subjects, including current and future political relationships and on the means of resuming formal status negotiations" (emphasis added).[27] The new format had been set.

At the follow-up "roundtable" on Guam in July, the American representatives presented a two-tiered approach toward negotiations: "Under the U.S. proposal ... multilateral negotiations would focus on those aspects of the relationship with the United States ... common to all six districts. The United States further envisions bilateral negotiations between the United States and a district or a group of districts addressing elements of the free association status which are special or local, such as ...in substantial part, provisions for U.S. financial assistance.... Either function [bilateral or multilateral negotiation] could be delegated by a district to the Congress of Micronesia or its negotiating commission."[28] The United States had succeeded in shifting the locus of negotiations from the Congress to the district legislatures, and each now enjoyed the discretion to decide whether the Congress would play any further role with respect to its area. The status commission of the Congress continued to contend that negotiations with the separatist factions "violated United Nations precedent on the territorial integrity of a non-self-governing territory. Nevertheless, a decision was made to participate in status talks to forestall a dismantling of the Trust Territory by the United States, so that Micronesia's people could speak in the ... constitutional referendum."[29]

A unified Micronesia had not been premised upon any shared sense of "nationalism"; it did not constitute a movement based on unfulfilled common needs; it lacked any "traditional" affinity in shared cultures. In opposition to a "common enemy," diverse groups had joined forces, but once it became apparent that the United States was willing, reluctantly, to remain the fairy godmother--and more so for some than others--there was no longer any compelling purpose for cohesion. The identity of the antagonist shifted. In the words of Senator John Mangefel, the wry philosopher of the Congress of Micronesia destined to become Yap's first elected governor, "If Micronesian unity collapses, it is because we failed to understand each other and to accommodate each other's particular wishes, not because of some American Secretary, or ambassador, or high commissioner, or CIA agent.[30] We have found the enemy and they are ourselves."[31]

When formal negotiations resumed in October 1977, representatives of all three Micronesian status commissions participated as equals on a "multilateral" basis with the United States on issues which concerned the entirety of the Marshalls and the Carolines, and "bilaterally" on matters affecting their respective districts.[32] Prior thereto, the Americans had attempted to promote acceptance of "some form of all-Micronesian entities [sic] which would operate in the economic and to a limited extent, in the political field."[33] "The United States ... [had] determined to establish its bilateral relationship with each entity in a manner to allow for cooperative development among the entities, should that be their desire at some future date."[34] The Territory-wide adoption of the Federated Constitution was already being written off by the Americans. On the part of the Micronesians, the seeming willingness of the three negotiating groups to accept the concept of an "all-Micronesian entity,"[35] to be vested with such powers as all agreed upon, apparently was premised upon the "Congress of Micronesia delegation hoping that the draft Constitution would be approved for all districts, and the other two in the expectation that it would not."[36]

The cue that Washington's opposition to a vote on the Federated Constitution was abating appeared in Acting High Commissioner Coleman's 1977 "State of the Territory" message. In that he indicated he would select an "earlier" date for the constitutional referendum because of the "urgency for Micronesia to begin to set its affairs in order."[37] For its part, the Congress was now ready to abandon its reluctance to force action, despairing that political education would secure the constitution a better reception at the polls. Its response was to pass a bill requiring the High Commissioner to fix the time for the referendum between June 15 and August 15, 1978. The Acting High Commissioner signed Public Law 7-31 on April 1, 1977, this after Washington had issued its invitations for all parties to attend the first "roundtable" discussions in Honolulu. Next, Acting High Commissioner J. Boyd Mackenzie proclaimed July 12, 1978, as the election date, exactly three years from when the Constitutional Convention had first met. Later, the Congress appropriated both $100,000 to fund election costs and nearly $200,000 more for political education. It also created an ad hoc Constitutional Referendum Board and special election machinery for holding the referendum, feeling strongly that the Congress should have a voice in the conduct of the plebiscite.[38] The Board, half of whose members were named by the Congress, issued its own voting regulations, required new voter registers be prepared, and named the members of district referendum boards and the various vote tabulators. All of this reflected Congressional concern that the political leadership in districts opposed to the adoption of the constitution would not accurately report the voters' free choices. The Congress remained the sole judge of the referendum and its results.

The Trust Territory's Education for Self-Government Program and the Commission on Future Political Status and Transition separately distributed information on the Federated Constitution.[39] The latter enlisted the support of the traditional leaders, who visited the various districts, reassuring their counterparts about the constitution. Proponents and opponents made use of the district radio broadcasting facilities, posters were plastered broadside in a number of the district centers, television debates and noisy rallies erupted in Palau, and even a caravan of placarded automobiles wound its way through Koror. Some voters in Kusaie (Kosrae) expressed discomfort with the constitution's provision for freedom of religion. On Ponape the return of lands became an issue, with opponents of the constitution charging that the national government would inherit all public lands and might not return them to the states. The Marshalls had long objected to the Federated Constitution not ensuring an equitable distribution of revenues nor recognizing the sovereignty of the Marshall Islands with respect to fishing rights and lease negotiations.[40] One of the candidates for the post of governor on Truk included rejection of the constitution as a plank on his platform for election; the imminence of the gubernatorial elections to occur there in the following month drew popular attention to personalities and away from the issues implicit in the constitutional referendum. In some cases the anti-constitution charges were patently false, having their genesis in past political quarrels.[41] In the Marshalls, the pro-unity Voice of the Marshalls protested the immorality of using profanity in a radio broadcast directed against the constitution's proponents. On the whole, debate on the constitution was wide-ranging, spirited, and with particularly strong campaigns mounted in Palau and the Marshalls.

As of midnight, July 11, all electioneering came to a halt, and approximately fifty-five thousand registered voters (out of an estimated sixty thousand eligibles) prepared for the forthcoming contest.[42] Members of both political parties in Palau spent the election day shuttling people to and from the polls. In the Marshalls, voters demanded that the booths remain open until midnight to accommodate those queued outside them.[43] Each district maintained a voting place for non-residents; on the closing of the polls, their ballots were dispatched to the appropriate district for counting. Trust Territory citizens from other districts present in the Northern Marianas and registered there were barred from the referendum. After Truk turned seven voters away at the polls, a court order held up the counting of that district's ballots until all were permitted to participate.[44] The largest mission of the United Nations ever to visit the Trusteeship had previously spread out across the Territory to observe the course of the voting, and it reported no objections to the conduct of the election.

The results of the referendum both vindicated the Constitutional Convention and undercut most of the compromises so laboriously reached. Three-fifths of the voters in a majority of the districts expressed their approval of the constitution. This ratification in four of the districts--Kosrae, Ponape, Truk, and Yap--assured the establishment of the Federated States of Micronesia.[45] Palau and the Marshalls opted out from the Federation, a discretion which legally first became available to them only after the Constitutional Convention had commenced its deliberations. The growth of the separatist movements within the two districts since 1975, as confirmed by unofficial plebiscites held before the referendum,[46] pressaged the possibility of their rejection of the constitution. Even so, there were reports that advocates of the constitution had been gaining ground.[47] In the Marshalls, however, the opposition of the entrenched leadership easily prevailed. In Palau, the cleavage between the parochial party forces, which had been successfully papered over in the positions expressed by the district delegation in the Convention, surfaced in the contest over the constitution, and the shift of but 310 tallies[48] would have reversed its defeat. Recalling the principal protagonists in the events leading up to the Constitutional Convention, there was some opinion that if Dwight Heine had been active in the pro-constitution forces in the Marshalls, the result there might have been closer, and that a decisive factor in Palau's rejection of the constitution was the failure of Senator Lazarus Salii to campaign aggressively for unity. Significantly, in the two districts of Micronesia in which the traditional leaders exert the greatest political influence, the Yap chiefs' strong endorsement of the constitution closely correlated with the 95 percent "yes" vote registered there, while in the Marshalls where most Iroij expressed vehement objection to the constitution, only a little over a third of the voters supported ratification. Countering the democratic processes introduced during the thirty-five years of American rule, the influence of the traditional remains a major force to be reckoned with in Micronesian governance.

The fate of the Federated States of Micronesia at last determined, the Administering Authority prepared to tackle two related tasks. To a considerable extent, one appeared mechanical, consisting of dismantling most of Headquarters, equitably dividing up the Trust Territory's functions and bureaucracy among the three emerging polities, and retaining executive powers "only in the area of fiscal responsibility for federal funds, foreign affairs, and responsibilities required under the Trusteeship Agreement. In the area of legislation, the High Commissioner [would] no longer ... [exert a veto over] laws passed by the constitutional governments" but could suspend them.[49] The High Court would reserve jurisdiction over a limited range of sensitive matters. While this divestiture was underway, simultaneously the negotiations on the compact for future status would be concluded, and termination of the Trusteeship could then follow. Given the near decade of past negotiations, and the reaching by all parties of full conceptual agreement on status just before the constitutional referendum, the task of completing the compact seemed easily manageable. Belying appearances, the winding up of the compact and the devolution of government proved onerous and protracted.

The experience gained in the splitting off of the Northern Marianas counseled moderation in the speed of the divestiture. The unseeming haste of the United States to separate the Northern Marianas administratively from the rest of the Trust Territory, which occurred a bare week after the Commonwealth Covenant had been signed by President Gerald Ford,[50] had spawned numerous unnecessary difficulties. Eventually, delegates to a Marianas convention were chosen to draft their own constitution, but not until after the Resident Commissioner had twice vetoed enabling legislation because of its failure to provide for minority representation. Late in 1977, executive and legislative officers were elected, after the Commonwealth Constitution was ratified. Only in 1978, two years after the Northern Marianas were detached, did constitutional government under commonwealth status become effective for most practical purposes.[51] With respect to the remaining portion of the Trust Territory, the assumption of administrative responsibility proceeded at a more leisurely pace.

In anticipation of the adoption of a national constitution, and after allaying Washington's objections since future political status had not yet been resolved, the four central districts in the Carolines drew up their own "charters" under Congress of Micronesia authorization. Later, with the districts' transmogrification, for the nonce these served as "state constitutions," so that the Federated States was in position to function as a federation upon the dismantling of the Trust Territory Headquarters. For the most part, these state documents hewed closely to the pattern set by the provisions of the Federated Constitution, although that of Yap struck boldly out in new areas.[52]

The year 1978 ended with an elected executive installed in Truk, and by early 1979, Yap, Kosrae, and Ponape had followed. Article XVI of the Federated Constitution directed that, in the absence of action by the Congress of Micronesia, the document was to become effective one year after ratification insofar as not in conflict with existing law. This would have had the Federated States, shrunk in size to but four states, launched on July 12, 1979. But the symbolism of Micronesia Day was not to grace the inauguration of the new Federated States Government. Shortly after the referendum on the constitution, a Secretarial Order required the national government to be organized no later than May 15, 1979. Conforming to these time strictures, the first members of the Federated States Congress were elected in March of that year, its fourteen Senators met on May 10 to organize, and on the following day by acclamation chose the Federation's chief executive officers from their ranks. With Tosiwo Nakayama (Truk) selected as President and Petrus Tun (Yap) as Vice-President, and the Speaker and Vice-Speaker of the Congress elected from Ponape and Kosrae, respectively, the highest offices in the executive and legislative branches of the new government were neatly distributed among the four states. The formal inauguration ceremonies were then held on May 15, 1979, with the ceremony fittingly opened by a Ponapean choir singing the Preamble of the Constitution set to music.[53]

The Federated States Congress readily took up its responsibilities of legislating for the new federal polity, but the consultations between the High Commissioner's staff and both Federation and state officials for the devolution of executive functions proceeded more slowly. Agreement was complicated by difficulties over the transfer from Saipan of personnel and of necessary funds. If anything, reassignment of the judicial function proceeded with even greater caution.[54] Finally, the year 1980 opened with the requisite national laws in place, supplemented by a Federation executive order, establishing a highly specific, executive branch in the central government, in many ways mirroring that which it had partially superseded at Headquarters. The state governments had been operational for up to six months, their officers during that period enjoying direct access to the High Commissioner, so all had to adjust to a new set of relationships. As to be expected, the states' roles in the functions of health and education predominated. The transition did not proceed smoothly, and the Ponapean Legislature, particularly, remained the champion of state rights under the Federated Constitution.

Outside of the Federated States, the Marshall Islands--already acting as though a separate entity, and frequently ignoring Headquarter's directives--was still engaged in drawing up its own constituent document as the referendum on the Federated Constitution was held in mid-1978. However, a preliminary draft[55] already foretold that the Marshallese would be asked to take the radical step of approving a Westminster-style government, deliberately rejecting their long exposure to the presidential system.[56] By March of 1979 the Marshallese Constitution was ratified, and by May of that year the first Nitijela (Parliament) under the constitution elected, the Marshallese president coopted by parliamentary vote, and a cabinet of ten ministers installed.

Palau's parturition proved to be exceedingly prolonged, touching on the comedy of the absurd. A Palauan constitutional convention held in the spring of 1979 produced a document which Ambassador Rosenblatt told the district legislature violated the negotiated terms of the status compact. He objected to its provisions on eminent domain, nuclear prohibitions, marine boundaries, and return of public lands.[57] Senator Tmetuchl's group within the district convention had favored a parliamentary system of government, but had been defeated by a rival bloc headed by Senator Salii, which adopted a more conventional--that is, American--system of government and a harder line on matters crucial to the future relations with the United States. A court decision in effect nullified the popular referendum accepting this document.[58] Next, the district legislature, in which the Tmetuchl faction dominated, attempted to have the constitution rewritten so as to bring it in line with the compact to which the Tmetuchl-led Palau Status Commission subscribed. The revised constitution then met a decisive popular defeat. The following year, in mid-1980, a new legislature now controlled by anti-Tmetuchl forces resubmitted the original constitution to the voters, and it was overwhelmingly reaffirmed at the polls, the third constitutional referendum in less than twelve months![59] Long after the date fixed by the Secretary of the Interior for the governmental structures of the three emerging Micronesian entities to be in place, that of Palau was finally ready to function.[60]

The reaching of final agreement on the compact proved far more attenuated than even Palau's metamorphosis to self-governing status within the framework of the Trust Territory. A few months before the scheduled referendum on the Federated Constitution, all of the parties had reached agreement upon a set of fundamental principles within whose constraints further formal sparring could proceed.

This Hilo Statement of Principles reflected the prime concerns of both the United States (defense and security) and the Micronesians (self-government, financial assistance, and an open-option political future). They provided the means for incorporating features which once had been rejected by the United States: unilateral termination by the Micronesians with the United States to continue financial grants; independence recognized as an option for bargaining;[61] minimal control from Washington over self-government, and that primarily as tied to military needs. Future status previously had been linked with military considerations; Hilo separated them, with the United States receiving an assured minimum fifteen years of access to land and water (and eventually longer in the Marshalls and Palau). Compromised, if not abandoned, was "a cornerstone of United States policy; the closer the political relationship, the greater the level of fiscal support which the United States would provide."[62] The Statement's neutrality on unity meant that all parties looked to the imminent referendum on the Federated Constitution for definitive resolution of that issue.

The Hilo Statement furnished the foundation of all subsequent negotiations during the remainder of the Carter Administration, enabling the incremental rewriting of a new compact. The advent of the Presidential elections of 1980 next triggered the performance of what periodically had become almost a ritualistic rite of political passage. Before the Republican Administration took over the reins of power, all parties initialled a draft compact,[63] one which Ambassador Rosenblatt claimed to be complete other than for subsidiary agreements "which would pose no very difficult problems."[64] The incoming Reagan Administration then placed everything in a holding position again for a full policy reveiw, this time for nine months. With the naming of Ambassador Fred Zeder as the President's "Personal Representative," by the end of 1981 bargaining resumed, fleshing out the compact's subordinate agreements. "Complete"[65] accord was reached with Palau and the Federated States in the second half of 1982. Contemporaneously, the growing dissatisfaction of the Kwajalein Marshallese with the terms of the compact, followed by a protest occupation of the Kwajalein Missile Range, forced reopening of the bilateral aspects of the Marshallese talks.[66]

In the course of the negotiations between 1977 and the final compact, much of the language of the Federated and Palau Constitutions designed to reduce the impact of the United States military presence was negated in return for concessions the Micronesians obtained. Thus the prohibition in the Palau Constitution against nuclear and other harmful materials, and its restrictions which may have prevented acquisition of land for military use, were reconciled with the compact by means of subordinate agreements, as were similar provisions in the Federated Constitution.[67] The Carter Administration in one stroke finessed away its objections to many of the provisions of both constitutions by conceding control of foreign affairs to all three new political entities. This was a step beyond what New Zealand had formally[68] accorded its associated states. Although the exercise of this function remains subject to overriding American military security concerns, the Micronesians are to enjoy an expanded measure of self-government broad enough to permit their seeking entrance into many international organizations.[69]

Long term "denial rights" to third countries were always in the background of the negotiations, but surfaced for the first time only in 1978 when the Marshallese and Palauan status commissions demanded $60 million annually for their surrender.[70] Meanwhile, a number of United States Senators held reservations about the brevity of the fifteen-year limitation on United States security and defense authority in Micronesia as incorporated in the evolving compact. The Senatorial objections brought the whole matter to the fore in 1980. The Marshallese then proposed to tradeoff unlimited "denial rights" in the Marshalls to the United States in return for the latter's maintaining the levels of economic assistance already agreed upon should the Marshalls unilaterally decide to terminate the compact before the full fifteen years had run. (The right so to sever free association ties without suffering loss of future grant payments was eventually included in the compact for all three entities.) The Reagan Administration desired to keep the Islands in perpetuity within the American military sphere, euphemistically referring to this in the negotiations as "for the longest period of time."[71] The two non-Marshallese parties resisted, but eventually all consented in principle to applying the concept of "long term denial." For a short while the minimum one hundred year formulation arrived at in the Palaun subordinate "Military Use and Operating Rights" agreement initialed in 1980 appeared to set the mode for all.[72] Eventually, the United States succeeded in obtaining what in effect are permanent denial rights in all three Micronesian entities,[73] although the sentiment growing in the Federated States treats the agreement as potentially breached should the United States fail to continue adequate economic assistance.[74]

With respect to American military usage, as distinguished from compact provisions denying third countries access to Micronesia, by early 1982 it appeared that the United States had firm user rights for half a century in both Palau and the Marshalls, the latter by a thirty-five year renewal clause applying to Kwajalein. Only the Federated States rejected any ties exceeding fifteen years. Objections of dissident Marshallese necessitated their negotiators shortening their terms and compromising on but fifteen years, renewable for an equally long period. Similarly, the impasse over Palauan renegotiations has left unresolved the length of military usage there.

Viewed from the cold perspective of political reality, there was probably little else that the Micronesian entities could have done in reconciling their constitutions with the compact: they recognized that the United States Congress would refuse complete independence for Micronesia unfettered by some form of military constraint;[75] on the other hand, the Islands lacked economic self-sufficiency. In the Federated States, at least, independence without the guarantee of some external financing would have been completely irresponsible as well as politically suicidal for its Carolinian leaders. In the Marshalls and Palau, so long as the American military desires basing options, these entities can anticipate receiving some form of "support." As the terms of the defense and security relationship continued to be spelled out with ever more precision, concomitantly the Micronesians became assured of a greater scope of self-government and ever-larger financial benefits. To them, the former was a natural right and the latter but a righting of the wrong suffered due to the American Administration's failure to erect a viable economy with accompanying supportive infrastructure. A measure of the United States response to the Micronesian charge, as well as of the national security value placed on the region,[76] is provided by comparison with two adjoining island nations which recently became independent. The American per capita grant assistance under the final compact is estimated to be approximately eleven times greater than Australia's aid to Papua New Guinea and eighteen times more than Great Britain's to Kiribati.[77]

The year before the Constitutional Convention met on Saipan, projected grant funds as offered by the United States, excluding the Marianas, totaled approximately $700 million over the anticipated fifteen year period of the compact. By 1982, grant funds alone had reached almost $1.5 billion for the same period. Beyond this sum, the "final" compact also contracts for the provision of a wide swath of Federal Government services (at an estimated cost of $3/4 billion), and special programmatic assistance ($94 million more).[78] Not computed into these totals are the costs to be added by the inflation adjustment clause in the compact, the separate monetary payments contemplated for land to be used by the military, or the assistance contracted to continue after the initial period elapses. Despite the magnitude of the $2.2 billion figure for economic assistance over the first fifteen years of the compact, Ambassador Zeder claimed it would be exceeded by a $3.1 billion projected expense should the Trusteeship be retained for the same period.[79]

On February 10, 1983, the citizens of Palau became the first Micronesians to vote on the compact of free association; 62 percent of those who went to the polls approved of its terms, including the subordinate agreements.[80] Surprisingly, they also indicated the desire to be more closely linked with the United States should the compact be defeated.[81] Notwithstanding the show of majority support for the compact, in effect they rejected its provisions permitting the introduction of nuclear materials into Palau,[82] thus reconfirming the three referenda in 1979 and 1980 on Palau's nuclear-free constitution. A particularly sensitive issue turned around the phrasing of the constitutional-waiver question on the ballot, a matter which remained in dispute practically up to the date of the election.[83]

Upon the tallying of the Palauan election returns, the United States assumed the stance that the compact had been approved, and that the waiving of the Palauan constitutional prohibition was an internal matter for the Palauans themselves to resolve.[84] Eventually, the Palau Supreme Court ruled that the failure to secure a 75 percent vote to remove the constitutional ban on nuclear materials constituted rejection of the entire compact.[85] A new vote on the compact was then scheduled for late in 1983, but was withdrawn when compact negotiations remained stalemated over the entry of nuclear materials and the amount of economic assistance to be provided by the United States.[86]

The Federated States of Micronesia was the second of the entities to submit the compact and its ten related agreements to public vote. Kosrae, Truk, and Yap registered almost 90 percent confirmation at the June 21, 1983, election, in contrast to Ponape's voting the compact down by 51 percent.[87] Reportedly, "the leadership on Ponape was angry that the plebiscite was not postponed to allow for further time for voter education."[88] Failure to assure protection of state rights against the anticipated burgeoning of the national government also contributed to the defeat, and probably even more fundamental was the amorphous, fairly widespread sentiment in Ponape favoring independence.[89]

The next step for the Federated States was ratification by the state legislatures of the surrender of major powers of government to the United States under the compact. Much to the surprise and chagrin of the Ponapean legislators, the Truk Legislature quickly registered approval.[90] As the legislators of Kosrae and Yap were assumed to be favorably disposed, which indeed later proved to be the case,[91] the Trukese action assured the necessary concurrence by two-thirds of the states. The Ponapean legislators then rejected the compact, secure in the knowledge that their decision would not negate the compact.[92] This was followed by the Federated States Congress unanimously taking the final formal step necessary to conclude acceptance of the compact.[93] The entire operation demonstrated the capacity of the Federated Constitution to be brought into concordance with the provisions of the compact, and also foreshadowed its ability to adapt to a status other than free association should at some later date this be the will of the people of Micronesia.

Within a week of the action by the Federated States Congress, the compact was submitted to popular vote in the Marshall Islands, and upon its ratification, approval by the Nitijela quickly followed.[94] The proportion of Marshallese voting affirmatively corresponded roughly with that which defeated the Federated Constitution, both positions advocated by the dominant political leadership. Given the voters who had defied the boycott on the election for delegates to the Micronesian Constitutional Convention, for a decade a third or more of the Marshallese (although not always the same persons) have recorded opposition to the course of political events in their homeland.

Over the years stretching from the Constitutional Convention to the ratification of the "final" compact and its subordinate agreements in 1983, many of the principals of the 1975 constitutional drama remained central to the newer political developments. As noted earlier, Senator Tosiwo Nakayama from Truk, who had chaired the Convention, easily moved into the post of Federated States President, and the Convention's vice-chairman from Yap was chosen to be his Vice-President. The people of Ponape elected as their first governor Leo Falcam, who had also served as a vice-chairman of the Convention. Senator Lazarus Salii, who had not sought reelection after the Convention, again gained political prominence as a negotiator on future status, this time as ambassador solely for Palau. One of his chores was to renegotiate earlier funding levels to cover the salary increases the Palauan government had reluctantly granted its striking employees, the latter represented by Senator Roman Tmetuchl, Salii's political party antagonist. And Senator Amata Kabua, whose non-presence at the Convention had as tangible an impact on its proceedings as if he had personally participated, led his district to complete severance from the rest of Micronesia, and as part of the process became the first President of the Marshall Islands. Later he saw the compact negotiations through to their successful conclusion. The sweep of political events which followed hard on the adjournment of the Convention failed to dim the political saliency of these and the other key Micronesian leaders who helped shape the Federated Constitution.

The same sense of uncertainty which prevailed throughout the whole of the Constitutional Convention continues to engulf the final phases of terminating the Trust Territory of the Pacific Islands. The compact and its many attachments finally assumed a shape to which all of the parties could accede, with but the "unconventional" weapons provisions of the Palau constitution delaying ratification there. Nevertheless, the entire process was replete with crises, and had to be concluded piecemeal, rather than with a single Micronesian referendum as originally planned. Apparently the same will hold true for review by the United States Congress. Domestically, this will be a "congressional-executive agreement and a 'treaty' in international legal terms."[95] The financial commitment and the other unique benefits assure debate on these features of the compact, at least, before majority approval is obtained. The difficulty which the Northern Marianas Commonwealth Covenant experienced suggests lengthy scrutiny.[96] Moreover, the deaths of Senator Henry Jackson and Representative Phillip Burton removed the two Congressional leaders most familiar with the full ramifications of the Micronesian negotiations, and upon whom reliance had been placed to ease passage of the compact in the Congressional halls.

Assuming the American national barrier is overcome, an international one of indeterminate dimensions remains. The United States now concedes to the United Nations some part in ending the Trusteeship, and also that besides referral to the Trusteeship Council there must be a submission to the Security Council.[97] "While ... free association has been adjudged a valid alternative to independence, the international community and the United Nations require the metropolitan nation and the future associated state to bear the burden of proof that there has been self-determination."[98] A move to end the Trusteeship without resolving the Palau problem would be certain to encounter opposition in the Trusteeship Council;[99] with its acquiescence received to the genesis of all three Micronesian associated states, the possibility of rejection by Soviet veto in the Security Council cannot be ignored.[100] The United States refuses to disclose its next course of action should this "sensitive issue"--the phraseology is that of a President of the Trusteeship Council[101]--materialize. But as another U.N. Trusteeship Council source has pointed out, no precedent exists for ending a strategic trusteeship, and "no one can say how and in what manner the United States can seek to terminate it."[102]

To the Micronesian polities desirous of forging international linkages, anything unilaterally undertaken by the United States after a Trustee Council rejection or a Soviet veto in the Security Council offers an unsatisfactory solution. The transition to full internal self-government may proceed as contemplated, limited only by the constrictions of American defense strategy, but each such entity will lack the de jure character necessary to insure international acceptability. In addition, so long as the region remains a captive of the Cold War, the traditional enclaves within Micronesia may seek realignment, and possibly completely separate political status.[103]

To those who hold to the devil theory of Micronesian-American relations, the postponing of the referendum on the Federated Constitution was intentionally designed to further the process of Trust Territory disintegration initiated with the forming of the Northern Marianas Commonwealth, enabling the Americans to confront smaller, weaker Micronesian entities to the end of assuring a permanent United States presence throughout the area. This view treats the objection of incompatibility between the proposed constitution and the laboriously accreted Compact of Free Association nearing completion as but a sham behind which to hide Washington's more sinister purpose. The position has an aura of tenability, but, upon balance, is incomplete. Rather, long-term American policy was more general, to assure retention of all Micronesia as a security screen and access to specific parts as integral to United States military activity. The details were malleable. The principals in Washington, while countenancing self-government, attempted to turn when they could not truncate every move which threatened these objectives. The Micronesians, on their part, were bent on using the thrust of the constitutional effort to narrow the authority delegated to the United States under the draft compact, so as to approach as closely to independence as they dared. Meanwhile, disagreement within the leadership of each negotiating collectivity complicated everything. So, from their particular perspectives, everyone partially succeeded, and in the course of the trade-offs, the Marshalls and Palau attained separate status while the United States appeared to obtain a longer span of access for the American military in these two more desired parts of Micronesia, and the likely perpetual denial of the area to all third nations.

Whether or not by sheer ineptitude, the United States so delayed the termination of the Trusteeship of the Pacific Islands that the regional cleavages inherent in the artificiality called "Micronesia" were encouraged to reassert themselves. Today, three separate political entities stand aborning as associated states, their relationships with the United States still to be implemented. Borrowing from the jargon of the environmental impact statement being prepared for the United States Congress, "it is difficult at this point to predict with any high degree of precision just what the long-term effects will be on ... the [Micronesian] physical and biotic environment, the economic environment, the social and institutional environment and the military uses."[104] From the American position, in retrospect, the division of the Carolines and the Marshalls into associated states and the abandoning of a unified Micronesia under the Constitution of the Federated States of Micronesia now assumes the dimensions of a tactical mistake. Given the inconclusiveness of the ratification vote in Palau, the uncertainty surrounding the review processes in both the United States Congress and the United Nations, and all of this against a background of pettifoggery, wrangling, and Micronesian distrust, only the future will tell whether dismemberment constitutes a fundamental strategic error, as well.

---

1. Minutes of the Pre-Convention Committee: September 19, 1974, pp. 34-39, passim.

2. Statement of Ambassador Haydn Williams, issued through Saipan Liaison Office, March 6, 1976. See *Highlights*, March 15, 1976, p. 3.

3. *Highlights*, March 15, 1976, p. 2.

4. Letter dated July 16, 1976, referred to in *Marianas Variety* 5:20 (August 4, 1976), p. 6.

5. *Ibid*. The Micronesian's identification of conflicts between constitution and draft compact, completed within several weeks of the Convention's adjournment, did not fully coincide with the contents of the Washington analysis issued much later. See "A Comparison and Cross-Analysis of the Constitution of the Federated States of Micronesia as Approved by the Micronesian Constitutional Convention, and the Draft Compact of Free Association, October 31, 1974, Draft," prepared by Michael A.

White, dated November 18, 1975. (My own comparison, completed while the constitution was being concluded, did not fully jibe with either. In short, areas for disagreement existed.)

6. *Marianas Variety* 5:20 (August 4, 1976), p. 6.

7. *Highlights*, January 15, 1977, p. 12.

8. *Honolulu Star-Bulletin*, December 30, 1977, p. A-24.

9. *Highlights*, January 1, 1978, p. 3.

10. *Honolulu Star-Bulletin*, December 30, 1977, p. A-8.

11. *Honolulu Advertiser*, July 12, 1978, p. C-4.

12. *Micronesia Support Committee Bulletin* 3:4 (May-June 1978), p. 4.

13. See exchange of letters between Senator Bailey Olter for the Committee on Future Political Status and Ambassador Peter R. Rosenblatt, all dated April 9, 1978.

14. Congress of Micronesia, *Senate Journal*, Fifth Congress, 2nd Regular Session, February 1, 1974, p. 100.

15. A preparatory twenty-page lexicon of technical terms used in the constitution was issued in February, 1976, and followed by a translation of the constitution into twelve Micronesian languages, a project completed by teams drawn from each language area.

16. In January 1976 the chiefs' actions again caused the lack of a quorum in a fight over voting rights for traditional leaders. In both cases, former delegates to the Constitutional Convention led the walkouts.

17. At this time the Palauan delegation in the Congress met with the Palauan community on Saipan, and a letter was sent to the Palau District Legislature rejecting the Federation Constitution and pressing for separate status negotiations. The District's Speaker responded by pledging total support for their position. *Honolulu Star-Bulletin*, February 16, 1976, p. A-18.

18. *Highlights*, May 1, 1976, p. 2. The same Palau Legislature also endorsed the oil superport by an overwhelming vote (*Ibid*.). Later, the project died.

19. *Marianas Variety* 5:20 (August 4, 1976), p. 9.

20. *Highlights*, September 1, 1976, p. 1.

21. *Highlights*, May 1, 1976, p. 2.

22. See note 2, *supra*. After the Northern Marianas split, it was "reported that Williams agreed there would be no more separate talks with the remaining five districts." See *Honolulu Advertiser*, April 14, 1976, p. H-6.

23. See quote in Arthur J. Armstrong, "The Emergence of the Micronesians into the International Community," *Brooklyn Journal of International Law* 5:2 (Summer 1979), p. 257. Also see Roger S. Clark, "Self-Determination and Free Association: Should the United Nations Terminate the Pacific Islands Trust," *Harvard International Law Journal* 21:1 (Winter 1980), pp. 78ff.

24. Here see claim of the legal counsel/Department of Defense advisor to the President's Personal Representative for Micronesian Negotiations that the Carter "administration sought to mount a convincing case against further fragmentation.... Armstrong, 1979, *op. cit.*, pp. 224-25.

25. *Honolulu Star-Bulletin*, May 3, 1977, p. A-19. See implication that there was no other alternative than call the "roundtable conference," in "Draft Environmental Impact Statement for the Compact of Free Association," Office for Micronesian Status Negotiations, Washington, D.C., January 30, 1984, p. 51.

26. Armstrong, 1979, *op. cit.*, p. 223.

27. *Highlights*, June 1, 1977, p. 2.

28. *Highlights*, August 1, 1977, p. 2.

29. Letter of Andon Amaraich, Chairman of Commission on Future Political Status and Transition, in *Honolulu Advertiser*, April 18, 1978, p. A-11. Later, with the bargaining stance of the Commission undercut by the direct talks with the Marshalls

and Palau, the Congress of Micronesia relaxed its mandate to the Commission that in its negotiations it conform to the proposed constitution. See ESG Notes, No. 74, October 21, 1977.

30. It was confirmed in 1977 that the American Central Intelligence Agency had engaged in clandestine intelligence operations in Micronesia from early 1975 until December 1978. See U.S. Senate, "News Release of Senate Select Committee on Intelligence," June 17, 1977. Whether this included the Constitutional Convention remains unknown.

31. Honolulu Advertiser, February 27, 1978, p. A-6.

32. Micronesia Support Committee Bulletin 3:1 (December-January 1977), p. 4.

33. Honolulu Star-Bulletin and Advertiser, October 9, 1977, p. F-2.

34. Arthur J. Armstrong, "Strategic Underpinnings of the Legal Regime of Free Association," Brooklyn Journal of International Law 7:2 (Summer 1981), p. 189. See, also, statement of Deputy Assistant Secretary of State Robert Oakley at first "roundtable" discussion in Honolulu that even if the Federated Constitution is not accepted by all, "there is still the possibility of maintaining common links affecting important services and furthering mutual interest" (Armstrong, 1979, op. cit., p. 224). Joint effort has been minimal: see The Washington Report 2:7 (January 1, 1984), p. 4.

35. The proposed draft of an "Agreement Establishing the Central Pacific Commission" contemplated that the territorial scope could be expanded to include polities other than the three negotiating with the United States, and had the South Pacific Commission as an analogue.

36. Honolulu Star-Bulletin, December 14, 1977, p. A-24.

37. Highlights, January 15, 1977, p. 2.

38. Highlights, April 1, 1978, p. 2.

39. Doubts about the ESG Task Force were publicly evidenced as early as 1977 by the Micronesians' request to the Trusteeship Council for a U.N. agency

to develop an informational program for the constitutional referendum and to monitor the ESG efforts. See Highlights, July 1, 1977, p. 5. See also, Micronesia Support Committee Bulletin 2:10 (November 1977), p. 5.

40. Highlights, April 15, 1976, p. 6. See also "Analysis of Proposed Constitution of Micronesia issued by Marshallese Status Commission," 1976.

41. E.g., the Palau Status Commission's charge, in referring to the section of the constitution giving the Federated Congress power to determine the election and qualification of its members (Art. IX, Sec. 17), that "no other constitution known in the democratic world so clearly ignores the votes and wishes of a society which freely elects its own chosen representatives." See Micronesia Support Committee Bulletin 3:4 (May-June 1978), p. 4. Ignored was paralleling language elsewhere, as in the United States Constitution. Significantly, it was under a similar power that the Congress of Micronesia had recently expelled Senator Roman Tmetuchl for neglect of duties and violation of his oath, after he absented himself following the informal referendum in Palau favoring Palauan separatism (Honolulu Advertiser March 1, 1978, p. A-9). Tmetuchl at this time was chairman of the Palau Political Status Commission, and a "Proclamation of Palau Leaders" alleged the expulsion was motivated "to force Palau into an intolerable future political status" (Honolulu Advertiser, March 6, 1978, p. A-7). However, see explanation of John Ngiraked, in renouncing the Proclamation which he had originally signed (Micronesia Support Committee Bulletin 3:3 [March-April 1978], p. 6).

42. Highlights, August 1, 1978, p. 1.

43. Highlights, July 15, 1978, p. 12.

44. Honolulu Star-Bulletin, July 25, 1978, p. A-16.

45. Certified returns of the July 12, 1978, Constitutional Referendum in Highlights, August 15, 1978:

Dist.	"yes" votes	"no" votes	percentages	reject./ spoiled
Kosrae*	1,073	685	61-39%	N.A.
Marshalls	3,888	6,217	38-62%	N.A.
Palau	2,720	3,339	45-55%	114

continued

Dist.	"yes" votes	"no" votes	percentages	reject./ spoiled
Ponape	5,970	2.020	75-25%	518
Truk	9,762	4,239	70-30%	609
Yap	3,359	186	95- 5%	83

#unofficial

46. In September 1976, of the Palauans who voted in a non-binding district referendum (about 50% of the electorate), 88% favored separate Palauan negotiations on future political status. The following year, also in an incomplete return, 63% of the Marshallese voters approved of separate status (Honolulu Star-Bulletin, August 10, 1977, p. A-16). The Congress of Micronesia, in a letter to the Security Council, alleged there were serious irregularities in these referenda (Honolulu Star-Bulletin, February 25, 1978, p. 2).

47. Honolulu Advertiser, July 7, 1978, p. A-14.

48. The Congress of Micronesia ordered an investigation into the allegation that the Palau election returns should be invalidated because of alleged misconduct. Special Committee Report No. 7-13 failed to find substantiation of the charges sufficient to effect the results. Congress of Micronesia, Senate Journal, Seventh Congress, 2nd Sp. Session, 1978, pp. 57ff.

49. Micronesian Reporter 27:4 (Fourth Quarter, 1979), p. 23.

50. The separation occurred on April 1, 1976. Honolulu Advertiser, March 25, 1976, p. B-11.

51. "Practical" is advisedly used, for without termination of the Trusteeship, problems regarding the status of the Northern Marianas continued to arise, such as over unrestricted entry of its peoples into the United States and use of foreign-built vessels in its territorial waters.

52. Yap's constitution created two councils of chiefs, one for the Yap Islands and the other for the Outer Islands, with veto powers over state legislation concerning traditions and customs. The corresponding Council of Iroij subsequently structured into the Marshallese Constitution provides for only consultative and delaying powers. See Norman Meller, "On Matters Constitutional in

Micronesia," *The Journal of Pacific History* 15:2 (April 1980), p. 88.

53. *Micronesian Reporter*, 2nd Quarter, 1979, pp. 17-18.

54. See Bruce M. Turcott, "Beginnings of the Federated States of Micronesia Supreme Court," *Univ. of Hawaii Law Review* 5:2 (Winter 1983), p. 361; also see Addison M. Bowman, "Legitimacy and Scope of Trust Territory High Court Power," *Univ. of Hawaii Law Review* 5:1 (Spring 1983), p. 57.

55. For analysis of the first draft of the Marshallese Constitution, see Norman Meller, "The Ralik Ratak Draft Constitution," *Micronesian Perspective* 1:3 (December 1977), p. 1.

56. The Marshallese assert that a parliamentary system more approximates custom, with the paramount Iroij surrounded by his *alabs* (heads of senior clans) for advice. This view of the past ignores the reality of the little autocracies existing in traditional Marshallese culture, with the absolute power of the Iroij tempored only by his need of the *kajur's* (commoner's) services and the fear of deadly reprisal should he become intolerably arbitrary.

57. *Micronesian Reporter*, 4th Quarter, 1979, p. 24.

58. See Donald R. Shuster, "Palau's Constitutional Tangle," *The Journal of Pacific History* 15:2 (April 1980), p. 74.

59. The two Palauan constitutions drafted in 1975 (see p. 97, *supra*) had long slipped into oblivion.

60. Once the new Palau Government had commenced functioning, successive strikes of governmental employees occurred, the first marked by the dynamiting of the Presidential offices. The granting of a series of raises eventuated in further changes in the terms of the Palauan bilateral compact to meet the increased costs of the Palauan government. See *Pacific Islands Monthly* 52:12 (December 1981), p. 29; also *Honolulu Star-Bulletin*, December 2, 1982, p. A-3.

61. Later, the Reagan Administration apparently backed away from independence as an alternative option, at least if not accompanied with a mutual

security treaty as illustrated by the precedent of the Philippines.

62. In Armstrong, 1979, op. cit., p. 218. For full "Statement of Agreed Principles for Free Association," dated April 9, 1982, see *Micronesia Support Committee Bulletin* 3:3 (March-April 1978), p. 4.

63. Lack of knowledge about Republican Ronald Reagan's stand on Micronesia, and fear that his administration would force the acceptance of a commonwealth status, encouraged Micronesian initialling of the compact. See *Honolulu Star-Bulletin*, November 22, 1980, p. A-8.

64. *Honolulu Star-Bulletin*, May 27, 1982, p. A-27.

65. *Honolulu Star-Bulletin*, August 27, 1982, p. A-6. The hyperbole is noted, for as early as 1980, negotiations were supposed to have resulted in a complete compact package, while the compact and agreements signed on August 26, 1982, still left some tag ends dangling.

66. The refusal of the courts to rule the Marshallese "homecoming" illegal embarrassed the positions of both the United States and Marshallese negotiators. See Darlene Keju and Giff Johnson, "Kwajalein: Home on the 'Range,'" *Pacific Magazine* 7:6 (November/December 1982), p. 26.

67. Despite the strong prohibitions in both the Federated States and Palauan Constitutions against the presence of nuclear materials, according to one commentator, about all that will be foreclosed is further nuclear testing. See Henry M. Schwalbenberg, "Nuclear Weapons and the Compact," Micronesian Seminar No. 3, Truk, FSM, February, 1982. Subordinate agreements waive the constitutional provisions giving the Federated States and Palau jurisdiction over waters extended two hundred miles seaward, a claim which could challenge United States naval transit. The Marshallese Constitution posed no threat to the compact; to make doubly sure, the Marshall Islands Nitijela adopted a bill declaring the compact controls over any constitutional inconsistency. See *The South Seas Digest* 12:3 (September 9, 1983), p. 1.

68. "Formally" as there is some ambiguity surrounding the Cook Islands' scope of power over foreign

affairs. See Arnold H. Leibowitz, *Colonial Emancipation in the Pacific and the Caribbean* (New York: Praeger Publishers, 1976), p. 141. A difference clearly distinguishing the Micronesian Associated State status from that of the Cooks and Niue is that Micronesians will not be citizens of their former trustee. However, they may at will enter, live, and work in the United States.

69. For status of the three new Micronesian entities under international law, see Armstrong, 1979, *op. cit.*, pp. 244ff.

70. *Micronesia Support Committee Bulletin* 2:10 (November 1977), p. 11.

71. *Honolulu Star-Bulletin and Advertiser*, October 4, 1981, pp. 2-3.

72. See Henry M. Schwalbenberg, "FSM & Denial," *Pacific Magazine* 8:2 (March/April 1983), p. 22.

73. The Marshall Islands and the Federated States of Micronesia agreements on mutual security require concurrence of the United States *and* the Micronesian entity to terminate American denial rights (Article VIII, Marshalls; Article IX, Federated States of Micronesia). The Palau Military Use and Operating Rights Agreement declares the "denial right" provision of the compact (Sec. 311[b][2]) is to remain in effect "until otherwise mutually agreed" (Article IX, par. 4).

74. See Schwalbenberg, "FSM & Denial," *op. cit.*

75. Despite the American statement to the United Nations that independence was a negotiable alternative (published in full in *Pacific Islands Monthly* 53:8 [August 1982], p. 31), the Micronesians remained convinced that the United States had resolved not to end the Trusteeship until its national security interests were preserved. Henry M. Schwalbenberg, "American Military Needs in Micronesia," Micronesian Seminar No. 7, Truk, FSM, October, 1982, pp. 8-9. Thus the placing of "independence" on the Marshallese ballot as an alternative in a 1982 vote supposed to end Trusteeship status was vetoed by Washington. See *Honolulu Star-Bulletin and Advertiser*, August 22, 1982, p. F-3. In retrospect, the Micronesian threat of unilateral declaration of independence appears to have served primarily as a useful negotiating ploy, as illus-

trated by the Marshallese use prior to May 30, 1982, and later by the Palauans on their breaking off of negotiations late in 1983. See The Washington Pacific Report 2:7 (January 1, 1984), p. 4.

76. The differential weighting of the two factors (after excluding military impact and atomic test payments) may be roughly indicated by the smaller per capita benefits to be received by the Federated States with its limited national security importance. According to the estimates of Henry S. Schwalbenberg, over the first fifteen years the annual per capita average payments will be $816 for the Federated States, $937 for the Marshalls, and $1268 for Palau. Data from "Compact of Free Association: Class Notes," Micronesian Seminar, Truk, FSM, 1983, Pt. 3: Economic Affairs - p. 24.

77. Peter Larmour, "Compact of Free Association," Papua New Guinea: Foreign Affairs Review 2:2 (July 1982), p. 27. (Although the comparison was based on the compact as initialled in November 1980, changes in the compact since then only increase the disparity, if anything.)

78. "Briefing on the Micronesian Political Status Negotiations, [United States] Senate Committee on Foreign Relations," delivered by Ambassador Fred Zeder, December 10, 1982: Appendix. (Note: these monetary data are only approximate, as minor changes keep occurring.)

79. Ibid., p. 2.

80. 4,452 to 2,715, Micronesia Support Committee Bulletin 7:4 (Winter 1982), p. 4.

81. Closer association: 2,250; independence: 1,800 (Ibid).

82. With a 75 percent vote necessary to waive the constitutional ban on nuclear materials entering Palau, only 53 percent of the voters approved. See Micronesia Support Committee, "Palau; Self-Determination vs. U.S. Military Plans," Honolulu, May 1983, p. 17.

83. Micronesia Support Committee Bulletin 7:4 (Winter 1982), p. 4.

84. Several years earlier, Ambassador Peter E. Rosenblatt assured the writer (in a letter dated Jan-

uary 6, 1980) that "it is understood that if the nuclear agreement fails of ... [three-fourths] approved margin, the compact will fail...."

85. The South Seas Digest 12:3 (September 9, 1983), p. 1.

86. The South Sea Digest 19:3 (December 16, 1983), p. 1. A revised compact reducing the specific areas identified for military defense use in Palau, deleting some provisions on United States nuclear usage, and restructuring economic aid was submitted in September 1984. While a two-thirds majority approved, the failure to secure a 75 percent affirmative vote leaves the compact subject to challenge in the Palau courts as violative of the Palauan Constitution.

87. The National Union 4:13 (July 15, 1983), p. 1. As pointed out by the Ponape State Legislature, despite the 79 percent affirmative tally, only about 53 percent of the eligible voters participated throughout the Federated States, so that the "no" votes plus the "no shows" constituted a majority. The National Union 4:17 (September 15, 1983), p. 5.

88. Honolulu Star-Bulletin, June 22, 1983, p. A-12. The Ponape State Legislature had adopted a resolution asking postponement of the plebiscite to January, 1984, citing inadequate time for public information.

89. "Governor Resio Moses, citing the large percentage of Ponape voters [70%] who marked their ballots for independence [as an alternative, if free association were not possible] ... said, 'Upon entering into free association with the United States, FSM leaders should prepare for independence, as far as Ponape is concerned.'" The National Union 4:12 (June 30, 1983), p. 5. It should be noted, however, that in Truk an even higher percentage of voters (81%) preferred independence as a second choice, while still favoring the compact.

90. The Truk Legislature vote was not even close (21 to 1, with 6 excused absences). Honolulu Star-Bulletin, August 5, 1983, p. A-3.

91. For Yap, see The National Union 4:15 (August 19, 1983), p. 1. No one raised the constitutional objection that the Yap State Legislature was prohibited from ratifying the compact due to Article

XIII, Section 4 of the Yapese State Constitution barring the introduction of radioactive and nuclear substances.

92. The Ponape State Legislature cited provisions implying a United States military and nuclear presence in the Federated States as reasons for its rejection of the compact by a vote of 17 to 2. See *The National Union* 4:17 (September 15, 1983), p. 1.

93. *Ibid.* Yet to be completed and approved are the long-range economic development plans for expending 40 percent of the compact's grant funds, specifically required in the compact.

94. *Marshall Islands Journal* 14:74 and 75 (September 16 and 20, 1983), p. 1.

95. Armstrong, 1981, *op. cit.*, p. 227.

96. See to the contrary, Henry M. Schwalbenberg, "The Ballot and the Plebiscite," Micronesian Seminar No. 5, Truk, FSM, March 1982.

97. *Honolulu Star-Bulletin*, April 30, 1980, p. G-14.

98. J. Ross MacDonald, "Termination of the Strategic Trusteeship," *Brooklyn Journal of International Law* 7:2 (Summer 1981), p. 280.

99. *Honolulu Star-Bulletin*, December 16, 1980, p. A-14.

100. The Soviet Union has long accused the United States of imposing associated state status and working to break up the Trust Territory so as to annex its various components. E.g., see *Honolulu Advertiser*, February 27, 1978, p. A-6.; *The National Union* 3:11 (June 15, 1982), p. 2.

101. *The South Seas Digest* 10:2 (August 13, 1982), p. 2.

102. *Honolulu Star-Bulletin*, December 16, 1983, p. A-14.

103. The southern islands of Palau are inhabited by mid-Carolinians, and not Palauans. For long, minority regional representatives sought a part in the Marshallese negotiations with the United

States. The region between Yap's main islands and Truk is reported as ripe to break away from the state of Yap. In November 1977, at an advisory referendum called by the Truk State Legislature, of 3,181 ballots cast in the Faichuk area of the Truk lagoon, 84 percent voted in favor of separation from Truk; of 2,262 votes in the Mortlocks, 71 percent voted in favor of separation. See _Micronesia Support Committee Bulletin_ 2:10 (November 1977), p. 6. The action of the Federated States Congress supporting the Faichuk separation was subsequently vetoed by the President. In 1982, the Ponape State Legislature debated a bill calling for a plebiscite on the state withdrawing from the Federated States and negotiating its own separate status.

104. "Draft Environmental Impact Statement for the Compact of Free Association," Office for Micronesian Status Negotiations, Washington, D.C., January 30, 1984, p. 1.

APPENDICES

Appendix A

Table 1. Area, Population, and 1975 T.T. Operating Budget

Peripheral Districts	lagoon area m2	land area m3	land area %	public land % dis.	pop. %[a]	TT Oper. Budget %
Marianas	n/a	184.5	25.5	88	12.5	51.4[b]
Marshalls	4,307	69.8	9.5	3	21.8	10.1
Palau	525	191.0	26.4	74	11.0	9.0
Central Districts						
Ponape	341	187.0	25.8	66	20.3	11.3
Truk	2,030	45.7	6.3	16	27.5	11.9
Yap	405	46.0	6.4	4	6.9	6.3
T.T.			100%	--	100%	100%

a as of January 1, 1975
b includes 40.9% T.T. Headquarters

Source: Congress of Micronesia, Trust Territory of the Pacific Islands-Five Year Indicative Development Plan (1976-1981), July 1976, pp. 10, 24, 84. Task Force on Education for Self-Government, Economic Briefing Information on Micronesia's Economy, 1974, pp. 5-6.

Table 2. Agriculture, Wages, Gross Domestic Product, 1975

Peripheral Districts	Agriculture			Taxable Wages				Gross Domestic Product		
	copra mkt. %[a]	all ag. mkt. %[a]		public service %	private service %	total %		total $ mil.	per capita %	$
Marianas	1.3	12.1		34.2	43.1	37.1		40.6	32.5	2,713
Marshalls	54.0	45.4		17.6	17.8	17.6		22.3	17.9	853
Palau	0.8	1.9		12.8	12.2	12.6		14.6	11.7	1,103
Central Districts										
Ponape	16.2	16.8		14.1	11.7	13.3		19.5	15.6	803
Truk	21.7	18.6		14.1	10.2	12.8		19.8	15.9	600
Yap	5.8	5.3		7.3	5.1	6.6		8.0	6.4	974
T.T.	100%	100%		100%	100%	100%		124.8	100%	1,051

[a] as of 1973

Source: Congress of Micronesia, op. cit., p. 24; Task Force, op. cit.

Table 3. Total Taxes Collected by COM (COM FY 1975)

Peripheral Districts	Income %	Imp./Exp. %	Other %	Total ($000)	% Dist. GDP	Return to Dis. ($000)	COM share ($000)	COM Share % of Dis. GDP
Marianas	23.8	30.9	46.8	1,934	4.8	466	1,468	3.6
Marshalls	50.1	14.3	11.6	2,479	11.1[a]	215	2,264	10.1
Palau	7.6	14.8	24.3	775	5.3	219	556	3.8
Central Districts								
Ponape	8.3	15.7	8.2	782	4.6	232	550	3.2
Truk	7.0	17.1	5.2	759	3.8	241	518	2.6
Yap	3.2	7.2	3.7	336	4.2	99	237	3.0
T.T.($000)	4,122	2,676	267	7,065	—	1,472	5,593	—

[a] Elimination of income taxes paid by non-Micronesians in the Marshalls would give a tax rate of 4%, which is more in line with the other districts (p. 31).
Source: Congress of Micronesia, op. cit.

Table 4. Actual Budgets by Program Area, 1975[a]

Trust Territory Government Department	Operations ($000)	CIP ($000)	Total ($000)	Per Capita Operations ($)	Per Capita CIP ($)	Total P.C. ($)
Judiciary	737	-0-	737			
Health Services	8,085	4,545	12,630			
Education	13,120	1,467	14,587			
Public Affairs	1,996	-0-	1,996			
Resources & Development	7,743	80[b]	7,823			
Prot. to Pers./Prop.	2,349	-0-[c]	2,349			
Administration	6,021	390[c]	6,411			
Transportation & Communication	3,718	5,139	8,857			
Public Works	9,475	3,186[d]	12,661			
	53,244	14,807	68,051	444	124	568

[a] Does not include Federal expenditures of approximately $11.9 million, nor territorially-raised funds.
[b] Legal Affairs.
[c] General Support—$40; Maintenance and Rehabilitation—$350.
[d] Community Development—$1,392; Water, Sewage, Power—$1,794.

Source: Congress of Micronesia, pp. 26,27; pop. p. 24.

Appendix B

General Referendum on Future Status
of Micronesia, July 8, 1975

Area	Registered voters	Ballots cast	Independent yes	Independent no	Commonwealth yes	Commonwealth no
Truk	16,322	7405	3270	719	144	908
Ponape	12,724	7184	3507	2153	484	4366
Marshalls	9,203	3237	119	2175	409	2300
Palau	5,888	2486	455	869	171	905
Yap	4,283	2950	135	1906	86	1741

Area	Free Association yes	Free Association no	Statehood yes	Statehood no	Present Status yes	Present Status no	Other Status yes	Other Status no
Truk	1139	689	129	901	2583	542	28	571
Ponape	2841	2623	371	4427	2851	2637	–	–
Marshalls	826	1926	199	2302	2317	687	129	2011
Palau	1120	526	183	880	1288	370	38	754
Yap	1779	852	45	2479	1109	1370	14	1975

Appendix C

Miscellaneous Communication No. 23, printed in the MCC Journal, Vol. I, pp. 349ff, and answering the Communication cited in Chapter 9, note 6, supra, contained an appendix which was distributed to all delegates. Its contents well illustrate the problem of drafting discussed in Chapter 9.

On August 20, 1975, a note was received for the preparation of a Delegate Proposal, reading as copied below. Opposite [in this Appendix following] the two elements of the request are the sections prepared in the Proposal printed. During the course of the drafting, discussions were had with at least one of the interpreters of the requestors, and fuller explanation of intent was ascertained:

    1. Constitutional interpretation

Note received

"The interpretation of this constitution shall not be made in the light of any other constitution known in Micronesia, immediately before the effective date of the constitution."

Draft prepared

The provisions of this Constitution shall be interpreted so as to be compatible with the Constitution's Micronesian context, and not necessarily interpreted as having the same meaning as comparable provisions in other constitutions; nor shall they necessarily be interpreted so as to continue the law introduced into Micronesia by the various administering authorities prior to the effective date of this Constitution.

    2. No continuation of past judicial precedents

Note received

"Commencing with the effective date of this constitution, all common law, foreign to Micronesia, shall cease to exist. All legal interpretations shall henceforth be drawn from this Constitution."

Draft prepared

The Courts of Micronesia shall decide cases in a manner compatible with this Constitution, laws enacted thereunder, Micronesian customs and traditions, and the total social and physical configuration of Micronesian life. Judicial decisions rendered prior to the effective date of this Constitution shall not constitute precedents which must be observed by the Courts of Micronesia.

Explanation on element No. 1: Supplementing the written instruction, orally communicated was the information that the requestors did not want the Micronesian courts to interpret the Micronesian Constitution in the same way as interpreted by the courts of another jurisdiction whose constitution contained identical or similar language. It was pointed out that literally this would mean if a judge in another country decided "X", a Micronesian judge would have no alternative but to decide "non-X", regardless of what "non-X" was. The instructions were then changed so that the Micronesian judges were to be free to interpret the Constitution's language within the Micronesian context and not to have to follow the interpretations made by courts in other countries. Similarly, they were to be free to use their judgement without being influenced by the fact that the law introduced into Micronesia might lead them to another conclusion, in the effort to continue that law. On the belief that we had now ascertained the requestors' intent, the portion of the Proposal on "constitutional interpretation" was prepared.

Explanation of element No. 2: Analyzing the written instructions, it should be noted at the outset that the reference to "common law, foreign to Micronesia" raises problems. Common law refers to those principles and rules of action which derive their authority from ancient usage or from judgements of the courts enforcing them and elaborating upon them. In actual practice, it is the "recognition" of those customs by the courts which gives them a legally operational role, constituting the common law. Judge-declared law is foreign to Micronesia, for courts and judges are introduced institutions. Literally taken, all judicial decisions which purport to do anything other than enforce statutes according to statutory terms (that is all decisions which help build the common law) are to be nullified. As another factor, to draw "all legal interpretations" from the Constitution would be to ignore all those matters outside of the Constitution on which a Micronesian-oriented common law could ultimately be shaped.

Once again, after oral communication with at least one of the interpreters, it was ascertained that what was desired was that judges, after the Constitution becomes effective, should not have to follow the rule of law contained in decisions rendered before that time. Carefully the concepts of <u>res adjudicata</u> (the law of a case binds the parties to that case, after the time for appeal is past, even though the principle is subsequently overturned) and <u>stare decisis</u> (the principle of law decided by a case becomes a precedent binding other judges in the future when rendering decisions on the same subject with respect to other parties) were explained. The response from the interpreter was that it was desired to prevent pre-Constitution precedents having to be followed after the Constitution becomes effective. It was also ascertained that it was desired to build up a body of Micronesian common law, through court decisions based on Micronesian customs and traditions and the total social and physical configuration of Micronesian life. All these were included in the Delegate Proposal prepared.

Appendix D

Introduction of Proposals
Micronesian Constitutional Convention

Convention Day	For Week Ending	New Delegates Propositions		New Committee Propositions*		New Resolutions
		Number	Pages	Number	Pages	
7	July 18	5	5	—	—	1
14	July 25	25	36	—	—	5
21	Aug. 1	43	64	—	—	3
28	Aug. 8	39	83	—	—	3
35	Aug. 15	14	30	3	3	6
42	Aug. 22	18	26	3	4	5
Recess Subtotal		144	244	6	7	23
48	Sept. 20	6	6	—	—	2
54	Sept. 27	6	7	5	8	4
60	Oct. 4	3	3	3	7	—
66	Oct. 11	2	2	—	—	1
72	Oct. 18	2	2	12	43	—
78	Oct. 25	—	—	4	11	1
84	Nov. 1	—	—	4	4	2
90	Nov. 8	—	—	—	—	4
Subtotal		19	20	28	73	14
TOTAL		163	264	34	80	37

*First Reading in Journal

Appendix E

PALAU DELEGATION
MICRONESIAN CONSTITUTIONAL CONVENTION

OUTLINE OF POSITION

I. MICRONESIAN UNITY

The Palau Delegation to the Micronesian Constitutional Convention will support the Unity of Micronesia <u>if and only if</u> the following terms and conditions are incorporated in the final draft constitution(s) of Micronesia:

1. The central government of Micronesia shall have only those powers as may be <u>expressly delegated</u> to it by the people of the districts.

    a. each district shall be recognized as the basic political unit of government in Micronesia.

    b. each district, as the basic political unit of government, shall have all other powers of government <u>not expressly</u> delegated to the central government and which are characterized as the <u>reserved</u> or <u>residual</u> and <u>implied</u> powers.

    c. the jurisdiction of the central government of Micronesia shall be limited to subject matters which are of common concern and mutual interest to all the districts of Micronesia, and hence, shall necessarily be limited to international, inter-district and kindred matters, such as:

        i. International relations and national defense

        ii. immigration, international travel and postal service

        iii. international and inter-district transportation and communication

        iv. international and inter-district
            trade and commerce

        v. promotion of the standards of
            health and education services
            in the districts, with the district
            government having the primary
            responsibility and policy-making
            concerning the delivery of these
            services.

2. The central legislative authority of Micronesia shall be uni-cameral in structure consisting of equal number of representatives from each district -- equal district representation.

3. The district governments shall have full authority and control over ownership and use of land.

    a. the power of eminent domain in the
        central government shall be conditioned
        upon the approval of the appropriate
        district government.

    b. ownership and use of land by foreign
        governments, corporations, nationals
        or international organizations shall
        be the responsibility of the district
        governments.

4. Financial grants or aids by foreign governments or international organizations to Micronesia shall be divided and shared equally by all districts and the central government of Micronesia with exception of those grants which shall by their own special nature and terms provide for a different method of division or distribution.

5. District governments shall contribute equally to the national treasury of Micronesia.

    a. central government shall have no general taxing authority except the power
        to levy fees and taxes, other than
        a personal income tax, on business
        transactions and services falling

within its jurisdiction, such as fees or taxes on the following:

    i. transactions and activities of business entities engaging in international and inter-district trade and commerce.

    ii. air and ocean transportation and communication business transactions and activities.

  b. the central government shall derive needed additional revenues from the district governments on the basis of equal contributions.

6. Constitutional recognition of the right of political self-determination for each district to withdraw unilaterally from the Micronesian union over a specified period of time in order to afford each district an opportunity to reassess the desirability and advantages and disadvantages of unity of Micronesia.

7. The seat of the central government of Micronesia shall be located in Palau.

II. FUTURE STATUS

The Palau Delegation supports a status with the United States that is terminable and alterable and which leaves open the options for independence, commonwealth status, and other kinds of status with the United States or other nations.

III. ALTERNATE DRAFT CONSTITUTION

In the event the Convention will not incorporate any of the above terms and conditions in any of the proposed draft constitutions, the Palau Delegation will put together an ALTERNATIVE DRAFT CONSTITUTION incorporating all of the above terms and conditions and shall present the same to the Convention and, hopefully, to all the Micronesian voters for final consideration and approval.

Appendix F

Constitution of The Federated States of Micronesia

Preamble

WE, THE PEOPLE OF MICRONESIA, exercising our inherent sovereignty, do hereby establish this Constitution of the Federated States of Micronesia.

With this Constitution, we affirm our wish to live together in peace and harmony, to preserve the heritage of the past, and to protect the promise of the future.

To make one nation of many islands, we respect the diversity of our cultures. Our differences enrich us. The seas bring us together, they do not separate us. Our islands sustain us, our island nation enlarges us and makes us stronger.

Our ancestors, who made their homes on these islands, displaced no other people. We, who remain, wish no other home than this. Having known war, we hope for peace. Having been divided, we wish unity. Having been ruled, we seek freedom.

Micronesia began in the days when man explored seas in rafts and canoes. The Micronesian nation is born in an age when men voyage among stars; our world itself is an island. We extend to all nations what we seek from each: peace, friendship, cooperation, and love in our common humanity. With this Constitution we, who have been the wards of other nations, become the proud guardian of our own islands, now and forever.

ARTICLE I

Territory of Micronesia

Section 1. The territory of the Federated States of Micronesia is comprised of the Districts of the Micronesian archipelago that ratify this Constitution. Unless limited by international treaty obligations assumed by the Federated States of Micronesia, or by its own act, the waters connecting the islands of the archipelago are internal waters regardless of dimensions, and jurisdiction extends to a marine space of 200 miles measured outward from appropriate baselines, the seabed, subsoil, water column, insular or continental shelves, airspace over land and water, and any other territory or waters belonging to Micronesia by historic right, custom, or legal title.

Section 2. Each state is comprised of the islands of each District as defined by laws in effect immediately prior to the effective date of this Constitution. A marine boundary between adjacent states is determined by law, applying the principle of equidistance. State boundaries may be changed by Congress with the consent of the state legislatures involved.

Section 3. Territory may be added to the Federated States of Micronesia upon approval of Congress, and by vote of the inhabitants of the area, if any, and by vote of the people of the Federated States of Micronesia. If the territory is to become part of an existing state, approval of the state legislature is required.

Section 4. New states may be formed and admitted by law, subject to the same rights, duties, and obligations as provided for in this Constitution.

ARTICLE II

Supremacy

Section 1. This Constitution is the expression of the sovereignty of the people and is the supreme law of the Federated States of Micronesia. An act of the Government in conflict with this Constitution is invalid to the extent of conflict.

ARTICLE III

Citizenship

Section 1. A person who is a citizen of the Trust Territory immediately prior to the effective date of this Constitution and a domiciliary of a District ratifying this Constitution is a citizen and national of the Federated States of Micronesia.

Section 2. A person born of parents one or both of whom are citizens of the Federated States of Micronesia is a citizen and national of the Federated States by birth.

Section 3. A citizen of the Federated States of Micronesia who is recognized as a citizen of

another nation shall, within 3 years of his 18th
birthday, or within 3 years of the effective date
of this Constitution, whichever is later, register
his intent to remain a citizen of the Federated
States and renounce his citizenship of another
nation. If he fails to comply with this Section,
he becomes a national of the Federated States of
Micronesia.

Section 4. A citizen of the Trust Territory
who becomes a national of the United States of
America under the terms of the Covenant to Establish
a Commonwealth of the Northern Mariana Islands
may become a citizen and national of the Federated
States of Micronesia by applying to a court of
competent jurisdiction in the Federated States
within 6 months of the date he became a United
States national.

Section 5. A domiciliary of a District not
ratifying this Constitution who was a citizen of
the Trust Territory immediately prior to the effective date of this Constitution, may become a citizen
and national of the Federated States of Micronesia
by applying to a court of competent jurisdiction
in the Federated States within 6 months after the
effective date of this Constitution or within 6
months after his 18th birthday, whichever is later.

Section 6. This Article may be applied retroactively.

ARTICLE IV

Declaration of Rights

Section 1. No law may deny or impair freedom
of expression, peaceable assembly, association,
or petition.

Section 2. No law may be passed respecting
an establishment of religion or impairing the free
exercise of religion, except that assistance may
be provided to parochial schools for non-religious
purposes.

Section 3. A person may not be deprived of
life, liberty, or property without due process
of law, or be denied the equal protection of the
laws.

Section 4. Equal protection of the laws may
not be denied or impaired on account of sex, race,
ancestry, national origin, language, or social
status.

Section 5. The right of the people to be

secure in their persons, houses, papers, and other possessions against unreasonable search, seizure, or invasion of privacy may not be violated. A warrant may not issue except on probable cause, supported by affidavit particularly describing the place to be searched and the persons or things to be seized.

Section 6. The defendant in a criminal case has a right to a speedy public trial, to be informed of the nature of the accusation, to have counsel for his defense, to be confronted with the witnesses against him, and to compel attendance of witnesses in his behalf.

Section 7. A person may not be compelled to give evidence that may be used against him in a criminal case, or be twice put in jeopardy for the same offense.

Section 8. Excessive bail may not be required, excessive fines imposed, or cruel and unusual punishments inflicted. The writ of habeas corpus may not be suspended unless required for public safety in cases of rebellion or invasion.

Section 9. Capital punishment is prohibited.

Section 10. Slavery and involuntary servitude are prohibited except to punish crime.

Section 11. A bill of attainder or ex post facto law may not be passed.

Section 12. A citizen of the Federated States of Micronesia may travel and migrate within the Federated States.

Section 13. Imprisonment for debt is prohibited.

ARTICLE V

Traditional Rights

Section 1. Nothing in this Constitution takes away a role or function of a traditional leader as recognized by custom and tradition, or prevents a traditional leader from being recognized, honored, and given formal or functional roles at any level of government as may be prescribed by this Constitution or by statute.

Section 2. The traditions of the people of the Federated States of Micronesia may be protected by statute. If challenged as violative of Article IV, protection of Micronesian tradition shall be considered a compelling social purpose warranting such governmental action.

Section 3. The Congress may establish, when needed, a Chamber of Chiefs consisting of traditional leaders from each state having such leaders, and of elected representatives from states having no traditional leaders. The constitution of a state having traditional leaders may provide for an active, functional role for them.

ARTICLE VI

Suffrage

Section 1. A citizen 18 years of age may vote in national elections. The Congress shall prescribe a minimum period of local residence and provide for voter registration, disqualification for conviction of crime, and disqualification for mental incompetence or insanity. Voting shall be secret.

ARTICLE VII

Levels of Government

Section 1. The three levels of government in the Federated States of Micronesia are national, state, and local. A state is not required to establish a new local government where none exists on the effective date of this Constitution.

Section 2. A state shall have a democratic constitution.

ARTICLE VIII

Powers of Government

Section 1. A power expressly delegated to the national government, or a power of such an indisputable national character as to be beyond the power of a state to control, is a national power.

Section 2. A power not expressly delegated to the national government or prohibited to the states is a state power.

Section 3. State and local governments are prohibited from imposing taxes which restrict interstate commerce.

ARTICLE IX

Legislative

Section 1. The legislative power of the national government is vested in the Congress of the Federated States of Micronesia.

Section 2. The following powers are expressly delegated to Congress:

(a) to provide for the national defense;
(b) to ratify treaties;
(c) to regulate immigration, emigration, naturalization, and citizenship;
(d) to impose taxes, duties, and tariffs based on imports;
(e) to impose taxes on income;
(f) to issue and regulate currency;
(g) to regulate banking, foreign and interstate commerce, insurance, the issuance and use of commercial paper and securities, bankruptcy and insolvency, and patents and copyrights;
(h) to regulate navigation and shipping except within lagoons, lakes, and rivers;
(i) to establish usury limits on major loans;
(j) to provide for a national postal system;
(k) to acquire and govern new territory;
(l) to govern the area set aside as the national capital;
(m) to regulate the ownership, exploration, and exploitation of natural resources within the marine space of the Federated States of Micronesia beyond 12 miles from island baselines;
(n) to establish and regulate a national public service system;
(o) to impeach and remove the President, Vice-President, and justices of the Supreme Court;
(p) to define major crimes and prescribe penalties, having due regard for local custom and tradition; and
(q) to override a Presidential veto by not less than a 3/4 vote of all the state delegations, each delegation casting one vote.

Section 3. The following powers may be exercised concurrently by Congress and the states:

(a) to appropriate public funds;
(b) to borrow money on the public credit;
(c) to promote education and health and
(d) to establish systems of social security and public welfare.

Section 4. A treaty is ratified by vote of 2/3 of the members of Congress, except that a treaty delegating major powers of government of the Federated States of Micronesia to another government shall also require majority approval by the legislatures of 2/3 of the states.

Section 5. National taxes shall be imposed uniformly. Not less than 50% of the revenues shall be paid into the treasury of the state where collected.

Section 6. Net revenue derived from ocean floor mineral resources exploited under Section 2(m) shall be divided equally between the national government and the appropriate state government.

Section 7. The President, Vice-President, or a justice of the Supreme Court may be removed from office for treason, bribery, or conduct involving corruption in office by a 2/3 vote of the members of Congress. When the President or Vice-President is removed, the Supreme Court shall review the decision. When a justice of the Supreme Court is removed, the decision shall be reviewed by a special tribunal composed of one state court judge from each state appointed by the state chief executive. The special tribunal shall meet at the call of the President.

Section 8. The Congress consists of one member elected at large from each state on the basis of state equality, and additional members elected from congressional districts in each state apportioned by population. Members elected on the basis of state equality serve for a 4-year term, and all other members for 2 years. Each member has one vote, except on the final reading of bills. Congressional elections are held biennially as provided by statute.

Section 9. A person is ineligible to be a member of Congress unless he is at least 30 years of age on the day of election and has been a citizen of the Federated States of Micronesia for at least 15 years, and a resident of the state from which he is elected for at least 5 years. A person convicted of a felony by a state or national government court is ineligible to be a member of Congress. The Congress may modify this provision or prescribe additional qualifications; knowledge of the English language may not be a qualification.

Section 10. At least every 10 years Congress shall reapportion itself. A state is entitled to at least one member of Congress on the basis of population in addition to the member elected at large. A state shall apportion itself by law into single member congressional districts. Each district shall be approximately equal in population after giving due regard to language, cultural, and geographic differences.

Section 11. A state may provide that one of its seats is set aside for a traditional leader who shall be chosen as provided by statute for a 2-year term, in lieu of one representative elected on the basis of population. The number of congressional districts shall be reduced and reapportioned accordingly.

Section 12. A vacancy in Congress is filled for the unexpired term. In the absence of provision by law, an unexpired term is filled by special election, except that an unexpired term of less than one year is filled by appointment by the state chief executive.

Section 13. A member of Congress may not hold another public office or employment. During the term for which he is elected and 3 years thereafter, a member may not be elected or appointed to a public office or employment created by national statute during his term. A member may not engage in any activity which conflicts with the proper discharge of his duties. The Congress may prescribe further restrictions.

Section 14. The Congress may prescribe an annual salary and allowances for members. An increase of salary may not apply to the Congress enacting it.

Section 15. A member of Congress is privileged from arrest during his attendance at Congress and while going to and from sessions, except for treason, felony, or breach of the peace. A member answers only to Congress for his statements in Congress.

Section 16. The Congress shall meet in regular, public session as prescribed by statute. A special session may be convened at the call of the President of the Federated States of Micronesia, or by the presiding officer on the written request of 2/3 of the members.

Section 17. (a) The Congress shall be the sole judge of the elections and qualifications of its members, may discipline a member, and, by 2/3 vote, may suspend or expel a member.

(b) The Congress may determine its own rules of procedure and choose a presiding officer from among its members.

(c) The Congress may compel the attendance and testimony of witnesses and the production of documents or other matters before Congress or any of its committees.

Section 18. A majority of the members is a quorum, but a smaller number may adjourn from day to day and compel the attendance of absent members.

Section 19. The Congress shall keep and publish a journal of its proceedings. A roll call vote entered on the journal shall be taken at the request of 1/5 of the members present. Legislative proceedings shall be conducted in the English language. A member may use his own language if not fluent in English, and Congress shall provide translation.

Section 20. To become law, a bill must pass 2 readings on separate days. To pass first reading a 2/3 vote of all members is required. On final reading each state delegation shall cast one vote and a 2/3 vote of all the delegations is required. All votes shall be entered on the journal.

Section 21. (a) The Congress may make no law except by statute and may enact no statute except by bill. The enacting clause of a bill is "BE IT ENACTED BY THE CONGRESS OF THE FEDERATED STATES OF MICRONESIA:." A bill may embrace but one subject expressed in its title. A provision outside the subject expressed in the title is void.

(b) A law may not be amended or revised by reference to its title only. The law as revised or section as amended shall be published and re-enacted at full length.

Section 22. A bill passed by Congress shall be presented to the President for approval. If he disapproves of the bill, he shall return it with his objections to Congress within 10 days. If Congress has 10 or less days remaining in its session, or has adjourned, he shall return the bill within 30 days after presentation. If the President does not return a bill within the appropriate period, it becomes law as if approved.

ARTICLE X

Executive

Section 1. The executive power of the national government is vested in the President of the Federated States of Micronesia. He is elected by Congress for a term of four years by a majority vote of all the members. He may not serve for more than 2 consecutive terms.

Section 2. The following powers are expressly delegated to the President:

(a) to faithfully execute and implement the provisions of this Constitution and all national laws;

(b) to receive all ambassadors and to conduct foreign affairs and the national defense in accordance with national law;

(c) to grant pardons and reprieves, except that the chief executive of each state shall have this power concurrently with respect to persons convicted under state law; and

(d) with the advice and consent of Congress, to appoint ambassadors; all judges of the Supreme Court and other courts prescribed by statute; the principal officers of executive departments in the national government; and such other officers as may be provided for by statute. Ambassadors and principal officers serve at the pleasure of the President.

Section 3. The President:

(a) is head of state of the Federated States of Micronesia;

(b) may make recommendations to Congress, and shall make an annual report to Congress on the state of the nation; and

(c) shall perform such duties as may be provided by statute.

Section 4. A person is ineligible to become President unless he is a member of Congress for a 4-year term, a citizen of the Federated States of Micronesia by birth, and a resident of the Federated States of Micronesia for at least 15 years.

Section 5. After the election of the President, the Vice-President is elected in the same manner as the President, has the same qualifications, and serves for the same term of office. He may not be a resident of the same state. After the election of the President and the Vice-President, vacancies in Congress shall be declared.

Section 6. If the office of the President is vacant, or the President is unable to perform his duties, the Vice-President becomes President. The Congress shall provide by statute for the succession in the event both offices are vacant, or either or both officers are unable to discharge their duties.

Section 7. The compensation of the President or Vice-President may not be increased or reduced during his term. They may hold no other office and may receive no other compensation from the Federated States of Micronesia or from a state.

Section 8. Executive departments shall be established by statute.

Section 9. (a) If required to preserve public peace, health, or safety, at a time of extreme emergency caused by civil disturbance, natural disaster, or immediate threat of war, or insurrection, the President may declare a state of emergency and issue appropriate decrees.

(b) A civil right may be impaired only to the extent actually required for the preservation of peace, health, or safety. A declaration of emergency may not impair the power of the judiciary except that the declaration shall be free from judicial interference for 30 days after it is first issued.

(c) Within 30 days after the declaration of emergency, the Congress of the Federated States of Micronesia shall convene at the call of its presiding officer or the President to consider revocation, amendment, or extension of the declaration. Unless it expires by its own terms, is revoked, or extended, a declaration of emergency is effective for 30 days.

ARTICLE XI

Judicial

Section 1. The judicial power of the national government is vested in a Supreme Court and inferior courts established by statute.

Section 2. The Supreme Court is a court of record and the highest court in the nation. It consists of the Chief Justice and not more than 5 associate justices. Each justice is a member of both the trial division and the appellate division, except that sessions of the trial division may be held by one justice. No justice may sit with the appellate division in a case heard by him in the trial division. At least 3 justices shall hear and decide appeals. Decision is by a majority of those sitting.

Section 3. The Chief Justice and associate justices of the Supreme Court are appointed by the President with the approval of 2/3 of Congress. Justices serve during good behavior.

Section 4. If the Chief Justice is unable to perform his duties he shall appoint an associate justice to act in his stead. If the office is vacant, or the Chief Justice fails to make the appointment, the President shall appoint an associate justice to act as Chief Justice until the vacancy is filled or the Chief Justice resumes his duties.

Section 5. The qualifications and compensation of justices and other judges may be prescribed by statute. Compensation of judges may not be diminished during their terms of office unless all salaries prescribed by statute are reduced by a uniform percentage.

Section 6. (a) The trial division of the Supreme Court has original and exclusive jurisdiction in cases affecting officials of foreign governments, disputes between states, admiralty or maritime cases, and in cases in which the national government is a party except where an interest in land is at issue.

(b) The national courts, including the trial division of the Supreme Court, have concurrent original jurisdiction in cases arising under this Constitution; national law or treaties; and in disputes between a state and a citizen of another state, between citizens of different states, and between a state or a citizen thereof, and a foreign state, citizen, or subject.

(c) When jurisdiction is concurrent, the proper court may be prescribed by statute.

Section 7. The appellate division of the Supreme Court may review cases heard in the national courts, and cases heard in state or local courts if they require interpretation of this Constitution, national law, or a treaty. If a state constitution permits, the appellate division of the Supreme Court may review other cases on appeal from the highest state court in which a decision may be had.

Section 8. When a case in a state or local court involves a substantial question requiring the interpretation of the Constitution, national law, or a treaty, on application of a party or on its own motion the court shall certify the question to the appellate division of the Supreme Court. The appellate division of the Supreme Court may decide the case or remand it for further proceedings.

Section 9. The Chief Justice is the chief administrator of the national judicial system and may appoint an administrative officer who is exempt from civil service. The Chief Justice shall make and publish and may amend rules governing national courts, and by rule may:

(a) divide the inferior national courts

and the trial division of the Supreme Court into geographical or functional divisions;

    (b) assign judges among the divisions of a court and give special assignments to retired Supreme Court justices and judges of state and other courts;

    (c) establish rules of procedure and evidence;

    (d) govern the transfer of cases between state and national courts;

    (e) govern the admission to practice and discipline of attorneys and the retirement of judges; and

    (f) otherwise provide for the administration of the national judiciary. Judicial rules may be amended by statute.

Section 10. The Congress shall contribute to the financial support of state judicial systems and may provide other assistance.

Section 11. Court decisions shall be consistent with this Constitution, Micronesian customs and traditions, and the social and geographical configuration of Micronesia.

ARTICLE XII

Finance

Section 1. (a) Public money raised or received by the national government shall be deposited in a General Fund or special funds within the National Treasury. Money may not be withdrawn from the General Fund or special funds except by law.

    (b) Foreign financial assistance received by the national government shall be deposited in a Foreign Assistance Fund. Except where a particular distribution is required by the terms or special nature of the assistance, each state shall receive a share equal to the share of the national government and to the share of every other state.

Section 2. (a) The President shall submit an annual budget to Congress at a time prescribed by statute. The budget shall contain a complete plan of proposed expenditures, anticipated revenues, and other money available to the national government for the next fiscal year, together with additional information that Congress may require. The Congress may alter the budget in any respect.

    (b) No appropriation bills, except those recommended by the President for immediate passage, or to cover the operating expenses of Congress, may be passed on final reading until the bill appropriating money for the budget has been enacted.

    (c) The President may item veto an appropriation in any bill passed by Congress, and the procedure in such case shall be the same as for disapproval of an entire bill by the President.

   Section 3. (a) The Public Auditor is appointed by the President with the advice and consent of Congress. He serves for a term of 4 years and until a successor is confirmed.

    (b) The Public Auditor shall inspect and audit accounts in every branch, department, agency or statutory authority of the national government and in other public legal entities or nonprofit organizations receiving public funds from the national government. Additional duties may be prescribed by statute.

    (c) The Public Auditor shall be independent of administrative control except that he shall report at least once a year to Congress. His salary may not be reduced during his term of office.

    (d) The Congress may remove the Public Auditor from office for cause by 2/3 vote. In that event the Chief Justice shall appoint an acting Public Auditor until a successor is confirmed.

ARTICLE XIII

General Provisions

   Section 1. The national government of the Federated States of Micronesia recognizes the right of the people to education, health care, and legal services and shall take every step reasonable and necessary to provide these services.

   Section 2. Radioactive, toxic chemical, or other harmful substances may not be tested, stored, used, or disposed of within the jurisdiction of the Federated States of Micronesia without the express approval of the national government of the Federated States of Micronesia.

   Section 3. It is the solemn obligation of the national and state governments to uphold the provisions of this Constitution and to advance the principles of unity upon which this Constitution is founded.

   Section 4. A noncitizen, or a corporation not wholly owned by citizens, may not acquire title to land or waters in Micronesia.

Section 5. An agreement for the use of land for an indefinite term is prohibited. An existing agreement becomes void 5 years after the effective date of this Constitution. Within that time, a new agreement shall be concluded between the parties. When the national government is a party, it shall initiate negotiations.

Section 6. The national government of the Federated States of Micronesia shall seek renegotiation of any agreement for the use of land to which the Government of the United States of America is a party.

Section 7. On assuming office, all public officials shall take an oath to uphold, promote, and support the laws and the Constitution as prescribed by statute.

ARTICLE XIV

Amendments

Section 1. An amendment to this Constitution may be proposed by a constitutional convention, popular initiative, or Congress in a manner provided by law. A proposed amendment shall become a part of the Constitution when approved by 3/4 of the votes cast on that amendment in each of 3/4 of the states. If conflicting constitutional amendments submitted to the voters at the same election are approved, the amendment receiving the highest number of affirmative votes shall prevail to the extent of such conflict.

Section 2. At least every 10 years, Congress shall submit to the voters the question: "Shall there be a convention to revise or amend the Constitution?" If a majority of ballots cast upon the question is in the affirmative, delegates to the convention shall be chosen no later than the next regular election, unless Congress provides for the selection of delegates earlier at a special election.

ARTICLE XV

Transition

Section 1. A statute of the Trust Territory continues in effect except to the extent it is inconsistent with this Constitution, or is amended or repealed. A writ, action, suit, proceeding, civil or criminal liability, prosecution, judgment, sentence, order, decree, appeal, cause of action, defense, contract, claim, demand, title, or right continues unaffected except as modified in accordance with the provisions of this Constitution.

Section 2. A right, obligation, liability, or contract of the Government of the Trust Territory is assumed by the Federated States of Micronesia except to the extent it directly affects or benefits a government of a District not ratifying this Constitution.

Section 3. An interest in property held by the Government of the Trust Territory is transferred to the Federated States of Micronesia for retention or distribution in accordance with this Constitution.

Section 4. A local government and its agencies may continue to exist even though its charter or powers are inconsistent with this Constitution. To promote an orderly transition to the provisions of this Constitution, and until state governments are established, Congress shall provide for the resolution of inconsistencies between local government charters and powers, and this Constitution. This provision ceases to be effective 5 years after the effective date of this Constitution.

Section 5. The Congress may provide for a smooth and orderly transition to government under this Constitution.

Section 6. In the first congressional election, congressional districts are apportioned among the states as follows: Kusaie - 1; Marianas - 2; Marshalls - 4; Palau - 2; Ponape - 3; Truk - 5; Yap - 1. If Kusaie is not a state at the time of the first election, 4 members shall be elected on the basis of population in Ponape.

ARTICLE XVI

Effective Date

Section 1. This Constitution takes effect 1 year after ratification unless the Congress of Micronesia by joint resolution specifies an earlier date. If a provision of this Constitution is held to be in fundamental conflict with the United Nations Charter or the Trusteeship Agreement between the United States of America and the United Nations, the provision does not become effective until the date of termination of the Trusteeship Agreement.

INDEX

Aafin, Lambert, 135
Adams, John, 94
Agnew, Spiro T., 22
Albert, Chiro, 135, 140
Amaraich, Andon, 135, 140
American Articles of Confederation, 71, 118, 172, 182
American security, 16, 23-24, 51, 53, 56-58, 59-60, 62, 71-72, 76, 77-78, 94, 181, 197, 315-316, 319, 329-331, 335-337
Andrus, Cecil, 320
Archipelagic state, 23, 315, 328
Associated state status. See Free association; Compact of free association
Atomic testing. See Nuclear materials, tests, etc.
Australia, 231, 332

Bahamas, 71
Balos, Ataji, 93
Bank of Micronesia, 42
Basilius, Polycarp, 71, 134
Bigler, Carman Milne, 90, 91
Borja, Olympio, 135
Bossy, Popuisom Fichita, 141, 265, 268, 298
British Guyana, 71
British Honduras, 71
Burton, Phillip, 335

Cabrera, Lorenzo L. G., 114, 116, 232, 314
Canham, Erwin D., 79
Capital, national, 172, 173, 176, 177, 196, 298-301, 305, 318
Capital punishment, 194, 242
Caribbean, 71, 196
Carolinians in N. Marianas. See Marianas
Carter Administration, 317, 320, 329, 330
Chamorro. See Marianas; Micronesian: culture and tradition
CIA, 16, 322
Citizens, citizenship, 243-244, 305, 315
Civil liberties, 34, 62, 194, 201, 203-204, 223, 240-243, 250, 260-263, 270-272, 275-276
Civil service, 244-245
Commission on Future Political Status and Transition, 320-323
Commission on National Unity, 125
Common law, 192-194, 234-235
Commonwealth, 55, 64, 66, 75-76. See also Commonwealth Covenant of N. Marianas
Commonwealth Covenant of N. Marianas, 55, 66, 75-82,

95, 97, 99, 117, 243-244, 335, 336
Compact of free association, 29, 47, 53, 54-55, 57-59, 61-65, 76, 82, 86-87, 94, 109-110, 180, 181, 196-197, 231-233, 246, 265-266, 298-299, 313-322, 325, 328-337. See also Free association; Joint Committee on Future Status
Congress of Micronesia, vii-x, 21, 37-47, 51-52, 53, 55-56, 59-61, 63-66, 73-74, 75-76, 79, 81-82, 84-87, 88, 90, 91-92, 107, 110, 115-116, 117-118, 123-124, 127, 131, 134-136, 148, 157, 158, 160, 162, 164, 171, 174, 178, 191-192, 218, 231, 243, 292, 293, 299-300, 302, 316-318, 320-323. See also Convention, Micronesian Constitutional: enabling legislation
Constitution of Federated States of Micronesia
    Articles: I, 238, 315; II, 233-234, 314, 315; III, 243-245, 304-305, 315; IV, 194, 196-197, 201, 241-243, 250, 260-263, 267, 270, 272, 275-276; V, 257-277; VI, 244, 268-269, 270; VII, 237, 241; VIII, 238-240, 266, 315; IX, 233, 238-240, 244-245, 290-294, 295-298, 314, 315; X, 239, 242, 243, 244, 269, 270, 291-294, 296, 298; XI, 234-237, 291-292, 315; XII, 245, 286-290, 304-305; XIII, 240-241, 244, 298-300, 301, 315; XIV, 301; XV, 245-246, 296, 297, 301; XVI, 302, 326
    bill of rights. See Article IV above; Civil liberties
    citizens, 199, 243. See also Article III above; Citizens
    commerce, 239, 285-286
    common law, 192, 193
    compact compatability. See Compact of free association
    corporations, 244, 305
    eminent domain. See Eminent domain
    executive branch, 180, 192, 195, 198-201. See also Article X above; Plural executive
    federation, 235, 237, 304. See also Federalism, federation
    foreign affairs, treaties, 197, 314. See also Foreign affairs
    foreign aid, 285-290, 305, 325
    ideology, 200, 201
    interpretation, 192-194
    judicial branch, 192-193, 195, 234-235, 237. See also Article IX above
    land, 198, 244-245, 263-264, 269, 301, 305, 315-316. See also Public lands
    language, 192, 317
    legislative branch, 180, 192. See also Article IX above

"mock up," 217, 224-225, 246-247, 248-249, 285
preamble, 178-180, 203, 250, 285, 327
radioactive, toxic, etc. substances, 301, 315.
See also Nuclear materials, tests, etc.
ratification, 88-89, 93, 111, 146, 211, 221,
237-238, 259, 276, 300, 302, 305, 313, 317,
318, 319, 320, 322-325, 328-329, 334, 335
states, 233, 235, 237-242, 245, 267-277, 286,
297, 298, 305
style, 192-193
supremacy, 232-234, 314, 315
traditional leaders, 194, 201, 257-277. See
also Traditional leaders
Warnecke draft, 178-180, 199-200
Constitutional Referendum Board, 323
Constitutions, 193
Federated States. See Constitution of FSM
Kosrae, 326
Marianas, 78, 326
Marshalls, 328
Palau, 95, 97, 98, 175, 328, 330
Ponape, 326
Truk, 326
Yap, 326
Convention, Micronesian Constitutional
administration, 150-151, 153, 163, 217, 246,
259. See also committees: Administration;
and procedures, below
boycott, 88, 93, 114, 126, 135, 181, 219, 270-277, 283, 334
Chiefs' meetings, 259, 260, 268, 269, 271
committees: general, 1, 146-148, 152, 155,
156, 159, 162, 163, 173, 177-178, 189-192,
201-205, 214, 223-224, 234-235, 245, 246,
248-249, 259, 284, 285, 293, 300; Administration, 119, 122-123, 162-163, 184, 202-203,
211-212, 213, 215, 216-217, 224; Civil Liberties, 147, 159, 160, 190, 194, 203, 204,
214, 223, 234, 240-243, 250, 260, 261, 262,
263, 264, 268, 270, 275-276; Credentials,
116, 117, 139-141; General Provisions, 67,
138, 146-147, 159, 160, 189, 194, 203, 223-224,
231, 234, 237-238, 243-244, 298, 299-300;
Governmental Functions, 145, 159-160, 161-162, 176-177, 189, 190, 202, 205, 223, 233-240,
242, 245-246, 260, 262, 264-265, 266, 267,
271; Governmental Structure, 145, 159-160,
161-162, 189, 190, 192, 200, 223, 234-237,
244-245, 268-269, 270-271, 290-291, 292; Pre-Convention (see Pre-Convention Committee);
Public Finance and Taxation, 146-147, 159,
160, 202, 203, 212, 223, 234, 245, 246, 285,

286-287; Special, 294-301; Special Conference, 155-156, 161, 177, 237, 259, 261-262, 275, 285; Special Credentials, 140, 141; Style and Arrangements, 147, 160, 204, 205, 248, 249
Convening formalities, 156
Delegate Proposal 100. See "Palauan Constitution"
delegates, 85, 89-92, 93, 95, 116, 122, 123, 131, 134-139, 149, 150, 153, 158, 159, 201, 214, 217, 218, 220, 221, 302, 303
delegations: general, 113, 123-125, 138-139, 147, 154, 155, 157, 163, 164, 177, 178, 182-183, 190, 202, 214, 259, 264, 274, 288 (see also election of delegates; representation, below); Marianas, 81, 112, 114, 139, 151, 157, 212, 284; Marshalls, 85, 87, 91-94, 98, 112, 114, 117, 139, 141, 151, 219-222, 288, 295; Palau, 1, 54-55, 88, 98, 99, 112, 114, 116, 117, 119, 125-127, 138, 139, 141, 151, 157, 160-162, 171-184, 195, 202, 203, 211, 214, 217-219, 222, 224, 245, 250, 285, 287-290, 295, 296, 298-301, 304, 305; Ponape, 114, 124, 139, 151, 157, 219, 220, 283, 287; Truk, 114, 138, 139, 151, 199, 297, 313; Yap, 114, 125, 138, 151, 158, 199, 212, 275, 277, 288-289, 298, 303
election of delegates, 88, 89-93, 110, 116, 131, 132-135, 139, 334
enabling legislation, 2, 53, 87, 89, 93, 107-116, 117-120, 122, 131, 135, 140, 153, 211, 218, 257, 317
feasting and entertainment, 283, 284
funding, 108, 116, 119, 122, 123, 124, 145, 163
interpreters, 136-138, 148, 151, 162, 192, 219, 258-259, 260
length, 118-120, 145, 147, 249, 260, 293
meeting date, site, etc. See physical arrangements, below
"mock up" of Constitution, 217, 224-225, 246-249, 285
officers, 113-114, 138, 149, 150, 152, 155, 156, 157-159, 160, 162, 200, 213, 214-215, 224. See also under name of person
official language, 192, 193
physical arrangements, 114, 115-118, 119-121, 152-153, 154, 155, 211, 212, 213, 221
procedures, 1, 89, 91, 92, 98, 110, 111-113, 116, 118, 119, 136, 145-150, 152, 153, 154, 155, 156, 163, 183, 192, 201-203, 204, 214-217, 221, 231, 248-250, 257, 262, 273, 275-276,

284, 288, 293, 294
public information, 150-152, 162, 163-164, 211, 213, 217, 221-222, 225, 248, 275
recess, 2, 116-117, 118, 119, 123, 201, 202-203, 204, 211-225, 231, 232
representation, 108, 109, 131-136, 141-142
rules, 145, 148, 150, 155, 157, 158, 160, 183, 202, 214, 216, 265, 267, 274, 284, 303. See also procedures, above
signing constitution, 290, 302-305
staff, 1, 2, 92, 110, 117, 118, 119-120, 121, 123, 145, 150-154, 162-164, 189, 190-193, 214, 215, 216, 217, 218, 219, 221, 231, 248, 261, 264, 271, 302
traditional leaders, 257-277, 283, 294. See also Chiefs' meetings; enabling legislation, above; Traditional leaders
workshop, 150, 151-157, 172, 231, 258
Conventions, general, 5, 6, 236, 249
Cook Islands, 7, 52
Cooperation among Micronesian entities, 321, 322-323
Cruz, Jose R., 136, 216

Defense. See American security
Delegate Proposal 100. See "Palauan Constitution"
Democracy, 29-30, 35-36, 48, 53, 62, 84, 109, 153, 200, 237, 264
"Denial rights", 330, 331, 336
District government, 30, 31-33, 34, 37, 45-47, 53, 72, 73, 219

Education, 17, 29, 34, 65, 79, 84, 115, 137, 142, 197, 222, 240-242, 302, 322, 323, 327
Edwards, Edgar, 191
Elections. See Convention, Micronesian Constitutional: election of delegates; Referenda
Emergency, 242, 243
Eminent domain, 53, 55, 58, 60, 61, 77, 194, 198, 234, 263-268, 305
Eperiam, William, 261
ESG (Education for Self-Government), 65, 115, 215, 222, 248, 323

Falanruw, Sam, 161
Falcam, Leo, 114, 157, 158, 184, 195, 261, 262, 263, 272, 273, 288, 299, 334
Federalism, federation, 72, 172, 177, 182, 194-197, 235, 237, 304
Federated States of Micronesia, 197, 198, 250, 326, 327, 331, 333. See also Constitution of FSM
Fiji, 7, 193

Fishing rights, 238, 323
Ford, Gerald, 296, 326
Foreign affairs, 52, 56-58, 62, 77, 174, 196-197, 239, 315, 330, 335
Free association, 52, 53, 64-66, 95, 231, 232, 233, 315. See also Compact of free association
Fritz, Soukichi, 136, 139, 161, 235
Fundamental human rights. See Civil liberties
Future political status, 25, 51, 52, 54-56, 57, 59, 62, 63, 65, 66, 80, 91, 108, 117, 154, 175, 194, 202, 231-234, 313, 329, 332, 333. See also Commonwealth Covenant of N. Marianas; Compact of free association; Independence; Joint Committee on Future Status

Germans, Germany, 12, 13, 14, 21, 59, 74, 83, 84, 176
Gilbert and Ellice Islands Colony, 7, 25
Gladwin, Thomas, 97
Government functions, 34, 37
Government systems, 35, 36, 55-57, 62, 109, 146, 192, 193-196, 235-236, 292, 296, 328
Great Britain, 71, 107, 193-194, 332
Guam, 8-9, 12, 54, 71, 74, 75, 283

Hana, Maui, 57
Haruo, Sasauo, 135
Hawaii, 7, 57, 60, 145, 320
Health, 198, 240, 243, 327
Hefner, Robert, 235
Heine family, 83, 84-85, 89. See also Lanwi
  Carl, 85, 90, 114, 117, 136, 141, 160, 190, 201, 203, 219, 220, 250, 261, 262, 263, 271
  Dwight, 84, 89, 325
  John, 135, 289
Henry, Bethwell, 49
Hilo Statement, 329
Hitler, Adolf, 62
Human rights. See Civil liberties

Ibedul Y. Gibbons, 126, 219
Income tax, 47, 49, 76, 85-89, 90, 91, 285-290
Independence, 25, 51, 52, 53, 54, 56, 58, 64-66, 68-69, 97, 231-233, 316, 329, 331, 333, 335, 336
Inter-district Advisory Council of Micronesia, 84, 176
Interest groups, 45
Iran, 96. See also Superport, Palau oil
Iriarte, Heinrich, 136, 157, 161, 190, 257, 259, 268-270, 272, 276
Iriarte, Nanmarki Max, 136, 257-259, 268

Iroij, 82, 83, 88, 89-90, 92-93, 219, 220. See also Marshalls; Traditional leaders
Ismael, Dr. Hirosi, 136, 161, 190, 205, 233-234, 262, 264

Jackson, Henry, 335
Jamaica, 71
Japan, Japanese, 13-15, 18-20, 59, 74, 83, 84, 96, 176, 264
Johnston, Edward E., 136, 156, 303
Joint Committee on Future Status, 56, 57, 58, 60, 73, 76, 77, 82, 84, 107, 118, 125, 178, 181, 232, 263-264. See also Commission on Future Political Status and Transition; Compact of free association
Joseph, Chief Kintoki, 313, 314
Judiciary, 33-34. See also Constitution of FSM: judiciary branch

Kabua, Amata, 83-84, 85, 87, 90, 91, 96, 111, 334
Kabua, Iroij Lejellan, 83, 126
Kajur, 82, 83
Kapingamarangi, 10
Kendall, Wilfred, 91, 135, 141
Kiribati, 7, 332. See also Gilbert and Ellice Islands Colony
Kluge, Dr. P. Fred, 162
Koror. See Palau
Kosrae, 9, 10, 25, 131-132, 161, 297, 323, 324, 327, 333
Kusaie. See Kosrae
Kwajalein, 71, 83, 85, 329, 330

Labor unions, 258
Land. See Constitution of FSM: land; Public lands
Land and title court, 33, 236, 237, 270
Lanki, Iroij Jeltan, 220, 221
Lanwi, Dr. Isaac, 136, 161, 204-205, 260, 261
Lanwi, Mary, 89, 303
Law, 192-193, 235
Law of the Sea Conference, 23, 43, 238
League of Nations, 7, 35
Legal services, 241
Legislature, viii, 136, 236, 249, 293
Leiroj, 83, 90, 220
Liberal Party, Palau, 73, 96, 97, 124, 132, 134, 217
Limes, Louis, 157, 260
Local government, 29-31, 37-38, 48, 82, 237
Localization, 20, 37
Luii, Itelbang, 174

MacKenzie, J. Boyd, 322
Malaya, 198
Mangefel, John, 321
Mandate, League of Nations, 7, 35
Manglona, Ben, 136
Manhard, Philip W., 320
Marianas, 8, 11, 12, 17-20, 25, 44, 45, 47, 55, 56, 59, 62, 63-66, 71-82, 89, 94, 95, 98, 109, 111, 115, 117, 132, 135, 136, 151, 152, 243, 324, 326. See also Commonwealth Covenant of N. Marianas; Convention, Micronesian Constitutional: delegations, Marianas
  constitution, 78, 79, 326
  constitutional convention, 77-78, 324
  status commission, 76
Marshalls, 8, 9, 11, 19, 32, 46, 47, 62, 66, 71, 72, 73, 82-95, 96, 98, 109, 126, 135, 136, 219, 220, 283, 319-320, 323-325, 327, 328, 329, 331, 333, 334. See also Convention, Micronesian Constitutional: delegations, Marshalls
  constitution, 328
  status commission, 86, 87, 320-322, 330
Mason, Dr. Leonard, 320
McKnight, Robert, 171
Micronesia
  culture and tradition, viii-ix, 10-12, 20, 29-30, 48, 51, 74, 82-83, 90, 97, 152, 164, 165, 171, 193, 200, 201, 204, 216, 257-277, 283, 305, 321, 325. See also Micronesian Way
  Day, 39, 49, 116, 118, 156, 317, 322, 326
  economy, 13-17, 18, 19, 20, 22-24, 43, 44, 64, 85, 238, 330, 331, 332
  geography, 7-10, 221, 336
  population, 7-10, 18, 296-297
  unity. See Unity of Micronesia
Micronesian Anthem, 303
Micronesian attitudes, 19-22, 36-38, 65, 85, 336, 337
Micronesian News Service (MNS), 222
Micronesian Way, 283-286, 288, 289, 293-295
MIECO, 86
Military. See American security
Ministates, 24. See also specific place name
Modogkne, 94
Municipality, municipal government. See Local government
Mussolini, Benito, 62
Mwety, Soiter, 184, 265-267, 274, 298

Nakamura, Kuniwo, 218

Nakamura, Tosiwo, 160, 218, 289, 299-300
Nakayama, Tosiwo, 49, 113, 135, 156-157, 218-220, 225, 260, 274, 294, 295, 300, 313, 316, 317, 327, 334
National capital. See Capital, national
Naturalization, 243-244
Nauru, 7, 25
New Hebrides, 7
New Zealand, 7, 52, 107, 330
Ngiraked, John, 73, 114, 116, 119, 136, 141, 157, 158, 160, 161, 162, 173, 189, 212, 215, 217, 219, 250, 267, 272, 273, 275, 285, 287, 289, 290, 293, 299-300
Nimwes, Chutomu, 114, 136, 272, 300
Nitijela, 46, 84, 85-88, 89, 90, 91-93, 220, 328, 334
Niue, 7, 330
Non-negotiability, 55, 56, 171, 173, 182, 224, 240, 285, 290, 291, 298, 300, 301, 304. See also "Palauan Constitution"
Nuclear materials, tests, etc., 21, 301, 315, 328, 330, 332-333, 335
Nukuoro, 10

Olikong, Santos, 274
Olkeriil, Timothy, 99
Olter, Bailey, 135, 160, 232, 289, 317
Organic act, 54

Pakistan, 196
Palacios, Dr. Francisco T., 136, 139
Palau, 1, 2, 9, 17-19, 32, 44, 48, 60-62, 65, 66, 71, 72, 73, 93-99, 109, 116, 119, 124-127, 131-136, 140, 141, 146, 153 154, 165 171-173, 176, 217, 219, 298, 299, 317-320, 323, 324, 325, 328, 329, 331, 332, 335. See also Convention, Micronesian Constitutional: delegations, Palau
  constitutional conventions, 72, 95, 97, 172, 328
  constitutions. See Constitutions: Palau
  Status Commission, 95, 97, 98, 118, 173, 320-322, 328, 330
"Palauan Constitution," 178-184, 195, 201, 202, 203, 214, 219, 224, 240, 285, 286, 288, 289, 291, 292, 296, 298, 304, 305
"Palauan Petition," 175-178
Pangelinan, Edward D. L. G., 77, 132
Papua New Guinea, vii, 7, 180, 193, 196, 200, 231, 332
Parliament. See Legislature
Parochial schools, 242

Peace Corps Volunteers, 17
Philippines, 71
Philippo, Tipne, 216, 274
Pingelap, 10
Plebiscite, Northern Marianas Covenant. See Commonwealth Covenant of N. Marianas
Plural executive, 56, 199-200, 269, 270, 291, 392
Political parties, 44, 61, 75-76, 132-134. See also name of specific party
Political Status Delegation, 53, 56
Ponape, 10, 39, 47, 72, 109, 126, 131-132, 135, 152, 156, 165, 213, 283, 284, 323, 324, 326, 327, 333. See also Convention, Micronesian Constitutional: delegations, Ponape
Popular Party, Marianas, 75
Population. See Micronesia: population
Pre-Convention Committee, 81, 92, 98, 113, 114-120, 122-124, 145, 148, 150, 156, 181, 189, 199, 313
Procedures of Convention. See Convention, Micronesian Constitutional: procedures
Progressive Party, Palau, 73, 114, 117, 124, 127, 132, 217-218, 318
Public auditor, 245
Public lands, 21, 47, 53-54, 58-61, 94, 198, 264, 323, 328. See also Constitution of Federated States of Micronesia: land
Puerto Rico, 55

Radioactive materials. See Nuclear materials
Reagan Administration, 329, 330
Recess. See Convention, Micronesian Constitutional: recess
Referenda, 66, 73, 80, 98-99, 117. See also Commonwealth Covenant of N. Marianas; Constitution of Federated States of Micronesia: ratification
Reklai (acting), Eusevio Termeteet, 126, 218
Religion, 156, 241, 242, 303, 323
Rosenblatt, Peter, 316, 317, 328, 329
"Roundtable" discussions, 320, 321, 322

Sablan, Vincente D., 156
Saipan, 16, 74, 114, 119, 120, 283
Salii, Lazarus E., 2, 49, 54, 61, 96, 97, 109, 114, 118, 132, 135, 160, 162, 171, 177, 181-182, 214, 216-218, 264, 300, 317, 328, 334
Sawaichi, Jacob, 136, 157, 161, 162, 177, 217, 274
Secession, 63, 173, 175, 177, 180, 298, 299, 305, 318. See also Unity of Micronesia
Secretarial Orders, 60, 61, 79, 117, 191, 198, 326-327,

Silk, Ekpop, 64
Social security, 240
Solomon Islands, 7
Solomon Report, 37
Sony, Iskia, 160, 289, 290
South Pacific Commission, 43
Sovereignty, 54, 56, 57-58, 110, 232, 238, 315
Soviet Union, 319, 336
Spain, Spanish, 8, 12, 14, 21, 25, 59, 74
Statehood, 66
Status Commission. See specific name
Stephen, Naniken Heinrich, 259, 269, 291
Superport, Palau oil, 97, 175, 180, 181
Switzerland, 196, 200, 291

Tacheliol, Hilary, 139, 161, 269, 292
Takesy, Asterio R., 150
Tanzania, 72
Territorial status, 54, 64
Tinian, 72, 77, 78
Tman, Luke, 135, 138, 150, 158, 177, 184, 202, 204, 261, 265, 273, 284, 290
Tmetuchl, Roman, 65, 97, 124, 328, 334
Tomeing, Iroij Litokwa, 220, 221
Toribiong, Johnson, 160, 217, 261, 267, 289, 290
Toxic chemicals. See nuclear materials, tests, etc.
Traditional Chiefs' Conferences, 61, 125-127
Traditional leaders, 30-32, 61, 82, 83, 89, 91, 109, 111, 112, 126, 131, 138, 140, 141, 152, 154, 155, 159, 194, 201, 219, 257-277, 283, 294, 297, 313, 322. See also Micronesia: culture and tradition
Travel rights, 243
Treaties, 57, 232, 233, 234, 238, 314
Trinidad and Tobago, 71
Truk, 9, 10, 47, 61, 72, 76, 109, 125-127, 135, 136, 139-141, 199, 266, 323, 324, 333. See also Convention, Micronesian Constitutional: delegations, Truk
Trust Territory
  Budget, 16-17, 18, 19, 36-37, 42-43, 44, 46, 48-49, 85
  Code, 60, 241, 243
  government, 15, 29, 31-33, 44-45, 46-48, 65, 199, 264
  Headquarters, 8, 16, 19, 32, 37, 176, 325, 327
  High Court, 33-34, 325
Tun, Petrus, 114, 135, 138, 160, 161, 232, 243, 276, 327
Tuvalu, 7

Udui, Kaleb, 145
Uhberlau, Victorio, 150
United Nations, 7, 8, 18, 22, 29, 43, 47, 48, 51, 52, 59, 77, 85, 87, 157, 176, 231, 302, 313, 318, 319, 321, 324, 335-337
United States
    administration of Micronesia, 15, 29, 30, 33, 34, 37, 40-44, 48, 51, 80. *See also* Secretarial Orders
    House of Representatives, 80
    Senate, 78, 80, 81, 87
Unity of Micronesia, 2, 9, 11-12, 37, 52, 64, 71, 76, 77, 79, 83, 86, 88, 89, 91, 95, 97-99, 118, 125-127, 171, 173, 181, 250, 275, 276-277, 283, 289, 298, 299, 303, 313, 318-322, 324, 329, 337. *See also* Secession

Vance, Cyrus, 320
Vanuatu. *See* New Hebrides
Vermont, 71
Virgin Islands, 54
Voice of the Marshalls, 324. *See also* Marshalls

Wainit, Tatasy, 161
Weital, Daro, 136, 161
Welfare, 241
Western Samoa, 7, 193
West Indian Federation, 71
White Sands Hotel, 120-121, 213
Wiliander, Hans, 136, 160, 183, 203, 233, 246
Williams, F. Haydn, 61, 80, 88, 95, 107, 314-316, 319
Williams, Rev. Mack, 242
World Wars, 7, 19-21, 24, 59, 71, 74, 86

Yap, 9, 47, 72, 109, 126, 135, 139, 157, 158, 165, 271, 276, 277, 288, 292, 298, 324, 325, 333. *See also* Convention, Micronesian Constitutional: delegations, Yap
Yoma, Strik, 136

Zeder, Fred M., 157, 225, 329, 332

Constitution of the Federated States of Micronesia

PREAMBLE

WE, THE PEOPLE OF MICRONESIA, exercising our inherent sovereignty, do hereby establish this Constitution of the Federated States of Micronesia.

With this Constitution, we affirm our common wish to live together in peace and harmony, to preserve the heritage of the past, and to protect the promise of the future.

To make one nation of many islands, we respect the diversity of our cultures. Our differences enrich us. The seas bring us together, they do not separate us. Our islands sustain us, our island nation enlarges us and makes us stronger.

Our ancestors, who made their homes on these islands, displaced no other people. We, who remain, wish no other home than this. Having known war, we hope for peace. Having been divided, we wish unity. Having been ruled, we seek freedom.

Micronesia began in the days when man explored seas in rafts and canoes. The Micronesian nation is born in an age when men voyage among stars; our world itself is an island. We extend to all nations what we seek from each: peace, friendship, cooperation, and love in our common humanity. With this Constitution we, who have been the wards of other nations, become the proud guardian of our own islands, now and forever.

Tosiwo Nakayama, President

YAP DELEGATION
Petrus Tun
Samuel Falanruw
Francisco Luhluv
Hilary Tacheliol
Luke Tman
Delarmino Kathey

TRUK DELEGATION
Shulomy Nimwes
Erhon Albert
Ichila Dossy
Soukichi Fritz
Sasauo Haruo
Kotaro Heldart
Kimiuo Joseph
Sailer Wevely
Frank Nifon
Makelo Robert
Ishiu Sony
Manuel Sound
Tolensom Wainit

PONAPE DELEGATION
H.H. Salem
Leo Falcam
Kikuo L. Apis
Rikus Bois
William Egerium
Heinrich Triarl
Hirosi Ismael
Rubel Mateak
Bailey Olter
Iadao Sigrah
Hadwich Stephen
Haro Weital
Striks Yoma

PALAU DELEGATION
John Ngiraked
John Gibbons
Ibedul Gibbons
Tosiwo Nakamura
Santos Olikong
Lazarus Salii
Jacob Sawaichi
Ucting Roklai Termetet
Johnson Toribiong

MARSHALLS DELEGATION
Carl Heine
Jetton L. Lonkin
Atlan Anki
Ataloye Jameing
John Heine
Langue Kolles
Wilfred Kendall
Tom Kijiner
Isaac Lanni
Mary Lanni
Ninjin Rainin
Nijio Radrik

MARIANAS DELEGATION
Lorenzo S. Cabrera
Olympio T. Borja
Alonzo Igisomar
Luis Limes
Benjamin Manglona
Olfonso C. Rosa
Rilonso Rosa

published by
The Institute for Polynesian Studies
Brigham Young University—Hawaii Campus
funded by the
Polynesian Cultural Center

LIBRARY OF D